AN INTEGRATED APPROACH TO SOFTWARE DEVELOPMENT

AN INTEGRATED APPROACH TO SOFTWARE DEVELOPMENT

RUSSELL J. ABBOTT

A Wiley-Interscience publication
JOHN WILEY & SONS

New York • Chichester • Brisbane • Toronto • Singapore

Library of Congress Cataloging in Publication Data
Abbott, Russell J., 1942-
  An integrated approach to software development.

  "A Wiley-Interscience publication."
  Bibliography: p.
  Includes index.
  1. Computer software—Development. I. Title.

QA76.76.D47A23   1985   001.64'25   85-9427
ISBN 0-471-82646-4

Printed in the United States of America

10 9 8 7 6 5 4 3 2 1

PREFACE

This book is intended as a text in software engineering courses and as a day-to-day working reference for practicing software engineers.

1. It could be used as a software engineering text in computer science departments and in systems analysis courses in business and engineering. In the latter capacity chapters 2 and 3 would be most relevant.
2. For practicing systems analysts, software engineers, and programmers this book can serve as a useful reference for the development of requirements and software design documents, system specifications, and testing documentation.

The format of this book makes it easy to adapt to both purposes. It is organized as a collection of annotated outlines for technical documents that are important to the development and maintenance of software. These documents are not just provided in bare form. Their annotations explain why they are organized as they are and why their contents are as shown. Thus the annotations are used for tutorial purposes when necessary. To varying degrees the documents rely on relatively sophisticated concepts and in some sections require a certain amount of formal notation. Therefore this material is presented in the context of the documents in which it appears rather than in the traditional academic manner. In that way its relevance is immediately apparent. In addition, the outlines may be used by practitioners as models for their own documents.

SIGNIFICANT FEATURES

1. A clear distinction is made between *requirements* and *behavioral specification*. Requirements refer to the needs of the end user, behavioral specifications, to a behavioral description of a system that meets those needs.

2. To express a user's requirements we must first understand the user's world. Techniques from the disciplines of artificial intelligence and databases serve as an approach to the analysis of an arbitrary world. The ideas inherent in these techniques provide the book with a unifying theme.

3. To specify the behavior of an arbitrary system requires precision and clarity. A method of expressing behavioral specifications is presented in a way that is both rigorous and intuitive. It also includes the following:

    a. The user's view of a system in terms of *user conceptual model*.
    b. Operations in road-map form available to the user for manipulating that conceptual model.

4. For an organization to operate a system requires *procedures* and *administration*. These topics are discussed as a complement to behavioral specifications.

5. The approach to system *design* stresses design in terms of reusable components and combines into a single methodology techniques from object-oriented programming, dataflow design, and stepwise refinement. A theory of interpretive systems is developed to show how programming languages and application systems alike may be understood as interpreters. A new construct, the *component,* captures the essense of modularity and unifies the notions of types, subprograms, tasks, and objects. This methodology places input and output in their proper perspective and is particularly oriented toward design in terms of reusable components and implementation in a modern programming language such as Ada.*

6. *Validation, verification,* and *testing* are integrated into the development procedures to rescue them from their roles as the expensive black sheep of software development.

7. The book contains recommended outlines of documents for requirements, behavioral specifications, procedural and administrative manuals, and system and component design documentation.

8. An appendix presents an easy to understand formal notation for expressing specification. It is structured to parallel the syntax of programming langauges. Thus it is comfortable for most programmers to read and write.

---

*Ada is a trade mark of the United States Department of Defense.

USE OF THIS BOOK IN LECTURE COURSES

The software engineering curriculum is still rather fluid. Schools package systems analysis, specification, design, and management in various ways. This book can be used in any of a number of senior or graduate level courses:

1. *Software Engineering.*   It can serve as the primary text in a course in software engineering. The entire book can be covered in a single semester, although the pace may be somewhat rapid. Readings from the references may be used to explore in more depth topics of particular interest to the instructor. A supplementary software engineering survey book (e.g., Pressman, 1982; see the annotated bibliography at the end of this preface) may be used for breadth.

2. *Software System Design.*   It may be used as the primary text in a software system design course in which only the chapters on system specification and design would be covered. Readings from the literature may be selected to explore particular topics in more depth.

3. *Software Architecture.*   It may be used as the primary text in a course on software architecture and design in which only the chapters on design would be covered. It should be supplemented by readings from the literature.

4. *Systems Analysis.*   It may be used as a primary text in a systems analysis course in which only the chapters on requirements and specifications would be covered. It should be supplemented by readings in the organizational use of computer systems.

5. *Software Engineering Project Management.*   It may be used as a secondary text in a course on the management of software engineering projects.

The exercises throughout the book provide ample practice material and are structured to allow (if desired) concentration on a single system. A set of exercises is included for an appointment-scheduling system; if all are completed a full set of development documents for such a system will be written.

USE OF THIS BOOK IN A PROJECT COURSE

This book is ideally suited for a software engineering project course, in which the students compose their own requirements, behavioral specification, design, and text documents.

It is best to organize this class into four groups:

1. *Requirements.*   This group is responsible for defining the requirements of the system to be built.

2. *Specification.*   This group is responsible for explaining how a system that meets those requirements would look to the user.

3. *Design.*   This group is responsible for designing a system that acts as the specification group says the system should act.
4. *Prototype.*   This group is responsible for building a working prototype system to display the behavior that the specification group indicates. To the extent feasible the prototype should match the design created by the design group, although time limitations may force the two to diverge.

The instructor serves both as executive director to make sure that fundamentally the work stays on track and as "coach" to help the various groups to carry out their assignments. For the most part the instructor should avoid making project-related decisions because it is best for students to assume that responsibility.

Parallel Development

The major difficulty in teaching such a course is the limited time. Even in semester courses there is never enough to prepare the documents in the normal sequential manner. To accommodate the constraints documents must be developed in parallel. Starting out, of course, is difficult in that the students who initiate the behavioral specification, the design, and the prototype have nothing on which to base their work.

Yet parallel development is not so impossible as it seems. First, it takes a while for students to get used to the idea of producing large documents. Most computer science students, although comfortable in program preparation, are not accustomed to writing English and often have a rough time at the beginning. Second, it takes a while for most students to develop a feeling for these documents. The students must work with outlines and attempt to express their ideas within the framework that the documents provide before they can be confident enough to begin constructive work.

Third, in general it is not absolutely necessary to complete a requirements document before beginning a behavioral specification or to have a final behavioral specification before starting a design. With the basic idea in hand of what a system is intended to do it is generally possible to begin the behavioral specification and design. Finally, given a spirit of cooperation between groups and the appropriate perspective of each group's functions, parallel development can be a very positive approach. Each group will understand that the other groups are working out the details that its own group needs to do its work.

Parallel development can be considered constructive rather than disadvantageous. It is often said of large systems that "One should expect to throw the first version away." No matter how disciplined, the mistakes made the first time in a complex development are generally significant enough to determine that a second try would make a qualitative difference in the final product. Parallel development helps to mitigate this effect. If all the documents and a prototype version of the system are developed simultaneously each development group can benefit from the problems encountered and the lessons learned by the others.

Parallel development forces an orientation somewhat different from the usual "waterfall" chart approach. By the use of this methodology each document is driven by documents developed earlier and in turn drives documents developed later; that is, if the requirements document is fixed before work is begun on a specification the specification must be written to satisfy the requirements stated. Similarly, if the specification is fixed before the design is begun the design is forced to implement the system as specified. Of course, it never works out that way; problems that appear in later phases of development force compromises with decisions apparently made earlier once and for all. These compromises are frequently awkward to accommodate and often result in hard feelings.

On the other hand, if it is understood that the documents are to be developed in parallel, that no document drives any other absolutely, and that the primary constraint is that the documents (and the final system) be mutually consistent at the end of development, a spirit of cooperation and mutual respect can prevail. Each group represents an area of expertise that it brings to bear on the result and each group can represent its interests while understanding that the needs of the other groups must be heard.

1. Members of the requirements group think of themselves as experts in the definition of requirements. Although requirements are important, without the help of the other groups nothing would be accomplished except stating the problem. They recognize that the other groups are building a system to meet the needs that they discover and document. This, of course, is traditional.

2. Members of the specification group think of themselves as experts in the definition of user-friendly systems that are easy to understand and that fit the user's needs. All that is needed is to have someone tell them what the user is like and what the user-needs are. As far as they are concerned, these are details to be incorporated into their system-defining methodology. The specification group needs the requirements group to provide these details and the design and prototype groups to carry them out, but they do not see themselves as subservient to any other group any more than a photographer is subservient to the person whose portrait is taken or to the people who develop the prints.

3. Members of the design group think of themselves as experts in the design of clean, easily understandable, well organized software. All that is needed is to have someone tell them what the software is supposed to do. As far as they are concerned, that is a detail to which they apply their design methodology. The design group needs the specification group to work out the details of the appearance of the system and the requirements group to determine whether there are other constraints to be obeyed, but they do not see themselves as subservient to any other group any more than any other designers are subservient to their customers. Designers bring to their jobs a knowledge of design techniques that permit more to be accomplished than nondesigners might imagine and design constraints that set a limit to what is possible. Because of these talents designers often have the final say on what the product will do.

4. Finally, members of the prototype group think of themselves as experts in getting a computer to do what they want it to do. They can make the compiler do tricks, they can make terminals stand on their heads, they can make the operating system sit up and beg, and they have a bagful of other tools that turn building systems into a video game. They see the computer as their instrument and they are its masters. All they need is to have someone give them specifications to animate. The prototype group needs the other groups to tell them what to make the system do, but they do not see themselves as subservient to any other group any more than a musician is subservient to the designer of the instrument to be played or to the composer of the music selected. Without the prototype group there would be nothing but paper; so in the end they are most important. Also, it is often the prototype group with their knowledge of making an actual system do real work that makes or breaks a design and the system that depends on it.

In developing documents in parallel, we expect a lot of rewriting, but we should expect a lot in any case. The rewriting due to too early commitments made in the behavioral specification and design is really no different from that required to remedy internal consistency or errors made in interpreting or ignoring parts of earlier documents.

The experience of working in the dark proves valuable. Students appreciate all the more the importance of a well defined set of requirements when developing a behavioral specification and the value of a behavioral specification when constructing a design. They learn from their own experience that the decisions they make from a limited perspective can sometimes get them into trouble and lead to extra work. They also learn how each part of the job depends on all the other parts.

Finally, it is important to point out the effects of working in groups. Even students who began with no particular affinity for the groups in which they were placed find themselves identifying with their thinking and defending them against the other groups whenever disagreements occur. Each group develops its own identity and way of working together and each group tends to think of itself as beset by the others. Groups bargain with one another to make their own jobs easier and to bend the system to their own points of view. It is the instructor's obligation to hold up a mirror so that the students who are emersed in the process can recognize and understand the interpersonal and intergroup interactions as well as the technical issues.

Choosing the Project

The class project is selected from proposals written by the students themselves. At the start of the semester each student submits a project proposal which consists of a one-paragraph summary of its contents and one-paragraph preliminary versions of the requirements, behavioral specification, and design documents. The class reviews these proposals and selects one as its semester project.

Project Organization

In addition to the four groups the class is divided into committees in a form of matrix organization. Each group has a representative on each committee. The groups are responsible for the technical work, the committees, for management and quality assurance.

1. *Management Committee.* The management committee directs project planning, scheduling (and rescheduling as necessary), configuration management, and any other management and administrative functions that can be handled by the students themselves.

The management committee must produce a development plan, which consists mainly of a schedule of milestones for the production and review of documents. A typical plan calls for the production during the semester of four review versions and one final version of the documents to reflect complete descriptions of partial versions (i.e., ''builds'') of the final system.

To the extent that the instructor wants to give the students this responsibility the management committee may also allocate class time. A great deal of class time may be devoted to reviewing documents. This is best if the class is scheduled in part as a laboratory and in part as a lecture. It is also best if the lecture and laboratory times run sequentially to allow work started in one period to continue into the other.

Scheduled laboratory time is also important for another reason: the students must be assured of having some time to work together in groups. Individual student schedules are often so different that whole groups can get together only during class time. A total of five to seven scheduled hours a week works reasonably well. For a three-unit class the hours are best scheduled as two hours of lecture and three hours of laboratory or as one hour of lecture and six hours of laboratory.

Management is also responsible for additional structuring; for example, it is often useful for each group to appoint a liaison with the other groups. It is the job of the liaison to meet periodically with groups to which he or she is assigned and to report back about the work of these groups. It is a good practice to schedule a time for these meetings to take place during the next to last minutes of the class session once a week. During that time the liaisons can make their reports to their home groups.

Finally, management is responsible for keeping track of the progress of all projects. A good method is to appoint one of its own members as *project historian.* The project historian's job is to record decisions made by the committees, to keep track of the memberships of the groups and committees, and to record and follow up on action items. The historian should submit three weekly reports to the management committee which would contain the following:

a. *The current project plan and the events scheduled until the end of the semester.*

b. *A record of decisions made and brief rationales for the decisions.* These records play an important part in all projects. Recording the decisions made saves a great deal of energy in preventing the same issues from being reargued and rethought. In large projects, decisions are frequently made but inadequate records are kept. The result is that later, when it is necessary to refer to a decision (What did we decide about that question last week?) there is no reliable means of confirming it. Either no one remembers clearly or everyone remembers clearly but differently. A definitive, authoritative record of decisions made will save a great deal of wasted time.

c.   *A list of problem reports yet to be resolved and other items that require action, each item to include the name of the individual or group responsible for that item.* This list serves as a subsidiary project agenda, parallel to the schedule of document submissions and reviews of the project plan. Each action item should have a scheduled completion date. The actual date of completion should also be recorded as part of the project history. This list of action items provides a quick reference to trouble spots. Any document with an unusually large number of unresolved problem reports should receive extra attention.

2.   *Quality Assurance.*   The quality assurance committee is responsible for guaranteeing the overall quality of the project. It sets documentation standards and determines that each group's work is internally consistent and complete and that the groups are consistent with one another.

The quality assurance activity is concerned with consistency within and between documents and with document quality in general; for example, clarity of the writing.

As its first task quality assurance should define a problem report form for recording problems and a separate problem report should be issued for each problem. Problem reports may be initiated by anyone in the class (e.g., a member of a working group) as a way of anticipating a potential problem with another group's document and by the Quality Assurance group itself. There should be a problem report issued for each problem quality assurance (or anyone else) finds in reviewing the documents. All problem reports should be submitted to quality assurance for coordination (to prevent multiple reports from being issued on the same problem) and then issued formally by the quality assurance group.

Many students find writing difficult. Therefore, in addition to its responsibility for document consistency, quality assurance should note awkward phrasing and help to put the documents into simple language.

For the most part it is unreasonable to expect quality assurance to produce documentation or programming standards that go beyond the document outlines included in this book. Students do, however, sometimes enjoy defining document formatting conventions such as the use of alphabetic and roman numerals for section numbers, indentation guidelines, and page-heading style guides.

3.   *Presentation Committee.*   Each group makes periodic review presentations of its draft documents to the rest of the class. These presentations should be conducted with relative formality and records should kept of any action items that result from these reviews. The presentation committee, which runs the reviews, should make sure that it stays on the subject and gets bogged down neither in resolving problems nor in name calling or other nonproductive activities. It is also responsible for pointing out the issues raised at the review sessions for recording by the project historian and must set standards for the presentations, provide a moderator, and in general encourage the groups to take the matter seriously.

4.   *Technical Committee.*   The technical committee makes recommendations to the management group about technical topics that are not within the purview of individual groups. It is responsible for analyzing conflicts that develop between groups and for providing the objective, technical information on which resolutions may be based. As an example, it may be that a number of systems could conceivably serve as host to a project. After listening to arguments for each of the possible systems this committee would report to management on the issue. As another example, different groups may have different ideas about the scope of a project. Although this is primarily a requirements matter, other groups may have good reasons for wanting to define scope somewhat differently. It may, for example, be possible to include in the initial version of the system features that the requirements group would otherwise have left as future enhancements. Again after listening to all sides the technical committee must produce a report that defines the problem. If it so desires it may also make recommendations.

These committees should schedule meetings approximately once a week. If there is no work be be done at a meeting it can be adjourned quickly, but it is important that meetings be scheduled regularly so that the committees can develop an understanding of their responsibilities.

THE PLACE OF THIS BOOK IN THE SOFTWARE ENGINEERING LITERATURE

Much as been written recently on the subjects covered or touched on by this book. The general field is commonly known as *software engineering*. Because it involves the application of technology to the development and maintenance of software, it naturally divides itself into two subfields: software engineering technology and software engineering management. This book is about software engineering technology; it is not about software engineering management. As such it contrasts with many of the other books in the field.

In addition to the technology/management dimension, books in this field may be measured on a formality scale. At the informal end they are primarily anecdotal; at the other end they are formal and theoretical. This book is in the middle; it presents material rigorously but does not sacrifice intuitive understanding. It is intended to be accessible to practitioners in the field and to senior level computer science undergraduate students.

The following annotated bibliography discusses selected works. They were included if they are widely known or of significant interest. With this contour map of other publications current books may be located. References in the annotations are to other works in this list. //

Representative Books

Bersoff, E.H., V.D. Henderson, and S.G. Siegel, *Software Configuration Management,* Prentice-Hall, Englewood Cliffs, New Jersey, 1980. Software product assurance through configuration management. A thorough, management oriented, presentation.

Booch, G., *Software Engineering with Ada,* Benjamin-Cummings, Menlo Park, California, 1983. The "object-oriented" approach to software design based on ideas in Abbott (1983). Relevant to the design of software architecture and algorithms. Presented on a level accessible to most programmers.

Brooks, F.P., *The Mythical Man Month,* Addison-Wesley, Reading, Massachusetts, 1975. Good advice about managing software development.

Jackson, M. *Principles of Program Design,* Academic, New York, 1975. A semi-formal approach to program design that maps the syntactic structure of a program's input into a structure for an algorithm to process that input. Similar to Warnier (1974).

Jensen, R.C. and C. C. Tonies, Eds., *Software Engineering,* Prentice-Hall, Englewood Cliffs, New Jersey, 1979. A relatively informal collection of articles. Primarily management oriented. Topics include management issues, algorithm design (structured programming), testing, security, and legal aspects.

Jones, C.B., *Software Development: A Rigorous Approach,* Prentice-Hall, Englewood Cliffs, New Jersey, 1980. An attempt to make formal approaches to algorithm specification and verification accessible to practitioners. Focuses on abstraction and formal specification and verification. Too difficult for most programmers.

Metzger, P.W., *Managing a Programming Project,* Prentice-Hall, Englewood Cliffs, New Jersey, 2nd ed. 1981. A step-by-step guide through the development cycle. Greatest emphasis is on managing the programming and testing activities.

Myers, G., *Composite Structured Design,* Van Nostrand, New York, 1978. A relatively informal data flow approach to program design. Similar to Yourdon (1979).

Pressman, R.S., *Software Engineering, A Practitioner's Approach,* McGraw-Hill, New York, 1982. A survey that covers most topics in the standard life cycle. Relatively informal. Includes separate chapters on each of the traditional structured design approaches: stepwise refinement, cohesion versus coupling of subprograms (called "modules") (Stevens, 1974), and dataflow (bubble charts) (Myers, 1978; Yourdon and Constantine, 1979), and data structure (Jackson, 1975; Warnier, 1974).

Procedings: Specifications of Reliable Software, IEEE Catalog No. 79CH1401-9C, 1979. A comprehensive collection of original and review papers on methods of formal specification and verification.

Tausworthe, R.C., *Standardized Development of Computer Software,* Prentice Hall, Englewood Cliffs, New Jersey, 1979, two volumes. Discussions and outlines of standardized documents developed for NASA at JPL to cover the entire development cycle. Medium formality. Covers management and technical aspects. A good presentation of the state of the art in industry in 1979.

Warnier, J.D., *Logical Construction of Programs,* Van Nostrand, New York, 1974. A semiformal approach to program design that maps the syntactic structure of a program's input into a structure for an algorithm to process that input. Similar to Jackson (1975).

Yourdon, E. and L. Constantine, *Structured Design,* Prentice-Hall, Englewood Cliffs, New Jersey, 1979. A relatively informal dataflow approach to program design. Similar to Myers (1979).

Zelkowitz, M.V., A.C. Shaw, and J.D. Gannon, *Principles of Software Engineering and Design,* Prentice-Hall, Englewood Cliffs, New Jersey, 1979. A somewhat disjointed collection of articles that covers aspects of the development cycle. Focuses primarily on programming techniques, that is, algorithm implementation.

Representative Papers

Abbott, R.J., "Program Design By Informal English Descriptions," *Communication of the ACM,* November 1983. An approach to algorithm design based on the idea of identifying common nouns with abstract data types. Forms the basis of Booch (1983).

Alford, M.W., "A Requirements Engineering Methodology for Realtime Processing Requirements," *IEEE Transactions on Software Engineering,* 1(3):60-69, 1977. Describes SREM, a tool for high-level system design by functional decomposition. Intended for requirements analysis. Competes with PSL/PSA.

Blazer, R. and N. Goldman, "Principles of Good Software Specification and Their Implications for a Specification Language," *Proceedings: Specifications of Reliable Software,* IEEE Catalog No. 79CH1401-9C, 1979. Discussion of requirements for languages for system specification. See also Goldman (1980).

Goldman, N. and D.S. Wile, *A Database Foundation for Process Specification,* USC-ISI Report RR-80-84, 1980. A language for system specification derived from the requirements in Balzer (1979). A promising approach that uses techniques and notations from relational databases and formal specification to build a model of the system specified.

Guttag, J.V., E. Horowitz, and D.R. Musser, "Abstract Data Types and Software Validation," *Communications of the ACM* 21(12):1048–1064, 1978. The formal algebraic approach to abstract data types. Relevant to the design of software architecture and algorithms.

Heninger, K.L., J.W. Kallander, J.E. Shore, and D.L. Parnas, *Software Requirements for the A-7E Aircraft,* NRL Memorandum Report 3876, Naval Research Laboratories, Washington, D.C., 1980. An informal but rigorous specification of an existing software system. Demonstrates that software can be well documented without excessive formalism.

Luckham, D.C. and W. Polak, "A Practical Method of Documenting and Verifying Ada Programs with Packages," *Proceedings of the ACM-SIGPLAN Symposium on the Ada Programming Language,* 1980, pp. 113–122. An attempt to apply the algebraic method of abstract specification (Guttag, 1978) to Ada packages.

Parnas, D.L., "On the Criteria to be Used in Decomposing Systems into Modules," *Communications of the ACM,* 15(12):1053–1058, 1972. One of the original works that defined software architecture as something other than algorithm design.

Stay, J.F., "HIPO and Integrated Program Design," *IBM Systems Journal,* 15(2):143–154, 1976. An early approach to stepwise refinement and dataflow design.

Stevens, W., G. Myers, and L. Constantine, "Structured Design," *IBM System Journal* **13**(2):1974. A discussion of criteria for decomposing programs into subprograms. Introduces the notions of *coupling* and *cohesion*.

Teichrow, D. and E. Hershey, "PSL/PSA: A Computer Aided Technique for Structured Documentation and Analysis of Information Processing Systems," *IEEE Transactions of Software Engineering* **3**(1):41–48, 1977. A tool for high-level system dataflow design. Intended for requirements analysis. Competes with SREM. Lately has evolved into an automated document production system capable of integrating text with automatically generated reports and diagrams.

ACKNOWLEDGMENTS

I should like to acknowledge the work of all those who preceded me in this field. I hope that I have done justice to their conditions. In addition, I should like to acknowledge Jane Radatz for her enthusiastic support during the early work of writing this book and for her technical assistance, Ric Cowan for his aid, especially during the final period, and the Aerospace Corporation and California State University, Northridge, for their support.

RUSSELL J. ABBOTT

Chatsworth, California
August 1985

CONTENTS

PART 2   SYSTEM SPECIFICATION

引论说明书

APPENDIX   ABSTRACTION AND SPECIFICATION

AN INTEGRATED APPROACH TO SOFTWARE DEVELOPMENT

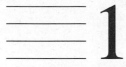

1

INTRODUCTION

1.1 SOFTWARE-DIRECTED SYSTEMS

This book is concerned with systems in which the primary responsibility for directing their operation rests with their software. We call them *software-directed systems*, some of which consist almost entirely of software, with hardware serving as input and output devices and processors. Most business data processing and information-management systems are examples. Other software-directed systems include significant hardware components. An automated factory, for example, includes equipment to perform most of the system's work; the software serves to direct and control the operation of the factory's machines. As another example, most communication and surveillance satellites are directed and controlled to a greater or lesser extent by software running on-board the satellite.

Some systems are not software-directed. Most mechanical systems and devices (e.g., steam shovels) get along quite well without software, and although some mechanical systems contain software (e.g., an automobile with a computer-controlled carburetor) the system should not be called software-directed if it is not controlled by the software. Many systems with fairly sophisticated internal controls, (e.g., automatic elevators) function adequately without software, hence should not be called software-directed. A system is software-directed if either of the following applies:

1. Software is responsible for its direction and control.
2. A central function of the system is information processing, and that information processing is directed by software.

In a software-directed system the software serves as the principal source of direction. Because in this sense it is the "brains" of the system, we take it to be primary and, in effect, we view the other elements of the system as peripheral devices. Thus in software-directed systems software is not just another component; it is the principal component. Other components may be important, even vital, but it is the software that is the ultimate core of the system.

1.2   A FRAMEWORK FOR TECHNICAL INFORMATION

The purpose of this book is to provide an integrated framework for the technical information needed in the successful development and maintenance of software. Much attention has been paid lately to software development and the various phases inherent in a disciplined development cycle. Development, however, is only the beginning of the life of a software-directed system. After its initial development it often changes considerably and the same sort of documentation is needed for system modification as for initial development. In fact, a reason for producing high-quality documentation is to provide material for the system's later modification. Thus the documentation described here is a framework to be used throughout the system's life. This information, however, should not be considered as applicable solely to one phase or another of the life cycle. It is essential from the time the system is developed until it is no longer in use.

We divide the information into three categories:

1. *Requirements.*   System requirements characterize the user's needs with respect to the system and define the objectives to be achieved—objectives that may evolve with experience. In discussing requirements our goals are as follows:

   a. To characterize these requirements as a distinct and important form of documentation. In the past the notion of requirements has often been confused with that of system specification.

   b. To outline and discuss the important categories of requirements.

   c. To provide a rigorous framework for expressing requirements. This framework encourages the requirements author to analyze the world with which the system will be concerned and within which it is expected to function. The framework we present contains a means for building a model of that world.

2. *Behavioral and Other Specifications.*   A behavioral specification describes the externally visible (thus behavioral) characteristics of a system. By describing its expected behavior a behavioral specification characterizes a system that is intended to achieve the objectives expressed by the requirements. Our goals are these:

a. To clarify for the general, that is, mathematically less sophisticated, reader the notion of a rigorous behavioral specification. We recommend an approach that lends itself to rigor without excessive formality.

b. To provide a framework and the tools for specifying interactive systems.

c. To identify other behavioral elements important to fitting a system to its environment. These elements are the following:

(1) The structure and functioning of the organization that *uses* the system. We describe a document, called a *procedures manual*, in which that information may be recorded.

(2) The support required from the organization that *operates* the system. We describe a document, called an *administrative manual*, in which that information may be recorded.

3. *Design.* A design describes the internal organization of a system. It shows how a system that functions as the behavioral specification describes may be built. Our goals for the design discussion are these:

a. To distinguish between design on the level of software architecture and the design of algorithms. We take software architecture to be concerned with the structure of a system in terms of its component parts and the interaction between those parts.

b. To provide a taxonomy of software component types. This taxonomy will give software designers conceptual tools to use in developing software architectures.

c. To illuminate the design notions of types, objects, dataflow, components (modules), abstraction, and encapsulation and to make these notions accessible to working software designers.

The following questions should fix in mind the place of the various documents:

1. *Why* is a system needed and for what purpose(s)? The requirements document answers this question.

2. *What* does a system that fills these needs look like and how is it used? The system specification answers this question.

3. *How* can a system be built to behave as described? The design documents answer this question.

In the past system documentation has been a concern mainly in large and complex systems. We believe that the recommendations in this book apply equally to all systems, large and small. No matter what the system, it is important that this information be available in some form. This form will vary, depending on a number of things: for example the size of the system and the value or risk of the functions it performs. The more numerous, more valuable, or riskier the functions, the more formal the documentation. The less numerous, less significant, or less risky, the less formal the documentation. In either case all the information should be available in some form—

be it formally in controlled documents or informally on napkins or the backs of envelopes.

Many organizations have their own formats for these or similar documents [U.S. Department of Defense, 1968; Gunther, 1978; Tausworthe, 1979]. Some of them differ from the formats presented here, but that is not critical. Their exact form is less important than their contents. When the form we discuss in this book differs from that of the reader's organization appropriate adjustments should be made.

Each category of information has a chapter to itself, and for each category an annotated outline which lists the intended contents is provided. Each also explains the reasons for including or excluding information.

1.3   SOFTWARE SUPPORT ENVIRONMENTS

A secondary goal of this book is to contribute to the evolution of software support environments. As we have suggested, the information given can be organized in the traditional document form. The book is organized to facilitate that approach, and most readers will probably want to follow it. Alternatively, the information may be kept in computer-processable form in a software support environment. The field of software support environments is growing rapidly, and environments that contain tools to aid in the development of software systems will soon be available. We hope to contribute to that development by discussing the information necessary for software development. We look forward to the widespread use of these environments and hope that this work will speed their development.

1.4   CONTINUING DEVELOPMENT

The field of software engineering is developing rapidly. The guidelines we have set out reflect the current state of the art to the extent that we have been able to capture it. We encourage readers to correspond with us, via the publisher, about ideas beyond those presented. In addition, we would like to hear from readers about their experiences in applying these guidelines. In particular, we would like to hear about cases in which the suggested organization of information did not quite fit and in what ways readers have changed the guidelines to accommodate them to their projects.

EXERCISES

1.   Is the notion of software-directed systems too one-sided? Develop the argument that software is no more important than any other component in a complex system. Evaluate the argument developed.

2.   The traditional system life cycle is often described in terms of a number of phases. The activities that occur during these phases typically result in the production of documents.

a. *Requirements Phase.*   The primary objective of this phase is to character-
    ize the user's needs.

    (1) The requirements document is developed.
    (2) A preliminary version of the system validation tests is written.

b. *Requirements Validation, Behavioral Specification, or Proposal Phase.*
    This phase has a number of different names and in some cases somewhat
    differing goals, depending on the particular development methodology
    adopted. In all cases the primary objective is to clarify the likely shape of
    the eventual system and to determine the cost of meeting the user's state-
    ment of requirements.

    (1) The initial versions of the behavioral specification documents are pro-
         duced.
    (2) The top level of the design documents is given draft form.
    (3) A preliminary system verification plan is developed.

    These drafts should provide enough information about the shape of the pro-
    posed system to allow it to be evaluated in terms of its functionality, overall
    design feasibility, proposed cost, and proposed schedule. Except for
    known, high-risk design difficulties, these documents do not provide de-
    sign details. Proposed solutions to the high-risk design problems are spelled
    out in enough detail to permit their feasibility to be determined.

c. *Preliminary Design.*   The primary objective of this phase is to develop a
    convincing architectural design of the system. To do so a more complete
    behavioral description is required:

    (1) A functionally complete specification document is produced.
    (2) An architectural design, which includes specifications of all software
         and hardware components, is developed.
    (3) For each element of the design verification tests are specified. In ad-
         dition, the validation tests are completed.

d. *Detailed Design.*   The primary objective of this phase is to complete the
    design:

    (1) The internal designs of the software and hardware components are
         completed.
    (2) Any functional details remaining in the specificiation documents are
         completed.

e. *Implementation.*   In this phase the system is built and the low-level ele-
    ments are debugged.

f. *Integration, Test, and Evaluation.*   In this phase the system is examined
    according to the tests defined earlier.

g. *Operation and Maintenance.*   In this phase the system is used. Any en-
    hancements or other revisions follow the same cycle as the original devel-
    opment. Instead of rewriting them from scratch the existing documents are
    modified according to the desired changes.

This same document development plan may be followed for a phased development strategy, that is, in which the system is delivered in terms of "builds." The first development phase follows the initial steps of document development. Each is treated as an enhancement/revision. In following this approach, in which the development phases succeed one another closely, care must be taken to ensure configuration integrity: the configuration management plan must be well thought out and executed.

Describe the information needed during each of these phases. Are there other approaches to a system life cycle in which different information would be needed? Could some work be saved by organizing things differently?

3. We have claimed that the technical information that pertains to a system should be organized into requirements, behavioral information, and design. Suggest another organizational strategy for the same information? Compare and contrast it with the proposed approach.

4. Do you agree that the information discussed should be recorded for systems of all sizes and not just large systems? Why or why not.

5. In what ways can you envision this information being incorporated into a software development and support environment? Describe briefly how such an environment could be organized and used. What automated tools might it contain? In your opinion what software development tasks will never be completely automated? Why?

REFERENCES

U.S. Department of Defense, Specification Practices, MIL-STD 490, 1968.

Richard C. Gunther, *Management Methodology for Software Product Engineering*, J Wiley, New York, 1978.

Robert C. Tausworthe, *Standardized Development of Computer Software (two volumes)*, Prentice-Hall, Englewood Cliffs, New Jersey, 1979.

PART 1

REQUIREMENTS

2

REQUIREMENTS DISCUSSION

A requirements document defines the problems that a system is to solve or the objectives it is to achieve. A requirements document describes the needs that the system is to satisfy for the expected user(s) and the constraints imposed by its intended environment. A requirements document should contain all the relevant information that a prospective user could possibly supply to those who will develop the system. In effect, a requirements document is a description of the world into which the intended system must fit and the goals that it is to meet. As such, it answers the first of the three questions posed in the introduction to this book.

1. *Why* is a system needed and for what purpose(s)? The requirements document answers this question.
2. *What* does a system that fills these needs look like and how is it used? The system specification answers this question.
3. *How* can a system be built to behave as described? The design documents answer this question.

The reason for writing a requirements document is to clarify ahead of time the problem the system must solve and what characteristics it must have to provide a solution. Too many systems have been built that are simply not capable of doing the job the users really need done; but once a user is presented with an inadequate system three principal options become available: accept the system as it is, even though it does not solve the problem, send the system back to be fixed, or discard it and start again. None is attractive; all are expensive.

To illustrate the importance of requirements consider the following story:

Bottom Line Technology (BLT) was such a large, busy, and successful company that its employees frequently found themselves pressed for time. They sometimes scheduled two meetings for the same hour; often they simply forgot where they were supposed to be and what they should be doing. BLT management became increasingly distressed by the disorganization and it was decided that an appointment and scheduling system was essential.

BLT hired The Rapid Coders Company, known in the trade as the rabid coders or just "Rabid" because of the frenzy with which they worked, to build the appointment system. Rabid assured BLT that they knew what was needed—in fact, they had recently built a similar system for a similar company, Rip-Offs International (ROI)—and could easily build one for BLT. BLT was pleasantly surprised when in less than three months Rabid delivered the system. Perhaps, they thought, not all software people are crooks after all.

BLT got its first disappointment when it found that the system Rabid had delivered did not run on the BLT computer. Of course, BLT had told Rabid what brand of computer it owned. What BLT forgot to tell Rabid was that a special operating system had been built for that computer; the standard operating system supplied by the computer manufacturer was not being used.

After a few weeks of retrofitting Rabid did get the system up and running. Rabid's additional charge, although not modest, was certainly within the budget of a company as large and successful as BLT.

A few days of operation revealed another problem. It seems that the system provided a means for users to make entries in their on-line appointment books about upcoming appointments. BLT employees naturally took advantage of this capability and frequently made brief notes to themselves about what they expected from the people they were going to see. Unfortunately the system had no means of preserving the privacy of these notes: anyone could look at anyone else's appointment book. When some BLT employees found out what some of their colleagues thought of them BLT morale declined precipitously.

BLT had Rabid change the appointment system to maintain privacy. This time, the Rabid charge, again not outrageous, was significant and BLT was forced to postpone plans for a new building.

All of this happened so quickly that BLT hadn't yet noticed that the system did not allow for the automatic scheduling of meetings, that is, a mutually convenient time for all attendees and an appointment for each of them. Of course, no one had told Rabid that BLT wanted the system to be able to schedule meetings. BLT, however, had assumed that any reasonable appointment system would have that capability.

The charge for this fix was so great that BLT had to cancel the new building entirely. In addition, BLT withdrew its favorable view of software people and vowed never again to buy another software product from an outside source. They would do all their future software development in-house.

Six months later, with the system working fairly well, BLT discovered that they could no longer add new people to the system: the system had been designed for a fixed number of users. Because of its rapid growth (especially with all the new programmers needed to do in-house software development) BLT had saturated the system in just half a year.

BLT was understandably reluctant to go back to Rabid for repairs, but when they consulted another software company they were told that the design of the system was so contorted (apparently true to its reputation, Rabid had adopted the *get-it-running-and-out-the-door* standard for system design) it would cost almost as much to unravel the code and make the correction as it would to throw the system out entirely and start from scratch.

But BLT did not want to start all over. So with fear in their hearts (and a lot less money in the bank) they went back to Rabid and asked for an estimate for this latest modification. There was good news and bad news. The good news was that some of the original programmers were still with Rabid and remembered how the system worked. The bad news was that that did not help. The system design was fundamentally dependent on the particular number of users and any change would be extremely costly. (It was reported that some of the Rabid programmers were heard mumbling, ''If they wanted more than 256 users, they should have bought a machine with larger bytes,'' a rumor that Rabid's management denied.) Faced with the prospect of having to omit its next quarterly dividend to pay for the latest change and still lacking a system about which they could feel confident, BLT decided to scrap the Rabid system and do the job correctly. As their first step they wrote a requirements document.

A requirements document should contain any information that might be important to the eventual use of the system to be developed. The only a priori limitation placed on the subject matter in a requirements document is that it must pertain to the possible *usefulness* of the system; that is, it must be part of the problem description rather than the solution description. Examples of information not appropriate for a requirements document are a description of a management plan for developing the system and a design for its implementation. Information of this sort is not appropriate for a requirements document because it is not relevant to the system's eventual use. Beyond that constraint anything that might be important for the system developer to know about the intended use of the system is reasonable to include. When relevant, and when truly required for the system to be *useful,* the requirements document should discuss the following points:

1. Why the user wants the system: the user problem the system will solve.
2. How the user intends to use the system.
3. Other systems and procedures that will interface with the planned system.
4. The technical expertise of the people who will actually operate the system.
5. The information the system must be able to handle.
6. Any integrity contraints the system must enforce; for example, access limitations.
7. Any legal constraints; for example, privacy, record retention requirements.
8. The data processing functions the system should perform for the user.
9. The hardware on which the intended system must operate.
10. The programming language in which the system must be written (if for some reason it must be written in a particular language).

11. The operating system on which the system must be installed.

12. The expected load the system should be able to serve; for example, the number of transactions per hour.

13. The response time needed from the system.

14. The expected enhancements that the system might undergo after initial use.

15. The design qualities and characteristics expected of the system.

16. Any auditing requirement; for example, the need for an audit trail.

17. Any physical constraints; for example, because of its intended location, the system cannot be run on a computer that needs air conditioning.

18. Any peripheral devices the system must use or control.

19. Anything else the user must have that the system developers should know about.

The purpose of a requirements document is to provide a place to express information of this sort in a clearly organized way. As such it serves two roles:

1. A place where the user can express his needs and limitations.

2. A place where the system developers can find a complete statement of the user's needs and limitations.

In this way the requirements document serves as the initial agreement between user and developer about what the eventual system should be.

A note on terminology. In business applications of computers the process of analyzing a business with respect to its data processing needs and constraints and formally documenting those needs is commonly referred to as "systems analysis." In nonbusiness applications the process of defining needs is often called "system definition," "requirements analysis," or "requirements engineering." The goal is the same. In all cases the needs and constraints found during analysis are called "requirements."

Requirements Only or Requirements Plus Rationale

When writing a requirements document we are faced with the problem of how much information to include. Should only a bare-bones statement of the requirements be made or should there be a rationale for and explanation of the requirement? We could argue either way.

1. *Include Requirements Only.* The purpose to be served by a requirements document is as a contract between the person or organization acquiring the system and the person or organization building it. The system developer will be constrained by this contract to build a system that satisfies the requirements as stated. The developer does not care *why* those requirements are needed or even if they make sense. On legal grounds all the two sides really care about is exactly *what* the requirements are.

When validating the system to determine that the developer did the job fully all we can go on is whether the system meets the requirements as stated. It dooesn't matter that the requirements statement may be incorrect or no longer what the user needs. It is the written statement of the requirements that matters. A requirements document that includes nothing but a list of plainly stated requirements makes the work of the developer and validator much simpler and more straightforward. If statements of requirements are mixed in with other information and with rationales for the requirements they will have a much harder job deciding what is and what is not a requirement.

2. *Include Rationale and Explanation.*   In the long run the requirements document should be useful as more than just a starting point for the developer. Once the system has been built inevitably operating changes are wanted. It is at this point that the requirements document can be especially useful. If the requirements document includes a rationale for the system as built potential changes can be evaluated in the light of the original reasons for having it as it is.

Consider the requirement that the system be available for certain activities during certain hours (and perhaps other activities during other hours). There could be any number of reasons for that requirement:

a.   The organization might be open for business between certain hours.

b.   The organization may not want its employees to use the system after hours because it doesn't want to pay them overtime.

c.   The organization may not want anyone to use the system after hours because it doesn't want the system in operation when there is no other activity and there is a greater likelihood of a security breach.

d.   The organization may want to use the computer facility on which the system will operate for other purposes during other hours.

e.   The system may be controlling factory devices that should not be allowed to operate except during normal production hours when supervision is available.

f.   The system is part of a weather-monitoring, satellite-tracking, or air-pollution control system and its responsibility is for exactly the hours stated.

If some time after the system is installed the issue of extending the hours of operation is raised it would be useful to know why the requirement was originated. If it was included as a security measure, it should be determined whether other means are now available to control the security risk that a change in operating hours would entail. If the requirement had been added simply because those were the desired hours of operation and additional hours of operation are now needed there would seem to be no reason not to permit them. If the requirement had been intended to be part of the cost-benefit strategy for using the system we must determine whether that strategy is still valid and how a change in the use of the system will effect it.

If the rationale for a requirement is not included we frequently hesitate to change the requirement for fear that something dreadful might happen. We think, "There must have been a good reason for it or it wouldn't have been required. Therefore we had better not change it.'' And if no one remembers what that good reason is the requirement remains unbudgeable. That is certainly not a good way to make decisions.

Both positions have merit. Is there a compromise between them? We recommend the following approach. Include statements of requirements with relevant information and rationales (when not overly sensitive) in a requirements document but highlight the requirements. Thus there could be a discussion that would lead up to a statement of a requirement to explain the background and explore possible alternatives. The actual statement of the requirement that embodied the decisions reached on the basis of that analysis follows that discussion. This approach has a number of advantages:

1. The actual requirements are clear to the system developers and validators.
2. Should questions of changing the system be asked we can look back and see exactly why the requirements were written as they were and what consequences a change in them might have.
3. The system developers might think of a way of achieving the objectives implicit in the requirement rationale that differs from the actual statement of the requirement. They then have the option of suggesting another approach and requesting that the requirement be modified.

Expressing Requirements

Requirements have been expressed traditionally by listing properties required of the system to be developed rather than by describing the problem to be solved; for example, a user may stipulate as one of his needs that certain information be kept secure from unauthorized access. That requirement would be expressed as
The system shall ensure the security of information about . . .
rather than by the statement
information about . . . must be kept secure.
This practice is unfortunate. It leads the authors of requirements documents to focus too much attention on the system to be developed and too little on the problem to be solved. There are, however, a number of valid reasons for this practice.

1. *There will be a system.* Presumably it is known that a computer system will be developed to meet the needs described. To pretend that we are not talking about a system to be developed is deceptive. (On the other hand, it may be that a noncomputer solution would provide a better answer to the problem. We might miss the noncomputer solution by focusing too much on *the system.*)
2. *The system is the solution.* When describing the system to be developed we are really not talking about a particular design. (This is true even if ''the system'' has been given a preliminary name.) *The system* should be read to mean *the solution*

to the problem or *the means of achieving the objectives or meeting the needs the requirements document describes.* Thus to say

    the system shall ensure the security of information about . . .

is the same as saying

    the solution to the problem shall ensure the security of information about. . . .

Hence we are not really discussing the solution instead of the problem. Certainly the first method is shorter.

In addition, reference to the solution as a system does not constrain it much. The word *system* means *a set of interrelated elements that forms a unified whole.* Presumably any solution will satisfy that definition.

    3. *The requirements author may know what is wanted.* It is best that the author of a requirements document have some familiarity with the sort of system for which requirements are to be written. Perhaps the new system is replacing a similar but outdated version or perhaps it resembles some other system with which the requirements author is familiar. With this familiarity the requirements author may know (or believe that he or she knows) the best approach to take when dealing with some aspect of the problem. A concern may be that the developers may not have the same experience, hence may not hit on so good an approach. Given these circumstances, it seems perfectly justifiable for the requirements author to mandate the approach wanted rather than hinting at it. When mandating an approach the requirements author takes the responsibility for the consequences if that approach does not work out; that is, the requirements author is assuming some of the responsibility of the developer. In some situations, however, that might be acceptable. In addition, if, as we suggested in the preceding section, the requirements author includes a rationale in the requirements document the developer is free to suggest some other approach believed to be better.

As an example, consider a system intended for computer-naïve users. The requirements author may believe that a menu-based system is better than a command-based system. Yet to require menus is to do more than state requirements, for the requirement is only that the system be comfortable for computer-naïve users. If the requirements author has reason to suspect that the developer is unfamiliar with menu-based systems or for one reason or another is more likely to produce a command-based system it seems justifiable for the requirements author to require menus.

We define a *requirement* as

    any function, constraint, or other property that must be provided, met, or satisfied to fill the needs of the system's intended user(s).

Although this seems to be a simple enough definition, requirements can be tricky. A personal illustration may be helpful.

A text-editing system was used to write this book. I decided to buy a computer terminal and work at home. Soon the choice was narrowed to a certain class of terminal. It happened that that class included models that offer as an option the capability of displaying 132 characters on each line of the screen. (The normal line width is 80.) Neither the text editor, the computer on which the book was stored, nor the computers I used most frequently generated a 132-character output. Therefore it seemed reasonable to consider the 132-character line option as adding little value. So for a while the wide-screen option was ignored in the evaluation of terminals until a colleague pointed out that my wife used a computer that often produced the greater output and that she would find it convenient if the terminal acquired for use at home supported that feature. At that point the option became a requirement.

The interesting thing about this requirement is that it was not overlooked originally because it wasn't considered; it was not a requirement that "fell through the cracks." It was weighed many times—once for each terminal manufacturer who offered the option at his own special rate; none would permit it to to be ignored, but each time we found it unneeded. It was missed because in working on requirements only the specific problem at hand was important. We asked: What is needed to work on this book at home? We didn't ask: Given the system we are going to acquire, what else could it be used for if it had the capabilities?

Most systems suffer from this narrow-mindedness of focus. In fact, it is usually considered commendable to restrict our search for requirements to a particular objective or to a particular problem to be solved. Yet, like it or not, all systems exist in a broader environment, no matter how narrowly defined their specific requirements. In that broader environment other uses would inevitably become apparent— if only the system had those added capabilities. From these newly conceived uses the list of possible applications will grow, often seemingly without bounds. There is probably no way to avoid contemplating extensions of the system's intended use. Therefore if some of the additional functions could be imagined during the requirements stage the system could be built to facilitate their inclusion.

Knowledge of Software

When writing requirements how important is it to know about computers and software? We could argue that user needs should drive the requirements and that a knowledge of computers should not be a factor. Unfortunately that is an impossible position. We cannot really describe a problem that we expect a computer to help solve unless we have some idea of the kind of things a computer can do. There is just no point, for example, in describing as a problem the need for a conversational companion for bedridden hospital patients. The current state of the art of computer science is just not up to producing such a system.

At the other extreme, lack of knowledge might lead us to ask for too little. Sometimes we demand something that is easy to provide just because the requirements writer does not know that it is easy. Consider, for example, the requirements for the appointment-scheduling system we have already discussed. Presumably we would want some sort of automatic reminder capability which would remind us of events scheduled for the following day. We face the question of how many reminders the system should be able to accommodate. If, as computer-naïve requirements authors, we assume that asking for some number (k) of reminders each day requires a system with k positions allocated in advance for reminders for every day we would feel obliged to keep k low to avoid the need for too much storage (which might make the system too expensive). But computer system design is more advanced than that. Designers know that the maximum required does not always imply that that maximum will be used. Generally, systems are not used to their utmost, and if some additional information about expected usage were incuded a better system could be designed.

In fact, there are at least two better ways of approaching the requirement of the maximum number of reminders to require each day:

1. We could require the ability to include as a maximum as many as k reminders each day but also agree* that the *average* number of reminders per day is some smaller number, say $k/5$.

2. We could require that the system keep track of some large but reasonable number of reminders all together and allow the users to decide how they are to be distributed over their calendars: evenly spread out or all on one day.

Given either of these versions, a competent system designer can develop a system with a much larger limit on the maximum number of reminders allocated for any one day.† To be aware of the alternate ways of expressing user-needs requires some knowledge of how to design a system to fill them. Anyone who lacks this knowledge is at a great disadvantage.

Additional Reading

For additional discussions of system requirements consult the following sources. [Alford, 1977; Chen, 1980; Chen, 1983; Davis et al., 1983; Ross, 1979; Tausworthe, 1979; Teichrow, 1977; and Yeh and Zave, 1980]. One should be cautious in reading the literature, however, because many authors do not agree with the distinction we draw between requirements and specifications. The two terms are often taken as synonymous:

> Software requirements engineering is the discipline for developing a complete, consistent, unambiguous specification . . . describing what the software product will do (but not *how* it will do it . . .) [Boehm, 1976].

> [A requirements document should specify] the functions to be performed by the system, from the viewpoint of the user or external environment. [For example], the requirements specification for a point-of-sale system would describe system responses to users' keystrokes [Davis and Rauscher, 1979].

> A requirements document should specify . . . the external behavior of a system, without implying a particular implementation [Heninger et al., 1980].

---

*This *agreement* that the average number of reminders per day is $k/5$ is an example of information about the system that is not truly a requirement; the requirement is that the system provide a maximum of k reminders each day. This other information helps the developer to provide a more cost effective system and it should definitely be included in a requirements document.
†This approach could be taken even further and the requirement could be written to permit reminders, appointments, and messages to share storage resources.

The specification is a means for precisely stating the system requirements. [Wasserman and Stinson, 1979].

For a more complete survey of this silent dispute see [Abbott and Morehead, 1982]. As we show in subsequent chapters, these descriptions of "requirements" are closer to our sense of behavioral specifications.

Our view is closer to that of Ross in his chair message with which he opened the 1979 IEEE Conference on Reliable Software:

Specification fits solidly between Requirements Definitions and Design. If we have good statements of requirements, they can only be translated into a valid design through adequate specification methods [Ross, 1979].

We continue this discussion in the chapter on system specifications in which we provide illustrations of the differences between requirements and specifications.

EXERCISES

1. Do you think it is really necessary for the developers to know as much about the user-needs as suggested at the beginning of this chapter?
2. Comment on the requirements-only versus requirements-plus-rationale debate. Why do you suppose the requirements-only side has been more widely adopted?
3. Present cases for both sides of the practice of stating requirements in terms of *the system shall*.
4. Develop arguments for and against considering possible system uses that are beyond the motivating problem narrowly defined. In the long run, doing so will probably save money. Why is it that the standard budgetary process generally requires requirements to be defined as narrowly as possible?
5. Write a brief set of requirements for a companion for bedridden hospital patients.
6. If a requirements author knows too little about computers, impossible requirements may be written; if too much is known there many be the temptation to design the system while writing the requirements. Is there a perfect amount that requirements authors should know about computers?

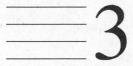

3

REQUIREMENTS DOCUMENT OUTLINE

To express requirements it is useful to have a preexisting outline in which there is a place for all functions, constraints, and properties that a user may need. This outline can be filled in to produce a requirements document for any particular set of user needs. The sections of this chapter provide such an outline. That is, section 3.n may be taken as section n of a typical requirements document.

The requirements document is the first in a series of documents produced during the life of a software system. As we indicated in the introduction, the following questions characterize the places of the various documents.

1. *Why* is a system needed and for what purpose(s)? The requirements document answers this question.
2. *What* does a system that fills these needs look like? The behavioral specifications answers this question.
3. *How* can a system be built to behave as described? The design document answers this question.

3.1 OVERVIEW OF THE DOCUMENT, ORGANIZATION, AND CONVENTIONS

This section sets the context for the rest of the document. It tells what the document (requirements) and the system are about. It also explains the organization of the rest of the document and any conventions used to write it.

3.1.1   Scope of the Document

This section is a brief statement of the ground covered by the document. It should give the reader an idea of what to expect.

3.1.2   Organization of the Document: Annotated Contents

This section will help the reader to understand how the remainder of the document is organized. It highlights the motivation behind the remaining sections and shows how the document should be approached. Most reference documents are not intended to be read straight through. This section tells the new reader what the goals are for the various sections and what use can be made of them.

3.1.3   Conventions Used in the Document

This section defines the definitions, notational conventions, and abbreviations used in the document. All should be listed and defined in a simple, clear, and concise manner. If any of these subsections are lengthy they should be included as appendixes and referred to as such.

Definitions

This section serves as a glossary of definitions used in the document. It contains definitions of all the terms that are neither standard English nor technical.

Acronyms

This section lists all the acronyms used and the terms for which they stand. When an acronym is introduced in the text of the document the term for which it stands appears in context, followed immediately by the acronym in parentheses; for example, we might say that this textbook is about requirements, specification, and design (RSD) documents.

Notations

This section introduces the mathematical or other special notations in the document that readers are not expected to know beforehand.

Terminology

This section introduces conventions that concern the interpretation of the wording of the document.

EXERCISES

1. Write a description of conventions to be used in writing dates. Allow at least two *formats*, such as Jan. 1, 1990, 1/1/90, or 1 Jan 90. Permit (and explain) *wild card* dates; for example, *Jan *, 1990* means every day in January in 1990 and *Jan 1, ** means every January first. Provide a direct explanation, not one by example as we have done.
2. Find a glossary of computer terms. Find five definitions with which you disagree. Make better definitions.
3. What are the advantages of acronyms?

3.2   SYSTEM OVERVIEW AND ORGANIZATIONAL CONTEXT

This section of the requirements document presents an overview of the system and its intended use. It also describes the system's expected operational context and the organization that will be using the system and identifies the features of that organization's structure and operation to be reflected in the system's functioning.

3.2.1   System Definition

This section defines the overall goals and limitations of the system. It describes the user's organization and reflects the policy decisions taken by that organization. All further development must exist within this framework.

Purpose(s)

The statement of the system's purpose should be a concise characterization of the intended direct result(s) or effect(s) to be produced. On the most general level it answers the question: why develop this system? Examples include the following:

Faster processing of orders with fewer clerks (for an order entry system);

Automatic control of a factory (for a factory automation system);

The production of higher quality, less costly technical reports (for a word/text processing system).

Scope

The statement of scope should identify the functional areas for which the system is to be responsible. It should also define the limits of those functional areas and identify the boundaries of the system's responsibilities; for example, a word processing system may be intended for text entry and modification but not for text formatting or document filing.

Anticipated Market/Users

The intended market/users for the system are listed here. If the potential user-community is fragmented the fragments should be listed separately. Examples of possible users include "any office with 3 to 10 people" (for a word processing system intended for sale) or "the personnel department of the XYZ company" (for a human resources tracking and development system intended specifically for that company).

Anticipated Uses

The primary intended use(s) of the system should be examined here. Its applications, rather than the particular operations it is expected to perform should be given: for example, a system that enhances and facilitates the examination of geographical terrain photographs might be used to pinpoint sites of energy or mineral deposits. The uses rather than the system functions should be listed here. Functions appear in Section 3.4 of the requirements document. It should be clear how these uses would achieve the purposes set out above; for example, the purpose associated with the primary use would be to discover more energy and mineral resources.

Range of Configurations and Options

Many software products are intended to operate in different configurations and to have multiple options. Although the complete details of all possible combinations of configuration elements and options cannot be described here, this section should list the primary objectives; that is, is the system intended for both large and small computers, for single and multiple users, or for direct and remote use? Does it contain special features that will be made available in a "deluxe" version and not normally in the "standard" version? These alternatives should be outlined.

3.2.2   Overview of the User Organization

This section and the subsections within it provide an overview of the structure and functioning of the expected user organization. The overview is intended to provide a conceptual framework for an understanding of the needs of that organization. The amount of detail should be appropriate to the degree to which its structure and functioning are expected to be reflected in the system.

One of the most important functions of a requirements document is to define the conceptual structure of the world into which the system is to fit. This is often a difficult job, even though that world may not be exceptionally complex or sophisticated. Identification and expression of the concepts in terms of which the expected user organization functions is often difficult just because those concepts are understood primarily on an intuitive level by people in the organization rather than in a formal way; there is often the matter of being so close to the problem that it is hard to see it for what it is. Thus a successful requirements document will, as one of its accomplishments, formalize the terms in which the user organization operates. This section of the requirements document bears the main burden of that formalization task.

It is frequently useful to begin with whatever formal structure the user-organization has already worked out for itself. Thus, if it has descriptions of its relevant portions, say in terms of organization charts, then those organization charts should be included in the next section of this document: structural organization. Similarly, if the user-organization has developed administrative forms in terms of which it transacts parts of its business relevant to the system, then those forms are valuable for isolating the entities and relations required in Section 3.3. Every hint of its existing conceptual structure should be exploited.

Not every feature of the user-organization's structure need be included. The requirements document is not intended to be a complete description of the world with which it deals. This document should concern itself only with that portion of the user-organization relevant to the system under consideration. This section of the requirements document describes the system's operational context from as many structural points of view as are relevant. The four that follow are generally most important, but if there are others that matter in the operation of the system they too should be presented.

Logical Organization

This section discusses the relevant details of the user-organization's logical structure. Logical organization refers to the traditional business/command/decision-making structure of the organization reflected, for example, in an organization chart. To the extent that this structure must be known by and reflected in the operation of the system it should be described here or in a referenced document.

Physical Organization

This section discusses the relevant details of the user-organization's physical structure. Physical organization refers to its geographical arrangement; for example, are there branch offices located across town, across the state, across the country, or around the world that must be connected? How many? To the extent that this structure must be known by, reflected in, and be otherwise relevant to the operation of the system it should be described here or in a referenced document.

Temporal Organization

This section discusses the relevant details of the user-organization's temporal structure. Temporal organization refers to a schedule of relevant events and may include the following:

1. The budgeting cycle and other activities based on the fiscal year.
2. A regular (e.g., daily, weekly, monthly, production, or sales) reporting cycle.
3. The calendar for administrative activities such as personnel reviews, curriculum revisions, or legislative processes.
4. Schedules of events such as airline flights or television broadcasts.
5. Specifically scheduled individual events such as baseball games, trade shows, or rocket launches.

Information Flow Organization

This section describes the current information-flow structure of the organization. It should be included here only to the extent that it is relevant. Information flow is relevant if:

1. The information that is flowing is relevant to the system.
2. The information flow corresponds to an organizational structure that is more or less fixed or that reflects organizational policy in regard to the division of responsibility.

Information flow is often described by ''bubble charts.'' Each bubble represents an operational part of the organization and each is labeled to identify the name of the organizational unit and the information processing task it performs.

Labeled arrows connect bubbles to show how information passes from one part of the organization to another. The labels identify the information that passes between the organization's two parts.

Bubble charts also reflect information souces, sinks, and storage units to indicate the points at which information enters the organization, where it leaves the organization, and where it is stored within the organization. We discuss information flow diagrams in more detail in the procedures manual.

3.2.3 Anticipated Operational Strategy

This section describes the way in which the system is expected to be integrated into its operational environment. It also describes the owner of the system, the administrators, the users, and the system-funding strategy.

System Ownership

This section identifies the owner of the system. In many cases the owner is simply the anticipated user-organization. In others the owner expects to run the system as a service to other users; for example, in a time-sharing service or one that copies floppy disks from the format of one micro computer company to the format of another. In still others the owner offers the system on a royalty basis to administrators who run the system as a service or directly to the users (e.g., leased software packages). To the extent that system ownership is a factor in the system's use it should be spelled out here. Ownership may be important if the owner wishes to supply users with a working but unmodifiable version of the system (e.g., object code).

System Administration

This section describes the anticipated plan for running and servicing the system.

Operational Control.   This section identifies the organization expected to provide the system with basic operational support. Frequently this will be the user-organization's ''computer center.'' Operating the system will be another of their service responsibilities.

There may also have to be a new service organization set up to operate the system. An organization that lacks a computer center, for example, must develop a strategy for supporting the system's operational needs which include buying supplies and changing the paper on the printer (if there is one).

In addition, operational policy decisions must often be made (e.g., which of two contending users has higher priority). The mechanism for making those decisions should be considered ahead of time and at least outlined here.

Modification Policy and Change Support.   This section outlines the expected policy for changing the system after it is built. It answers such questions as these: will the owners be the only ones with authority to make changes? May the administrators (e.g., the computer center) modify the system? May users make their own changes? If a user feels the need for a change to whom should the modification request be addressed? What agency is responsible for tracking the changes and for ensuring their compatibility? If the system exhibits a fault who is responsible for fixing it? If a system change causes a fault who is responsible for fixing that? What agency has the authority to decide which of the possible changes will be requested/made?

Users

To the extent that they are known this section identifies the system's users in the context of the overall organization. These are the people who interact directly (or most nearly directly) with the system and those whose job needs the system was intended to serve. It also identifies the departments and job descriptions of the intended users.

The description should be more specific than that of the users in 3.2.1, in which only general categories are defined. Yet, although specific, the identification should be relatively brief because 6.1 details the user classes.

The primary purpose of this section is to discuss the system's intended functional interfaces with the user-organization. It may be that the best interface between it and the system is not yet known—that part of the job of system development is to define the most propitious interface. To the extent that the interface is known or constrained (e.g., only certain people in the organization are permitted access to information in the system or only a certain department has the information needed by the system) the interface is defined here. To the extent that the developer is expected to solve this problem that requirement is described in this section.

Funding Strategy

This section describes how the system is expected to be supported financially. Some systems are supported by their own budgets; others must be supported by the budget of the administering organization. Still others are supported by royalty fees paid monthly or yearly by the users, whereas still others are supported by charges levied on system services and resources required.

3.2.4   Currently Used Procedures

This section describes the procedures currently applicable to the performance of the functions intended for the system. The description is best given by reference to documents that define the system itself and its use by the organization. Also indicated are the parts of the current procedures that must be maintained in the new system.

EXERCISES

1. Write two statements of scope, one overly broad (e.g., almost a complete office automation system) and one overly narrow (e.g., only a record of appointments in a file) for an appointment scheduling system. How might company politics affect a system's statement of scope? What might the consequences be of building a system of this scope? Can you identify two systems that deal with the same area but have radically different scopes? What are they and how do they differ?

2. Write a realistic statement of scope for an appointment scheduling and reminder system. Does it include a mail-message capability (to allow users to make appointments with one another)?

3. Write a statement of scope for an on-line mail system. Does it include editing and formating capabilties?

4. Write statements of scope for word processing, text editing, and text formatting systems. How are you drawing the boundaries between them?

5. Write two statements of scope that distinguish between (a) a business graphics system to be used to produce graphics for vu-graphs and (b) a graphics system to be used to make television commercials.

6. Write a statement of scope for a spreadsheet system.

7. Characterize five distinct markets for an appointment scheduling system to be sold as a commercial product. (One market might be the owners of a particular brand of micro-computer.) How does the anticipated market affect the system's scope and uses?

8. List uses for an appointment scheduling system.

9. What advantages and disadvantages do multiple configurations and options give the developer and user?

10. Provide a top-level description (logical, physical, temporal, and information flow) for some aspect (e.g., the instructionally related activities) of your school or some other organization familiar to you.

11. When a company produces a software product for sale they are the owners but not the users. Does this produce a conflict of interest as far as requirements are concerned?

12. Why is system ownership/administration relevant in a requirements document?

13. Who are the users of payroll systems, appointment scheduling systems, factory monitoring systems?

14. In large organizations distinct units are often responsible for acquiring new systems from external sources (e.g., purchasing), operating the systems once they have been acquired (e.g., a computer center), maintaining them (e.g., the data processing department), and using them in jobs (the end user). What are the interests of these organizations? How do these separate interests conflict with one another?

15. List five different ways in which the operation of a system may be supported financially. How do these funding approaches affect the system's requirements? Is a system's funding strategy relevant in a requirements document?

16. Define the anticipated operational strategy for an appointment scheduling and reminder system.

17. Describe the current procedures for (a) a relatively informal activity like arranging meetings and making appointments and (b) some more formalized activity like enrolling in classes or transferring from one department of your company to another.

    a. Are there changes that could be made in these procedures to improve the process?

    b. Would any group of people feel threatened if these changes were made?

    c. How difficult politically would it be to make these changes? Why?

18. Why might an organization benefit from obstacles that make changing an organization's procedures more difficult?

19. Why are a company's current procedures relevant in a requirements document?

3.3   WORLD MODEL

This section discusses the elements in the world with which the system is expected to interact and their relation to one another. It also identifies the amount and significance of this information and the length of time for which it must be retained. Because the purpose of this section is to describe in as much detail as necessary the conceptual world with which the user deals, hence with which the system must deal, this material is fundamental to an understanding of the system requirements. Unfortunately no firm guidelines can be given for its presentation. The user's world may consist of anything at all. No field of knowledge, neither computer science, data processing, metaphysics, nor any of the physical sciences, provides the guidelines for defining arbitrary parts of the world in terms meaningful to an arbitrary level of abstraction; that is, if we tried to use the language of physics to describe payroll information we would be just as unsuccessful as if we tried to use the language of accounting to describe satellite orbits.

The information presented in this section represents the user's expertise. The best way to express expertise information is generally in terms of the language of experts in that particular field. If the system is to provide medical monitoring services, for example, the objects to be measured and the measurements to be made are best given in medical terms. If, on the other hand, the system is about banking the language describing the information manipulated should be that spoken by bankers. Workers in the still highly research-oriented field of artificial intelligence have recently developed systems capable of dealing with certain specific and limited areas of knowledge (e.g., see [Hayes-Roth et al., 1983]). Notwithstanding this success, means are neither currently available nor on the horizon for describing arbitrary segments of the real world, yet it is the purpose of this section to present that segment with which the system is expected to deal.

Unfortunately, although the best language for a particular field is that of its experts, that language is often not well defined. Sometimes the field under consideration is not an academic discipline. It consists, perhaps, of accumulated practical knowledge that has never been formally organized. Those in the field have become experts as a result of their day-to-day work. The language they speak and the concepts with which they deal, although as specialized and sophisticated as those of any of the more formal disciplines, may never have been thought through. This is one reason why writing requirements is sometimes so difficult. Before the requirements can be written we must describe the world that the requirements are to be written for; if that world has never before been clearly explained describing it for the first time can be a demanding job. Yet doing so is essential, particularly in terms that are clear and precise. Once the description is committed to the requirements document it is the description itself that drives the further development of the system and not the actual world. If the world is not described accurately or in enough detail the system will not fit as intended and the work put into building it may be wasted.

Because clarity and precision are so important and to assist those who have to write requirements for unorganized fields, this section presents one way to build a world model. The proposed organization will certainly not fit all areas, for, as we already said, the world is too complex for a single framework to encompass any arbitrary part of it. To the extent that the proposed framework does fit, however, it may be used; to the extent that it doesn't fit, additional descriptive structures must be invented.

It is important to make one further point. This section approaches the user's conceptual world from a static rather than a dynamic perspective; it describes its fixed structures, the things that might be encountered in it, and all the possible ways in which those things might be related. It does not discuss the activities and processes that go on in that world. Activities, processes, functions, and operations belong in Section 4. If an analogy can be made to a recipe this section lists the ingredients and utensils to be used by the recipe; Section 4 describes the part those ingredients and utensils take in filling the recipe. If a further analogy can be made to a computer program, this contains declarations of types and objects; section 4 covers the operations to be performed on objects of the declared types.

Overview of the Framework

The framework presented here recommends describing the world in terms of entities, their attributes, and relations among entities. The entity-attribute-relation approach was developed in parallel by workers in the fields of databases [Chen, 1976; Chen, 1980; Chen, 1983; Davis, et al., 1983] and artificial intelligence [Barr, et al., 1982–1983]. The version presented here contains ideas from both areas. A similar approach is taken in [Goldman and Wile, 1980]. First we present a brief overview of the notions that are important to an understanding of entities, attributes, and relationships. We then explore these ideas in more detail.

Entities and Entity Types

An entity is a "thing": a person like you and me, a physical object like a chair, an organizational unit like a division in a company, and almost anything else that we can think of that would have a separate identity. One of the most useful conceptualization tools we use is categorization; we tend to group *things* together into *categories* to reflect the commonalities we see among them. Thus we find it useful to consider that the world consists of entity types that, in some sense, resemble one another. Examples of entity types that correspond to the entities mentioned above are

person	you and I are both persons
chair	any particular chair is (of the type) chair
department	any particular department in a company is (of the type) department

An entity *E* is *of an* entity type *T* if we can say *E is a T*. Thus we can say *I am a person. Your Bauhaus chair is a chair. The personnel department is a department.*

We say that an entity of a particular type is an *instance* of that type. Thus to say that I am a person is the same as saying that I am an instance of the type of person, and to say that your chair is a chair is the same as saying that your chair is an instance of the type of chair. Although the basic idea of entities and their types should seem to be relatively intuitive and straightforward, some details are somewhat more difficult.

Attributes

Entity types frequently have *attributes* or properties that characterize or differentiate one member of that type from another. Typical of attributes are the following:

> *Measures of entities of the type*
>   height, weight

> *Labels for entities of the type*
>   name, driver's license number, alias

> *Characterizations and other properties of entities of the type*
>   style, birthday, salary, telephone number

Although most attributes are easy to describe and understand, dealing with them precisely is more complicated:

1. *Attributes with Multiple Values.*   Most attributes have single values; their value for any entity can be given as a single piece of information. *Birthday* is a single-valued attribute of a person because a person is born on just one day. Some attributes have multiple values. The attribute *alias* has a collection of values because a person may use more than one alias.

2. *Attributes with Component Parts.*   Most attributes are "atomic"; they have no parts. *Weight* is atomic because its value is a single number. Some attributes have parts; the attribute *name* may be understood to have the parts *first name, middle name,* and *last name.*

3. *Understanding Attribute Values.*   There are generally three distinct ways to interpret the values associated with attributes:

    a. *As a measure on some **unit of measure** scale.* The value of the attribute weight may be given in terms of pounds, kilograms, or some other unit of measure. The value itself is often just a number; the unit of measure must be specified separately.

    b. *As a name that stands for itself.* Attributes such as *model type* take their values from possible predefined sets. These values do not refer to a unit of measure scale; they stand for themselves.

c. *As something that matches a template.* The values of some attributes must take a certain form. Other than that, they may be considered meaningless, although the form may reflect an encoding of information that is not of current concern. Telephone numbers and social security numbers are examples.

Relations

The notions of *entity type* and *attribute* permit us to describe individual classes of entity. Entities are also related to one another: you *own* that chair; I *work for* my department. These relationships are *facts* about the world that establish connections between entities. It is important to be able to express them.

Just as entities may be categorized by type, relationships may be categorized by form. The relationship that *You own that chair* has the form

owner (*person, chair*)

Note that we are not talking about the grammatical form of the English sentence in which the relationship is expressed. We are talking about the form of the relationship itself, which establishes a particular kind of connection (**ownership**) between two particular entity types (*person and chair*):

That chair is owned by you.
You are the owner of that chair.
That is your chair (implying ownership).

All express the same relationship, the form of which is that the *ownership* relation holds between you and some particular chair. All relationships that identify a particular person as owner of a particular chair have that same form:

You own that chair.
I own the Victorian chair in the next room.
Joe owns the broken down chair in the garage.

All are relationships of the form

owner (*person, chair*).

All establish the same connection (**ownership**) between the same entity types (*person* and *chair*) We express relationships as

relationship name (*entity type, . . . , entity type*)

perhaps with some other information needed to pin them down completely. A class of relationships that can be expressed in a single form is called a *relation*; for example, the class of relationships that identifies people who own chairs is called the **(chair-)owner** relation.

As another example, the relationship
I work for the payroll department
has the form

work for (*person, department*).

Note that this relationship does *not* take the same form as the chair-ownership relationships even though both are concerned with two entities. The two relationships are different for two reasons:

1.   The name of each relation is different: **owner** and **work for**.
2.   The entity types related by the two relationships differ: *person* to *chair* in one and *person* to *department* in the other.

Thus a relation is characterized by its name and the entity types it relates.

Extensional and Intensional Attributes and Relations

The attributes and relationships we have discussed are all *extensional*. The actual entities and values are mentioned explicitly. We may also describe aspects of our world *intensionally*. We characterize an attribute or relationship intensionally by defining it in general terms; for example, when we say that a salesman's quota percentage is defined as *actual sales divided by quota* we are defining an intensional attribute of the salesman. When we say that everyone in the department eats lunch at Sir Lunch-A-Lot Restaurant we are defining an intensional relationship. (The relationship is the **eat-lunch-at** relation; it is defined between people and the restaurant where they eat lunch.)

Intensional attributes and relations are powerful tools. Most standard database systems do not provide a way of expressing them. They are more common in artificial intelligence systems and especially in systems that are equivalent to predicate calculus. [For an overview see Hayes-Roth et al., 1983.] The programming language Prolog [Clocksin and Mellish, 1981] is also in one view, a relational database system that provides for the expression of intensional attributes and relations.

This has been a brief introduction to a framework for expressing the user's world model by discussing entity types, attributes, and relations. The basic ideas are simple and intuitive, but because the world is not simple problems inevitably develop when an attempt is made to determine what the entities are in actual situations. The following sections examine some of these difficulties and provide guidance for dealing with them.

Entity Types and Substances in the Requirements Document

Entities are items in the world about which the desired system is intended to process information. This section of the requirements document identifies these entities types and characterizes the sort of information to be kept about them. Relevant characteristics, that is attributes, are given for each entity type. Attributes may include pay rates (for employees) or fuel status (for satellites). Keeping track of the values of entity attributes is often the primary responsibility of a system.

The notion of an entity type is taken quite broadly here. One way to acquire some understanding of entity types is by describing the system informally. Entity types are generally those things to which we find ourselves referring as a class or in terms of a typical, or generic, member of some class.

In an airline reservation system, for example, typical entity types are passengers, flights, airports, tickets, and reservation clerks. Any informal description of an airline reservation system will refer to these entity types or to generic instances of them; for example,

> . . . When the *passenger* orders a *ticket* the *reservation clerk* first checks to see whether the requested *flight* is full. . . .

The italicized terms identify four entity types: *passengers, tickets, reservation clerks,* and *flights*. This statement also identifies an attribute of the *flight* entity type: whether or not it is full. (Most likely it will not be the one maintained by the system. The more inclusive flight attribute, the number of seats still available, is more likely to be. The *is-the-flight-full* attribute may be defined in terms of the *number-of-seats-booked* attribute.) Note also that an action is mentioned: the clerk checks the full/not-full status of the flight. Actions are not considered in this chapter; they are discussed in Section 4.

A second way to begin picking out entity types is to consider the forms and reports used by the organization for the area under consideration. Most organizations record information on forms to be filled out and stored. Entries on a form or a report often represent an entity or an attribute of an entity.* Consider an airline ticket form. Simplified, it is shown in Figure 3.1.

A number of entity types are indicated more or less directly by this form: passenger, ticket, travel agency, flight, and city. For each certain attributes are requested. Note, for example, that the passenger is referred to by name, an attribute of the passenger. Similarly, the travel agency and the flight are indicated by reference to their identifiers.

One other entity type is identified by the airline ticket—only far less obviously. In airline parlance a flight identifies a trip made by an airplane from an initial departure point to a final destination point. That flight may stop at intermediate locations along the way. (If no intermediate stopping points are scheduled the flight is called nonstop.) Passengers are not required to fly entire flights; they may book passage from or to any of the intermediate locations. Each of the ticket lines that shows a flight number, departure city, etc., identifies a flight ''segment.'' Thus a passenger's itinerary consists of one or more segments. Segments are another entity type.

---

*Some forms represent actions, or requests for actions, and some of the entries on those forms correspond to parameters of the action and not to entities or their attributes. See Section 4 for further discussion of forms of this sort. It should not be assumed that all entries on all forms correspond to entities or attributes.

Passenger					Ticket ID #

Travel Agency

From	To	Flight #	Date	Time	Class

Price_____

Figure 3.1   Simplified airline ticket.

A flight segment is not identified on the ticket by a name of any sort. There is no number or code; it is not just a simple matter of looking at the form and guessing that flight segments are entity types. We must be fairly familiar with airlines' procedure to understand segments. This is one instance of the importance of expertise in the field. Although, as we have already indicated, it is perfectly reasonable to consider segments as entities, it is also possible to arrive at the same information in another manner. Section 3.3.4 shows how segments may be identified as examples as a relation instead of as an entity type.

Most entity types are simple and straightforward. A few are somewhat more difficult to recognize. We discuss these other entity types next.

The Name Versus The Thing

When writing a requirements document we sometimes wonder whether it is acceptable to define an entity type if there is no predetermined way of providing it with a unique name. Therefore, if we want to define an entity type *person* but have no *a priori* method of unique identification (e.g., no *employee identification number*) we often feel obliged to invent one on the spot. This is really a case of confusing an entity with its name. A person is a person no matter by what name (or number) he or she is known and independent even of having a name (or number). The very idea of an entity implies individuality. It is not necessary to create unique labels for entities before we are permitted to speak of them.

On the other hand, it is generally important to be able to refer to entities. After all, what is the point of keeping track of information if we cannot associate it with the entity to which it applies? This problem usually develops in configuration management: we have a number of things that we wish to keep track of but have no labels for them. (Consult [Bersoff et al., 1980] for a definitive discussion of configuration management.)

The standard but not the only way of dealing with this problem is to create unique labels. Consider courses offered by a university. Ignoring their titles, we usually identify them by a department and number; for example, *Math 101*. Although two labels in combination are adequate neither the department name *Math* nor the course number *101* is a unique identifier. Yet is it not necessary to create an additional identifying number or label; the reference *course number 101 taught by the Mathematics department* is sufficient.

In everyday life it is more often the case that things are uniquely identifiable even though they lack names. Thus *my left hand, the big toe on my right foot, the car you bought last year, the book by Abbott reviewed in ACM Computing Reviews last month,* and so on. None of these things needs a unique label or number to be identifiable as entities. It can generally be left to the system developers to provide a means of unique identifications.* The only reason, then, to insist on a particular identification system as a requirement is to provide compatibility with some other system.

Abstract Entities

As in the airline ticket example, most entity types consist of entities with physical reality such as people or things; for example, *passenger* and *ticket*. Other types of entity are abstractions. The *flight* and *segment* entity types are not physical objects; they are conceptual constructs. No physical object corresponds to a flight, although the object most closely associated with it is the airplane that makes the flight. No airplane is permanently assigned to any flight, and if the airplane making a particular flight on a particular day is replaced by another the flight itself is not considered to be a different one.

As another example, consider a system to keep track of information about a company's organization. The organizational units such as departments are abstract entities. A department in a company is not a physical object. The identity of a department is independent of the people assigned to work in it and of the location in which it is situated. A department exists as an entity just because the people in the company want to think of it that way; that is, because it is designated as an entity in the company's organization plan. A department may be said to exist as an entity even if it is newly designated, has no people assigned to it, no location from which to operate, and no telephones.

---

*A well designed system will not impose an arbitrary identification system. The system developers should find a way to identify entities without imposing an unnecessary additional burden on the system users. A requirement to that effect should be written as part of the Human Factors section.

Substances

For the most part entity types are designated by count nouns; for example, *passengers, clerks, tickets,* and *departments*. The entities identified by these types are recognizably discrete units; that is, people, things, and abstract objects. There are two other entity types: substances (or materials) and those in which the entities themselves are collections of other things. This section discusses the first of these; the second can be found in the next section.

Substances and materials are generally referred to by "mass nouns"; for example, earth, air, fire, water, iron, steel, information, software, documentation, and text. Substances do not come in discrete, well defined units. We may argue that substances may always be reduced to their molecular or atomic components, but people certainly do not think of them that way. *Water,* to most people, is different from a pair of hydrogen atoms linked to an oxygen atom; *earth* does not have a single molecular component; and *cloth* is meaningless on the molecular level, where it lacks the two dimensionality we associate with it.

Although substances have no well defined instances, we do deal with them in discrete units. We talk of a glass of water or a yard of cloth. What are we doing? Because substances and materials do not come in conveniently predefined, discrete units, we create artificial ones for them. These units are not always formal, but when they are they are called units of measure. Units of measure may subdivide a substance or material in any of a number of ways. Examples include by volume (e.g., *pint* of water), by weight (e.g., *ton* of iron), and by measures specific to the particular substance (e.g., *line* of text or code, *slice* of cheese, *volume* of documentation, *head* of hair, or *bit* of information).

With this additional understanding it makes sense to identify substances as entity types and to treat them in more or less the same way we treat others. The primary constraint is that an *instance* of a substance entity type is not an object in the usual sense but is an artificially defined amount of the substance indicated in terms of some unit of measure.

There are two kinds of information about substances and materials with which we are generally concerned.

1. Information about the substance or material as a substance or material; for example, *water freezes at 0 degrees centigrade.*
2. Information about individual units of the substance or material; for example, *this pint of water is mine.*

Information of the first sort may easily be associated with the substance or material as an entity type in the same way as information is associated with other entity types. Information of the second sort may be associated with unit-of-measure instances of the substance.

Collections

As distinguished from mass nouns with which we refer to substances, collective nouns identify entity types in situations in which the entities are themselves groups of other things. Examples include *team, herd, mob,* and *jury.* In a system that keeps track of information about baseball the players and the teams are entities (i.e., a *player* entity type and a *team* entity type) and it is important to identify the properties of both.

When a system is to deal with entity types in which the entities themselves are collections it frequently must also deal separately with members of the collection. In a system that will store information about wildlife there will be entity types for *herd* (e.g., of moose), *pride* (of lions), *flock* (of ducks), and *gaggle* (of geese) as well as for *moose, lion, duck,* and *goose.* In such cases, in which the collection is treated as a unit in some situations and members of the collection are treated separately in others, we should be careful to identify the collections and the members as entity types.

This situation is not so different from that in which individuals are associated with some other entity; for example, employees with the departments for which they work. There is a difference, however. *Department* is not a collective unit because departments exist independently of their members. *Mob* is a collective because there cannot be a mob without members. What about a team? In sandlot games the team is the collection of its members. In sports as a business a team is far more than its players; it includes owners, managers, coaches, and, perhaps most important, its status as a corporation and its charter as a member of a league.

What about juries? Does a jury consist of its members and nothing more, or is it an abstract judicial object that is independent of its members and to which people are assigned? In most cases we probably do not have to provide an abstract answer. The issue is settled when it is determined whether the collective object has an identity that persists beyond all its members. In most cases it probably doesn't matter whether we think of a collective unit as existing apart from its members. In all cases collective units, when relevant, are entity types and should be recognized as such.

Collective nouns differ in another way from objects (such as departments) with which groups of individuals are associated. The existence of a collective noun implies what we might call a conceptual substance (for which we may or may not have corresponding mass nouns) in much the same way that a unit of measure implies the existence of a substance. The collective noun functions as a unit of measure for the conceptual substance; for example, *herd* may be a unit of measure for the conceptual substance named by the mass noun *cattle* and *mob* is a unit of measure for the conceptual substance *rabble* (these, of course, are inexact units of measure). Other collective nouns may be units of measure for other conceptual substances even though we may not have the equivalent names for these substances. Thus as a collection of its members, *gaggle* has the same sense as *herd*, but we have no word that refers to geese as undifferentiated material in the same way as *cattle* refers to cows. When no such word exists we often use the plural form of the count noun that identifies the group members: **gaggle** of **geese**.

General Types and Specialized Types

The issue of dividing up the world into entity types needs some discussion. Consider requirements for a system that will keep track of baseball information. This system will certainly need to gather information about both players and managers. Are players and managers two different entity types or a single one? We could argue that they are two types because players play one sort of role and managers one that is entirely different. One could also argue that they are the same entity type because both are people. Not only that, the same person can be a player at one time and a manager at another. A playing manager is both player and manager at the same time.

Notwithstanding these reasons for merging the types, the best strategy is to define *player* and *manager* as separate entity types. There is nothing in the notion of an entity type to force it to be disjoint; that is, to require that an entity of one type is not to be considered as another. There is no reason why a person cannot be a player and a manager. The job of developing a system to keep track of nondisjoint entity types may be somewhat more difficult than if there were no overlapping. That is the responsibility of the system developers, not of the people defining the requirements. When defining requirements we should make as many distinctions as necessary to characterize properly the world with which the system is to deal. While writing the requirements we should not worry about how difficult it will be for the developers. There will be plenty of time to back down on requirements later.

There is somewhat more to this issue than simple overlaps. Players and managers have things in common: for example, they both wear uniforms and have uniform numbers. It would make sense to "factor out" the common features of these two types and to define one called *team member*. (It especially makes sense to create a more general type if that type makes sense intuitively. If the new type did not make intuitive sense it would probably be better not to force its creation.) Players and managers are both team members. By defining the entity type *team member* in addition to *player* and *manager* we can then define for team members those properties common to both players and managers. We can also consign to the more specialized types the properties that apply only to them. Thus a team member has a uniform number; a player (in addition to a uniform number) has a batting average; and a manager (in addition to a uniform number) has a won-lost record.

This type of organization is called *generalization* and *specialization*: the *player* type is a specialization of the *team member* type and the *team member* type is a generalization of the *player* type. To associate attributes of more general entity types with their specialized subtypes is called attribute *inheritance*. Players *inherit* the attributes associated with team members because players are a particular kind of team member. Similarly, because managers are also a specialization of team members they too inherit the team-member attributes. In addition, each specialization may have attributes that are unique to themselves such as **batting average** for players.

We need not stop at two levels. If we were concerned with other employees of baseball clubs, we could define a *team employee* type. It would have specializations such as *administrative personnel* and *scout*. An attribute of the *team employee* might be *salary* and all specializations of that type would have a *salary* attribute.

On a still more general level we could define a *person* entity type. Its specializations would include *team employee* as well as, for example, *ticket holder*. Attributes of the *person* entity type would include *name* and *address*.

Roles

It is often appropriate to define overlapping entity types that are specializations of other entity types. In fact, to the extent that such a structure would clarify the nature of the entities involved, the more informative they are, the more important it is to identify them. Most entity types turn out to be specializations of a certain sort and most define the *roles* entities play rather than the actual differences between them.

If an *entity type* is a way of categorizing "things" on the basis of the thing's properties, a *role* is a way of categorizing "things" on the basis of the thing's function, position, or use. Thus the entity types *player* and *manager* do not really characterize differences between the *people* who are players and managers; they characterize two roles any person can perform. The differences in attributes between players and managers are differences with respect to the roles rather than to the people. Thus a player's batting average or a manager's won-lost record has nothing to do with the player or manager as a person or even with the player manager in some other role like *father* or *mother*.

For our purposes it is not necessary to differentiate entity types that characterize things on the basis of property differences (*dog* entities versus *building* entities) from those that characterize things on the basis of role differences (*student* entities versus *employee* entities). It is worth being aware of the two ways of defining categories, however, to avoid confusion when both occur.

Units of Measure as a Specialization of Substances

The notions of specialization apply in a special way to substances and their units of measure. When concerned with substances or materials we generally treat them as one entity type and their units of measure as a specialization of a substance entity type; for example, for a system concerned about automating whiskey production there would probably be "whiskey," "barrel-of-whiskey," and "bottle-of-whiskey" entity types. The whiskey entity type would be used as a focal point for information about whiskey in general, such as ideal color and acidity. The barrel-of-whiskey entity type would serve as a focal point for information about individual barrels of whiskey which would probably include the color of the whiskey in that barrel. The bottle-of-whiskey entity type would relate to the whiskey in individual bottles. (For more discussion on how substance entity types are related to their units-of-measure entity type see the sections on types and specialized types.)

It is important not to confuse units-of-measure entity types with those for the containers of the units of measure. Thus in the whiskey factory, even though there would be a barrel-of-whiskey entity type for whiskey aging in separate barrels, there would also be a "barrels" entity type for the separate barrels in which the whiskey was aging. The barrel in which whiskey ages is different from the whiskey aging in the barrel and each must be considered separately. There would also be a relation (see below) that would link specific units of aging whiskey with the barrels in which they were aging.

One particularly interesting ''substance'' is time. We treat time in the same way as we treat other substances. We say, for example, *how **much** time* rather than *how **many***; and time does not come in predefined instances. Instead we have created units of measure for time: *year, month, week, day, hour, minute,* and *second.*

Records Versus Entities

In the example of the airline ticket the ticket itself is an interesting entity. It is both an entity on its own as well as a record of information about other entities.

As an entity.   The ticket is an entity in that it is an item that the airline prints and sells, that the passenger buys, and that the airline accepts from the passenger in exchange for admittance to a flight. It is identified as an entity by its ticket number—an attribute of tickets used to identify them in the same way as passenger names are used to identify them.

As a record.   Besides being an entity, however, the ticket also records information about itself and other entities. The entries on the ticket record information about the passenger, the scheduled flight, and the sites to be visited.

A driver's license is a similar example in that it, too, is an entity and a record of information. Tickets and licenses are unusual in that in any definition of a system's entities we should not be concerned with records or forms. Only in cases like this in which the record or form serves a separate role should it be mentioned as an entity.

It is important not to confuse an entity with its record of information. People working with computers are especially likely to make this mistake. When writing a requirements document always remember that the focus is on things in the world and not on their records of information. Only later, when the system is actually under development, is it determined exactly how the information is to be stored.

This is not to say that records are not essential. In most cases records of information (as distinguished from the information itself) will eventually be of central importance to the system. Their accuracy, consistency, and integrity should be ensured by identifying and tracking them. But it is not the place of a requirements document to decide *how* this job is to be done. That is the responsibility of the behavioral and design specifications. A requirements document merely serves to identify (in section 3.9) the required integrity constraints.

Therefore records and forms are not entities unless they function independently of their roles as records. Integrity, security, privacy, and similar requirements should be expressed in terms of access to and accuracy of the information.

Decision Rules for Entity Types

Just because we think of something as an entity type, does that automatically mean that we can always tell whether something is of that type? That is, does an entity type always come with a decision procedure that determines whether an entity is or is not of that type? In this section we argue that such rules may not always be available (in fact that they *cannot* always be available) but that we are quite accustomed to working without them and that not having them is not really a problem.

Consider a system for building expert systems in which *hypothesis* might be an entity type. In still more general artificial intelligence systems *idea, belief,* and *thought* might be entity types. Imagine a system that will help people to write requirements. *Entity types, attribute,* and *relation* might themselves be entity types. If we are not careful, permitting *entity type* to be an entity type could lead to standard self-referential paradoxes. For if *entity type* is an entity type we could define a specialization of that type for entity types that do not describe themselves. [Most entity types do not describe themselves. The entity type *chair* is not itself a chair (it is the idea of a chair); the entity type *person* is not itself a person (it is the idea of a person)] Some entity types are self-descriptive. The entity type *idea* is an idea and the entity type *entity type* is an entity type.

We could then ask the question: does the nonself-descriptive entity type describe itself? That is, is the nonself-descriptive entity type a nonself-descriptive entity type? The ususal paradox is there. If the nonself-descriptive entity type is nonself-descriptive it is descriptive because it describes all entity types that are not self-descriptive. Similarly, if the nonself-descriptive entity type is not self-descriptive it does describe itself. Either way there is a contradiction.

The problem arises from the assumption that for any entity type we always have a way of telling whether it belongs to that type. Thus, given an entity type T and an entity E, it may not be possible to tell whether E is a T.* An example may clarify this difficulty. Is the stool at the bar a chair; that is, is the stool of the entity type chair? It depends on how we understand the idea of *chair*. Does it include stools? Further, is an automobile seat a chair; is a rock a chair; would an automobile seat or a rock be a chair if it were being used as a chair? The problem is that the notion of *chair* does not necessarily come with decision rules that will always tell whether or not something should be considered a chair. Certainly we could make up rules for deciding when something should be *called* a chair but they would most likely be somewhat artificial, and, given any particular rules, we could probably find an example for which they would violate our intuition.

A similar problem is posed by units of measurements. Is $15^{1}/_{2}$ oz a pint? How far can we be from exactly 16 oz and still be entitled to say that we have a *pint*? The answer cannot be given as another measurement (e.g., a pint is 16 oz plus or minus 0.01 oz) because we can again ask how far can we be from that error factor and still be entitled to say that we are within it? If 16.01 oz is a pint, isn't it unreasonable to say that 16.01 plus another 10^{-200} oz is not also a pint?

*or even whether there are any Ts at all. Are there any *angels*?

This lack of rules can be quite bothersome; in some circumstances it leads to serious ethical and moral difficulties. Even in situations with significant implications we often cannot agree on a set of rules; for example, what is a *person*? Is a body with no brain function but with artificially maintained respiration and other physical functions a person? When does a human sperm and a human egg become a person? At the moment of birth? At the moment of conception? Some time in between? If some "moment" is selected, when exactly does that moment occur? Does birth occur when the head is first visible, when the child is completely out of the mother's body, or some time in between? When does conception occur? When the sperm and egg first make contact? When the sperm "enters" the egg? When their genetic materials combine? When does each of these more precise "moments" occur?

In difficult cases that affect us profoundly we make artificial rules called laws. We have, however, had enough experience to know that any legal definition will probably not always match our desired views of the world. There will always be exceptions and special cases, and it takes a human judge and jury to interpret the law and decide when something fits a given description. Yet we do manage to get along without precise answers in some situations and with artificially precise answers in others.

Of what relevance is this in defining requirements? Fortunately these problems are of minimal concern. In nearly all cases the computer system will not be required to determine whether something presented to it is of a certain entity type. For the most part all the computer system will be required to do is to keep track of information about entities of known types; that is, entities whose types are determined by the system users.

Even in those rare cases in which the system is required to determine the type of some entity it will probably be possible to make decision rules that will permit it to do as credible a job as the law does now—not perfect but good enough. In systems in which such decisions are made, mechanisms should be provided to permit those decisions to be appealed to a human decision maker.

The point we wish to make is that we generally use ideas (entity types) without having well defined decision procedures for prospective entities of those types. The logical paradoxes tell us that if we wish to continue to use the notion of entity type in our normal intuitive way then for some entity types it may be theoretically impossible to develop definitive rules for the inclusion or exclusion of entities.

Attributes

An attribute is a value that in some sense is directly connected to an entity. The most familiar attributes are measures of various sorts such as *height, weight,* and *age*. Other familiar attributes are identifying tags like *name* or *ID number*. Somewhat less directly connected to an entity, but still considered attributes, are characterizations like *make* and *body style* for automobiles. In general it is not difficult to identify attributes.

Sometimes we are tempted to classify as an attribute something that is better characterized as a separate entity; for example, in discussing the requirements for a company information system, we might be tempted to list *department* (to which an employee is assigned) as an attribute of the entity type *employee*. After all, an employee's assigned department is part of the characterization of an employee as far as the company is concerned. This would be inappropriate. It would be inappropriate because *department* itself should be an entity type and an entity type cannot also be an attribute of some other entity type. To consider department as an entity type and an attribute of an employee confuses the notion of department. What we are really defining in this situation is a relation between departments and employees.

Similarly, *supervisor* should not be listed as an attribute of the entity type employee. Instead, the information that certain employees supervise other employees is captured as a relation between employees.

Unfortunately it is not always easy to determine whether a prospective attribute should be treated as an attribute or whether it should be an entity type with a relation to another entity type. Consider the attribute *name*. In almost all cases *name* would be considered an appropriate attribute and should not be considered as an entity type, but what if the application area were concerned not only with people who have names but also with the names themselves? For example, we may wish to keep track of the countries of origin of names, in which case names are entities. Then a name is something of interest on its own; and the requirements for a system with these concerns should identify names as entities. Once names are characterized as entities they may no longer be considered to be attributes of people, and the information relating a person to a name must be characterized as a relation between *person* entity and *name* entity types.

In general we suggest the following guideline:

> *If a prospective attribute has an attribute of its own it should not be treated as an attribute but as an entity type.*

Therefore, if we are concerned with the attribute *country of origin* for *name,* we cannot let *name* be an attribute but must make it an entity type. Of course, if we are not concerned with any attributes of names but use them simply as ways of referring to people, they may be considered to be attributes of people.

Attribute Values

As the preceding section indicated, an attribute refers to a *value,* whereas an entity refers to a *thing*. Just as there is sometimes a problem in deciding how to name (i.e., identify) entities, there is a similar problem with attribute values: how should they be expressed? Consider the attribute *height*. Its values can be measured in feet and inches, in meters and centimeters, or in any of a number of different units of measure. Often users will require a particular measurement system (the English or metric system), but at other times they will not care. It is the job of the requirements writer to determine whether a specific way of expressing attribute values is preferred.

On the other hand, if no choice is made it is not necessary for the requirements author to invent and then require one; for example, assume that we are defining a *priority* attribute for factory production jobs and that there are three priorities:

1. *Drop everything and work on this job immediately.*
2. *Work on these jobs in the order received.*
3. *Work on these jobs when there is nothing else to do.*

If desired we could create names for these values such as *urgent, normal,* and *background,* or *high, medium,* and *low priority,* or *top, standard,* and *fill priority,* but if no names are currently in use and there are no problem-based reasons to prefer one set to another we could let the system designers make their own suggestions.

In the examples mentioned so far the attribute values have had *meanings.* Thus height means something independent of the unit of measure. So does priority. Some attributes have no meanings. Their "values" are not references; they are *nothing but* numbers or character strings. Thus an ID number just represents itself. Most attributes of this sort are used as labels or tags, and there is usually a requirement that their values be different for each entity. (In addition, there may also be a requirement that the tag be the same as that used by some other system.) In such cases we should be clear about whether these attributes are tags and must be unique and also whether the attributes must be compatible with their use elsewhere.

Default Values

Attributes frequently have default values, that is, values we would assume unless told otherwise. In a manufacturing system, for example, the color of the product manufactured may be a standard gray except in unusual situations, in which case the attribute *color* would have *gray* identified as its default value.

Multiple Values

Most common attributes are single-valued but some have multiple values; for example, a police information system may wish to keep track of the aliases used by criminals. *Alias* is an attribute, but it may have many values because any number of aliases may be used by one suspect. If an attribute has multiple values that fact must be indicated.

Compound Values

The values of some attributes are divided into components; for example, an *address* attribute may be said to consist of *street, city, state, country,* and *postal code.* The *street* component itself may be a *street number,* a *street name,* and a *suite* or *apartment number.* It is important to notice that the components of a compound attribute are attributes of a single entity; that is, the *street* is the entity's street, the *city* is the entity's city, and so on. This is different from the situation in which we are concerned with attributes of an attribute, the *country of origin* of a *name. Country of origin* is an attribute of *name*; it is not an attribute of the entity having that name.

In the case of compound attributes it is necessary to indicate for each of the components the possible values the parts may have and the format or other limitations that apply.

Compound, Multivalued Attributes

Consider the attribute (educational) *degrees* of the entity type *person*. It is both compound and multiple-valued. It is compound in that it consists of components: the degree held (BA, BS, MA, etc.), major, year, school, and perhaps other values. It is multiple-valued in that a person may have more than one degree.

Other examples of compound, multivalued attributes are time series and historical records; for example, a medical record of a person's height taken at each visit to a doctor's office is a multivalued attribute of the person. It is also compound in that the value has two components: *measured height* and the *date* on which the measurement was taken. A similar example is the price of a stock. It has multiple values: one for each buy/sell transaction. The attribute is compound in that its components are the price and some transaction identification, possibly a time stamp.

These examples are somewhat troublesome. Some of the components apparently are properties of the attribute rather than of the entity; that is, the school component of the *degree* attribute seems to be an attribute of the degree (the school that issued the degree) rather than of the degree holder. The *date* component of the historical height record seems to be an attribute of the height rather than of the person, and the *transaction identification* component of the stock price attribute seems to be an attribute of the transaction rather than of the stock. Why, then, having made the rule that attributes, which themselves have attributes, should be entity types, do we not insist that these be entity types instead of attributes?

We could, in fact, take the alternate approach. It is possible to define anything as an entity. We could, for example, define height as an entity type: the entities would be the various heights that people could have; that is, 5 ft 2 in., 6 ft 4 in., etc. We would then define a relation to link each person with his or her own height. The date would be an attribute of that relation. (See below for more details on relations and their attributes.) The pure relational [Codd, 1977] database method does not distinguish between entities and attributes. Everything is a domain from which values may be drawn.

This approach, however, seems unintuitive. We do not normally consider heights (i.e., the numbers themselves) as entities. Let's look more closely at the role played by *date* in the medical record. Is the date really an attribute of *height* (as *country of origin* may be an attribute of *name?*) No, the date is not a property of the height itself; it is an attribute of the fact that the person has (or had) that height. It says *when* the person had that height; thus it is an attribute of the connection between the person and different values of his or her height.

Seen in this light, it makes more sense to leave *height* as an attribute of *person* and to consider *date* as an attribute *of the fact* that people have heights; that is, *date* is an attribute of the property of having a height rather than of the height value. We could argue further that height is not a well defined attribute of a person because the height of a person varies at different times. To be more rigorous we would have to define the height attribute as *height at a given date*. Then both *height* and *date* would clearly be components of that attribute.

Similarly, we could argue that *price of a stock* is not a well defined attribute because a stock has no single price. The price of a stock is really the price at which the stock was bought or sold in a particular transaction. Thus to define the attribute more precisely requires that a particular transaction be identified.

To consider our other example, however, a degree can be considered as a well defined attribute without additional information related to the school from which the degree was earned or any other facts that might pertain. In this case we must determine whether the other information is, in fact, desired. If it is, the correct attribute is not just *degree* but *degree-school-date*-etc. The attribute is compound in the same way that the address attribute is coumpound—because that is the information desired. On the other hand, if we are treating schools as entities, the school at which a person received a degree would not be part of the degree attribute. We would define a relation between people and schools to identify that information.

Like the examples illustrated, records of events, occurrences, or actions are frequently difficult to characterize. Intransitive actions can be especially tricky. (Transitive actions are easier because they usually identify a relation at least between the subject and the object.) Imagine the requirements for a system to be used by a museum to record information about its members. One of the entity types presumably would be *member* and one of the member attributes might be (monetary) *donations*; that is, acts of donating. Donating is an intransitive act: from the point of view of the museum the donor produces a donation in much the same way that a tree *bears* fruit.

For each donation the museum wishes to keep track of the amount, the date on which it was made, the check number, and, if it was restricted in any way, the purpose. We could decide that each of these pieces of information is an attribute of the donation itself and that *donation* should be another entity type. Alternatively, we could decide that *donation* is a compound attribute of the member. Both decisions are acceptable. The question really is how does the museum feel about donations? Have they lives of their own? Do we exclude the donors from discussions of particular donations? In that case they make sense as entities. Or are donations always associated with the donors and always considered in that light? In that case they are better as attributes of the donors. The answer to these questions should determine how donations are described in a requirements document.

Let's consider further the approach that considers donations an entity type. What are the entities; that is, what are the things of that type? They must be the actual money contributions. The museum probably does not think of the money itself as a separate entity; once received it is deposited in a bank account and loses its individual identity. Thus there really is no entity type of *donation* as such.

Let's imagine that the donations are separate objects; each monetary contribution maintains its identity until completely spent. The museum still wants to keep track of donation attributes: date made, check number, amount, and purpose. In addition, the museum wants to record the name of each donor. A relation is needed to link donations and members. (The donor could not be an attribute of the donation because the donor is another entity type and entities cannot be attributes of other entities.) We then have a choice between saying that the donation attributes are attributes of the entity type *donation* or that they are attributes of the relation that links the donations to the members. It seems to make little difference which approach is taken for this.

It really is not reasonable to treat the actual money contribution as entities. If we wished to identify donations as entities a better approach would be to define the *donation* entity type as the *act* of contributing; that is, the *donation* entity type would consist of actions as abstract objects. The attributes of that type would be the date, amount, and so on. We would still need a relation to link these donations as abstract objects to the members because again the members as entities could not be considered attributes.

Although this approach is logically consistent, it is unnecessarily complicated. It forces us to consider the act of donating to be an object independent of the donor, the author of the act, and then to define an additional relation to link the actor to the act. Having come this far, it is a small and simplifying step to describe the act of donating as a compound attribute of the donor. The attribute describes a donor action and as such its components are parts of the description of that action.

In general, then, some attributes are compound just because the information they represent is not atomic. This is often the case when the attribute records an action, especially an intransitive action. Therefore there is no harm in defining compound attributes.

We should always be mindful of the possibility, that what we are really interested in is not a compound attribute of a single entity but a relation among a number of entities. If, in the donations example, we are keeping track of donations of objects (e.g., paintings) to the museum and the objects themselves are an entity type, a donation *is* a relation that links the members to the objects and the attributes (date, etc.) are attributes of the relation. Similarly, if, in the degrees example, we treat schools as entities, we may wish to define a *degrees-granted* relation that links schools to people by degrees granted. Such a relation would have the other pieces of information (date, degree type, major, etc.) as attributes of the relation.

In the end it all comes down to the point of view taken by the users of the system.

Computed and Intensional Attribute Values

Often it happens that attributes may be defined in terms of other information that is already defined. In an airline reservation system, for example, an attribute of a flight may be *percent booked*. That attribute may be defined as the number of seats sold divided by the number of seats on the plane. This is a computed attribute because it is defined in terms of other attributes.

Computed attributes differ from most attributes in that the eventual system will have to be told what value most attributes have (e.g., the system cannot know what a person's height is without being told). With computed attributes the system can determine the value of the attributes from other known information.

Computed attributes may be defined in terms of relations as well as other attributes. As an example, consider the attribute *has children*. For any person this attribute has the value *yes* if the person has children and *no* if not. Assume that in defining our world model we have already defined the **parent of** relation. We could then define the *has children* attribute as having the value *yes* if the person is shown in the **parent** of relation as having at least one child.

Computed attributes are a form of intensional definition of attributes. In the examples given so far we are really interested in the value computed rather than in the means of making the computation. Imagine expressing the requirements for a system having to do with retail sales. In this system we probably would want to associate price formulas with products; that is, an attribute of any product is the formula by which its price is computed—perhaps on the basis of the quantity bought or whether the buyer is entitled to an educational discount. We do not want a number as the value of the price attribute; we want a formula. The eventual system will have to be able to deal with the formula as such, for we may want to ask what the current formula is or we may want to change it.

Attribute values of this sort are said to be expressed intensionally. The information associated with the attribute is a description of the attribute's value and not the value itself. It is generally more work to build systems that have the following capabilities:

1. To allow us to express attribute values as descriptions.
2. To evaluate those descriptions to determine values.

The difficulty in building these systems is proportionate to the complexity of the intensional description. These difficulties however, are the responsibility of the system builders, not the requirements author. If in writing requirements, we have attributes for which intensional value descriptions are needed, they should be provided.

Individuals

An individual is a particular thing that is uniquely identified *a priori*. In a system that will help to control an automobile the automobile is an individual because it is the single thing being controlled. The parts of the automobile (e.g., engine and transmission) are also individuals because they are known separately and individually.

Sometimes an "individual" is a particular role to be played rather than the individual filling the role; for example, the *driver* in the car example. In a system dealing with the governmental structure of the United States *the president* is an individual. In this case, however, the presidency, that is, the office of or the role of being the president, is the individual rather than the person occupying that office.

When describing the system informally to ourselves the individuals are generally those things to which we find ourselves referring by name or other direct reference. For example, if an airline reservation system is developed for Jet Stream Airlines that airline company is an individual to the system, for in describing the system we refer to the airline company by name. Consider a system that will monitor the goings on around a house. The front door, that is the main entry, is an individual. Although it has no proper name, we refer to it by direct reference: "the front door."

Individuals as Instances of Entity Types

Sometimes it is questionable whether we should call a small, known class of things an entity type or a collection of individuals; for example, when describing the information needs of a large company with six divisions should each of the divisions be identified separately as individuals or should there be an entity type *division*? The advantage of identifying the divisions separately is that each is then seen as a unit on its own, with unique needs and capabilities. The advantage of identifying *division* as an entity type is that the features common to all divisions can be spelled out under that heading.

The disadvantages of each approach are the counterparts of the advantages. Identifying a *division* entity type makes it likely that the unique characteristics of each division will be less visible. The disadvantage of identifying the divisions as individuals is that the notion of *division* as a general concept may be lost, in which case the system designed to serve the company as currently organized, with its particular collection of specific divisions, may be less flexible to reorganizations that add new divisions or eliminate existing ones.

A good compromise is to define an entity type and some (or all) of its individual members. Just as we saw that certain entity types can be defined as specializations of more general entity types, individuals can be defined as *instances* of an entity type. An individual identified as an instance of a particular entity type inherits all the attributes of that type (except for those that are explicitly blocked).

Sometimes we define an entity type for which some individuals are known and others are not known ahead of time; for example, the entity type *regent* (of, say, the California State University System) consists of *ex officio* members such as the *governor* and the *chancellor of the university* and other members unknown in advance and appointed for fixed terms. The governor is an individual in any system that deals with the organization of state government. He or she is also a regent and thus a member of the *regent* entity type. The non-*ex officio* members are not individuals as far as the system is concerned but are merely instances of the entity type *regent*.

Notation for Entity Types

It is frequently possible to represent the required information regarding entity types in shorthand notation. Even if it is not possible to express all of it, a concise notation is useful as a summary. We recommend the notation shown in Figure 3.2 for displaying the outline of information about entity types.

Entity Type Name: Class Size: Specialization of <more general type>

   <If a substance an indication of that fact>

   Attribute_1: attribute information: = default value if any

   ...

   Attribute_n: attribute information: = default value if any

Figure 3.2.   Notation for entity types. The components of a compound attribute are listed under the attribute.

As an example, the entity type *pitcher* is sketched in Figure 3.3. Note that because *pitcher* is a specialization of the type *baseball player* we do not include attributes that are common to all baseball players but only those that are specific to pitchers.

```
Pitcher: 150  :  Baseball Player
Handedness    :  Right or Left :  = Right
Games Won
      This Year : 0 -  30   := 0
      Last Year : 0 -  30   := 0
            ...  (previous years)
      Lifetime  : 0 - 400   := 0
Games Lost
      This Year : 0 -  30   := 0
      Last Year : 0 -  30   := 0
            ...  (previous years)
      Lifetime  : 0 - 400   := 0
Games Saved
      This Year : 0 -  30   := 0
      Last Year : 0 -  30   := 0
            ...  (previous years)
      Lifetime  : 0 - 400   :=0
Earned Run Average
      This Year : 0 -  10   := 0
      Last Year : 0 -  10   := 0
            ...  (previous year)
      Lifetime  : 0 -  10   := 0
```
Figure 3.3:   A Pitcher Entity Type.

Relations Among Entities and Other Record-Keeping Requirements

The preceding section discussed the information requirements of individual entities. This section discusses relations between entities and identifies information that must be kept for them.

For our purposes a relation is any *connection* between entities. Following are some examples:

1. *Marriage.*   The *marriage* relation connects the two entities who are married. There are multiple instances of this relationship: one for each marriage. We may want to consider the marriage relation as a table with two columns:

Marriages

Husband	Wife

Each row of this table records an instance of the marriage relation. Note that the entity types *husband* and *wife* are most likely defined as specializations of the more general type *person*.

Note that if we do not care about *who* is married to whom but simply wish to keep track of *whether* a person is married that information may be kept as an attribute of the person rather than as a relation between two people.

2. *Parents-Child.* The *parents-child* relation connects parents and children. Potentially it involves a large number of entities: the parents and any number of children. We may want to consider the parents/child relation as a table with three columns.

Parents

Father	Mother	Child

In this table there is one row for each child, that is, for each instance of a child and that child's parents. Thus each set of parents is listed as many times as the number of children.

3. *Supervises.* The *supervises* relation connects the supervisor and the individual supervised. There are multiple instances of this relation: one for each person supervised. In addition, an individual may participate in more than one at a time; an individual may be both a supervisor and a supervisee, and an individual may supervise more than one supervisee.

   4. *Project Assignment.* This relation connects an individual and the project to which the assignment is made. Thus relations need not be between people. The entity types connected may include abstract objects such as projects.

   5. *Enrollment in a Course.* This relation connects students and courses. It differs from that preceding in that the relation itself has attributes: the semester of enrollment and the grade the student earned in the course. We may wish to consider this relation as a table with four columns:

Enrollment in a Course

Student	Course	Semester	Grade

   6. *Instructor in a Course.* A similar relation is Instructor in a Course. It connects instructors and courses and also has an additional "semester" attribute. Both the Enrollment in a Course and Instructor in a Course relations may be important to a system. The fact that the same entity type *course* appears in both does no harm; it simply means that there are (at least) two ways in which *courses* are related to other entity types.

   7. *Purchase.* This relation connects an item purchased, a purchaser, a store, and possibly a salesperson. In addition, it has a number of attributes of its own: the date of the purchase, a check number if the purchase was made with a check, a driver's license number if offered as identification, a purchase price, delivery instructions, a payment schedule, a finance charge if any, and anything else about a transaction.

   Note that the driver's license number is an attribute of the relation, although it presumably matches the driver's license attribute of the purchaser.

Part-Whole Relations

One of the most common relations is that of a part to the whole to which it belongs. Imagine a system needed for tracking parts for an automobile assembly line. Certainly one of the entity types of concern to such a system is the class *automobile*. An automobile is built of parts such as *door* (left and right side and perhaps front left and right and back left and right), *engine* and *transmission,* each of which is also an important entity type. Many of these parts also have parts that are themselves of concern. Doors have parts, *window, lock,* and *handle* and engines have parts, *block, pistons,* and *spark plugs*. It is important to keep track of the parts that are combined into larger parts and eventually into an automobile.

A collection of part-whole relations may be used to specify this information requirement. To indicate that automobiles are composed of their various parts we define an **automobile-parts** relation:

Automobile Parts

Automobile	Engine	Passenger Door	Transmission	. . .
				. . .
				. . .
				. . .
				. . .
				. . .
				. . .

Other relations would be used to track the parts of each of these parts. By defining a relation for each component that also has components to be tracked we can describe the entire hierarchical structure.

Notice that part-whole relations are *not* retained as attributes. The parts are not attributes of their containing elements. They remain relations because the parts are independent of the assemblage in which they are installed.

Attributes of Relations

Often, as some of the examples showed, relations will have attributes. This is to be expected because relations define connections between entities and those connections are frequently characterized by properties of their own such as time and date information (when did this particular connection occur) and other modifiers (why, where, how long, and how often). In general, attributes of relations record the same sort of information as recorded by attributes of entities. In some ways a relation parallels a sentence: the entities are the subject, object, direct object, objects of prepositional phrases, and other nouns and noun phrases; the relation is the verb; the attributes of the relation are the modifiers.

Just as we said earlier that a compound attribute of an entity type represents the intransitive action or actions of a single entity type, relations often represent actions of more than one. Thus if we were keeping track of donations to many museums a *donated* relation could be defined to link the *donor* and *museum* entity types. Attributes of the relation would include information relevant to the donation such as the date and amount.

In general, when focusing on a relation we are concerned primarily with connections defined *between* entities rather than with the entities themselves. Thus a primary reason for discussing relations is that the information does not fall naturally within the domain of a single entity but is more conveniently separated from the entities under discussion.

Computed and Intensional Relations

Just as there are computed and intensional attributes there may also be computed and intensional relations. An example of a computed relation in a world of team sports is one that records the overall won-loss record of each team against each other team. This information may be computed from the relation that records the result of each game. Another example is one that defines the cousin relation in terms of the parent and sibling relations; that is, X and Y are cousins if X and Y have parents who are siblings.

An example of an intensional relation is one that describes requirements for a degree. A person is granted a degree if the requirements have been satisfied: we want both of the following:

1. To be able to determine whether particular people have met the current requirements; that is, whether they have taken the appropriate courses successfully.
2. To be able to change the requirements, for example, by adding new required courses.

As in the case of intensional attributes, building a system that can deal with intensional relations is more difficult than building one that does not have to. Again, that is the responsibility of the system developers. The job can be done by using a modern language like Prolog [Clocksin and Mellish, 1981]; we should not limit our requirements unnecessarily because the system developers are unfamiliar with these techniques.

Additional Examples

Earlier we were shown how airline flight segments could be described as entities. Let's now consider how the same information could be applied in terms of a relation. Instead of a segment entity type, we could define a **Reservations** relation as a table, similar in appearance to the segment listing on the airplane ticket; here, however, the passenger is also identified:

Reservations

Passenger	From	To	Flight No.	Date	Class

This relation connects the entity types *passenger, city* (for both *from* and *to* columns), and *flight*. The *date* column is part of the identification of the flight (because the same flight number occurs day after day) and the *class* column is an attribute of this relation. Notice that as part of this relation there is no need to keep the information about time of departure. It is an attribute of the flight and not part of this relation. It is printed on the ticket for the convenience of the passenger but not because information is added.

This relation says that the passenger named has a reservation for that part of the flight that occurs between the cities indicated. The relation records information about the entity types it connects. It is then perfectly reasonable to print out that information on the passenger's ticket. Therefore the lines on the ticket that we previously called *segments* can now be said to be a record of information but are not themselves entities; that is, they express instances of the **reservations** relation.

As another example, consider again the tracking of stock-price information. Earlier we said that price information could be identified as an attribute of the stock. If the concern of the system were wider and included information about the people buying and selling the stocks, stock buy-sell transactions would be described best as a relation between the buyer and the seller. Thus the relation would link the entity types *stock buyer, stock seller* (both would be specializations of the entity type *stock owner*), and *stock*. The attributes of the relation would include *transaction price* and *date of transaction:*

Transactions

Buyer	Seller	Stock	Date	Price	. . .
					. . .
					. . .
					. . .
					. . .
					. . .
					. . .
					. . .

Which approach is better? Is it better to claim many entities or to identify fewer entities and record more information as relations? No firm answer can be given; it is really a matter of how the eventual users of the system will be served best. If the system users find that thinking in terms of segments as an entity type is more comfortable, the segments should be so identified. If the users find that classifying segments as an entity type clutters their world with unnecessary entities and that all they are really concerned about is the relation between passengers and flights that reveals where the passengers got on and off, then the information should be expressed as a relation. It is the job of the requirements writer to work with the eventual users, to understand their way of thinking, and to express the requirements in terms that match their manner of viewing the world.

Relations and Forms

Earlier we suggested that a good way to determine entity types would be to examine the forms and reports used by an organization. Forms and reports also provide a good way to acquire an initial set of relations. A form often records an instance of a relation; a report often summarizes one or more relations. Consider the form on which a credit-card purchase is entered. That form has spaces for the purchaser's credit-card number, the seller's identification number, a list of the items purchased and their prices, the total amount of the transaction, the date of the transaction, an authorization number if the transaction exceeds a certain amount, and other information. This form is a useful starting point for defining a purchase relation. In general, it usually records the following:

1. Attributes of entities.
2. One or more relations between entities.
3. Attributes of these relations.

Constraints

There may be limitations that are required to hold within or between relations; for example, it may be company policy that an individual may not earn a higher salary than his or her supervisor. This limits the possible pairs that may be included in the supervisor/supervisee relation (or it limits the possible salaries that someone may receive). It is a constraint on each instance of the relation (or the attribute).

As another example, a relation between satellites and ground stations may be a means of identifying which ground station controls which satellite. A limitation may be that each satellite is controlled by exactly one ground station at any time. This constraint limits instances allowed in this relation: no two instances have the same satellite and a different ground station.

As still another example, in a student registration system a student may not be permitted to register in a course for which the prerequisites have not been completed. If any limitations (or "invariants") are required they must be spelled out.

Dependencies and Hints for Constructing Relations

We often have a choice of relations to define; for example, in developing a set of relations for stock-market information we might define a **transactions** relation as shown earlier and a **state-of-incorporation** relation that connects each stock with, say, the state in which it is incorporated. Are there arguments for or against including these two pieces of information in a single relation?

The argument in favor of defining a single relation that tracks buy-and-sell transactions with information about a stock's state of incorporation is that it saves us from having to define two separate relations and provides a more efficient way of expressing that information.

The argument against presenting this information in a single relation is that the two kinds are not connected and it would be confusing to present them together. We believe that this argument is more telling and we suggest that relations should be defined to present just one sort of information each.

A convenient way to determine whether relations present more than one sort of information is to examine the *dependencies* inherent in the structure of the information. A dependency is said to be defined from some of the elements in the relation (said to be the *domain* of the dependency) to another one of the elements of the relation (said to be the *range* of the dependency) if, given particular instances of elements of domain, there is at most one possible instance of the range; for example, in the **Enrollment-in-a-Course** relation there is a dependency in which the domain consists of three components: student, course, and semester; the range is the component grade. A student can have at most one grade in a course in a given semester.

The **Automobile Parts** relation defines a number of dependencies; for example between the domain automobile and the range Engine, between the domain automobile and the range Passenger Door, and, in fact, between automobile and each of the other relation components. There are no dependencies in the **Marriages** relation. Because people may marry more than once, given either husband or wife, the other is not uniquely determined.

When writing requirements we should determine the dependencies that exist within relations. Multiple dependencies suggest the possibility that two independent pieces of information are being presented and that the relation might better be split into parts for each dependency. In fact, we suggest as a general rule that relations should have no more than one dependency unless all are derivitive of a single hierarchical structure (as in the automobile example). Even in hierarchical structures splitting relations with multiple dependencies should be seriously considered.

Applied to the example that began this section, this rule suggests that stock information should be kept in two relations: one for buy-sell transactions and the other for the state of incorporation.

Notation for Relations

It is convenient to use a notation for relations similar to that for entity types. To refer to a relation *Relation Name* rather than continuing to draw table outlines we write

Relation Name(Entity_Type_1: = default, ..., Entity_Type_k: = default)
  Attribute_1:   attribute information : = default;
  . . .
  Attribute_n: attribute information : = default;
  Constraints: constraints

This relation connects the indicated entity types. In addition, it has the indicated attributes. Note that defaults are allowed for entities being related as well as for attributes. An entity type would have a default value of one particular entity (i.e., some individual) if that individual were usually or standardly involved in the relation but if other entities of the type could be involved, given special circumstances.

An advantage of this notation is that it differentiates the entity types linked by the relation from the attributes of the relation. It is useful to be able to see at a glance the entity types that are involved in a relation.

Interpreted Relations

As we indicated at the start of this chapter, the world is more complicated than any simple modeling system can handle. As a way of expressing complex relationships, we permit what we call *interpreted relations*. An interpreted relation is one in which the relation components are connected in ways that defy a simple presentation.

As an example of this difficulty, consider the prerequisite relation for courses at a university. In most schools students are required to have completed certain more elementary courses, called *prerequisites*, before they are permitted to enroll in the more advanced. Often the prerequisites may be satisfied in more than one way; for example, the prerequisite for course *A* may be: the two courses *B* and *C* or the single course *D*.

Although the prerequisite relationship between courses is not particularly complicated, there seems to be no convenient way to express it as a simple relation. The most intuitive way is in words. The problem with using words, however, is that each set of prerequisites may require a different natural language statement and this does not fit our relation format. Thus we cannot define a prerequisite relation that, on its own, represents the desired information; additional language may be required and that language must be read and understood (i.e., interpreted).

We define an interpreted relation as any relation that can be defined in words. In doing so, we do not condone loose statements of relations—the prerequisite relation is rigorously stated. We simply acknowledge the fact that certain relationships cannot be conveniently expressed in the formats described so far. With the option of interpreted relations available, nearly all discrete relationships can be captured in a world model.

Time and Space and Other Continuous Structures

Although discrete relationships between entities may be expressed conveniently by relations, relations do not generally provide the best means of describing temporal, spatial, or other continuous structures within which entities exist. For example, it would be difficult to express geographical structures, population density variations, weather information, the shape of a factory floor, a satellite orbit and the areas of the earth visible to the satellite at any point in that orbit, or the structure of a calendar that permits time divisions that range from a microsecond to a century.

We may abstract certain discrete features of continuous structures by using relations: a graph is a reasonable abstraction of an airline route map, but it is generally not the duty of the requirements author to simplify the job of the system developer by making those abstractions. If a structure is continuous in the minds of the prospective system users it should be presented that way in the requirements documents.

When writing a requirements document we should use the best means available for providing the required information. When describing continuous structures a good representation may be a diagram. It could then be up to the system developers to find a way of incorporating the indicated continuous structures into a fundamentally discrete computer system.

Summary

This has been quite a long and involved discussion of entity types. We must realize that the job of picking out the entity types is a difficult one at best and the chances of getting them correct are miniscule. Most likely, the first attempt at defining the entity types will result in an incomplete and awkward collection. That is all right. As the rest of the document is written, other entity types may come to light, and some of the entity types originally defined may seem better characterized in some other way. These changes may be made. Requirements documents need not be written from front to back, nor from back to front. In general, they are written in a spiral manner: first patches here and there, then rough drafts, then revisions to earlier drafts, until eventually the product represents the user's needs adequately. At that point the requirements are defined.

We might question whether it is really worth all the trouble to describe the world model. After all, isn't it sufficient to identify the results (output) that the system is to produce (from given input)? If we could describe the desired output, perhaps in a general form that would not prejudice the design of the system, wouldn't that be enough?

In one sense the answer is "Yes, it would be enough; all one really needs is to know what results the system will produce." But if we thought about it, how would we describe the desired results? Perhaps specifically in terms of report formats or explicit command sequences for controlling external devices. Yet it is probably not wise to set detailed output formats in concrete before system development is even begun. All we really know is what information we want the system to deal with and what transformed information the system is to provide to the users.

So we are put in the position of describing output as (unformulated and uncoded) information, which means to describe the world to which the information relates. We could pretend that we are not describing a world model and that all we are doing is *explaining* the desired output. Here is a general picture of the output we want and here is what we mean by it. To explain "what we mean by it" means to explain a world model. In the end it all comes down to the same thing. To explain the desired output we must explain what the output is about; that is, we must construct a world model. This model may be hidden as annotation to an explanation of the required output but it must be there. Because we are finally forced to provide the reader with a world model we might as well be explicit about it and do it at the beginning.

3.3.1   Entity-Relation Summary

This section should use the notations for entities and relations we have described to summarize the entity types, the individuals, the relations, and their various attributes. These entity types and individuals should be shown hierarchically ordered in a tree structure that lists specializations and instances below the types from which. they come. The textual descriptions in the following subsections should be keyed to the diagram. To the extent that the summary provides sufficient information, the textual descriptions may be reduced or eliminated.

3.3.2   Entity Types

The subsections in this section discuss the various types of entity with which the system must deal.

Entity Type i

Each entity type is described in its own subsection. The following information should be presented:

   1. *Brief Description.*   This section names the entity type and provides a brief description of its significance to the organization and its place in the functioning of the system. If the entity type is collective the member entities should also be identified. If the entity type is a unit of measure of some substance or material it should be made known.
   2. *General Type.*   This section identifies the more general type, if any, of which it is a specialization.
   3. *Class Size.*   This section gives the maximum number of entities in this type with which the system may have to deal at one time. In an airline reservation system one of the entity types may be *city served.* This section tells how many cities the airline serves or expects to serve. Another is *passenger.* This section tells how many passengers the system will ever be required to keep track of at one time.
   This sort of information is often known as a *performance requirement.* It does not concern structure or content but the *amount* of information the system must be able to handle. Performance information is no less important than content information. If a system is unable to deal with the amount of information a user has it is as useless as if it handled no content information at all. In our approach to requirements we recommend including performance requirements with the related technical re-

quirements. Other approaches to requirements (e.g., see, [Heninger et al., 1980])
segregate them in their own chapters.

4. *Blocked Attributes.* If this entity type is a specialization of some other entity
type it inherits the attributes of the more general type. The inherited attributes need
not be mentiond explicitly here because they should be fully defined in the discussion
of the more general type. Sometimes attributes of a more general type are not inherited; for example the entity type *ostrich* is a specialization of the entity type *bird*.
It is convenient to associate the property ''capable of flying'' with the entity type
bird, but ostriches cannot fly. In cases such as these we must identify the attributes
of the more general type that are *not* inherited by the specialization. These attributes
are listed here.

Attributes

In addition to the general information about this entity type, each attribute should be
described on its own and should be characterized both intuitively (i.e., what does
the attribute mean) and in terms of the allowable attribute values. For each attribute
the following information should be given:

1. *Attribute Intuitive Description.* This section describes the meaning
of the attribute. It should provide enough information to allow someone not familiar with the organization to understand how the attribute is used and how its
values are determined; for example, a system that keeps records of students might
include an attribute Grade Point Average (GPA). This section should define GPA as
the weighted values of the student's grades and give the user's algorithm or formula
for calculating a student's GPA. This algorithm or formula is *not* normally a computer program; it is the definition of the attribute as understood by the user. In addition, this section should include a brief discussion of the use of GPAs (e.g.,
determination of Dean's-List and graduation honors and scholastic probation and dis-
qualification).

2. *Attribute Values and Constraints.* This section describes the allowable values of the attribute and any required formats and precision; for example, the preceding section gave the formula for calculating GPA. This section gives the actual
numbers used in translating letter grades to numerical values; that is, it indicates that
GPAs fall in the range of 0 to 4. In addition, this section indicates that GPA is determined to two decimal digits.

As another example, consider social security numbers. Social security numbers
have a specific form; they take values of the form DDD-DD-DDD, in which each of
the Ds is a digit.

Usually we must know something about the entities to determine value ranges for
most attributes; for example, the *height* attribute of the entity type person can reasonably be limited to a range of 1 to 10 feet and the weight attribute can reasonably
be limited to the range of 1 to 1000 lb. Both suggested ranges include extreme values
that occur infrequently, if at all. (Actual extremes may be determined by consulting
an almanac or book of records.) It is, of course, much better to overstate the allow-

able range than to understate it. If the allowable range is overstated the system may be slightly more expensive to build than it would otherwise have been, although the difference will probably be negligible if the range is not significantly overstated. If the allowable range is understated the system may be inadequate for dealing with entities that have values beyond the indicated range. The loss due to this inadequacy may be significant.

3. *Default Values.*   If there are default value(s) for this attribute they should be stated here.

4. *Multiple-Valued Attribute Class Size.*   If an attribute has multiple values this section indicates how many values of the attribute the system is expected to handle at once. If the amount of information to be handled is not spelled out as a requirement the system may turn out to be too big and needlessly expensive or too small and inadequate for the user's needs.

5. *Retention and Archiving Requirements.*   Some information must be retained indefinitely and other information may be archived or discarded after some period of time. This section indicates how long the information must be retained within the system.

Consider, for example, a system for use by a stock market trader that keeps track of stock prices. Most likely the trader is interested in the price of each trade for a recent period, say the current and last few days. For a few months before that the trader may be interested only in the maximum, minimum, and final price of the stock for each day; for a few years before that, it may be the maximum, minimum, and closing price for each week. Before that the trader may not be interested at all in end-of-a-period prices but only in the maximum and minimum price at which the stock traded.

Although it is often possible to deduce how long information is expected to be retained from the descriptions of the required actions (some of which may explicitly discard data; see Section 3.4), it is worthwhile to include this information here because it is a direct property of the information being described.

Systems sometimes choke on too much old information. It may not really be needed, but it is not discarded because no one can be sure that it will not be later. It is important to provide for the elimination or archiving of out-of-date information. This information, like class size information, is a performance requirement. By giving system designers a way to determine how long information must be kept and when it may be archived or discarded we are helping to determine how much data the system must be able to handle at once.

3.3.3 Individuals

This section identifies the individuals of concern to the system.

Individual i

Each individual is described in its own subsection. Ideally, each individual should be identified as an instance of some entity type and that entity type should be described on its own. Then we need only to name the individual and indicate its type.

For individuals not identified as an instance of some entity type all the entity type information (as outlined in the preceding section) should be presented. Of course, individuals have no "class size" because individuals are not types. Other than that, the same information should be provided and the guidelines presented for describing entity types and their attributes may be followed.

3.3.4 Relations

This section describes the relations of concern to the system.

Relation i

This section characterizes relation i. The following information should be presented:

1. *Relation Intuitive Description.* This section describes the relation intuitively and gives the meaning of the relation to the organization. A good way to be sure that the relation is completely characterized is by drawing a picture of it. A form on which the relation can be recorded is often a good method of presentation. It need not be one currently in use; it need only do the job of holding the information in the relation.

2. *Relation Size.* This section indicates how many instances of the relation will be of concern to the system.

3. *Relation Components.* This section describes the entity types connected by the relation and the attributes of the relation. Each component (i.e., entity or attribute) is described separately. The information presented depends on whether the component is an entity type or an attribute.

a. *Entity Type.* Each entity type included in a relation should be discussed in Section 3.3.2. Thus this section simply refers to the discussion of that type.

b. *Attribute.* If the component is an attribute of the relation the following information should be presented:

(1) *Intuitive description.* Attributes of relations are similar to attributes of entities. This section discusses the attribute *intuitive description*.

(2) *Value constraint.* This section describes the attribute *value constraint*. Refer to the preceding discussion for details.

(3) *Attribute rate of change.* Just as an attribute of an entity or individual may change with time, an attribute of a relation may change with time. If multiple values of a relation attribute are of concern, and if those values depend on a time series, this section describes that time series.

4. *Relation Invariants.* This section characterizes any applicable invariants.

5. *Relation Retention Requirements.* Just as information about entities may be discarded after some time, relation information may also age and lose its value. Required archival, retention, and permissible information destruction instructions pertaining to this relation should be included here.

EXERCISES

1. Create a world model for your school or university. *(Be careful not to express actions. A world model is a static description of entity types and the ways in which entities of those types may be related.)*

a. Define the entity types *student, teacher* (include both full-time and part-time instructors), *grader, teaching assistant, department, interdisciplinary program, school* (if your university is organized into schools), *course, section* (for multisection courses), and *tests* (such as qualifying tests that are independent of courses).

b. Define simple relations that deal with the relationship(s) between faculty and departments and between courses and departments, the enrollment of students in courses, the grades (A–F) received by students in courses and on tests, the assignment of faculty, graders, and teaching assistants to courses and sections, students' majors and minors, the chairs of departments, the deans of schools, the departments and programs within schools, and the schools within the university.

c. Define a student's GPA. Define the conditions under which a student is on the Dean's list, on probation, eligible for graduation honors.

d. Define the various possible undergraduate student statuses such as freshman and sophomore. Define the possible graduate student statuses such as classified and candidate.

e. Elaborate the enrollment and grade relations in (b) to allow for the possibility of cross-listed courses, pass-fail enrollments, pass-fail grades, audit enrollments, withdrawals from enrollments, incompletes in courses, completed incompletes, courses taken more than once (how would this affect the definition of GPA?), the possibility of double majors, and multisection courses with course coordinators.

f. Define a framework for expressing course prerequisites and corequisites.

g. Express your school's undergraduate general education and other general course requirements.

h. Express your school's top-level requirements for its the various undergraduate and graduate degrees (e.g., total units, general education, major, and tests).

i. Express this information as a database schema for some database system. Express it in Prolog or some other programming, design, specification, or requirements language. Express it in first-order predicate calculus.

2. Build a world model similar to that in the preceding question for an appointment scheduling and reminder system to serve some organization with which you are familiar. Are appointments entities? Will the system be required to find a mutually agreeable time for all those who should attend a meeting? (Such an activity is not part of the world model but does it imply the existence of particular entity types?) Will users be able to designate other people (e.g., secretaries) to accept appointments for them? Does this imply entities or relationships? Are reminders entities? Should we be able to enter, for example, a spouse's birthday in the system and be reminded of it a week in advance? Is the system going to find an available meeting room for meetings? If so, are rooms entities? Does it matter how large the room is? Will the system include a message service? If so, are messages entities? Are user-designated collections of messages (e.g., files) entities? In what way does the scope of a system affect the world model?

3.4 FUNCTIONAL REQUIREMENTS

This section describes the system's functional requirements. Functional requirements are understood to mean the actions or sets of actions that characterize the purpose or purposes of the system. In the past most requirements documents have tended to focus attention on functional requirements. Although the functions a system performs do generally provide a distinctive characterization of the system, functional requirements are not the only important aspect of system requirements. Although significant, this section is only one of a dozen.

This and the preceding section complement each other. This section describes the processing required of the system; but processing implies something to be processed, and the information available to the system for processing should be as described in Section 3.3. It should be possible to characterize the system's functional requirements in terms of transformations on this information. Processing requirements may imply entities, relationships, or attributes not covered in Section 3.3 in which case it should be revised to include a discussion of those entities, relations, or attributes.

A large number of potential actions is often required of a system and some framework is needed to determine how to list them. A reasonable strategy is to group the actions that are related to one another. We believe that it is useful to identify each related group of actions with some task that has a meaning to users of the system. In this section, then, we suggest that the required actions be grouped together in terms of the user-level tasks to be supported or directed by the system.

We recommend *against* describing functional requirements in terms of an input-process-output format. This format focuses too much attention on the system and its description and not enough on the needs of the users. A requirements document should describe the user's world and needs. The behavioral specification documents describe the system in terms of its input-output behavior, although, as we shall see when we come to the behavioral specification, an input-process-output format is not completely satisfactory there either. Most system actions involve a change to the system state and not only a response based on the currrent input.

We divide user-level tasks into two major categories: activities and processes. An *activity* is a task performed primarily under the direction of a person. A *process* is a task performed primarily under the direction of the system. Activities and processes are not intended as disjoint categories but more as poles of a continuum and as conceptual tools to help organize our thoughts about functional requirements. In a pure activity the user does all the work; the system serves as a (perhaps very) dumb servant. In a pure process the system will do all the work with little or no interaction with users.

Most tasks performed by the use of computer systems are neither pure activities nor pure processes. Therefore it will frequently be difficult to determine with certainty whether a task should be called an activity or a process. Consider an interactive computer program to monitor and control a factory. In most circumstances the system is in charge. Under abnormal conditions the system gives control to a human overseer. Most systems of this sort have shared control: in some cases the system determines what to do and in others the user makes the determination. These systems often request information or ask advice of their human users; likewise, the user may request information or ask advice of the system.

In the final analysis it does not make too much difference whether borderline tasks are categorized as activities or processes. What is most important is that the functionality of each task be defined clearly and that the responsibility of the system with respect to that task be spelled out. The use of the activity and process categories is primarily intended to provide the requirements author with conceptual tools in terms of which to express the user's needs.

Independent of the seat of responsibility, both activities and processes are characterized by the fact that they are seen by the system users as occurring over a period of time; that is, the length of time that it takes to accomplish an activity or process is significant to the user. This is in contrast to what we might call *actions*. Actions occur instantaneously, at least as far as the user is concerned. Of course, the determination of what is a significant period of time depends on what the user considers significant. But this is a requirements document. Its job is to characterize the user's needs and part of making that characterization is to determine how the user understands time.

Here, too, we should not worry about making a perfect distinction. No catastrophe will result if we initially characterize as an activity something that the user really thinks of as an action or *vice versa*. The primary purpose of making the distinction is to help organize our presentation of the user's functional needs.

Activities

An activity is a task in which people take an active and controlling role and in which the computer system is expected to serve a supportive function. Thus an activity is generally a series of steps or transformations for which people are primarily responsible but (some of) which may be performed with the help of the system. Activities are generally pursued to achieve a specific goal or to produce a specific result. A typical activity is that of developing a budget. If the system is to provide assistance in building a budget, budget building should be identified as one of the relevant activities. Other examples of activities are writing (using word-processing facilities), designing (using computer-aided design facilities), and programming (using program-development tools).

Processes

A process is an ongoing series of steps or transformations occurring to or performed by elements contained within the system. A process should be discussed if the system is expected to monitor the process and possibly to direct and control it. Processes are often defined for systems that control external equipment, as in a factory. Typical of processes are steps in a manufacturing sequence; for example, if a system is to direct the operation of an automobile assembly line one of the processes would be attaching the right front fender.

Processes occurring totally within a computer may also be defined. Typical are ongoing, automatic data analyses and transformations; for example, in a system to monitor weather information one process may be the continuing transformation of streams of raw data from weather-monitoring devices into a standard internal format. Another process in the same system may be the ongoing reporting of all instances of recognizably dangerous weather patterns. As with all processes both persist over time. Both are considered to be ongoing in the system—performing their jobs as the material presents itself.

A process should be discussed when the system has some responsibility for ensuring that the process is progressing satisfactorily. (Otherwise the system developers will have no way of knowing that the system has that responsibility.) The responsibility may be as minimal as monitoring the process and signaling distress should the process attributes go out of bounds or it may be as total as complete authority over the process. The system may be intended to monitor and control the equipment that performs the process and to direct it to modify its functioning as the process continues.

Subactivities and Subprocesses

Many activities and processes have known subactivities and subprocesses. Subactivities of a design activity might include structural analysis and cost analysis. To the extent that these are known, they should be included as functional requirements.

Phases and Modes

The notions of *phases* and *modes* are frequently used in characterizing functional requirements. *Phases* usually refer to a linear sequence of activities through which the system is expected to pass and *modes* usually refer to a collection of operations or capabilities that are related to one another in some way. Most systems have phases of operation to some extent or other, even if the phases merely reflect a daily cycle of starting, working, and stopping. Many systems also have various modes of operations; for example, an update mode of operation for a data base system. It is *not* good practice when writing requirements to define phases and modes of the system's operation explicitly. The definition of phases and modes is the job of the system designers. It may be that to set out phases and modes in the requirements document unnecessarily limits the design of the system. Instead, we recommend the use of activities and processes to characterize the various externally defined phases and modes of the system's expected operation.

Consider a data base system in which there is a need for certain summary reports. One way of defining the need for these reports is to require a "report phase" or "report mode" of operation in which the reports are produced and nothing else is permitted to happen. This is a poor requirement because it may be that the system could be designed to generate the reports dynamically as it performs its other duties. The reports could then be made available on request. Yet if we were to specify as a requirement that there be a "report phase" or "report mode" the system implementers would be constrained to provide one. This system would be less useful than one in which the reports were generated dynamically because the system with the report phase would be less available for normal operation than the one that generated its reports dynamically. In particular, it would not be available for normal operation during the report phase.

Therefore instead of requiring that the system perform in accordance with a rigidly defined set of phases and modes, it is better to identify the activities and processes that occur during the presumed phases and modes and to permit the system designers to determine the phases and modes that are actually needed.

System Actions

We distinguish activities and processes from another category of system functional capabilities: discrete system actions. Activities and processes are carried out in a series of system actions. While an activity or process is intended as a characterization of a higher level system function, an action is intended as a characterization of a direct system capability. As far as the user is concerned an activity or process occurs over a period of time; an action takes place (or can be thought of as taking place) more or less instantaneously.

As an example, consider a system to control the ovens in a bread bakery. Baking bread would be considered a process because it occurs over a period of time. During the baking process the system might monitor the bread and adjust the oven temperature settings. Imagine that ovens are built so that the flames themselves cannot be adjusted; that is, the flames may be turned on or off but not up or down. To maintain a particular temperature in the oven the flames must be turned on and off as appropriate. To the baker turning the flames on or off is an action, whereas maintaining the oven temperature within a specified range is a process. This is so even though, in fact, the flames neither ignite to the fullest nor go out instantaneously. As far as the baker-user is concerned turning the flames on or off is a single act and not one whose duration is of any consequence.

Depending on the application, however, the time scale by which we determine whether something is an activity (or process) or an action may vary from one system to another. A period of time considered as a duration by one user may be considered as an instant by another. In the oven example the oven manufacturer may consider the period between the time when the gas valve is shut off and the flames finally go out to be a duration of consequence. When testing the ovens (by computer-controlled test equipment) extinguishing the flames may be considered a process rather than an action.

Sometimes we just don't know whether to characterize something as an activity or an action. Thus something that seems like a discrete action may turn out to be a more involved activity. Consider, for example, canceling a flight in an airline reservation system. It may seem that this is a simple, straightforward action: the flight is listed as canceled. On further analysis we may decide that when a flight is canceled it is also necessary to cancel any reservations existing for that flight. In addition, the passengers holding those reservations must be notified and perhaps helped to reschedule their travel plans. Also, any special arrangements made for that flight (e.g., food service, medical facilities ordered for passengers) must be canceled. It may be possible for the system to take responsibility for these required side effects, in which case the act of canceling a flight would become a process. If it is necessary for a person to take some responsibility for some of these effects, canceling a flight becomes an activity. As part of this now complex process or activity changing the flight listing from scheduled to canceled remains an action.

Common System Functions

A number of functions are not directly associated with any particular system but are required in most:

1. *Audit Reporting.* If a system has an auditing requirement (see Section 3.9.3) it presumably includes some means to access the audit data gathered; for example, in a system in which information is recorded we may want to determine who recorded the information. The required auditing activities are described here. The concepts in terms of which those activities are defined are described in Section 3.9.3.

2. *System Tuning.* In many systems it is possible to improve resource utilization if we know how the resources are being used; for example, if some class of users typically uses a lot of computational capability and another class typically uses the system's mass storage it may be useful to try to balance system use between the two classes. To do so it is important to have reports of system resource utilization.

In both cases recording the relevant information is best expressed as a process and accessing the information, as an activity. These processes and activities should be included as functional requirements.

Activity, Process, Subactivity, or Subprocess i

We recommend organizing the description of system functional capabilities first in terms of the required activities and processes and within each activity or process by the actions known to be needed for carrying out that activity or process.

Each activity, process, subactivity, and subprocess is described separately. Generally it makes sense to describe the subactivities and subprocesses under the activities and processes within which they fall. We do not show this substructure explicitly in the outline because there may be arbitrary levels of substructures. The following information should be presented about each activity, process, subactivity, or subprocess:

1. *Purpose, Objectives, and Intuitive Description.* This section describes the purpose(s) served by the activity or process. It provides any context necessary for understanding that purpose and tells why this activity or process is performed. It tells what the user expects to accomplish. This section also includes a brief description of the activity or process itself given in terms of the world view defined in Section 3.3; for example, the *edit* activity in a word processing system may be described, in part, as follows:

> During this activity a user revises documents to bring them into a preferred form. The revisions may include adding, deleting, or changing parts of the modified document(s). A user may move parts of one document from one place to another and include parts of other documents in the one(s) being modified. If a document has a defined structure, such as a scheme of hierarchically numbered paragraphs, then if desired by the user that structure is maintained during modification, and all cross references using these structures within or between documents are kept current.

2. *Entity Types and Individuals Involved.* This section lists the entity types and individuals involved in the activity or process. Each of these is described in Section 3.3; therefore this section simply refers to those descriptions. For the activity of revising documents on a document-handling system, for example, at least two types of entity are involved: the documents being revised and the person making the revision. In the system that runs an oven in a bakery there is at least one individual, the oven (assuming a bakery with a single oven), and at least one entity type, the baking bread.

Sometimes a process or activity causes an instance of an entity type to be introduced into the system's world model. In an airline passenger reservation system the *help customer* activity will introduce a new passenger into the system if the customer is previously unknown. Frequently the effect on an entity is to change one or more of its attributes. If that is the case, the attributes likely to be affected should be identified.

3. *Relations Involved.* This section lists the relations that might be affected by the activity or process. If a document-handling system were expected to keep track of cross references between documents the cross-reference relation would be listed as one of those potentially involved during the revision activity. In the *serve customer* activity of an airline reservation system the *reservation* relation would be listed as potentially involved.

4. *Detailed Requirements and Constraints.* This section defines the activity or process in more detail. The following list describes the subjects that might be included. It is not necessarily a complete list: for some activities or processes other details may be included; for others, not all need to be discussed.

a. *Initial conditions and final results.* This includes a detailed description of the initial conditions with which the activity or process starts and the final result(s) to be achieved; for example, if the objective of an activity is to produce a budget this section would describe the nondiscretionary budget elements (the initial conditions) and the characteristics of a completed budget (the final conditions). If the objective is to bake bread this section would characterize unbaked dough and well baked bread.

b. *Conditions to be maintained.* This section includes a description of a state that is to be maintained, if any; for example, if this is a process whose objective is to maintain a satellite with its sensor oriented toward the earth this section would describe the metrics that characterize the satellite's orientation and the range within which the values are permitted to fall.

c. *User limitations.* Constraints here include restrictions on the types of user permitted to make use of this activity or to initiate or terminate the process. (Any such user groupings must be identified as a type in Section 3.3.)

d. *Conditions that limit this activity or process.* Another constraint would be any condition that precludes the use of this activity or the initiation of this process; for example, one user should be prevented from editing a document while some other user is editing the same document. Again, any such conditions should be stated in terms of concepts introduced in Section 3.3.

e. *Result constraints.* Another sort of requirement would be one placed on the overall effects produced by the activity or process. Consider an activity to help students register for classes. During that activity students may consider various trial schedules until they find one for which they are eligible and that contain classes with vacancies. A constraint on this activity could be that the activity would not be considered completed if a student's schedule included two classes with overlapping times.

f. *Display requirements.* If this is expected to be a cooperative activity or if it is a process with a human overseer it is important for the user to be kept informed of its progress. In such cases displays of the current state of the activity or process should be required.

g. *Report requirements.* Many activities and processes terminate with some final report or result. Any required report should be described here.

h. *Auditing requirements*. Still another sort of requirement may be that certain or all of the events occurring during the activity or process be logged to permit if necessary, history to be reconstructed.

i. *Timing requirements*. Some activities and processes must be performed within time limitations; for example, a system that acts as a chess-playing assistant must function within the constraint that the total amount of time the player may take cannot exceed a certain limit; otherwise the player loses the game. In addition, most process-controlled software, that is, software that runs machinery of any sort or that has direct control over physical processes, must function within real time constraints.

5. *System Responsibility*.   This section characterizes the responsibility of the system with respect to the activity or process. Note that the preceding section describes the activity or process itself. It should not allocate responsibility between the system and the user. This section indicates those aspects of the activity or process for which the system is to be responsible; for example, in the case of an *edit* activity in a text-processing system the system presumably has no responsibility for *achieving* the final objectives; its sole responsibility is to store the text and to provide text manipulation capabilities that permit the user to achieve those objectives. Generally the system is to be responsible at least for record keeping. This section should say what records the system is to maintain.

It is important to identify those capabilities the system is supposed to provide. Otherwise, if only the activity is characterized and the user were identified as having complete responsibility for its completion we might conclude that paper and pencil would meet the requirements.

6. *Triggering mechanism(s) and Conditions*.   This section describes the triggering mechanism(s) for performing this activity or process. Commonly there are three types of trigger: external request, internal decisions, or no trigger (in the case of ongoing processes).

External requests are the most familiar: a user at a terminal (or a command in a command stream) requests explicitly that the activity or process commence. Editing a document or baking bread are both good examples because the request to perform this activity or process originate from an external source: the user/writer or the user/baker. Shutting down a nuclear reactor in response to an operator's command is another good example because, again, the system begins the shut-down process as a result of receiving an explicit command from the operator.

Internal decisions reflect situations in which the system has built into it the capacity to initiate the activity or process on the basis of information available to it. Archiving information older than three months is a good example because the system initiates the archiving process on the basis of information (the date) available to it internally. Shutting down a nuclear reactor in response to a dangerous configuration of monitor readings is another good example because the system initiates the shut down on its own on the basis of information available to it. Of course, if the activity or process is said to be initiated on the basis of information available to the system internally that information must be described in Section 3.3.

In either of these cases, if this section is describing the triggering mechanisms or conditions for a subactivity or subprocess, the parent activity or process must have this trigger defined as one of its required actions or events.

Finally, some activities or processes are best considered as continuing indefinitely and not being triggered at all. In most process control systems the process of reading and logging the various device monitors is understood to occur continuously and without explicit initiation for each reading.

7. *Termination Mechanism(s) or Conditions.* As the preceding section described the mechanism(s) that initiate the activity or process, this section describes the mechanism(s) that terminate it. Again there are three types of terminator: external request, internal decision, or no terminator. Sometimes the internal termination decision is based on the simple fact that the job is done; for example, the process of closing down a factory production system terminates when everything is turned off.

8. *Expected Demand.* The subsections in this section describe the amount of use expected for this activity or process.* The expected demand can be categorized as follows:

a.   *Required number of parallel instances.* This section indicates how many of these activities or processes may be required to proceed in parallel. Consider a banking system in which one activity is *customer service.* This section indicates the maximum number of clerks or service stations that may be providing customer service at any one time. Alternatively, if this is a process to control some particular type of machine in a system to run a factory this section tells how many of these machines may possibly be operated at once.

b.   *Expected frequency.* This section indicates how frequently this activity or process is expected to begin; for example, in our banking customer service activity this section says how frequently customers are expected to arrive for service. Even better, this section should give a distribution that characterizes the expected arrivals. Better still, this section could provide the expected demand distribution as a function of certain conditions or time periods; for example, there may be normal and peak load demands.

c.   *Expected duration.* This section indicates how long each instance of this activity or process is expected to last. For the banking customer service activity, again, this section gives the expected average time required for each customer service. Even better, this section should contain a distribution to characterize the expected service lengths.

For guidance in providing information of this sort, consult a text on queuing theory (e.g. [Kleinrock, 1976]).

---

*This, like the class size in the world model, is known as a performance requirement.

Specifically Required Action

The preceding sections described an activity or process as a whole. The subsections of this section describe any action known ahead of time to be required for this activity or process. Recall that an action is different from an activity or process in that the system users consider that actions occur without a duration. Actions are indivisible system services. System users should understand them as atomic units of action and, if possible, instantaneous.

Required actions generally translate into system operations. We do not call them system operations here, however, because we wish to focus on the needs of the user rather than on the ways in which the system satisfies those needs.

The list of actions should not be expected to be complete. It is the job of those designing the system to complete the list of actions necessary to achieve the objectives of the activity or process. In many cases, however, certain actions are known to be needed. When describing them the requirements writer performs a number of services and makes more precise the description of the activity or process, gives the system developers a better understanding of the intent of the activity or process, and ensures that at least the listed actions will be provided in the final system. The following subsection presents the required information about required actions.

Actions as Responses to Events

Often an action is required in response to some event that occurs during the activity or process. An event is a change in some attribute or relation. Although events generally correspond to system inputs, again we focus on the user's world and not on the system's. Thus the objective here is to describe the happenings in the world (as laid out in Section 3.3) to which the system must respond.

In some cases the system has the means of experiencing events directly; for example, in a system that includes a process to monitor an experiment the system has measuring devices that react when particular events occur.

In other cases events occur about which the system must be informed explicitly; for example, in an airline reservation system one of the activities might be *serving a customer*. If, during this activity, the customer changes his or her mind about the date of departure the reservation clerk must provide the system with that information. The system has no direct means of perceiving this event.

Most events change an attribute of an entity or a relation between entities. In the baking system, for example, the event that the humidity of the bread reaches a certain level reflects a change in the humidity attribute of the bread. Any attribute changes should be stated in terms of attributes identified in Section 3.3.

Actions and Events as Triggering Mechanisms

Some actions and events reflect even more than a change to the attribute of some system entity or relation. They reflect a change from one activity or process, or subactivity or subprocess, to another; for example, in a system to monitor a building for unauthorized entry after hours the event that one of the sensors is disturbed might cause the system to log the disturbance and to switch to an "alert process" in which sensors in the area are monitored more frequently and additional sensors are activated. During a programming activity the user may wish to initiate a debugging subactivity of some particular piece of software. The following information is presented about each action:

1. *Information Required for Use and Information Acquired.* This section describes the information the system needs to perform this action; for example, in an airline reservation system one action (in the customer service activity) might be to make a reservation for the customer. To perform this action the information needed is customer's name, desired flight, and date of departure. All other information, such as the city and time of departure, can be derived from the desired flight.

All the listed information should be described in Section 3.3 as an entity, an entity attribute, a relation, or a relation attribute. If a piece of information appears to be needed but has not been described in Section 3.3, Section 3.3 should be augmented to include it. Because the required information appears in Section 3.3, there is no need to discuss it further. All that is necessary is to refer to the pertinent section.

In cases in which this action accesses the information from an existing source the external format of the required information is known in detail; for example, a system intended to read the commercial Universal Product Code (UPC) markings must be able to handle UPC codes exactly as they are defined. When such predefined constraints exist on the external availability of the information they should be expressed.

In many other cases the exact format of the information is not known ahead of time. Then no limiting constraints should be given. In accepting a customer's name as input, for example, it is inappropriate for the requirements document to insist that the name be put in a particular place on a terminal screen, formatted in some particular way on some other input medium, or be limited to a certain number of characters. If there is no reason for insisting on a constraint none should be given.

In the examples mentioned so far the information used by the action is provided as parameters for the actions. The number of pieces of information is known ahead of time. They correspond to the *information required for use.* Other actions perform larger scale data acquisition. An action to accept and store grades for all students in a course at the end of a semester is an example. Here the information required for use is probably the identification of the course; the information acquired is the collection of grades for all the students. For actions of this sort this section should describe the information in terms related to Section 3.3. This section should also give the amount of information expected.

2. *Results.* This section characterizes the results this action is supposed to produce. The following information should be presented to describe results:

a. *Overall description and constraints.* This section provides an overall description of the intended result(s) of this action. It describes any constraints or conditions placed on the use and outcome of this action. In a student registration system, for example, a student may be constrained from registering for a class if that student has not passed the prerequisites for that class.

b. *Required calculations.* Sometimes an action requires that a calculation be performed; For example, a computer-aided design system may have a required action to calculate the structural integrity of a proposed design. If a certain algorithm or approach for performing that calculation is desired that algorithm or approach should be specified here. If no particular algorithm or approach is desired, but only a final result is needed, a specification of that final result should be included here.

c. *Error processing*. Because this is an action rather than an activity, the system is not expected to interact with the user in case of error. This section must describe how errors that do arise should be treated. In general, it is worthwhile to log or report errors. In addition, there are other options:

(1) Errors may be ignored.
(2) Errors may be processed separately in some predefined ways. For example, an attempt may be made to correct them and the attempted correction, processed.
(3) An error may cause the action to be aborted.

d. *Changes of state*. This section describes any changes of state the action requires of the system in which these changes refer to a transition from one activity or process to another. Most actions do not change the system's state. Making an airline reservation, for example, does not change the state of an airline reservation system. Other actions are intended to change the state of the system. A command to terminate student registration and produce summary reports directs the system to change from its registration to its report activity. If this action is intended to direct the system to a change of state that intention is described here. Actions of this sort occur in one activity or process as a means of moving the system to another activity or process.

e. *Changes to the world model*. This section describes the changes to a user's world model (as described in Section 3.3) that this action brings about. This section is the key to describing the intended effect of the action. For most systems actions are not isolated and the effect of one action is normally felt by other actions performed later. This section describes how that effect is understood to effect the world model. In particular, the changes should be described in terms of the information defined in Section 3.3.

Normally there are three changes:

(1) Entities are added or deleted.
(2) Entity attributes change their values.
(3) Facts (i.e., instances of relations) are added or deleted.

Some actions cause more than one sort of change. Any change must be expressed in terms of the world model described in Section 3.3. The following are some typical examples:

A new entity is added to the system.

A student registering for classes for the first time is an example. In this case this section refers to the description in Section 3.3 of the student entity type and indicates the initial attributes and relations for the new entity.

New facts and attribute values are added to the world model.

At the end of a semester a student's grades are added to the record. If grades were described in Section 3.3 as a relation between the entity types *student* and *course* this corresponds to a change to that relation. In addition, the students grade-point average is recalculated to reflect the new courses taken. This corresponds to a change in the value of an attribute.

Facts are deleted from the world model.

In an airline reservation system, a flight completes satisfactorily and information about the flight may be deleted from the system. Again, reference is made to the descriptions in Section 3.3 of the information to be deleted.

f. *Reports, displays, or other products.* This section describes any reports, displays, display changes, or other products required to be produced by the system as a result of performing this action; for example, in an airline reservation system a query about available flights between certain cities would presumably be required to display a listing of those flights with information about their status (e.g., filled or canceled). Similarly, the act of making a reservation would presumably update a continuing display of the customer's tentative itinerary. (That continuing display should be required in the discussion of the overall reservation activity and not in the discussion of any particular action.)

Other output products would include material generated by computer-driven devices, such as printers, typesetters, tape drives, and music synthesizers, to be used elsewhere. In an order-entry system an invoice is a good example of another product.

As in the case of required information, the format of the information to be provided, and sometimes the exact information itself, may be known precisely. At other times it may not be appropriate to define the exact format until later in the system-development cycle. An example of information that must be in a known special format is information a payroll system must produce to fill W-2 forms. Because W-2 forms are defined by the government and are not open for modification by individual companies, systems that generate them must produce output in the precise format required.

An example of information better left for later specification is the output of a computer graphics system. We do not generally know, when writing the requirements of a graphics system, how that output will look. Part of the job of designing a graphics system is to define the appearance of the output. On the other hand, we may require that "hidden lines" be removed and surfaces shaded to indicate light sources.

g. *Control exercised.* This section describes the external controls this action is designed to exercise. If a device, such as a machine tool, is to modify its operation this section will explain the modification. Again, the device itself should be described in Section 3.3 as an individual or an entity. The manner in which it can be controlled should also be discussed either as its own attributes or as attributes of its relation to the materials on which it is operating.

This section should refer to those descriptions. However, it applies only to process control and other embedded systems and not to traditional data processing.

3. *Speed.*   This section identifies any speed constraints this action must meet. A speed constraint is placed on the action in terms of how fast it achieves its results. Speed constraints are most common in process control and other embedded systems which require directions that are fast enough to control the desired processes. Thus one of the actions of a computer system to control a factory machine may be to turn off the machine if it is malfunctioning. This action must be fast enough to turn the machine off before it does any major damage.

4. *Expected Demand.*   This section, like the throughput section for activities and processes as a whole, characterizes the expected demand for this action. Because it is part of some activity or process, the expected throughput requirements for the activity or process apply. Only additional information about this specific action need be supplied. Expected demand is described as follows:

   a. *Maximum parallelism required.* This section gives the maximum number of parallel instances of this action that may be required concurrently within the activity or process. It may be, for example, that a single process is responsible for controlling multiple factory devices, in which case the same actions may be required in parallel for each device.

   b. *Expected frequency of use.* This section defines the frequency with which this particular action is expected to be needed.

EXERCISES

1. Write a description of the activity of scheduling an appointment with someone.
2. Describe the activity of scheduling a meeting with a number of people. Include the problem of finding and reserving a room that has the required facilities (e.g., a movie projector if the activity includes screening a movie) and is available at an acceptable time.
3. Describe the activity of writing and debugging a program assigned for homework in a course. Describe the activity of writing and debugging a module to be included in a large system.
4. Describe debugging as an activity.
5. Describe debugging as a mixed initiative endeavor between user and system.
6. Describe debugging as a process, given, say, a specification of the results desired.
7. Describe the activity of registering for courses at the start of a term. Describe first only the subactivities directly related to building a schedule. Then describe the related subactivities such as paying fees. What are the minimal user-level actions?
8. Describe the activity of dropping a course during a term.
9. Describe the process of driving a car. Include the need to monitor other cars to avoid collisions (assume the ability to sense the size, location, and speed of ob-

jects), adjusting the speed to stay at the speed limit (computer readable speed limit signs) if no higher priority requires another speed, determining the best route to the destination, given current road conditions, and following the selected route (assuming computer readable road signs). What else does the process of driving entail? Assuming appropriate sensing devices, could it be completely automated?

3.5 COMPATIBILITY REQUIREMENTS

This section describes other systems with which the intended system is required to be compatible or interface directly. Interfaces and compatibilities are among the most important requirements to be defined. A system that fails to mate correctly with other systems will most likely fail in its basic mission and will not be serving its users as required.

3.5.1 Host System

This section and the sections within it describe the required interfaces between the system and the host computer, peripherals, and operating system. If there are no constraints in this regard there is, of course, no need to list requirements. Sometimes, however, the choice of host computer, peripherals, and operating system is limited and these limitations must be stated.

Host Computer

This section lists the constraints applicable to the choice of host computer. In particular, if the system must operate on a particular brand of computer that requirement must be given. A number of possible reasons are raised. Perhaps the system is needed for an organization already committed to a particular computer, or the system may be an anticipated software product for a particular preselected target computer, in which case that computer will be the required host.

Besides stating the limitations imposed by the brand of host computer, it is also important to list them with respect to that computer's hardware configuration; for example, if an existing computer which is required to serve as host has 1 megabyte of rapid access memory and no more will be installed (even though this particular brand of computer is capable of supporting 2.5 megabytes of rapid access memory) that constraint must be made known.

Host Peripheral Devices

Just as any limitations on the host computer must be made explicit, those with respect to the peripheral devices must also be clearly expressed. In some cases the peripheral devices may be special purpose devices such as interfaces to factory equipment. In others they may be more ordinary but still limited such as special printing or plotting devices which, for one reason or another, must be used.

Host Operating System

This section describes the limitations on a host operating system. Many computers are adaptable to a number of different operating systems (real time, time sharing, batch, etc.) for which there are frequently many different versions. Operating-system capabilities and limitations are strange and mysterious. Any applicable constraints with respect to the required operating system should be made clear. Those that are not will almost certainly return to haunt the project later.

3.5.2   Other Directly Interfacing Systems or Environments

This section describes any other interfacing systems or environments with which the system must interact. This refers to existing systems that perform functions to complement those provided by this system and with which this system must interact directly.

It is particularly important to include the limitations that cannot be avoided; it is equally important not to list as a requirement a possible interface that is not actually needed. An example may be a requirement that a proposed editor be able to interface with an existing mail system so that users can read their mail and send messages while within the editor. The proposed editor is the new system. It must interact with the existing mail system if there is a requirement as stated.

Another example is the unnecessary requirement that in a patient record-keeping system patient addresses be stored in the exact format expected by an existing form-letter system. The information need not be stored in the same format because it is always possible to write an additional program that will transform the information from one format to another. The primary requirements here are that the needed information be available; for example, that each patient have a zip code so that the form letters can be presorted and qualify for a lower postage rate.

Interfacing System or Environment i

Each interfacing system or environment should be described in its own subsection and each should be defined by detailed specifications for its relevant characteristics or by reference to its specification document(s). It should be made clear in what way(s) the interfacing system will be required to interact with the system under consideration, for it is only the actual interfaces that lead to interface requirements.

3.5.3   Other Required Compatibilities

This section should list any other required compatibilities. We supply three possible areas. More may be added as appropriate.

Upward and Downward Compatibility

Many software products are offered as a family in which, for example, low-end versions operate on smaller computers and provide minimal functionality and performance, high-end versions operate on more powerful computers and provide the system's maximum functionality and performance, and intermediate versions may be tailored to customer needs. This section is relevant to system families. It is almost always important that their different versions be compatible with one another so that as user's needs change they may switch from one version of the system to another. If these compatibilities are required they should be expressed here.

Compatibility with Other Products in This Product Line

Just as many software systems come in families, many also come in product lines. A product line is a collection of products that serves related user needs; for example, a product line for writing may include an editor, a formatter, a spelling checker, a style checker, and other text and word processing items. Because these systems do not necessarily have direct interfaces, they need not be compatible (see Section 3.5.2). Yet they must certainly be compatible in terms of being able to deal with the same information: the formatter must be able to take as input the text produced by the editor and vice versa. Similarly, the spelling corrector must be able to process the editor's text. All required compatibilities between products in a family are spelled out here.

Transition Compatibilities: Migration Paths

Many current computer systems do not automate a completely manual process. Computers have been around for 30 years and their use is now widespread. In many cases a new system will replace an existing system that probably already includes computers. If the proposed new system is to replace or improve an existing system the user has probably adapted to the existing system in a number of ways; for example, there may be forms and procedures to gather information for the existing system. A decision must be made regarding the continued use of these forms and procedures and, if they are to be changed, how the transition will take place. In addition, if the existing system has a database of any sort it is likely that it will have to be installed on the new system. Provision must be made for converting and installing that database. This is the appropriate place to specify this requirement.

This section describes the existing system directly or by reference to other documents. It also indicates those parts of the existing system that will be retained unchanged and those that represent information that must be retained but perhaps in some other form.

EXERCISES

1. Imagine that someone is to write a program to be run on a mainframe computer at your site. This person will write and test the program elsewhere and has neither *a priori* knowledge of nor access to your computer. Once finished, the pro-

gram will be delivered to you and must run. Describe a mainframe computer at your site in enough detail to permit a developer to write programs that will run on it. You might discuss the following issues:

How much about the hardware must you know? How much about the operating system or the terminals? If the program being written is a database program and a database system is available on your computer, how much about that system must you know? Which version of the database system have you? How much must you know about the languages available? Have you particular dialects of languages?

2. Describe an application system to which new application programs are frequently added. In what ways must the new programs be compatible with the existing system?

3. Examine a system family and determine the extent to which it is upward compatible.

4. Define a family of software products, including an appointment scheduling system, associated with general office activities. In what ways must these products be compatible with one another? Are there ways in which compatibility is not needed? Must they all be written in the same programming language?

3.6   HUMAN FACTORS

This section defines the required capabilities and constraints of human factors. These requirements tend to be among the most important and most difficult to characterize. They are important because the human factors engineering of a system can make it a success or failure. [Card et al., 1963; Shneiderman, 1981; Moreland, 1983; Black and Sebrechts, 1981; Ledgard et al., 1980; and Good, 1982]. They are difficult because the state of the art of discussing human factors in computer systems is not advanced and the terminology available to define their requirements is not well developed.

The suggested organization of this section is in terms of types of system use. In many cases there are a number of different user types: for example, operator, primary user, casual user, administrative user, and clerical user. It is more than likely that each has its own needs which should be carefully considered and expressed as clearly as possible.

User Type i

The human factors needs of each user type should be clearly defined in a section for that type. A number of categories are suggested. Others should be added as appropriate. Each user type should be identified and a basic characterization provided in Section 3.3. This section should refer to that characterization.

1. User Sophistication

This subsection describes the degree to which the user can be expected to be sophisticated with respect to the use of computers and the technical material with which the system deals. The system should be required to accommodate its operation to the described levels of user capabilities.

1.1 Level of Computer Sophistication.   This subsection characterizes the degree to which this user type is knowledgeable about computer systems. It discusses the computer assumptions that may be made about these users and the amount of coddling they will need. In particular, it discusses the extent to which they can be expected to understand and work with traditional computer concepts which include the idea of a *black box* and operations on it, a predefined sequence of operations, *loops*, conditional structures, other control structures such as finite state machines and recursion, data storage such as files, trees, and relations, and interactions such as type-ahead and standard editing operations.

1.2 Level of Technical Competence.   This subsection characterizes the degree to which this user type is knowledgeable about the technical application-specific aspects of the system. It discusses the technical assumptions that may be made about these users and the amount of coddling they will need. In particular, it discusses the extent to which they can be expected to understand and work with the technical details of the system's application area. It may be, for example, that certain users will be functioning solely as clerks and will have no understanding of the system's operation. On the other hand, some may be technical analysts and will be using the system primarily in that capacity. The technical competence of the user is an important factor in determining how the system should interact and it must be spelled out.

2. Physical Needs/Constraints

This section and the subsections within it describe the physical needs and constraints of these users. Their needs and constraints may be defined in terms of physical and response-time requirements.

2.1 Special Physical Limitations.   In most cases there will be no special physical needs or limitations, but when there are, they will generally be significant; for example, a type of user may be responsible for monitoring many different system displays at once and the system must be developed to make that job manageable. In other situations the user may be limited by other activities; for example, computer systems developed for pilots flying fighter planes typically incorporate "heads-up" displays. A heads-up display is one that may be read by the user without having to look down at a display panel. Heads-up displays are implemented by reflecting the display off the windshield of the airplane. Note that they are *not* a requirement. The requirement for which heads-up displays are a solution is that pilots should not have to look away from their primary focus of attention (enemy aircraft) to observe system indicators.

2.2   Response-Time Requirements.   Response-time requirements may derive from tasks required of the system users or emerge simply from human factors considerations. If the response time is too great the users will neither like the system nor use it.

Fighter pilots exemplify the first type of user; they need the information (e.g., that the system senses enemy aircraft) immediately. Users of a database management system exemplify the second type of user; they (usually) do not need an immediate response to do their jobs effectively, but if the response time is too long they are not likely to enjoy working with the system and may not work productively. Intermediate between these two examples is that of an on-line teller system, that is, a system that interacts directly with banking customers. Although an immediate response is not necessary for a functionally useful system, the customers will not like the system and may switch to another bank if the response time is too long.

3.   On-Line Tutorial Needs

This section defines the requirements for on-line tutorials for this type of user. If these users are expected to learn how to operate the system from the system itself these tutorial needs should be indicated. If it is not expected that the system will provide tutorial and training facilities few if any requirement should be listed here.

4.   On-Line Assistance Needs

This section sets forth requirements for on-line assistance during system operation. If the system is not interactive there are, of course, no requirements in this area. Many systems are interactive, and it is generally a nice feature to have the system provide assistance when the user is lost. This section should define the extent to which this sort of help is required for this type of user.

It may be that help should be available at every conceivable interaction point; that is, the system may be required to respond to a help request at any instant and to provide assistance with respect to the immediate context of the request: for example, for every command, every subcommand, and every parameter. On the other hand, perhaps help need be made available only at major turning points; for example, when the user has the ability to switch from one activity to another.

Another issue with regard to help is its expected depth. The system may be required to respond with new information to a help request that immediately follows a prior help request, or it may be required to provide only a single level of assistance and, if that is not enough, to refer the user to a manual. Perhaps the system should integrate the help and tutorial facilities so that if the user does not understand the help response a brief (or not so brief) tutorial on the troubling question can be given.

One consideration to keep in mind, however: the more requirements imposed on a system, the more expensive it is likely to be to build.

5.   Robustness Requirements

This section and the next discuss the human factors requirements with respect to system failures. Note that Section 3.10 covers the requirements imposed on the system with respect to system failures in general. This subsection simply tells how the system must interact with the user in the event of failure.

A system is considered *robust* if no matter what input is supplied it cannot fail because the input was unanticipated. It is most appropriate to require robustness for input supplied by people. When the system's input originates from a source known to produce valid data it may not be necessary to require robustness.

It is generally considered appropriate to require software systems to *validate* their inputs before use so that if the input is out of range or otherwise unacceptable the system will not fail. What does it mean for input to be valid? Presumably we would say that a social security number with a letter in it is invalid, but is a query to a database system that asked for the sum of all social security numbers invalid? Is a query that asked for the social security number of a person not known to the system invalid? Perhaps instead of requiring that a system check its input for validity we should simply require that the system never fail, no matter what the input.

6.   Failure Message and Diagnostic Requirements

This section sets forth requirements for error and other diagnostic messages from the system to this type of user. In general, the requirements should ensure that the messages from the system to these users reflect correctly the degree to which these users know the system and the amount of aid they require from the diagnostic messages. For the most part users with less familiarity with the system should be given more explicit instructions about how to handle various error conditions than those with more familiarity.

It is generally good practice to require that failure messages be self-contained and not force the user to consult other reference materials. They should be explicit about the cause of the failure and should describe that cause in terms relevant to the user (rather than in terms relevant to the internal structure of the system). It is generally good practice to require that failure messages include within them instructions about how the user is to proceed after the failure. At the same time it is good practice to require that messages be as short as possible.

7.   Input Convenience Requirements

Whether a system is easy and convenient to use can make the difference between success and failure for a commercial product. It can also make the difference between a system that is well liked and used productively and one that is resented and misused. This section and the next are concerned with capabilities built into the system to make it easier for users to do their jobs.

This section discusses requirements that make it easier for the user to provide the system with information. In particular, requirements should be promulgated that preclude the system from forcing the user to enter information that the system can determine on its own. Examples of these requirements are the following:

1. Default values shall be provided for all user inputs.

2. The system shall display the default values and give the user the option of accepting or changing them.

3. Default values shall be adjusted to the current context; for example, in an airline reservation system the default value for a passenger parameter is the current passenger and the default flight is the flight about which information was most recently requested.

4. The system shall make the relevant user data as visible as possible; that is, displaying it fully rather than displaying it only in part and requiring the user to construct a mental image of the rest of it.

5. The system shall permit users to act as directly as possible on that data; that is, as if manipulating the data with a screen editor rather than indirectly by commands.

6. The system shall scan all user input to ensure that it matches in form, type, and range the input expected. If the input fails to match, the system shall provide an informative message that indicates how the input fails to match and an example of acceptable input.

8. Output Convenience Requirements

This section sets forth the human factors requirements for outputs, displays, and reports. The detailed operational requirements for these areas are given in Section 3.4. This section lists requirements that apply to outputs, displays, and reports whose details are not completely defined in that section. The requirements should ensure that the output is consistent from presentation to presentation and with other uses of the same information. They should also ensure that the format will be clear and easy to understand. Examples include the following:

1. System outputs, displays, and reports shall be consistent with those of the user's organization.

2. When the system displays the same information in two different contexts that information shall be displayed in the same format unless different formats are specifically required.

3. When the system displays similar information that information shall be displayed in similar formats unless different formats are specifically required.

EXERCISES

1. Name an application area and identify a class of users that is sophisticated with respect to the use of computers but are not sophisticated with respect to the application area itself. What knowledge would you expect these users to have about computers in general? What knowledge would you expect them to lack about the application area?

2. Do the same exercise as in the preceding question but with the user's competence reversed; that is, knowledgeable about the application area but not about computers.

3. Identify some user classes for an appointment scheduling system and characterize their expected competencies and lacks. Does it matter if the company installing the system already uses computers for other office automation tasks?

4. Discuss an on-line tutorial system. What are its good qualities? What are its bad qualities?

5. How would you approach the development of an on-line tutorial system for an appointment scheduling system?

6. Discuss your favorite examples of on-line help. What do you like about them? What general principles can you draw?

7. Give examples of nonrobust systems with which you are familiar. How do they fail? To whom does it matter that they fail? How important is it to them? How difficult would it be to make them robust?

8. Imagine that the user of an appointment scheduling system has requested that an appointment be scheduled with another user who is not known to the system. Give five examples of failure messages that range from very bad to very good. Why are they good or bad?

9. Give examples of systems that make it particularly difficult (easy) to provide input. What makes these systems unpleasant (pleasant) to work with?

10. What are the advantages and disadvantages of menu-driven systems? Of command driven systems?

11. Full-screen editors always show their users the portion of text on which they are working. They also give their users the impression that they, the users, can act directly on the data. Line editors do neither. They require their users to request explicit displays of text. They force their users to give commands to an editor that acts as agent to carry out user demands. Imagine a hybrid system in which the text on which the user is currently working is always displayed on the screen, with the "current position" marked with a pointer of some sort, but on which the user still gives line editor commands, say in a buffer at the bottom of the screen. (We might call this a full-screen line editor). Because the commands are identical to those of a line editor, in what ways would this system be preferable to a line editor? In what ways would it be inferior to a good full-screen editor? Note that for many applications this compromise approach is often easier to implement than complete full-screen editing while providing many of the benefits.

12.   Give examples of systems that produce difficult-(easy-)to-read output. What is it that makes these outputs difficult (easy) to read?

3.7   MAINTENANCE AND CONTINUING DEVELOPMENT

This section and the sections within it set forth the requirements for system features needed to facilitate maintenance and continuing development. The first decision we must make is whether the organization that will own the system after it is developed will assume the responsibility for maintenance and continuing development.

The greatest costs associated with most software systems accrue during the maintenance phase of the system's life or that period during which errors are corrected and, more importantly, the system's functionality is enhanced and its performance, improved. It is therefore important to think about what we may require during the system's initial development to facilitate later modification and enhancement. We divide the possible requirements into two major categories: maintenance environment and standards.

3.7.1   Development/Maintenance Environment

This section and the sections within it set forth the requirements for facilities and capabilities to be provided for use during future modification and improvement. A good set of system development tools can make the job of system maintenance easy and straightforward. Inadequate tools can make the job virtually impossible. The field of software environments is developing rapidly; for example, [Druffel et al., 1983], presents a description of one major effort and includes references to other work.

The second decision we must make is the extent to which the development organization should be responsible for providing a maintenance environment for the system it builds. Traditionally we have expected the development organization to produce a product and nothing more. This seems shortsighted. If after the product is delivered we expect to assume any responsibility at all for its maintenance there are tools that must be provided, some of which the development organization will have developed.

Practicality dictates that the maintenance system be the same as the initial development system or some modification of it. If this does turn out to be the case the requirements stated in this subsection may force a choice of the initial development system. Although it is not normally a function of a requirements document to mandate anything about the method of development, the need to ensure the acceptability of the eventual maintenance system may force this effect. There are two ways to proceed:

1.   The organization that will own the system has (or will acquire) its own software development and maintenance environment. The new system must fit that

maintenance environment, in which case the developing organization is forced to do its development in the same (or an equivalent) environment. This environment should be characterized by completing the subsections to this section.

This owner presumably already has (or will have) most of the tools required to engage in further development. However, even if the eventual owner has (or will have) a full maintenance environment the developing organization should be required to deliver certain system-specific materials, such as test drivers and test data, that will help with future development.

2. The organization that will own the system has no software development and maintenance environment that it intends to use for this system. The only choice is to require the development organization to deliver the system itself and a maintenance environment for it. In this case we presumably are not concerned with the next three sections. We may still be concerned about the language in which the system is written (because a particular language is mandated by some higher authority, or because our programmers know only certain languages) and we should certainly be concerned about the maintenance tools to be provided.

Development/Maintenance Computer

This section identifies the computer system to be used in the maintenance system. If no computer system is required no requirements should be indicated.

Development/Maintenance Peripheral Devices

This section identifies the peripheral devices to be used in the maintenance system. If no particular peripheral devices are required, no requirement should be indicated.

Development/Maintenance Operating System

This section identifies the operating system that is to serve as host for the maintenance system. If no particular operating system is required, no requirement should be indicated.

Development/Maintenance Language

This section identifies the programming language to be used for future development and maintenance. If no particular programming language is required, no requirement should be indicated. Because a maintenance programming language effectively determines the language in which the system is to be written, we should be certain about the requirements imposed. On the other hand, if no programming language is required, and the programming language selected by the developer is one with which the intended maintenance organization has no familiarity or one that is not compatible with preferred tools and methodologies, we would have no recourse later.

Development/Maintenance Tools

This section identifies the maintenance tools to be supplied with the development/ maintenance system. Many tools are available for software development and their selection may be difficult, [Freeman and Wasserman, 1983; Squires, 1982; and Branstad and Adrion, 1981]. In fact, the selection of maintenance tools should be based on a decision to use a comprehensive software development and maintenance methodology.

If maintenance is to be done at all then we must at a minimum require an editor (or some facility to create and modify programs), a language processor (or some facility to translate and execute programs), and a file system (or some facility to store and retrieve programs). Besides these we may require test generators and test drivers, configuration management tools to keep track of the possible system versions and options, and debugging tools.

On a more advanced level we may also require tools for expressing system requirements and for analyzing the consistency of those requirements, various modeling and simulation tools for determining the effects of possible requirements, a tool for expressing the system specification, a rapid prototyping tool that would allow us to explore alternative system modifications, tools for relating the requirements to the specification and the specification to the design, a tool for relating the requirements, specification, and design to the tests performed and their results, a tool for verifying formally that the program matches the specification (and perhaps other program verification tools), program design tools and languages, a tool for auditing design and coding standards, and project management tools.

3.7.2 Standards

This section stipulates the design and coding standards to which the system must adhere. Standards as such are not normally part of a requirements document. (After all it shouldn't matter to the user of a system how the system has been designed as long as it meets its functional and performance requirements.) We include standards in a requirements document only because they may be needed to ensure that future modifications can be made effectively. It is for this reason that they are discussed in the section on maintenance and continuing development.

Design Standards

This section presents the design standards for the system. It may be appropriate to refer to an existing design standard because good design is not likely to vary significantly from one system to another.

Coding Standards

This section provides the coding standards for the system. It may be appropriate to refer to an existing coding standard because good coding is not likely to vary significantly from one system to another.

EXERCISES

1. What are the advantages or disadvantages to an organization in doing its own software maintenance?
2. Develop criteria for an organization to use in determining whether it should undertake software maintenance.
3. What software development and maintenance tools are available at your site? Are they used in an integrated fashion? Are there other tools that you know of that could be installed at your site and that you would like to see installed? Why are they not installed? Are there tools at your site that are not used? Why not?
4. Does your site follow (teach) a particular software development methodology? What tools do you use in that methodology? What additional tools would improve the process?
5. Are you currently following any design or coding standards? Are you willing to consider adopting as a standard the approach developed in the design part of this book?
6. If you were buying an appointment scheduling system for an organization that you owned what would your strategy be in regard to maintenance? Justify that strategy.

3.8   REQUIRED INFORMATION: SYSTEM DOCUMENTATION

This section sets forth what amounts to the documentation requirements for a system. In some software development methodologies the documentation is not considered part of the system but is a separate product that is called for as part of the development contract. An argument for this view is that in describing documents we are not referring to a user need. Documents, if they are anything, are a solution to a need and not the need itself. Documents therefore should not be characterized as requirements.

That argument raises this question: what is the need that is generally met by documents? The answer, of course, is information. To take full advantage of a system we need certain kinds of information—the kind that is generally supplied in documents. We believe that this need for information *is* a valid user need and that it should be expressed as a system requirement.

What information do the eventual users of a system need? Different systems have different information requirements. The following may be used as a guide. Information categories should be added or deleted as appropriate.

3.8.1   Requirements

We generally need a record of the requirements that a system was intended to meet. After the system is completed and when changes are being considered it is important to be able to look back to determine what the original requirements were and why the system was built the way it was.

3.8.2   Usage Information

There are three categories of usage information.

1. *User Information*. This is information needed by individuals to operate the system.
2. *Procedural Information*. This is information that explains how the system fits into the procedures of the organization that will be using it.
3. *Administrative Information*. This is information needed by those who will be administering and operating the system as a service to the system users.

We describe these needs in the following subsections and discuss the documents that satisfy them in Part Two, System Specification.

User Information

Some systems are (or are claimed to be) self-explanatory; that is, we can sit down at a terminal and use them without having to read external manuals. Most systems, even those that include on-line tutorials, require additional descriptions that provide more elaborate and complete information about their use. If it is anticipated that such elaborate and complete information is required that requirement should be expressed here.

Generally, when such information is required it is needed for two distinct purposes: tutorial and reference. Both should be expressed if appropriate. The need may be for several different system descriptions of this sort, one for each user type.

Procedural Information

To make use of a system an organization must often perform a number of activities to supplement its direct operation. These activities may include data gathering and dissemination and more generally transmission of information about the system and its functioning to people who may not have direct access to it. These activities must follow a schedule, and responsibility for completing them must be assigned to agencies within the organization. Thus organizational procedures must be developed and distributed and should be expressed here.

Administrative Information

Often it is not the user but a separate administrative and operations organization that is responsible for installing and operating the system. Installation and operation may be complex. The organization must be supplied with information that lets it do its job.

3.8.3   Maintenance Support Information

If we intend to maintain the system after it is delivered we will need information to help us to do that work.

Support Environment Information

If the developers are to deliver a software development environment or software support tools we need information about that environment and those tools.

Design Information

Detailed information about the design of a system must be supplied if we expect to modify it after it is delivered. This information should be provided in a form that facilitates its use for making system modifications.

Test Information

If we intend to modify a system after it is delivered we will have to test the modifications. Because the developers had to create tests, they should provide information about those tests for later use.

EXERCISES

1. In addition to the information mentioned above, what other facts may be needed about a system?
2. Documentation is considered by many to be an unproductive and unpleasant task. Can you think of any way to ease the pain of producing system documentation or of any documentation that can be done without?
3. Can you give examples from your own experience in which significant expenses were incurred because documentation was missing? If not, construct a hypothetical situation.
4. If you were buying an appointment scheduling system for your organization what information would you want delivered with it?

3.9   INTEGRITY CONSTRAINTS

This section defines the system integrity requirements. A computer system is said to have integrity with respect to a set of principles to the extent that the system enforces those principles itself or ensures that the system cannot be used to violate them.* Integrity requirements, that is, the principles that must not be violated, originate from a number of sources. The listed subsections identify some of them. Others should be added as needed.

---

*It may seem strange to use the term *integrity* to characterize a computer system, but its definition, *rigid adherence to a code of values,* is exactly what we mean: the system must neither violate the specified principles nor permit any user to violate those principles by its use. The term is a common one in the field of computer security [Turn, 1981].

3.9.1 Access Limitations

It may be important to limit access to (some of) the information or to (some of) the functions to be made available by the system. This section and the subsections within it should state these limitations.

Limitations on the Availability of Information

Many systems deal with information that is sensitive for one reason or another. This information should be made unavailable to those who should not have access to it. Two motivations for these limitations are listed. Others may be added as needed.

Security

Security concerns the protection of system resources such as information, functions, and computational capabilities from accidental or malicious access, modification, destruction, or disclosure [Turn, 1981]. If the system deals with data that is secret, classified, proprietary, or otherwise limited in distribution these limitations should be stated here [Parker, 1983]. Although the system does deal with such information, it may be that it has no responsibility for enforcing the limitations: the system may be housed in a locked room with access permitted only to those with authority to see the data, in which case there are no security requirements imposed on the system but only on the installation facilities.

Privacy

Privacy concerns the rights of individuals to storage, processing, distribution, and use of information about themselves [Turn, 1981]. Certain information should be kept private simply out of respect for individual sensibilities. The privacy of other information is mandated by law or custom. The privacy require-ments that are not spelled out elsewhere should be carefully and completely defined here.

Addition and Modification Limitations

In many systems the right to add or modify information maintained by the system should be restricted to limited groups of people; for example, only certain individuals should be authorized to add a name to a payroll roster or to change an individual's pay rate.

Functional Access Limitations

In many systems the right to request a system to perform certain functions should be restricted to limited groups of people; for example, only certain individuals, and then only when a number of them act in concert, should be authorized to start World War III.

3.9.2   Legal Requirements

This section describes the legal requirements that the system must fulfill. A law may require that certain records be retained for certain periods of time, or that personnel decisions be made (or not made) with (or without) the knowledge of an employee's race. Again, it may be that a law requires some information to be kept private unless permission for its dissemination is granted by an authorized agent. Whatever the applicable legal constraints, if the system is to be responsible for enforcing them they must be stated.

3.9.3   Audit Requirements

Many systems record financial or other auditable information. To the extent that the system will be responsible for maintaining auditable records, to the extent that the system is expected to ensure that the records are not tampered with, and to the extent that the system is expected to facilitate the auditing process these requirements must be defined.

Note that Section 3.4 (and not this section) presents the functional description of the auditing activity. Here we define auditing principles and terms. This section is related to the functional description of auditing in the same way that the world model is related to the system's other functional requirements. In the section that describes auditing as an activity we assume knowledge of the principles and definitions presented here and discuss the auditing activity in those terms.

3.9.4   Other Policy-Based Requirements

Most organizations have policies that restrict the flow of information; for example, employee compensation records are not made generally available. Any policy-based integrity requirements that are not covered elsewhere should be stated here.

EXERCISES

1.   Should a system impose maximal or minimal constraints on access to the function that shuts down a nuclear reactor? What if the process of shutting down a reactor were expensive? In general, what limitations should be imposed on access to life-preserving functions? What if performing those functions destroyed property and there was concern about sabotage?
2.   If a system imposes limitations on its use how can we be assured that the few people who are allowed to access the limited capabilities can be trusted?
3.   Define the privacy constraints for an appointment-scheduling system. Are there any circumstances under which it should be possible to violate these constraints? What if a user's appointment schedule were subpoenaed by a court?
4.   Imagine that you are producing an appointment-scheduling system as a software product to be sold, you hope, to a mass market. Because there is no preexisting

customer, there are no customer-unique integrity constraints. Specify three integrity constaints (other than privacy) that you would include in the system. Why would you want them?

5. What Federal law restricts the distribution of student's grades? What limitations does it impose? What constraints would such a limitation impose on an automated university records system?

6. Develop audit requirements for a banking system. How might employees steal money from the bank without detection even with those auditing requirements?

3.10   RELIABILITY AND FAILURE REQUIREMENTS

This section and the subsections within it set forth the requirements for system reliability and for the system's response to failures that is, the fault tolerance requirements [Anderson and Randell, 1979; Anderson and Lee, 1981; Avizienis, 1978; Randell et al., 1978; Siewiorek and Swarz, 1982].

3.10.1   Required Reliability: Mean Time to Failure

Reliability, especially software reliability, can be a tricky concept. For now we adopt the standard definition of reliability (see the additional discussion in section 8.2.1).

The reliability *of a system can be characterized by a function* R(t) *which expresses the probability that the system will conform to its specification throughout a period of duration* t *[Anderson and Lee, 1981].*

This definition characterizes reliability as the probability that a system will work correctly for a given period of time. According to this definition, reliability is not expressed as a single number. It is a function of time durations to probabilities:

reliability: duration   →   probability of correct operation

For any period of time there is the probability that the system will work correctly. The profile of these probabilities is said to be the system's reliability. Commonly, we want a single number to express this function. To accommodate the need we frequently use a variant of this probability profile: *mean time between failures* or *MTBF*; also called *mean time to failure, MTTF*. Either of these means of characterizing reliability will do. Of course, we do not really want the system to fail. Therefore these reliability requirements define the minimum acceptable reliability.

In discussing reliability, we are not considering the reason for failure. (Systems can fail for any of a number of reasons, including component wear and logical design flaws.) Also, we are not characterizing the type of failure. (Systems can fail in a number of ways; some serious and others not so serious.) Therefore reliability as a pure measure of the probability of failure is something of a blunt instrument.

3.10.2   Self-Diagnostic and Recovery Capabilities: Fault Tolerance

Probably of more importance than reliability itself is the system's responses to failures. What happens if the system does fail? Can it be prevented from doing significant damage? Can it be restarted? How long will it take? Can all the information be
recovered? This section sets forth the requirements for the diagnosis of and recovery
from failures. Certainly the system should not be built with known errors that will
lead to failure. Yet inevitably there are errors and precautions must be taken in an-
ticipation. There are two primary categories of failure: those that are due to external
factors and those are are due to internal factors. It is worthwhile distinguishing between them.

Externally Caused Failures

Systems do not operate in a vacuum; most are dependent to some degree on
their environment. This is especially true for software. If a software system is
operating on a single computer and that computer fails there is not much that can be
done about it. Without a computer to run it software is like a musical score in the
hands of someone who can't read music—just meaningless symbols. (Of course,
even in this case we may want to have a manual backup system capable of
taking over.)

   Software, however, is not responsible for the environment. Hardware is part of a
larger system and if it fails the larger system must take the responsibility. We simply
agree that if the hardware fails the system will also fail.

   An extreme case of that is the system which runs on a computer that is not considered part of the system (the standard case for software products) and has failed.
Systems may be dependent on their environment in less absolute ways; for example,
a system that accepts information from a monitoring device is dependent on that device to provide correct data. If the device malfunctions and begins to produce er-
roneous data should the system be responsible for detecting (and perhaps diagnosing)
that malfunction? Should it be responsible for protecting existing data from the bad
data?

Internally Caused Failures

Many systems consist of both hardware and software. (Don't forget, this is a requirements document. We don't necessarily know how the system will be designed.
All we are aware of is the problem the system is to solve or the objectives it is to
achieve. Often the problem or objectives can be stated without reference to hardware
or software.) Many systems consist of hardware and software integrated into an operational whole and both are considered part of the system. Therefore if the hardware
fails the system itself will fail and it may be responsible for taking some action; for
example, if reliability is extremely important (as in a medical system or one that will
operate a nuclear power plant) the system can be designed with redundant hardware. It may be required to reconfigure itself in case of hardware failure. Similarly,

when a system consists of software embedded in a larger system that necessarily consists of hardware and software the software may be responsible for taking protective and corrective action if the hardware fails. Consider a satellite. If its hardware fails, it must adapt itself to whatever remains functional; there can be no repair calls.

Some system failures are due not to worn components but to design errors. Software, in particular, does not wear out; therefore software failures are not due to the physical degradation of equipment. Software fails to operate as anticipated both because it is virtually impossible in large systems to ensure that no errors will remain and because new errors are frequently introduced as systems are modified. Because the software may fail for unexpected reasons, provision should be made for systems to protect themselves from or recover from their own design errors.

The following categories of requirements should be applied to external and internal failures.

Failure Detection

This section lists the failures the system is required to detect. These are often violations of constraints listed earlier. There may also be failures that are not listed as constraints simply because they are considered too trivial to mention; for example, a value should not change between the time it is stored and when it is next referenced. Here all the constraints for which the system is responsible should be given, a time limit should be placed on the constraint or condition may be permitted to exist before it is noticed, and the diagnostic report to be produced if the condition occurs should be indicated.

Error Confinement

This section lists the ways in which error conditions should be limited; for example, if a diagnoseable error occurs in the record of an employee's salary, presumably that error should be corrected before any checks are printed. If a system device or component malfunctions, that device or component should not be permitted to operate on other elements of the system. Finally, if a system transaction could cause an error if not fully completed (e.g., debit one account and credit another) it should be isolated; its effects should not be recorded unless it can be completed in full.

Error Recovery

This section describes the extent to which the system is responsible for recovering from errors. Error recovery is made possible, for example, by the use of redundant coding techniques. This section gives the extent to which recovery is required. In most systems information is periodically "checkpointed" so that the system can be restored to a condition known to be correct. In addition, records may be kept of system transactions in which the precise cause of the error may be pinpointed and its effects, eliminated. All recovery requirements should be listed here.

Recall, however, that this is still a *requirements* document. We should not be prescribing the means of achieving requirements, only the requirements themselves; for example, we should not demand checkpointing explicitly. Checkpointing is a solution, not a statement of an objective. Yet we may require at least the same recovery capability as a system that does checkpoint its data at some specified intervals. That is an objective and it leaves open the means of achieving it.

This section should also identify the extent to which the system is required to recover from failures automatically. Most systems have some failure-recovery mechanisms built in, if only as "try again if the first time failed," as in attempts to reread a storage medium a number of times. More can be done, however. Most systems have fairly standard recovery and restart procedures and at least one will succeed. Certainly systems that can detect errors can follow these procedures. There may be even more sophisticated exception analysis and recovery that can be performed. When writing requirements we should not define the recovery and restart procedures, but we must not be shy about requiring recovery and restart whenever possible.

Failure Modes and Priorities

System component failure or malfunction may force the sacrifice of some normal system functions. This section ranks these functions in priority order to maintain the most important. In particular, it tells how system failure or malfunction may threaten national security, human life, human safety or wellbeing, other life or safety or wellbeing, vital or otherwise significant records, objects or materials with monetary value, objects or materials with artistic, historical, or sentimental value, historical records, records of property ownership, business records, and user's time. It reveals the relative importance of each of these possible losses and it establishes priorites that, in the event of a malfunction, will permit the system to focus its resources in the most appropriate manner. In addition, this section indicates the extent to which the system is expected to isolate the cause(s) of the failure or malfunction(s) in preparation for repair.

One possible recovery policy may require that, when practicable, the system never cease to operate; that is, no matter what happens, the system must attempt to restart itself. This policy might be appropriate for a heart-lung machine. An alternate policy may require that at the first sign of failure the system inform the operator of a problem that needs resolution. This policy might be appropriate for a nuclear power generation plant.

A compromise policy would divide the system's functions into three classes: critical, dangerous, and others. The system would be required to perform its critical functions in all circumstances and to deactivate all dangerous functions if some malfunction is detected. Other functions should be performed to the extent possible. It may not always be easy to make these distinctions. Some functions may be critical *and* dangerous. It is worthwhile to attempt to reduce them into separate critical and dangerous components.

Mean Time to Recovery (MTTR)

Just as MTTF measures the reliability of a system in terms of the probability that it will be operating, MTTR measures reliability in terms of the length of time the system will not be operational if it fails. This measure exhibits the same inadequacies as MTTF—a single number cannot realistically capture the complexity of most systems, but when useful it should be included here.

EXERCISES

1. Name some ways in which an appointment-scheduling system might fail that would not make it totally useless.
2. Assume that an appointment-scheduling system is either operating correctly or not operating at all. What is the minimum MTTF that you would consider acceptable?
3. For which externally (internally) caused failures should an appointment-scheduling system be responsible? How would they be detected? Confined? To what extent should recovery be attempted? Don't forget to express these requirements in terms of user-level concepts and not implementation-level concepts.
4. Define failure modes for an appointment-scheduling system. What are the top priority functions? An appointment-scheduling system, let's assume, is pure software. It is dependent on hardware over which it has no control. Is it realistic to define failure priorities? Can a system of this sort have any control over the functions that it can perform? Isn't such a requirement really one for the developers to force them to allocate their resources so that the high-priority functions will be more thoroughly tested?

3.11 OPERATIONAL RESOURCES AND RESOURCE LIMITS

As we have stated, a requirements document describes a problem to be solved or an objective to be achieved. A problem is not completely defined until we have characterized the resources that may be used in its solution.

Imagine, for example, that we want a payroll system for a new division of a large company. Presumably the parent company already has a payroll system, but let's assume that for some reason that system is not completely satisfactory. It may be, however, that the current system is capable of performing satisfactorily some of the functions required by the new system; for example, printing W-2 tax forms. Let's assume that there is no reason why those functions cannot be provided by the old system, in which case there is no point in recreating the function in the new system if the existing one can do the job.

This is an example of the availability of an operational resource, here a computational capability, that if used would simplify the solution to the original problem—the need for a payroll system for the new division. If this resource were not mentioned explicitly its availability might not be known to the developers and they might not use it in their solution. Thus it is important to include in the requirements document the availability of any existing capabilities that may be usefully incorporated in the solution.

Presumably the expected solution to the payroll problem is some computer system, although that is not absolutely necessary. We could assign enough clerks to do the job manually, an approach that might satisfy the other requirements. (A well organized manual system might be able to do the job fast enough to meet our needs, and sometimes a manual solution is truly better.) A manual system in this case would probably be too costly to operate or, if cost were not an issue, it might not be possible to find enough clerks who could be trained to do the job. These are examples of constraints on operational resources. Two resources used in the operation of almost all systems, money and staff time, are almost always available in only limited supply.

Most systems consume other resources as well; for example, all computer-based systems consume computing power and most consume storage resources. Although the new system may not use more of these resources than is available at the intended site other systems may also be contending for them and only a certain portion of the total will be allocated to this particular system. Thus it is important to include in a requirements document constraints on the availability of resources to be used in the solution of the problem.

In this section we list all the operational resources that are available for use in the problem solution. We also list the limits on those resources. As the foregoing examples illustrate, operational resources may include computational and other functional capabilities, money, staff talent and time, computing and storage resources, and physical space. Other resources will depend on the user organization and the particular problem to be solved. A separate section should be devoted to each resource.

EXERCISES

1. What operational resource limits would you put on an appointment-scheduling system?
2. List three operational resources not yet mentioned.

3.12   OTHER REQUIREMENTS

Although the requirements topics listed so far cover a lot of ground, it seems that there are always other requirements that do not fit into any of the defined categories. Requirements that fit nowhere else should be listed here.

EXERCISE

1. Name one requirement for an appointment-scheduling system that does not fit
    into any of the categories discussed in this requirements outline. (Note that there
    are additional sections.) Send a copy of your answer to the author of this book
    via the publisher.

3.13   EXPECTED FUTURE ENHANCEMENTS

This section discusses the areas in which the system is expected to undergo enhancements in future versions. Expected enhancements are system requirements in that the
system should be designed to incorporate these enhancements without a major dis-
ruption of the original design. The system designers meet this requirement by showing how the enhancements can be added to the system, although they should not be
expected to design them.

   When writing this section we should review the entire requirements document and
identify anything that might change; for example, might the organization's structure
or calendar change? Might the world model change, perhaps by the addition of new
entity types? Might additional functions be required? In most systems the initial complement of available functions is not complete; there are almost always desired functions that were not included. Might there be a need to enhance the performance
requirements? In most systems it is expected that the amount of data to be handled
(the size of an entity type or relation) will grow, that the number of transactions will
grow, or that some other performance parameter will eventually have to be in-
creased. Might additional compatibilities be desired? This is the place to list those
requirements and to ensure that the system will be easy to modify to accommodate
them.

EXERCISES

1. Develop the argument that expected future enhancements are not a fair require-
    ment. We cannot really accommodate them without designing the system for
    them, and if we do the design they are not really future enhancements. Counter
    that argument.
2. Define three functional enhancements for an apointment-scheduling system.
3. Define three compatibility enhancements [(1) compatibility with some software
    system, (2) compatibility with some new hardware, and (3) one of your own
    choice] for an appointment-scheduling system.

3.14   TEST SITUATIONS AND SCENARIOS

The final two sections of the proposed requirements document are not often included
in a statement of requirements. This section is in many ways redundant with require-

ments stated elsewhere, and section 3.15, Development Requirements, may contain material that is too sensitive to be included in a public statement of requirements. We discuss it here as a means of indicating its usefulness but not to insist that it always be covered.

This section and the subsections within it should identify situations and scenarios in which the system is expected to be useful. They are intended to form the basis for system-validation testing; that is, each situation or scenario should eventually be used to define a set of system inputs and a set of appropriate system responses. Any situation or scenario that the user wants to be sure is included in the eventual test plan should be proposed here. The actual inputs and responses are not to be given; they cannot be because the precise inputs and outputs have not yet been defined. Only the situations are described.

A test situation is an event set in the context of a set of conditions. The system is expected to deal with that event in a useful way. A test scenario is a sequence of events that the system is expected to handle. In each case the conditions, the events, and the expected system services should be described in terms of user-level concepts.

3.14   Test Situations

The various test situations should be described here. For each of them the following should be provided:

Test Situation i

The name and a brief overview description of the situation should be given here. The following information should be presented for each test situation:

1. *Conditions in Effect.* This section should describe the conditions assumed to be in effect when this situation is encountered. Only the conditions relevant to the capabilities being tested should be described but all conditions important to the test situation should be included.

2. *Triggering Event.* The event that triggers the situation should be described in detail. The event may be external, such as a customer needing information from a catalog-sales support system or a machine tool breaking in a computer-aided manufacturing system. The event may also be internal, such as the discovery of an accounting inconsistency. Whatever the event, it should be described in terms familiar to the user.

3. *Expected Service or Result.* This section should describe how the system is expected to deal with the event. It need not give in detail the precise system outputs or responses; they cannot be known until the system is further developed. It should describe the way in which the system is expected to react and the services and information the system will provide to the user to deal with the situation.

3.14.2   Test Scenarios

The various test scenarios are described here. For each the same basic information is given.

Test Scenario i

Each test scenario is named and briefly described. The following information should be presented about each:

1. *Conditions in Effect*. The conditions in effect before the start of the scenario are described here.

2. *Sequence of Triggering Events*. The sequence of events making up the scenario are described here. Each event should be treated separately. It may be that the sequence of events is conditional: depending on the exact event and precondition, the next event may be selected from among a set of alternatives.

3. *Expected Services or Result*. The expected system responses for each event in the sequence should be described. As usual, they should not be detailed descriptions of system output but categorical characterizations of how the system will help in the given circumstances.

EXERCISES

1. Define three test situations for an appointment-scheduling system.
2. Define three test scenarios for an apointment-scheduling system.

3.15   DEVELOPMENT REQUIREMENTS

This section and the subsections within it describe support requirements that pertain to the *process* of developing the system. They are not requirements on the system itself but on the system development process. For this reason the information in this section is often not included in a requirements document but instead becomes part of a contract with the developers. Because these requirements do, in fact, tend to define the system to be developed, we include them here for completeness.

3.15.1   Development Support

The subsections in this section define the resources available for developing the system.

Budget

This section contains the budget for the system. The budget may be described in terms of the money available in given time periods or by naming the amount to be paid at the delivery of the system. It may be described by identifying the funding strategy; for example, cost plus fixed fee, fixed price, level of effort, or cost plus incentive fees.

People Available To Help in the Development

This section names the people who will be assigned to help the developers and the charges to be made for them. It identifies the time and dates when they will be available.

Development Facilities to be Provided

This section lists the facilities to be provided to the developers and the charges to be made for them. They may include offices in which the developers can work, computing equipment and development tools with which the development work can be done, and existing systems to which the new system must interface to be made available for testing.

System Components to be Provided

This section lists the hardware or software components to be provided to the developers for possible inclusion in the system and the charges to be made for them. Note that this is not the same as resources in the environment that may be used to solve the problem (see Section 3.11). This section discusses elements that may be incorporated as components into the system; they are not external components already in the environment to be used by the system. If the organization acquiring the system owns a large library of software components, the availability of that library for use in the system may make a significant difference in its cost.

3.15.2 Development Schedule

This section describes the constraints on the development schedule which may specify that the system be operational by a certain date (because some other event may be scheduled for that date and the system will be required to support that event; an automatic scorekeeping system for the Olympics), that the marketing strategy for the system requires the system to be available for demonstration/delivery by a certain date (because a competing organization will have their product ready by then), or simply that the system users need the system by a certain date.

EXERCISES

1. How much would you pay to have an appointment-scheduling system developed?

2. How long would you allow?

REFERENCES

R.J. Abbott and D. Morehead, Software Requirements and Specifications: A Survey of Needs and Languages, *The Journal of Systems and Software*, **2**:297–316, 1982.

M.W. Alford, A Requirements Engineering Methodology for Realtime Processing Requirements, *IEEE Transactions on Software Engineering*, **SE-3**:60–69, 1977.

T. Anderson and B. Randell, Eds., *Computing Systems Reliability, Principles and Practice*, Cambridge University Press, Cambridge, 1979.

T. Anderson and P.A. Lee, *Fault Tolerance, Principles and Practice*, Prentice Hall International, Englewood Cliffs, New Jersey, 1981.

A. Avizienis, Fault-Tolerance: The Survival Attribute of Digital Systems, *Proceedings of the IEEE*, **66**(10):1109–1125, 1978.

A. Barr, P. Cohen, and E.A. Feigenbaum, *The Handbook of Artificial Intelligence (three volumes)*, William Kaufman, Los Altos, California, 1982–1983.

E.H. Bersoff, V.D. Henderson, and S.G. Sigal, *Software Configuration Management*, Prentice-Hall, Englewood Cliffs, New Jersey, 1980.

J.B. Black and M.M. Sebrechts, Facilitating Human-Computer Communications, *Applied Psycholinguistics*, **2**:149–177, 1981.

B. Boehm, Software Engineering, *IEEE Transactions on Computers*, **C-25**:1226–1241, 1976.

M.A. Branstad and R. Adrion, Eds., NBS Workshop on Programming Environments, *ACM Software Engineering Notes*, **6**(45):1–52, 1981.

S.K. Card, T.P. Moran, and A. Newell, *The Psychology of Human-Computer Interactions*, Lawrence Erlbaum Associates, 1983.

P. Chen, The Entity-Relationship Model: Towards a Unified View of Data, *Transactions on Data Base Systems*, **1**(1):9–36, 1976.

P. Chen, Ed, *Entity-Relationship Approach to Information Modeling and Analysis*, Elsevier/North-Holland, New York, 1983.

P. Chen, Ed., *Entity-Relationship Approach to Systems Analysis and Design*, Elsevier/North-Holland, New York, 1980.

W.F. Clocksin and C.S. Mellish, *Programming in Prolog*, Springer-Verlag, New York, 1981.

E.F. Codd, A Relational Model of Data for Large Shared Data Banks, *CACM*, **13**(6):377–387, 1970.

A.M. Davis and T.G. Rauscher, Formal Techniques and Automatic Processing to Ensure Correctness in Requirements Specification, In *Specifications of Reliable Software*, 15–35, IEEE, 1979.

C. Davis, S. Jajodia, P. Ng, and R. Yeh, Eds., *Entity-Relationship Approach to Software Engineering*, North-Holland, 1983.

U.S. Department of Defense, Requirements for Ada Program Support Environments (Stoneman), 1980.

L.E. Druffel, S.T. Redwine, Jr., and W.E. Riddle, Special Issue on The DoD STARS Program, *Computer*, **16**(11):9–104, 1983.

P. Freeman and A. Wasserman, Ada Methodology Questionare Summary, *ACM Software Engineering Notes*, **8**(1):51–98, 1983.

N.M. Goldman and D.S. Wile, *A Database Foundation for Process Specification,* Technical Report, USC Information Sciences Institute, 1980.

M. Good, An Ease of Use Evaluation of an INtegrated Document Processing system, In *Proceedings of the Conference on Human Factors in Computing Systems*, 142–147, ACM, 1982.

F. Hayes-Roth, D.A. Waterman, and D.B. Lenat, *Building Expert Systems*, Addison-Wesley, Reading, Massachusetts, 1983.

K.L. Heninger, J.W. Kallander, J.E. Shore, and D.L. Parnas, *Software Requirements for the A-7E Aircraft*, Technical Report, Naval Research Laboratories, 1980.

A. Kleinrock, *Queueing Systems*, Wiley, New York, 1976.

H. Ledgard, J.A. Whiteside, A. Singer, and W. Seymour, The Natural Language of Interactive Systems, *CACM*, **23**(10):556–563, 1980.

D.V. Moreland, Human Factors Guidelines in Terminal Interface Design, *CACM*, **26**(7):484–494, 1983.

D.B. Parker, Congressional Testimony on Computer Security, *ACM Software Engineering Notes*, **8**(5):10–17, 1983.

B. Randell, P.A. Lee, and P.C. Treleaven, Reliability Issues in Computing System Design, *Computing Surveys*, **10**(2):123–165, 1978.

D.T. Ross, J.B. Goodenough, and C.A. Irvine, Software Engineering: Processes, and Goals. *IEEE Computer*, **6**(5):62–72, 1975.

D. Ross, Conference Chair Remarks, In *Specifications of Reliable Software*, iii, IEEE, 1979.

B. Shneiderman, *Software Psychology: Human Factors in Computer and Information Systems*. Winthrop, Cambridge, Massachusetts, 1981.

D.P. Siewiorek and Robert S. Swarz, *The Theory and Practice of Reliable System Design*, Digital Press, 1982.

S.L. Squires, Ed., Special Issue on Rapid Prototyping, *ACM Software Engineering Notes*, **7**(5):1–184, 1982.

Robert C. Tausworthe, *Standardized Development of Computer Software*, Prentice-Hall, Englewood Cliffs, New Jersey, 1979 (two volumes).

D. Teichrow. PSL/PSA: A Computer-Aided Technique for Structureed Documentation and Analysis of Information Processing Systems. *IEEE Transactions on Software Engineering*, **SE-3**(1):41–48, 1977.

R. Turn, *Trusted Computer Systems*, Technical Report, The Rand Corporation, 1981.

A.I. Wasserman, and S.K. Stinson. A Specification Method for Interactive Information Systems. In *Proceedings of the Symposium on Specification of Reliable Software*, pages 68–79. IEEE, 1979.

R. Yeh and P. Zave, Specifying Software Requirements, *Proceedings of the IEEE*, **68–69**;1077–1084, 1980.

PART 2

SYSTEM SPECIFICATION

═══4

DISCUSSION

If a requirements document defines the properties a system must have to be useful a system specification is a complete external description of a system that has those properties. We can imagine a requirements document as giving the shape of the world into which a system is supposed to fit and a system specification as providing a system that fits that shape. As such a system specification answers the second of the three questions posed at the start of this book.

1. *Why* is a system needed and for what purpose(s)? The requirements document answers this question.
2. *What* does a system that fills these needs look like and how is it used? The system specification answers this question.
3. *How* can a system be built to behave as described? The design documents answer this question.

Thus a system specification answers two questions:

1. How does the system act?
2. How should the system be used?

To reply to the first we must provide a description of a system from an external point of view; that is, one of the functions of a system specification is to give a "black-box'' description of the system. Therefore to write a system specification we must first decide in what terms black-box behavior should be characterized. The most common framework for describing black boxes is the *stimulus-response* model: construct a model that responds as the system would to any given stimulus.* We adopt this stimulus-response model for system specifications and call an external system description a behavioral specification.

To develop a complete stimulus-response model we must describe the system as it is seen at all its external interfaces, one of the most important of which is generally that with its user(s). There may also be any number of interfaces that the system will have with external devices or other systems; for example, a system to operate a factory has interfaces with the factory machines it controls and the devices it monitors, and the various airline reservation systems must interact with the reservation clearing house. Rather than include descriptions of all interfaces in a single behavioral specification, we suggest writing a separate behavioral specification for each external interface.

A user's manual, when it is complete enough, would be an excellent choice to include in a system specification as the behavioral specification for the user interface. Unfortunately, we are not generally in a position to write a user's manual when the system specification is needed. A user's manual usually has more tutorial material and more examples than are necessary in the behavioral specification. A good user's manual should have as its audience the individuals who will actually be using the system. They may be clerks, scientists, or administrators, depending on the system's area of application. This manual should make it easy for the users, whoever they happen to be, to learn and to make use of the system. To achieve that goal great care must be put into its design, but writing a document to assist users is not the goal of the behavioral specification.

A behavioral specification has as its primary purpose the presentation of a clear description of the system seen from outside at some particular interface. It should be rigorous and complete but need not be tutorial. A behavioral specification has as its audience the representatives of the using organization who are in a position to determine whether the system fits their organization's needs.

In addition, there is often some information that a behavioral specification must provide that a user's manual gives only implicitly, if at all; for example, a behavioral specification should discuss response times, whereas a user's manual may not; and a behavioral specification must discuss integrity constraints, whereas a user's manual may only imply them by the operations that are permitted to various classes of users.

Nonetheless, even though there may be some significant differences between a behavioral specification and the typical user's manual, the two are so alike that it is worthwhile to consider a behavioral specification as a preliminary user's manual.

A behavioral specification is a precise description of all the externally relevant

---

*Some systems initiate actions; that is, they respond without any directly related stimulus. Usually however, these cases may be described in terms of a series of responses to some initial stimulus. Therefore, even these systems can be handled by a stimulus-response model.

properties of a system at some interface. It should be complete enough that it can be used to describe the system to any potential user—and not just to the one who wrote the original requirements document. A behavioral specification should provide enough information about a system to enable any reader to determine whether the system will satisfy his needs, whatever they may be.

4.1 ADDITIONAL DOCUMENTS REQUIRED

Behavioral specifications alone are often not sufficient to permit a prospective user or organization to determine whether a system will really meet its needs. Just as a reference manual for a programming language describes the valid constructs in the language but does not explain how to use the language to write good programs, behavioral specifications tell us what a system is capable of doing. They do not tell us how that system fits the particular demands of a user or organization. To provide this information two other manuals are needed:

1. A procedures manual describes how an organization should function to make use of the system described in the system specification. It recommends organizational components (e.g., a data entry group, a database administrator) and identifies the information paths that should be provided between these groups and the information flows and operations that should be scheduled within the organization. Just as a style guide for a programming language tells us how to make effective use of the programming language described in the reference manual, a procedures manual tells us how to operate the system described in the behavioral specification.

2. It would be nice if we could buy a computer system and use it without thinking any more about it. Unfortunately, the acquisition of a computer system always brings with it a larger or smaller administrative commitment. The system must be installed; it must be updated when it is changed; it must be supplied with paper and other consumable resources; it must be fixed when it breaks and perhaps serviced on a regular basis to keep it from breaking; if there are users they must have account names assigned (and deassigned when they leave); system resources such as storage space must be allocated; accounting (and possibly billing) must be taken care of; the system must be configured and reconfigured if that is an option, and it must be turned on and off. Someone must be responsible for these jobs, and there must be some documentation to explain how these tasks are to be done. An administrative manual deals with these issues.

Thus a system specification includes three types of manual:

1. *Behavioral Specification.* These manuals describe the system at each of its external interfaces.

a. *Preliminary User Manual.* A preliminary user manual describes the system as the user will see it, although it doesn't provide the tutorial material usually found in a user's manual.

b. *Preliminary Interface Manual(s) (one for each of the required nonuser interfaces).* Each interface manual describes how the system will appear at a particular interface. Each interface manual is similar to a user's manual except that the "user" is whatever is outside the interface. Often the user is a device or another system. Because a user's manual is just a special interface, the one between the user and the system, we treat all the interface manuals in the same way.

2. *Preliminary Procedures Manual.* This manual describes how the user-organization must function to benefit from the system. In addition, this manual includes a preliminary transition manual (if a transition from a current system is anticipated).

3. *Preliminary Administrative Manual.* This manual describes how the system is to be administered and operated.

4.2 REQUIREMENTS VERSUS BEHAVIORAL SPECIFICATION

We may wonder what the difference is between a system specification and a requirements document. We have said that a requirements document describes the properties a system must have and that a system specification describes a system that has those properties. Is there any difference between the two? It is conceivable that there is no difference. If the properties laid out in the requirements document are restrictive enough the system specification will be just a repetition in other terms. In most cases, however, the properties set forth in a requirements document do not completely define a system; they only restrict certain aspects of it. Other aspects of the system are left for further elaboration.

As an example, consider the difference between a requirements document for a house and a floor plan plus elevation (i.e., artist's conception) for a house that meets those requirements. The requirements document might characterize the following:

1. *Entity Types*
   a. The people expected to live in the house and the people who might visit.
   b. The furniture, appliances, other equipment, and indoor plants, either already owned or to be acquired that must be accommodated.
   c. Clothing that will be stored.
   d. Pets.
   e. Food stuffs that must be stored and their properties; for example, package sizes and refrigeration requirements.
   f. Books and papers that must be available and protected.
   g. Automobiles that must be accommodated.

2. *Activities and Processes*

   a. Sleeping: whether the people living in the house sleep in private or in pairs. Any requirements that should help to limit noise during the sleeping hours.

   b. Eating and food preparation: any support required.

   c. Sanitation: support required for washing and toilet activities

   d. Relaxation, visiting, and recreation: sufficiently clear descriptions so that we can determine the space (such as family room or patio) and facilities (such as swimming pool) needed to support these activities.

   e. Temperature regulation: an ongoing process which requires that the temperature be maintained within user-specifiable ranges, perhaps with different ranges during different, possibly concurrent, activities.

3. *Compatibilities*

   a. Any requirement that the house be compatible with its environment; for example, with other houses in the neighborhood or with its physical setting.

   b. The requirement that the house be compatible with a particular plot of land on which it must be built.

4. *Interfaces.* Required interfaces to energy (gas, electricity), communication (telephone, broadcast and cable television, radio, computer networks, and newspapers), water, sanitation, and transportation (street access for automobiles, pedestrian access), and other external systems.

5. *Human Factors*

   a. Applicable human physical limitations such as restrictions on the ability to use stairs.

   b. Required amenities such as fireplaces and gardens.

6. *Maintenance.* Requirements and standards that facilitate cleaning, yard maintenance, and repairs.

7. *Security.* Requirements that the house be made safe from intruders.

8. *Legal.* Building codes that must be accommodated.

9. *Future Enhancements.* Additions to the family; more children, grandparents.

In contrast, the floor plan and elevation should describe the actual layout of the house, as it will appear and as its inhabitants will use it. (As Chapter 5 discusses, the *design* of the house should describe the materials to be used in construction, the routing of plumbing pipes and heating ducts, which walls are the "bearing walls," and so on.)

It is possible, of course, for a requirements document to include a floor plan and elevation; we could require a particular layout and appearance, but normally that is neither wise nor feasible. For one thing, the work involved in defining requirements is usually so demanding that there is generally little time left for constraining the requirements further.

In the second place the skills and knowledge appropriate for defining requirements are generally quite different from those best suited to the development of a system specification.

1. To do a good job with requirements we must be expert in the needs of the user organization. We must know the goals of that organization, the concepts with which it works, its style of operation, and the capabilities of its people. It is the job of a requirements document to characterize this sort of information in terms of properties needed in the system.
2. To do a good job of defining a system that meets stated requirements, that is, to develop a system specification, other skills and knowledge are required. We must have a good sense of the things computers can do well; we must know which interfaces are best for each kind of user; we must know what operations can be done easily and what would require tortuous designing.

In short, to do a good job of writing requirements we must be expert in the field for which the system is to be used; to do a good job of specifying a system we must be expert in human factors and computer systems.

Of course, some overlap will occur between the areas of expertise of the requirements writer and the system specifier. No one should write requirements for a software system without some basic understanding of what computers are and what can be expected of them. In fact, some sections of all requirements documents should be written by individuals who have a significant amount of knowledge of software and hardware. Similarly, someone specifying a system for an organization must have, or at least develop, some feeling for the use the organization will make of the system. By the time the system specification is written the system-specification author may have become somewhat expert in the field treated by the organization. Yet, by and large, the areas of skill of the requirements author and the system specification author differ; therefore it is worthwhile to keep the two documents as separate as possible.

4.2.1   Abstract Capabilities Versus Concrete Presentations

Another characteristic that distinguishes requirements from system specifications is that requirements often speak on a rather abstract level compared to the concrete level on which system specifications must speak. A requirement that a certain capability must be provided may be expressed in terms of the capability in the abstract; the system specification for a system that provides that capability must be concrete about exactly what is provided. Note, however, that when we say that requirements may be presented in abstract terms we are *not* saying that they may be stated loosely or imprecisely. We are saying that in requiring a capability we may express the requirement in terms of the abstract capability itself. A specification, in contrast, must indicate the exact form in which the capability will be provided.

Consider, for example, the difference between a requirements document and a system specification for a (digital?) watch for use by runners and as a regular time-piece. A requirements document would contain the ideas important to a discussion of time: the 24-hour day and the 12-hour cycle, the 60-minute hour, the 60-second minute, fractional parts of seconds (tenths and hundreds), time zones, the calendar (months and the number of days in different months), and the days of the week. It would also describe the functions that the watch would be required to perform: keep regular time, store some number of times for reminder purposes (e.g., alarm set-tings), show the day of the week for any requested date, have both count-down and count-up stopwatch capabilities, *beep* at a requested pace rate (given in miles per hour, minutes per mile, kilometers per hour, or minutes per kilometer) based on a runner-supplied stride length (given in feet and inches per stride or meters and centimeters per stride), and calculate distances covered, based on the given pace and running time. All these capabilities may be expressed abstractly in that they are given in terms of the precisely characterized but abstract functions to be performed.

In contrast, a system specification for such a watch would begin by describing the actual displays on the watch face. It would then explain how those displays may be understood as representing the abstract world model defined in the requirements document. It would also describe the actual buttons on the watch. It would tell what the effects on the displays would be of pushing the buttons and would explain how those effects may be interpreted as providing the abstract capabilities required. Thus the system is described concretely, and the concrete description is related to the abstract description in the requirements document.

4.2.2 Principles and Policies Versus Rules and Regulations

We present one more analogy to help clarify the differences between requirements and a system specification. Contrast an organization's principles and policies with its laws, rules, and regulations. We suggest that principles and policies are similar to requirements and that laws, rules, and regulations are similar to a system specification. (We also suggest that the enforcement techniques adopted by an organization are analogous to design. The enforcement rules stipulate how the laws, rules, and regulations are to be carried out.)

Principles and policies are abstract statements of basic beliefs that are intended to guide an organization in its overall approach to its affairs. Although they are (or should be) clearly and precisely expressed, they are generally stated in terms as abstract as possible. The point of formulating policies and principles is to clarify an organization's position on the fundamental issues it faces. This is similar to requirements; both face the job of clarifying these issues.

Laws, rules, and regulations implement* principles and policies. Laws, rules, and regulations are concrete statements of definitions and procedures that are intended to guide the organization in its response to specific events. Like principles and pol-

---

*Although not in the software design sense. Here *to implement* means simply to *put into practice or to put into concrete terms*.

icies, laws, rules, and regulations should be clearly and precisely stated, but unlike principles and policies they should be stated in terms as concrete as possible. Whereas laws, rules, and regulations may be stated in *general* terms (a single statement will cover as many situations as possible), they should also be expressed in such a way that there can be no confusion about their specific application. This is similar to a system specification; both characterize exactly how a system must function in response to specific conditions.

Although we do not discuss design until Chapter 5, the analogy can be carried one step further. Laws, rules, and regulations are really a description of how an organization *should* function; but there is frequently the question of ensuring that the organization *will* function in the specified way. To be sure that its regulations are carried out organizations structure themselves in certain ways (e.g., audit departments) and adopt certain (enforcement) procedures (e.g., by requiring multiple approvals before certain actions may be taken). This structuring and these enforcement procedures correspond to *design* in computer-based systems. For just as the structure and the adopted procedures of an organization are intended to ensure that the organization will carry out its obligations, it is the design of a computer-based system that determines whether it will carry out its system specification.

4.3   APPROACHES TO EXPRESSING SYSTEM SPECIFICATIONS

Although we indicated that a system specification should provide a stimulus-response model of a system, we have not stated the terms in which this model should be presented. Some possibilities are more suited to general computer systems than others.

1.   *Input/Process/Output Specifications.*   This approach is probably the one most commonly used in specifications. See [MIL-STD490, 1968, Gilbert, 1983, and Davis and Rauscher, 1979], for descriptions of this approach which range from the informal to the formal. Its strategy is to take the stimulus-response model literally and to require that systems be defined exactly in terms of an output for every input.

To specify a system with the input/process/output approach we first determine all the possible inputs the system might receive. (Usually the inputs come in classes that correspond to the system operations.) Then, for every input we specify the processing to be performed and the output that results from it. As an example, consider a specification for software that computes a mathematical function, for example the sine function. To specify a sine program we might state that the input must fall in a range of 0 to 2 *pi* and that it will be interpreted as radians. We then specify the computation that will be performed on that input, that is, a calculation of the sine of the input interpreted as an angle given in radians. If desired we may specify the algorithm by which the calculation is to be performed and the precision it must achieve. Finally we indicate that the result of the calculation will be produced as output.

Input/process/output specifications work quite well for systems that calculate mathematical functions, as in the example cited. Input/process/output specifications are not useful for systems that retain some of their inputs from one stimulus for use in processing future inputs. The input/process/output approach fails for these systems because it provides no way to discuss the information retained from one input to the next; for example, in an airline reservation system it is important that reservations be (at least) counted to allow the system to refuse new reservations when a flight is full. Using an input/processing/output model we can, at best, include some talk of a "side-effect" of the processing part that stores information (somewhere). There is no place in the input/processing/output specification structure to describe the information that may be stored or *how* we should understand it as being organized. Therefore there is no way to explain how future inputs can access the stored information.

Most data processing systems, as well as systems of other sorts, are required to store information from one input to another. A satellite inertial navigation system, for example, must be able to accept and store new and revised travel plans to compare them with actual travel results. Thus the input/process/output approach is inappropriate for general use because most computer systems are required to retain information from one use to the next. The input/process/output approach is appropriate for computer systems that can be described strictly as computing functions of their inputs.

2. *Algebraic Specifications.* The algebraic approach to specifications is one way around the problem of not being able to talk about stored information. It is one of the most formal approaches, and in many ways the most elegant, to specifications. See, for example, [Guttag et al]. See also [Chen and Yeh, 1983], for an extension of this approach to concurrent, distributed systems.

The algebraic approach to specifications also takes seriously the notion of a system as a black box for which a stimulus-response model is desired. It gets around the problem of system memory by defining the processing of each input in terms of that input *and all previous inputs (and operations)*. Because all previous inputs are available, there is no need to build a model of the inside of the system. We can always recompute it!

The simplest and most widely quoted example is the algebraic specification of a push down (i.e., Last-In-First-Out) stack. A push-down stack may be defined in terms of three operations.

Function Push(E : Element; S : Stack) return Stack;

The element E is pushed onto the stack S as its new top element. The new stack is returned as the value of this function.

Function Pop(S : Stack) return Stack;

The top element of the stack S is "popped" (and thrown away). The value returned by this function is the stack without that top element.

Function Top(S : Stack) return Element;

The stack S is examined and a copy of its top element is returned as the value of this function. The top element remains on the stack which is unchanged.

To complete the algebraic specification of a stack we provide algebraic rules that characterize the functioning of the operations. In expressing the rules we use nesting to indicate operation sequencing; for example, f(g(x)) means perform g(x) and then perform f on the result. The following two basic rules suffice.

a. Pop(Push(E,S)) => S. This rule states that if a Pop is performed immediately after a Push the stack returned by the Pop will be the stack originally input to the Push. This is exactly what we want: the Pop should remove the element pushed by Push and return the original stack.

b. Top(Push(E,S) => E. This rule states that if a Top is performed immediately after a Push the element returned by Top will be the element pushed by Push. Again this is exactly what we want: the Top should make a copy of the most recently pushed element.*

Consider
Top(Pop(Push(E1,Push(E2,S))))
We know, of course, that this expression should evaluate to E2 because it expresses the following sequence of operations.

a. Push E2 onto S.

b. Push E1 onto S over E2.

c. Pop the top element E1 off S, leaving E2 as the current top element.

d. Copy the top element, E2, and return it as a value.

Can we get that same result from our rules? They do not tell us what to do with Top(Pop(*something*)), but they do tell us that Pop(Push(E,*something*)) returns that *something*. In this case the *something* is Push(E2,S). We can use that rule to evaluate the middle of the expression, replacing Pop(Push(E1,Push(E2,S))) with Push(E2,S), leaving Top(Push(E2,S)). Now we have a rule that lets us deal with this expression; it tells us that the result will be E2 as expected.

It is possible to specify any system algebraically. A great deal of theoretical work has been done in this area. Nonetheless, we have not used this approach for the following reasons:

a. It is relatively unintuitive. Given a system of any complexity, the algebraic specification rules become quite complex; they are difficult to construct and to understand and they often fail to help a reader to decide how to think about the systems they specify.

b. Algebraic specifications are biased toward systems whose operations are naturally nested. Thus a stack is easy to specify algebraically, but a queue or a data structure of similar complexity becomes quite involved. We find our

---

*This is something of a simplification. We have not dealt with creating stacks, with attempts to pop an empty stack, or with attempts to copy the top of an empty stack; that is, we have not dealt with the exceptional and boundary conditions, but as a brief introduction to algebraic specifications what we have discussed will do.

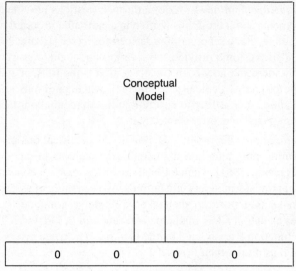

Knobs and dials for manipulating the conceptual model

Figure 4.1 A model.

selves writing algebraic transformation rules that are, in effect, recursive programs of the preceding inputs.

3. *Model Specifications.* The model approach to system specification suggests that the best way to specify a system is to define another system that models it. Thus the model approach suggests that to specify a stack we could build (or imagine) a physical device (e.g., a tray dispenser in a cafeteria) that acts like a stack. Similarly, to specify a queue we might imagine a tube with one-way valves on both ends: one end admits elements to the tube, the other allows elements to leave it.

As the examples illustrate, the model approach can be informal. On the other hand, the model approach can be quite formal; there is no constraint on the formality with which the model itself is defined. Either way, with a felicitous model we can present a clear picture of exactly how a system is expected to function.

We adopt the model approach to specifications because we believe that it provides the best way to explain a system. The models we recommend are rigorous but relatively informal; for example, pictures. When writing a system specification we may want to draw a picture (see Figure 4.1) to show the system's internal conceptual model and the "knobs" and "dials" for manipulating it. Yet there is nothing that requires such informality. A formal language which permits us to define formal versions of the same models is presented in the appendix.

In addition to the specification approaches we have sketched, there are two others in use today. We provide brief descriptions but do not go into detail. We relegate them to second place because their primary use is in specification of computer programming languages rather than computer systems [Pagan, 1981].

1. *Axiomatic Specifications.* Axiomatic specifications provide rules for proving statements about programs written in a particular programming language. Each language has a set of axioms defined for it (see [Hoare, 1963] and [London, 1978]). Axioms provide information about the constructs in the language and describe how each construct affects the truth of statements made about the program. Typically, axioms tell what conditions must be true before executing a construct to ensure that a statement about the program will be true after that construct is executed.

2. *Denotational Specifications.* Denotational specifications provide rules for transforming programs into mathematical functions [Tennent, 1978; Stoy, 1977, Tennent, 1981]. Denotational specifications are concerned with programs that transform inputs into outputs. We can think of a denotational specification D as a function that takes as input a computer program P and produces as output some mathematical function F, $D(P) = F$. The program P and the function F are related by the fact that if P, when given i as input, will produce o as output then $F(i) = o$.

EXERCISES

1. A white-box description of a system describes the system's behavior in terms of its internal design. Why is a white-box description inappropriate for a system specification?

2. A system may be said to be *autistic* if it has no external interfaces. Is it necessary to produce a behavioral specification for an autistic system? Some years ago Pet Rocks were a fad item. We might consider them autistic systems. Can you name any other autistic systems? Manuals were included with Pet Rocks. Do you suppose these were behavioral specification manuals, procedure manuals, or administrative manuals? Why? Find out.

3. Describe the information that should be included in a behavioral specification, a procedures manual, and an administrative manual for an automobile.

4. We have provided an outline to distinguish between requirements and behavioral specifications for a house and a watch. Make the same sort of outline to distinguish between requirements and behavioral specifications for a washing machine, a countertop toaster-oven, a chair, a city park, a state park, a national park, a communication (e.g., telephone) system, a government, and a plan for investing in the stock market.

5. The Bill of Rights establishes requirements. Select one of them and find a law in your state that helps to make the requirements of that article concrete.

6. Give specific examples of information that you might find in a behavioral specification, a procedures manual, and an administrative manual for an appointment scheduling system.

7. Give an algebraic specification for the following operations on sets:

```
is_a_member_of(S : Set, E : Element) return Boolean;
make_null_set( ) return Set;
make_singleton_set(E : Element) return Set;
union(S1 : Set, S2 : Set) return Set;
intersection(S1 : Set, S2 : Set) return Set;
```

≡5

BEHAVIORAL SPECIFICATION OUTLINE

It is generally useful, as in a requirements document, to develop a behavioral specification from a working frame. A behavioral specification outline provides a place for each of the pieces that we can anticipate.

Some (many) systems have multiple interfaces which may be present for any of a number of reasons; for example, multiple-user types that apply to different parts of a system or the system has interfaces with other systems. Generally a system is best explained separately for each of its interfaces. Therefore we recommend that a separate behavioral specification document be written for each one. We do not describe these documents explicitly because all can use the same format.

Sometimes the separate interfaces are *not* best explained in separate documents. Often they are so similar that they would be identical except for selected parts of their chapters on operations, in which case it is better to write a single document and to list the operations made available by each interface. In general, decisions regarding the amount of documentation to produce should be based on the usefulness of the documentation rather than on some formula or outline.

5.1 OVERVIEW OF DOCUMENT, ORGANIZATION, AND CONVENTIONS

This section is similar to Section 3.1 of the requirements document. Much of the material here can be taken from that document.

5.1.1. Scope of Document

This section defines the area covered by the behavioral specification.

5.1.2 Organization of Document: Annotated Contents

This section helps the reader to understand how the remainder of the document is organized. It highlights the motivation behind the remaining sections and guides the reader to an approach to behavioral specification. Most reference documents are not intended to be read straight through. This section tells the new reader what the goals are for the various sections and what use can be made of them.

5.1.3 Conventions Used in Document

The best way to write behavioral specifications is in terms as concrete as possible. A picture is worth a thousand words and behavioral specifications should be presented graphically. In particular, system specifications are best expressed by tables, arrays, forms, formats, templates, and any other regular organization of information that can get the point across.

People understand information best when it is shown in a regular form. Because a behavioral specification describes how a system deals with information, the best way is in terms that the reader can understand. Following are some of the most useful methods of presenting structured information.

Tables

Tables are regular, two-dimensional arrangements of information, extendable at the bottom, in which the columns but not the rows are labeled. Figure 5.1 is a table that lists the ages of a number of individuals.

Each row of a table represents a "fact," in Figure 5.1 that a particular person is a certain age. For that reason each row must be different from every other row because to repeat a fact adds no information. A table is frequently used to record instances of relations. It would have a column for each entity type and a column for each attribute of the relation. Thus a single table is written for each relation.

Some tables have *keys*. A key is a column or collection of columns that guarantees a unique entry in the table; that is, each row has a unique entry in the key column(s).

Person	Age
Jim	35
Jane	27
Jenny	15
Joan	21
John	42
JoAnne	27
Jason	19
Joe	30
Jake	25
Jeff	25

Figure 5.1 An example of a table.

If we assume that each person has a unique name, the *person* column is a key. The *age* column is not a key because two people may be the same age. We discuss tables in much more detail in the appendix.

Forms

Forms are irregular, two-dimensional arrangements of information in which the various pieces of information are labeled. Figure 5.2 is an example of a loan application form.

Forms are used to record information about an entity or an instance of a relation; for example, a form that contained information about the entities of some entity type would consist of entries that corresponded to the attributes defined for that entity type. Similarly, a form that contained information about a relation would consist of entries that corresponded to the entities in the relation and the attributes of the relation.

Forms of this sort are usually stored in collections—one for each entity or one for each instance of the relation. Thus information about a relation stored on a form is entered one fact per form. A complete relation consists of a collection of forms. Thus a form is analogous to a single row of a table and a table is analogous to a collection of forms.

Sets and Multisets

Sets and multisets are collections of objects that have no internal structure. Sets differ from multisets in that sets may not have two identical elements as members; multisets may. Note that the rows of a table are a set; no two rows may be identical. A table may be a set of forms. The following is the *multiset* of ages in Figure 5.1:

$$\{35, \ 27, \ 21, \ 42, \ 27, \ 30, \ 25\}$$

Last Name   First Name   Middle Name

Soc. Sec. Number

Amount Desired: _____

Term Desired (in months): _____

Current Employer: _____

Address: _____

_____

_____

Years on Current Job: _____

Figure 5.2   An example of a form.

The following is the *set* of ages in Figure 5.1:

$$\{35, \ 27, \ 21, \ 42, \ 30, \ 25\}$$

Arrays

Arrays are multidimensional (generally one- or two-dimensional) arrangements of elements that can be identified by reference to labels on its rows and columns. Labels are often integers but are not always required. Note that what we might consider a traditional table in which the rows and the columns are labeled is an array. Figure 5.3 is a two-dimensional array of words.

We identify an entry in an array according to the labels on the rows and columns in which it lies. The word in row 1 and column 2 is *above*.

Sequences

Sequences and their specializations, *strings, lists,* and *queues,* are one-dimensional arrangements of elements. They may be appended to one another, broken apart, and have elements inserted or removed internally or at the ends. Specializations of sequences are constrained by the operations that may be performed on them. A queue,

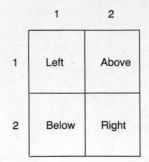

Figure 5.3   An example of an array.

<above, below, left, right>
Figure 5.4   An example of a sequence.

for example, is a special kind of sequence that may have elements added only to one end and removed only from the other. Figure 5.4 shows the words from the array in Figure 5.3 ordered alphabetically.

Graphs

Graphs and their specializations such as *trees* are abstract arrangements of elements, called *nodes*, connected by *edges*. The edges may be directed and the graph may obey other constraints such as connectedness (the requirement that there be some path between every pair of nodes). The edges and nodes may be labeled, but they are not required to be.

A tree is a special type of graph. It is connected and directed and has no cycles. A tree has a distinguished node called the *root* that has no edges leading into it. Each of its other nodes has exactly one edge leading into it. Figure 5.5 shows a binary sort tree of the ages in the set of ages shown in Figure 5.1.

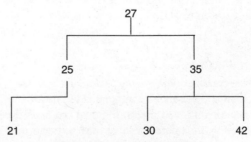

Figure 5.5   An example of tree.

Gear	Reverse

Figure 5.6   An example of a single-valued element.

Single-Valued Elements

Single-valued elements are values with associated names. A single-valued element is the simplest of all data structures. It is essentially a named *variable* to which values may be assigned and whose value may be retrieved. Figure 5.6 is a single-valued element named *Gear*. It may be used to keep track of the gear in which a car is traveling.

Composition of Data Structures

We permit combinations of these data structures; that is, there can be a *form* in which one of the entries is a *sequence* and another is a *table*. There can be a *sequence* of *sets* in which each element of each *set* is a *form*, or there can be an *array* of *trees*.

Not all seven classes of data structure are necessary. In fact, with the exception of the single-valued element any one of them is sufficient to express the information that any of the others could express; for example, it is possible to express anything desired in a table alone, a graph alone, or in a set alone, but because these structures are widely known and easy to use there is no harm in allowing all of them.

We do not define these data structures more formally here. To the extent that rigorous behavioral specifications of the operations to be performed on them are required those behavioral specifications should be made in context. For the most part most people are sufficiently familiar with these data structures that their intuitive understanding suffices as a behavioral specification.

EXERCISES

1. Express your driver's license (a form) as a row in a table.
2. Express the example sort tree of ages as a table. Why can't you define an array in which an arbitrary sort tree could be expressed?
3. Express the example array as a tree, form, and row in a table.
4. Express the set of ages as a table. Why can't a form be defined in which an arbitrary set could be expressed?
5. Divide the data structures into two classes: one in which each instance of the structure corresponds to a single fact and one in which each corresponds to a collection of facts. Find one property of data structures in general that determines in which of the two classes the structure is likely to fall.

6.   A table can be described as a set of forms. Find three other such correspondences among the data structures.

5.2   SYSTEM OVERVIEW AND ORGANIZATIONAL CONTEXT

This section of the behavioral specification and the sections within it present an overview of the system. It need be neither complete nor formal because Sections 5.3 and 5.4 provide the details. This section should introduce the system to the reader and provide an understanding of the details to follow.

5.2.1   System Definition

This section is an abbreviation of the corresponding section in the requirements document.

Purpose

This section can be taken from the corresponding section of the requirements document.

Scope

This section can be taken from the corresponding section of the requirements document.

Objectives

This section lists the requirements objectives that the specified system actually satisfies. Additional objectives may be added if they are satisfied by the specified system even if they were not mentioned as requirements.

Anticipated Market/Users.   This section should be a revised version of the audience market section of the requirements document. In particular, it should identify those individuals and organization for whom the system as specified is now intended.

Anticipated Uses.   This section can be taken from the requirements document.

Range of Configurations and Options.   This section should sketch the configuration and option choices. If they are complex they should be described in detail in an appendix or separate document.

5.2.2   Overview of the Using Organization

To the extent that it is relevant, this section is an overview of how the system fits the structure of the user-organization described in the requirements document. Details of the interface between the user-organization and the system are provided in the procedures manual. A reference to that manual should be given here. If the procedures manual is simple enough it may be included as an appendix to this document. If the interface between the user-organization and the system is minimal, it may be described completely in this section.

5.2.3 Operational Strategy

This section and the sections within it identify the person or group that bears the responsibility for the system. Because the responsibilities are numerous, each is explained separately.

System Ownership

The name of the system owner is given here.

System Administrator

This section names the person or group responsible for the day-to-day administration of the system.

System Operation

This section describes how the system is installed, revised, initiated, and shut down. Operational details are contained in the operations manual which should be referenced. This section is a brief overview.

Fee(s) for Use

If there are fees associated with the use of the system the formula(s) for calculating those fees should be explained here. A separate document or appendix will provide details if the fee schedule is complex.

Analogy to Existing Systems

If the system replaces or simply matches another system that the intended users already understand this section will explain the resemblance of the new system to the old and how the new system differs from it. The intention is not to provide a complete description of the new system but to help users to master it on the basis of their familiarity with some other system.

5.3 STATIC DESCRIPTION

This section and the sections within it provide a static description in terms of which the system may be understood by potential users. Although it need not be made in formal terms it should be presented rigorously enough so that someone who understands the model can be expected to make effective use of the system. The data structures already described exemplify an appropriate level of rigor.

5.3.1 Prerequisite Knowledge

The sections within this section provide the user with information needed to understand the system itself. This information defines a background in terms of which this system can be understood.

System Environment

To the extent that it is relevant this section and the sections within it describe the environment in which the system is embedded. If the system is a component of some larger system or interfaces with other systems or devices the enclosing and interfacing systems and devices should be explained here.

This section presents a *conceptual* environment; it need not correspond to the *actual* environment of the enclosing system or interfacing units. Its purpose is to provide the user with a concept of the larger environment into which the system fits. The best is one that is intuitively obvious rather than one that includes actual (but irrelevant) details. The primary constraint is that the picture given the user should be accurate enough for use as a model of the system.

Enclosing System.   This section describes the system in which the current system is embedded. It should stress the role this system plays in the context of that enclosing system. As an example, consider a system that processes images produced from data gathered by a satellite. The enclosing system includes the on-board systems that monitor and control the satellite's immediate operation, the world-wide network of ground tracking and receiving stations, and the other data processing systems that handle data produced by the satellite. This section describes the place of this image-processing system in the context of that more global system. The discussion should be intuitive; its primary purpose is to give the user bearings about the current system. For details reference should be made to the documentation for the enclosing system and its components.

Interfacing Systems and Devices.   This section describes the devices to which a system interfaces in a way that affects the user. As an example of an interfacing system, consider one that will keep track of state automobile registration records. This system might interface to a national system that in turn might provide a general interface to the many automobile registration systems run by the states.

Interfacing System or Device i   Each interfacing system or device should be described in its own section. The description should be intuitive and for details reference should be made to the documentation for the interfacing system.

Required Concepts

This section explains the basic concepts prerequisite to an understanding of the system. To the extent that they repeat the information in World Model (Section 3.3 of the requirements document) this section should refer to that section of that document. If further analysis has revealed the need for greater subtleties or has determined that not all the information provided there is needed for understanding the system as specified these clarifications should be explained here.

Generally we recommend that the world model in the requirements document be updated to reflect changes. If the differences do not express real or permanent changes but were adopted soley for this particular version of the system it is preferable not to change the requirements document and to describe the differences here. This situation may occur if the system is being delivered in versions in which the earlier ones are less complete. The behavioral specification of earlier versions would be based on a simplified world model. The real world model, however, is not changed and later versions of the system are expected to conform to it more closely.

5.3.2 Conceptual Model

This section and the subsections within it describe a conceptual model of the system and provide the framework for its use.

The behavioral specification treats the system as a black box. As such, it is not concerned with the actual design of the system. Yet some strategy must be adopted to describe the system's behavior. As discussed earlier, we adopt the model approach to specification. We believe that in explaining the behavior of a system as a black box it is almost always useful to provide a model of its interior. Without a model it would be virtually impossible to explain to the user how different operations are related to one another; that is, if one operation feeds information to the system and a later operation uses that information the user must understand that the information had been *stored* by the system. The user must also understand how that information is related to previously stored information. Theoretically we could get away without a model by explaining each operation as a function of all preceding inputs. This is the tack taken by the algebraic approach to specification.* For systems of any complexity, however, that approach is usually unintuitive. Our approach is to build what we call a *conceptual model* of the inside of the system and to explain the system's behavior in terms of that model.

A conceptual model is a mechanistic description of the inside of a system. Its purpose is to provide an understanding of the system's behavior. Thus it is a user's eye view of how the system works. A conceptual model should provide enough information to allow a working version of the system to be created simply by implementation of the model. On the other hand, a conceptual model is *not necessarily* a

---

*If we want a *constructive* specification of operations even that approach implies a simple model: all previous inputs and operations are *stored* exactly as they appeared as inputs; every new operation *accesses* that stored information for data relevant to its needs.

description of the system's actual construction. Although the conceptual model does provide an implementation strategy, this strategy may be inefficient to the point of foolishness. The purpose of the conceptual model is *not* to tell the user how the system is designed, but to provide *a way to think about* what is going on inside the system.

The Conceptual Model as a Representation of the User's World Model

Recall that a requirements document presents a world model to explain how the user sees the world. A system that solves the problems stated in the requirements document must include some *representation* of the user's world model. Ideally, this representation in the conceptual model should correspond directly to the actual world model presented in the requirements document. This is not always possible, however.

1. *Lack of Formality.* The world model in the requirements document may not be expressed in a formal language, but the conceptual model is implemented by a computer system and is necessarily formal. Given this possible lack of formality in the world model, it may not be clear what the correspondence should be or even if the world model as expressed in the requirements document has a formal counterpart.

2. *Economic Infeasibility.* The world model in the requirements document may be so complex that it would be economically unjustifiable to build a system with a conceptual model that matches it.

3. *Inadequate Abstraction in the World Model.* The world model may be inappropriate to serve as the conceptual model for either of two reasons.

   a. *Irrelevant details.* Some of the features described in the world model may turn out to be irrelevant in the implemented system.

   b. *Incompleteness.* Other features not considered in the world model may have to be included in the system's conceptual model.

For these reasons the world model described in the requirements document may not match the system conceptual model discussed here.

A reasonable way to regard the relationship between the requirements document and the system's conceptual model is a *representation.** of the world model. A representation is a *portrayal* and as such it differs from the world model. Figure 5.7 summarizes how a representation may differ from the world model it represents.

1. A representation is *concrete* in comparison to the abstract level of the world model. It is concrete in that it is presented in terms of structures and elements

---

*This is not to say that this section explains the internal *implementation* of the system's conceptual model. The implementation of the conceptual model may be quite different from the representation, that is, picture, the user is given of it.

World Model	Representation
Abstract	Concrete
Pure	Elaborated
Detailed	Simplified (abstract!)

Figure 5.7   Qualities of a representation.

that are intended to be presented visually. The presentation of the world model is unimportant because it is a description of the world. The world model is thus intended to be *abstract,* whereas the conceptual model is concrete.

2. A representation is *elaborated* in that it may require additional features not in the original world model, which is therefore *purer.* A representation sometimes includes information that is not really a part of the thing represented; for example, Chinese names in Roman characters include a roman spelling for each Chinese name. That spelling is not a part of the original name. The names themselves may be part of the (pure) world model; the Roman spellings may be part of the (elaborated) conceptual model.

3. A representation may be *simplified* (we might even say *abstract*) in that it may not include everything in the world model but only those elements that are directly relevant to the system. Because they often simplify, representations sometimes clarify issues that may not be quite so clear in the original world model. Thus a representation may not include all the details of the thing represented; for example, the representation of Chinese names in Roman characters generally includes neither the meanings of the Chinese words used in the names nor their correct pronounciations. The representation thus makes clear that the reason for using names is to provide labels and that their sound and meaning are considered irrelevant as far as the system is concerned. In this sense a representation is an abstraction of the world model. Because the world model itself is an abstraction of the user's actual world, the system's conceptual model is twice removed from reality.

For a representation to be an accurate portrayal of the world model there must be a mapping between the model and the representation; that is, it must be clear how elements in the world model are presented in the representation (if they are) and it must be clear to what parts of the world model elements of the representation correspond. This mapping is provided when the data structures are described later in this chapter.

The Conceptual Model as a Conceptual Design

In addition to serving as a representation for the user's world model, the conceptual model also provides the user with a description of the internal structure of the system to the extent that the user must understand that structure. Imagine that the best way to determine how to make use of the system is to explain it in terms of (real or imagined) components. The conceptual model includes those components, and this section and the subsections within it provide that explanation. As an example, consider a text processing system composed of an editor and a separate formatter; that is, not a what-you-see-is-what-you-get word processor. To operate the system the user must include formatting directives in the text. For the user to understand the role of the formatting directives and why they must be embedded in the text, the conceptual structure of the system must also be understood; that is, that the text is first edited and then sent to the formatter for formatting (and perhaps printing) and that the editor and the formatter are separate system components. This section and the sections within it provide this explanation.

Conceptual Dataflow Diagram

The description of the conceptual model is organized as an overview of its design in this, the first, subsection and then provides discussions of its components in subsequent subsections. This subsection includes a dataflow diagram that contains the system conceptual components as well as a top level description of the system. The dataflow diagram and discussion serve as a system overview of the discussions to follow. (For more detailed coverage of dataflow diagrams consult the section in the procedures manual and [Myers, 1978, or Yourdon and Constantive, 1979]. Figure 5.8 is a simple dataflow diagram of a system that includes a database and a means of interacting with that database. There are three components:

1. A user-interface component.
2. A processing component.
3. A database component.

This dataflow diagram explains that user input is processed first as keystrokes by a user-interface processor. The user-interface allows the user to edit commands before they are passed on to the command processor for execution. The command processor, in turn, consults the system database for information. In systems that provide a

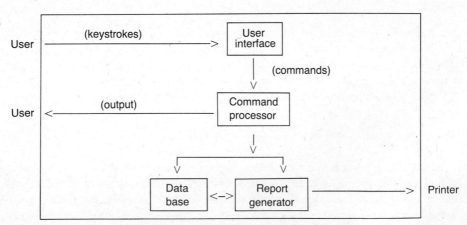

Figure 5.8   Example of a simple dataflow diagram.

sophisticated user-interface it is often best for the user to understand this structure. Of course, if the user does not need to know about a front-end user-interface, it should not be included in the conceptual model.

Object Types and Individuals Within the System

This section and the subsections within it identify the object types and individual objects that are maintained in the system. (More precisely, they identify the object types and individual objects modeled by the system's conceptual model.) At thisXXXX point we are distinguishing between the following:

1. *Entities* existing outside a system about which the system keeps records.

2. *Objects* existing within the system that the user must understand.

Some, probably most, systems focus primarily (even exclusively) on entities external to them. These are the entities described in the requirements document world model. Systems generally keep many records of the external entities, but they do not contain the entities themselves. Examples of external entity types are *wing, engine,* and *airplane* (an individual) in an avionics system, *guest* and *room* in a hotel reservation system, and *employee* in a payroll system. No instances of these entities are actually *within* the system; there are no flesh-and-blood employees inside the payroll system.

Other systems at least deal with some internal objects. Examples of internally stored object types are *document* in a word processing system, *figure* in a graphics system, *message* and *mail box* in a communication system, *image* in an image processing system, and *fact* and *rule* in an expert system.

We use the two distinct terms *entity* and *object* to highlight this distinction between things external and internal to the system. Other than the fact that entities exist outside a computer system and objects exist within it, entities and objects are quite similar. Entities and objects are *things* in terms of which it is useful to understand the world. Similarly, as entity types are categories of entities in the world, object types are categories of objects within the user's conceptual model of the system.

This section and its subsections are concerned exclusively with internally stored objects that the user must understand to use the system. For most systems there may be little to say in this section. Many systems, however, even those that focus primarily on external entities, have user-level internal objects or individuals; for example, some systems require their users to understand the idea of *files* or *workspaces* as object types. Although users generally do not need to know much about files or workspaces, they often do need to know that they can create and delete them.

Most objects (such as documents in a word processing system) correspond to entities that have been described in the world model in the requirements document. Some, like *files* do not correspond to entities described in the requirements document; they evolve from the representations selected for the system's conceptual model.

There is one further distinction to be made between objects and data structures as already described:

1. *Objects are things that the system processes.* In general, objects move along the paths in the dataflow diagram of the preceding section.

2. *Data structures* are *things the system uses to keep track of information about the things that it processes.* In general, data structures correspond to fixed components in the dataflow diagram of the preceding section.

It is sometimes difficult to make this distinction, but it can be made. Whether something is classified as an object or as a data structure depends on the point of view the user is expected to take.

Data structures are not discussed in this section; they are described later. As we have said, for most systems there are no internal object types. In general, it is better to omit some of them than to confuse data structures by calling them internal object types. The only damage done by not mentioning an internal object type is that the user may not have quite so clear a picture of the system's capabilities. On the other hand, if a data structure is described as an object, the user would probably be confused about how that data structure is more than just a record of information of other entities and why it is considered an object.

Object Type i. Each object type is described individually. For each we should state whether it represents an entity type in the requirements document and, if so, which one. If the object type does represent an entity type any variations from the entity type should be explained; for example, in the requirements for a word processing system there is probably an entity type *document* and it doubtless has a *name* attribute. In an actual word processing system the object type *document* may have a limit on the number of characters allowed in the name of any document.

If the object type does not represent an entity type in the requirements document it should be given completely in the same way that the requirements document describes entity types.

As an example, consider once again a word processing system. Assume that the system supports a number of different printing devices; for example, a line printer, a laser printer, and a letter quality printer. Documents are processed differently, depending on the intended output device. Assume that it is possible to store processed versions of documents before printing. We may then have a version of a document processed so that it can be printed on the line printer, another on the laser printer, and another on the special letter quality printer.

Clearly, each of these document versions is a different object. They are also different types because they are used in different ways. (We would not attempt to print the document version formatted for the laser printer on the line printer.) Thus each different output device defines its own object type. Most likely these object types were not described in the requirements document because if did not explicitly state that the documents were to be stored in different formats before printing. (In fact it would have been an overconstraining requirement if it had.)

Components

This section and its subsections describe the components that appear in the conceptual data flow diagram. This section continues to explain the system's abstract design. The only reason for providing this information is to enable the user to work with the system. The design, as explained here, may bear no resemblance to the actual system design.

Component i.   Each of the user level components is explained in its own section. Its function(s) should be described and its role(s) in the overall system, explained. These explanations should be given on a level relevant to the system user.

It is best if components can be explained simply. To accomplish this components should be classified primarily as processing or record-keeping components. (See the bubble charts in the procedures manual for a discussion of processing and storage components.) In Figure 5.8 all the components are processing components except the data base, which is a storage component. The description of the component will differ, depending on the type.

Processing Components

Processing components are described in terms of the user-level processing that they perform. The description should be on the same level of detail as the dataflow diagram.

In systems without a primary user, for example, an autonomous process control system, this section is the heart of the behavioral specification. Because the primary function(s) of the system are performed by the processing components (rather than as a result of user commands), the descriptions of the processing components are central.

Storage Components

Many components are used to store information. Each storage structure of which the user must be aware should be described as a component; for example, if the system keeps track of marriages and the user is supposed to think of marriage records as tabular, that table, perhaps called the ''Marriage Table,'' should be discussed as a component. Before we discuss the record-keeping components in a specification it is worthwhile to clarify the relationships among the following:

1.   Records kept by a system.
2.   Data structures in which the records are kept.
3.   The entities and relations in the user's world model about which the records are kept.

The World Model, Records, and Data Structures

The user's world model, as described in Section 3.3 of the requirements document, provides a way of looking at the world, much of which involves information about things in the world; for example, the value of an entity's attribute is information about the entity, and an instance of a relation is a fact about the entities involved in the relation. That information is presented abstractly in the requirements document; that is, we are told that the information exists but we are not necessarily told how that information is recorded or represented. That is how it should be. The requirements document talks about the information the system must deal with and how it must be transformed. It does not talk about how the information is recorded.

Most systems that meet the objectives of a requirements document deal primarily with information about the entities described therein, not with the entities themselves.* Thus most systems operate on a level once removed from the reality described by the requirements document; that is, the requirements document describes the real world as best it can; the world inside a computer system is (merely) information about that world.

In this sense a computer system is a shadow model of the real world. Information inside a computer system is about things outside the system; for example, this book, the object that you are holding in your hands, is an entity in the real world. It is not contained in any computer system. On the other hand, its price probably is. However, the book's price is not an entity in the real world; you cannot point to it.† Writing down a number that refers to its price and pointing to the paper on which the number is written is the closest you can come; but that is not pointing to the price of the book any more than pointing to a piece of paper on which the book's name is written is pointing to the book.

As a shadow model of the real world, it is only by means of internally stored information that a system is connected to the user's world; that is, the system's internal information is the only link between what the system does and what the user wants it to do. Our job here is to describe that internal information to the user.

Now a second problem develops. The best way to describe information is to present it in some concrete form; that is, in terms of some data structures. To tell a user how to understand the information that is kept within a system, we must make up a data-structure representation for that information. On the other hand, we do not want to claim that the form in which the information is presented to the user matches the form in which it is actually stored in the system.‡ Although the user may not be told how the information is actually recorded, there must be some picture given of how

---

*Recall that some systems also deal with objects in the system itself; for example, messages in a message-handling system.

†Of course, as we showed in the chapter on requirements not all entities are physical objects, but all entities do correspond to *things*. The price of a book is not itself a thing; it is a property of a thing.

‡In fact, when the behavioral specification is being written the system may not yet be designed, and we may not know how the information will eventually be stored.

that information may be recorded; that is, the user must have a conceptual data-structure representation for the information stored in the system.

Therefore we have made the following connections. A user's world is described in a requirements document. To deal with that world a system must store information about it. For a user to understand the information a system keeps some representation of that information must be provided.

Forms, tables, arrays, graphs (and their special case *trees), sequences* and their special cases *lists, strings, queues,* and *stacks), sets, multisets, variables,* similar data structures, and compositions of data structures, that is, the data structures sketched in Section 5.1.3, provide a computer system with methods of keeping records of information. We recommend their use in a specification that describes those records to users. In fact, we claim that

> *any information a computer can handle is best explained in terms of some data structure.*

We call this claim the *data-structure hypothesis.*

We recommend the use of all the data structures as appropriate. Although any information a computer system can store can be explained by the use of tables or forms alone, tables and forms are not always the most intuitive way of approaching some information; for example, in a program to play checkers the most intuitive way of representing the board is with an 8×8 array. In a system that will keep track of materials moving between machines in a factory the best way to represent the paths between the machines is with a graph. In general, we should describe information with a data structure that presents the information in the most intuitive manner.

For simplicity it is best to identify each data structure by a separate component. For each data-structure component the following information should be presented:

1. *Intuitive Explanation.* This part names the data structure (and presumably the component). A brief, intuitive description is provided; for example, a "Marriage Table" data structure would be identified as containing information about marriages.

2. *Logical Description.* The logical description of the data structure should be given here. The structure, that is, the form, table, set, multiset, tree, graph, array, or whatever, should be described in enough detail to permit someone not previously familiar with the structure to use it after having read the description. It is generally most informative to describe data structures graphically.

This subsection should display a picture of the data structure and identify the slits in which the data belongs. **It should be concrete!** It should be a two-dimensional representation of the data structure that will tell the user *exactly* how to imagine that structure.

3. *Mapping to World Model.* There should be a mapping to the world model that shows how the information in the data structure is related to the world model in the requirements document; that is,

mapping: system conceptual model —> world model

The mapping may be explicit by including a statement of the relation between the components of the data structure and the world model or implicit if the names used to label the data structure components identify the connections between the components and the world model clearly.

To show the mapping to the world model each information entry in a data structure picture should be (at least implicitly) identifiable as the attribute of an entity, an instance of a relation, or, rarely, the name of a relation. If the names used in a data structure picture are the same as the attribute names used in the world model it is not necessary to show the mapping explicitly. The names should be self-explanatory. If it is not clear from the names in the data structure exactly how the information is related to the world model an explanation should be provided. This often involves more detailed considerations than we might at first imagine; for example, in referring to a spouse we must indicate whether the reference is made by a name or by an identification number.* If the system is keeping some information that is not understandable in terms of the world model, that is, for which no mapping provides a sufficient explanation, there is an incompatibility between the system conceptual model and the world model of the requirement's document. That incompatibility should be repaired.

Although a mapping between the conceptual model and the world model must be made apparent, the conceptual model represented by data structures may be somewhat "sloppier" in its coverage of the world than the world model described in the requirements document. The world model is expected to describe *exactly* what entity types occur and what relations connect them. There is no room, for example, for confusing attributes with entities. In contrast, the conceptual model data structures need not be explicit about which pieces of information are attributes and which are relations. The data structures may show attributes of an entity type in exactly the same way as they show relations between entity types.

For example, information about a person may be kept on a "form," which might show an (apparent) "spouse" attribute. This attribute reflects the marriage relation and is not a real attribute at all. There is no harm in showing the marriage relation as an attribute as long as it is made clear to the user that the information about each spouse must be consistent; that is, each of a pair of spouses must be identified as being married to the other. This is sloppier than the world model because there is no differentiation between different sorts of information. Yet the concreteness of the presentation combined with the user's independent knowledge of the world makes up for the lack of abstract precision.

4.   *Size Limits.*   The maximum size of the data structure should be specified here. In some cases data structures themselves are fixed in size: for example, an array with a fixed number of rows and columns or a form with a fixed number of entries

---

*In describing the marriage relation in the requirements document it was not necessary to decide how references were to be made. All that was required was to indicate that the relation links the entity types involved. Only in the conceptual model of the behavioral specification is it necessary to be concrete about exactly how the entities are labeled. This is an example of how requirements may be abstract while the behavioral specification must be concrete.

in which each entry is a fixed size. In other cases data structures are variable in size and grow with increasing information: for example, a set of employees (in which each employee is represented, perhaps, by a form) is not fixed in size; another form is added for each new employee. Yet, because the system cannot be expected to handle unlimited amounts of information, the maximum that it is able to handle is indicated here.

Systems are often required to keep information indefinitely, in which case, the amount of information grows without bounds. Of course, that is not possible. Normally the strategy we use is to define various classes of accessibility. The two most common classes are on-line and archive; for example, assume that a company wishes to keep track of its payroll records "forever" but for the most part it expects to be making active use of records from the current fiscal year only. In the section that describes the payroll record data structure both classes are defined and their expected maximum sizes are given. The current fiscal year may be called "active" data and all earlier data is considered "archived." The maximum size of the archived data structure may be shown as "unlimited".

5. *Invariants.* Invariants indicate the relationships that must hold among data in the system. These are system consistency checks; for example, suppose that a system shows spouses as if they were attributes of the marriage partners. Consistency requires that each spouse have the other listed as his or her spouse.

Any such consistency requirements based primarily on the data structure being described are indicated in this section. If there are other variants that are related to this data structure but that are described under some other data structure they are referenced here but not described. Each invariant in the system is stated separately.

EXERCISES

1. Find a widely used program whose user's manual doesn't explain the data structures a user must understand. To understand the system do you find yourself constructing your own data structure descriptions? If so, describe those data structures. If not, how do you understand the information the system processes.
2. Describe the data structures that a user must understand to use a line editor, a full screen editor, a spread sheet program, a subset of commands from the command language of an operating system. (Of course, these may differ, depending on the particular system described.)
3. Imagine a system for appointment scheduling. Describe its conceptual model: the data flow diagram, the processors, the data structures.
4. Draw a user-level data flow diagram for a network message system. If you are not familiar with such a system make one up. Assume that the network consists of a number of geographically separated computers that are linked by lines fast enough for message transmission but too slow for significant CPU to CPU interactions. The system must route, forward, and return messages for which the addressee is unknown at the addressed location. Explain the system components.

5.4 OPERATION

This section of the behavioral specification describes the operations that the system makes available to its users. It is the traditional user's manual. The preceding sections set the stage by describing the system conceptual model. This section describes the operations that can be performed on that model, that is, how elements of the model can be manipulated. It also defines the constraints on the order in which those operations may be performed. We begin with a discussion of our approach to presenting system operations.

Road Maps

System operations are generally not available at all times. Systems are often organized into states in which different collections of operations are available. The user must *move* from state to state to accomplish this work. In many systems each state is characterized by a menu on which the possible operations available in that state are shown. Whether or not menus are shown explicitly, all but the simplest systems partition their operations into states. Even systems that do not may be said to consist of a single state in which all operations are available. So from here on we suppose that all systems partition their operations into states.

Given any system, we can construct the system's state transition graph to show the various states and the paths among them (e.g., see [Conway, 1963; Woods, 1970; Feycock, 1977; Robertson et al., 1977; Wasserman and Stinson, 1979; Shneiderman, 1981; Parnas, 1982; Reisner, 1982; and Jacob, 1983]). This state transition graph is, in a sense, a *road map* to show access between the various system operations. As we have suggested, it is particularly easy to think of menu-driven systems in terms of state transition graphs and road maps. Each menu corresponds to a state, that is, a node, of the state transition graph; each operation corresponds to the next menu available to the user.* We find road maps particularly felicitous for describing operations in behavioral specification and we adopt their use here. Because road maps are so central to behavioral specifications, we take some time to discuss them in some detail.

Road maps usually consist of multiple graphs. A main graph characterizes the primary interaction skeleton, and for each primary transition that requires additional (sub)interactions with the user a subgraph shows its interaction subsequence. A road map is thus a collection of planar-directed graphs in which states correspond to decision points and transitions correspond to actions. Road maps are similar to syntax diagrams for programming languages [Jenson and Wirth, 1974]. Just as a syntax diagram characterizes the possible sequence of symbols that make up a program in a language, a road map characterizes the possible user† input sequences that make up a valid interaction session.

---

*The "next" menu may be the same as the preceding menu; that is, the user may stay in the same state.
†Here and in the following discussion we refer to *the user* as the source of system input. *User* should be interpreted to mean *any* source of input; that is, anything on the other side of the interface being described. In some cases the user may be a machine or some other system.

Terminal Session

Local Model:
  Accepted : Boolean
  Account : Account_Number;

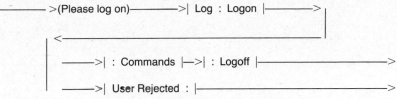

Figure 5.9 A road map for a terminal session.

Because road maps are important as the framework on which to present a system's operations, we develop a set of conventions for drawing them. The conventions may be easier to understand from an example than from an abstract presentation. Therefore we present an example road map that uses the conventions. Then we discuss the conventions more abstractly.

A Road Map Example

Consider the road map of a terminal session in Figures 5.9, 5.10, and 5.11. Figure 5.9 shows a terminal session as a sequence of transitions consisting of the following:

1. A logon operation.
2. Commands.
3. A logoff operation.

Logon

Local Model:
  Password : String;

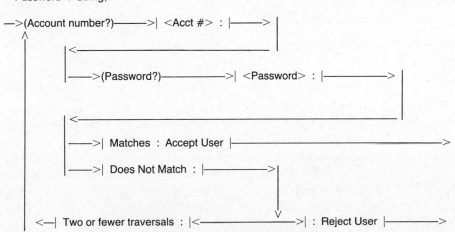

Figure 5.10 A road map for logging on.

Commands

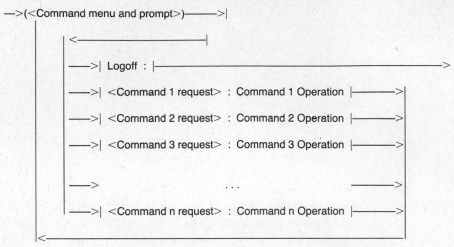

Figure 5.11   A road map for performing commands.

Figure 5.10 contains the internal details of the logon operation. Figure 5.11 is the command sequence.

The road map in Figure 5.9 is a main graph, labeled Terminal Session. It describes the three primary activities in an interaction terminal session. Two of these activities are subgraphs. The road map is interpreted as follows:

1. The user is first prompted to enter l o g as a request to log on.
2. When the user enters the characters l o g the system enters the logon subgraph.
   a. At that point the user is prompted to enter an account number.
   b. After that the user is prompted to enter a password.
   c. The account number and password are checked against the system's records and either of two actions occurs:
      (1) If the account number and password match the user is accepted and the system returns to the main graph.
      (2) If not the user is given a second and, if needed, a third attempt to log on. If the user is unsuccessful in logging on after three attempts the user is rejected and the system returns to the main graph.
3. After the system returns to the main graph either of two paths is taken.
   a. If the user had been rejected the system terminates.
   b. If the user had been accepted the user's account number is stored in Account (a single-value element data structure) and the system enters the commands subgraph.
      (1) In the commands subgraph the user is prompted with a menu of the available commands.

    (2)   The user selects a command.

        (a)   If the user selects the logoff command the system leaves the commands subgraph.

        (b)   Otherwise the system performs the selected command and returns to the commands menu.

  4. When the user again returns to the main graph the system goes through the logoff operation and terminates.

Road Maps and General Systems

It is interesting to note that the idea of road maps applies to systems in general, although in two distinct ways:

1. *Explicit Control.*   Road maps are explicit in some systems: they *control* the operation of the system. As we have noted, most computer systems are examples of explicit road maps.

2. *Implicit Control.*   Road maps are implicit in other systems; they *characterize* the operation of the system. Most man-made physical systems are examples of this form. As an example, consider a car with a manual transmission. Its road map requires the clutch to be disengaged before the gear is shifted. If we do not disengage the clutch first there is no guarantee that the transmission will respond. Yet there is nothing to prevent us from attempting to shift gears without disengaging the clutch; that is, from attempting to take a short cut across the road map. The road map does not explicitly control what we can do; it characterizes what we should do.

Reading and Writing Road Maps

We hope that the Terminal Session example has provided an understanding of road maps. We now describe road maps more generally.

As the example suggests, road maps consist typically of a main graph and a number of subgraphs. For the most part each graph and subgraph may be considered independently. Each road-map graph or subgraph is a micro behavioral specification for some part of the system. As such, like behavioral specifications in general, each (sub)graph has two components: a conceptual model part and an operations part. We call the conceptual model part of a graph or subgraph a *local conceptual model*. The operations part is simply the body of the graph itself.

The Local Conceptual Model

Each road-map graph may include a local conceptual model. Like the system conceptual model, a local conceptual model is a description of information the user needs to use that (sub)graph. For road map graphs the local conceptual model contains information that pertains to the user's progress through this particular graph.

Often the local conceptual model contains information that the system uses to suggest default parameters.

As an example, consider an appointment-scheduling system. Assume that the user has just read a message and is now asking the system to schedule an appointment. It would be a good guess that the appointment should be scheduled with the sender of the message the user has just read. That guess could serve as a default value. This is the kind of information that may be kept in local conceptual models.

One element that is always assumed to be available in every local conceptual model (and that need not be specified explicitly) is the number of times the user has traversed each transition in the subgraph. The traversal count for each transition of a graph or subgraph starts from zero each time the user enters or reenters that graph or subgraph. In the logon example the traversal count is used to determine when the user has made three unsuccessful attempts to log on.

The Operations: The Graph Itself

In addition to the local conceptual models, the main elements of any road map are the graphs themselves. Graphs consist of states and transitions. It is important to understand each of them. Most of the labels on road-map graphs, the labels inside the boxes, are *transition* labels! The only labels that refer to states are those in parentheses. For example, in the Terminal Session graph (Figure 5.9) there are exactly three states:

1. One state is labeled (please log on).
2. A second state is not shown explicitly on the graph; it is an implicit state. It is the state that is entered by the transition labeled Logon and exited by the two transitions labeled Commands and User Rejected.
3. The third state is also an implicit state. It is the implied state that is entered by the transition labeled Commands and exited by the transition labeled Log-off.

We may distinguish states from transitions by asking ourselves who has the initiative—the user or the system:

1. The user has the initiative at states. States represent points at which the next step is up to the user, that is, where user input is required. The action taken by the user, that is, the input supplied, determines the transition to be taken; that is, at any state each possible input is associated with an exiting transition.
2. The system has the initiative during transitions. Transitions correspond to actions that the system takes. Some of these actions may be single operations, such as logoff. Others may be complex actions that are refined into subactions. Some of these subactions may even have internal states that involve user inputs, such as logon. In either case, whether the action is simple or complex, transitions correspond to system actions.

This way of looking at state transition graphs is just the opposite of the way we normally think of syntax diagrams. In syntax diagrams the nodes represent specific syntactic elements or user inputs. In road-map graphs the nodes represent any of a number of possible user inputs and the transitions out of the nodes represent particular user inputs. We should examine syntax diagrams again and try to imagine the syntactic elements as labeling transitions and the points between them as nodes.

States

Because states correspond to points at which the user has the initiative, that is, when user input is required, prompts are generally associated with states. When prompts are shown in a graph their labels appear in parentheses. An example is the (please log on) prompt in the main graph. Although there is a state between every pair of transitions, not all states correspond to prompts; for example, there are no prompts associated with implicit states.

When so much information is presented to the user that it all cannot be shown directly within a graph it should be presented in a nearby figure and a reference should be made from the state to the figure; for example, when a menu is presented to the user at some state the state may be labeled with the name of the menu, which is shown elsewhere.

One final rule about states: when in a state it must be possible to determine the exit transition to be followed. This implies that graphs are not general context-free grammars. Unlike general syntax diagrams, no backtracking is permitted. Once the system has made a transition there is no going back. The next section discusses transitions more thoroughly.

Transitions

Transitions between states are represented by arcs in the state transition graph. A transition reflects a change of state, a passage from an old state, or the state left by the transition to a new state, the state entered by the transition. Transitions are characterized by two elements. We list them briefly and then expand on them.

1. *Selector: Input or Condition.*   Most states have a number of transitions that leave them. Selectors associated with transitions determine the transition to be followed. A selector distinguishes the transition with which it is associated from all other transitions that leave the same state. Selectors may refer to user inputs or to conditions in the system.

   a. *Input selectors.* When the user's input determines the exit to be taken from a state the selectors on transitions leaving that state refer to the possible user inputs (and determine the valid user inputs at that state); for example, in a menu state the selectors are the possible menu choices. We call these selectors *input selectors.* In the example Commands subgraph all the selectors are input selectors. In characterizing user inputs, input selectors may be arbitrary patterns. This is a useful feature.

Selectors are not limited to simple character strings. We may specify as selectors arbitrarily complex syntactic structures such as commands and their arguments or completely filled out forms with particular entries having particular values. The only constraint is that the inputs matched by selectors leaving the same state must be pairwise disjoint.

   b. *Condition selectors.* When the internal state of the system is used to determine the exit to be taken from a node the selectors are conditions. The information on which those conditions depend must be comprehensible to the user. This means that the information on which the conditions depend must be contained within the system conceptual model, the local conceptual model, or both; for example, if only a limited class of users is permitted to perform a certain action the selector on the transition that provides access to that action may express the condition that the user be in that limited class. In the Terminal Session example User Rejected and Matches are condition selectors.

2. *Action.*   The passage from one state to another is generally accompanied by an action performed by the system. An action may be something as simple as recording information, such as the user's name, or it may be as complex as analyzing a digitized image and producing a report. Actions are generally understood as discrete units of action. They frequently correspond to user-issued commands or to user-requested menu choices. In the example each of the command transitions is an action.

Each transition is identified with a selector and an action. These transition components are shown in a diagram of a state transition graph as a box through which the transition passes. The two components of the transition are listed sequentially, separated by a semicolon.

$$|\text{selector : action}|$$

Starting Transitions

Each graph has a single starting transition. Starting transitions are always shown in the upper left of a graph and enter the graph from the left.

Final Transitions

A graph may have many final transitions. Final transitions are shown leaving the graph to the right; that is, not entering any other state. If a graph has no final transition it is assumed to represent a process that continues indefinitely.

Graph Names

A graph may have a name associated with it. Graph names are used when one graph refers to another as a subgraph. Graph names are shown at the upper left corner over the starting transition.

Subgraphs

Actions may name subgraphs. When an action names a subgraph the system goes directly to the starting transition of the subgraph and proceeds as it would in any other graph. When a final transition of the subgraph is traversed the system returns to the transition that referred to the subgraph and follows it to the next indicated state. In the example, actions from the Terminal Session graph call the Logon and Commands subgraphs. This is similar to a program that calls a subprogram.

When a graph calls a subgraph, information may be passed in one or both directions. In our example the Terminal Session graph calls the Logon subgraph. When the Logon subgraph finishes two pieces of information are passed back to the Terminal Session graph:

1. A Boolean value that indicates whether or not the user has logged on successfully.
2. If the user has logged on successfully, the user's account number.

Also, in the example, when the Terminal Session graph calls the Logoff subgraph it passes the user's account number to it (so that the logoff graph can know which user to log off).

Multiple Main Graphs

A system may have multiple main graphs. Generally, each distinct user-type is associated with a separate main graph that characterizes the actions the user-type is authorized to perform. For example, a system may have separate main graphs for each of the following user types:

1. *Users.*   These people have access to the "normal" main graph.
2. *Data Base Administrators.*   These are the people authorized to modify the structure of the database.
3. *Auditors.*   These people are authorized to trace and analyze the work performed by others.
4. *Billing and Collections.*   These people bill customers for their use of system resources and are authorized to access information pertaining to that use.

Conventions for Writing Road Map Graphs

The preceding section set out the basic structure for state transition graphs. To facilitate the writing of road-map graphs we adopt the following conventions:

1. *Null Components.*   Either transition component (selector or action) may be null.

a. Depending on the type of state, a null *selector* component means that no input is expected or that no constraint limits the traversal of that component (see below in regard to the priority of such transitions).

b. A null *action* component means that if the associated transition is traversed no system action is performed.

c. If both components are null, then whenever the system traverses this transition it moves from the state at the tail of the transition to the state at the head of the transition, but no input is accepted, no condition limits the transition, and no action is performed.

Selectors are considered prioritized and the null condition is the lowest priority selector. It is lower than all the condition selectors and all the input selectors. If a transition is labeled with the null condition, that is, if no condition is indicated, then the transition is followed *only* if none of the selectors of the other transitions that leave that state is satisfied. Thus a transition with the null selector is followed only if all other transitions from the same state are blocked; that is, their conditions do not hold or the input they require is not provided. This provides for an *all other cases;* that is, an *else* or *otherwise* alternative.

2. *Time-Out Selectors.*   A *time-out* selector is a special kind of input selector. It is satisfied if the user supplies *no* input within the time specified by the selector. Time-out selectors provide a means for the system to continue operation if the user does not respond to a system request for input within a certain time.

A time-out selector is *not* satisfied as long as the user provides some input within the specified time, even if that input satisfies none of the explicitly indicated choices. Thus it is quite reasonable for a state to be left by a transition with a time-out selector and one with a null selector. In fact, it is generally wise to include both exit transitions from all states that depend on user input.

No time-out selectors are shown in the example. A time-out selector may be specified by writing

$$\text{Time Out}(n - <\text{duration}>) : <\text{action}>$$

where *n* is some number and <duration> is some unit of time such as *millesecond, second, minute,* or *hour,* as appropriate for the interaction.

3. Required user inputs may be specified in either of two ways:

a. *Syntactically or in terms of required data types.* Inputs shown in angle brackets, <input>, indicate that input of the type *input* is required. The angle brackets refer to a syntactic or data-type category that is defined elsewhere. Thus <Acct #> in the example means that the user is expected to enter an account number. It may be that account numbers come in specific forms (like social security numbers). We may assume that the required form is satisfied; that is, if the syntactic form of the input is specified in an input selector we may assume that the selector is not satisfied unless the input satisfies that form. The road map itself need not take any further responsibility for the form. (See user interfaces for a discussion of where this responsibility does lie.)

b. *Literally*. Inputs shown as character strings, for example, log and logoff in the example, indicate that the exact character string shown is required. In the case of log the user is expected to enter the characters l o g as a way of requesting the logon sequence.*

The Transitions Revisited

Transitions are the key elements in road-map graphs. Most typically, a transition identifies an input to the system (with the selector part) and an action performed by the system (with the action part); for example, in a menu driven system each transition leaving a state corresponds to the following:

1. One of the allowable inputs in that state (i.e., the menu selection).

2. The action performed in response to that input.

Similarly, in a command oriented system the transition that leave a state represent the different commands available in that state.

The following is a discussion of the transitions in more detail:

1. *Inputs to the System.* The term *input* is taken quite generally to mean *any information entered into the system from an external source.* An input may be one of the following:

a. A menu selection made by a user.

b. A command issued by a user. The command may consist of a command name and command parameters.

c. Data supplied by a user in response to a request from the system. The input may be compound and may include, say, all components of a form.

d. Data supplied "spontaneously," that is, interrupts. (Inputs of this sort come through a different interface from "normal" user inputs and the state transition graphs for these two interfaces are generally disjoint.)

The foregoing list may seem to imply that there are two sorts of input:

a. User-initiated, such as an interrupt or a user request for a system service; for example, a command.

b. System-initiated, such as a request for data from the user.

---

*The use of log is admittedly rather poor human factors design. When the user is required to enter the word *log* there is no other choice. There are no alternate transitions in the road map from that state. Instead of requiring the user to enter l o g, the system should go immediately to the logon subsequence without requiring user input. We have retained the log example solely to show a required character string input. The logoff example is a better design. When the user completes the terminal session and wishes to issue no further commands l o g o f f is entered. At that point the system leaves the Commands subgraph and in the main graph logs the user off.

We do not distinguish between them.* In both cases the input must be shown as an input selector on some transition. We make the following rule:

No input is allowed except as specified in an input selector.

Every element of information the system accepts must be specified by the selector of some transition and the input may be accepted only when that transition is traversed. Thus a state transition graph is central in describing a system's interface. The only way a system may receive input is by traversing a transition in which that input is expected.

This limitation on inputs is important. It implies a significantly different way of thinking about systems from the way most programmers are accustomed;

We can no longer think of a system as containing read statements embedded within the body of a program. All inputs occur between system actions.

2. *Conditions Holding Within the System.*   A transition with which a condition is associated may be traversed only if that condition holds.

In the Logon subgraph in Figure 5.10 a condition placed on one of the transitions requires that the password supplied by the user match the password of the user account number. If the user fails to supply the correct password, another transition (with the inverse condition) returns the user to the state at the start of the logon sequence.† In addition, the transition that returns to the start state has a condition that prevents it from being traversed more than three times. This limits the user to three attempts to log on and thus reduces the risk that an unauthorized user may hit on a correct password by repeated guesses.

Note that the conditions are expressed informally. The primary requirement is that they be expressed clearly and rigorously enough to convey their meaning accurately.

Note also that the example Terminal Session graph tests as one of its conditions the result returned by the Logon graph, that is, whether the user was accepted.

Finally, note that some of the conditions refer to the system's global conceptual model and some refer to the local conceptual model. The correct password for this user is presumably in the global conceptual model; the actual password and account number supplied by the user is in the local conceptual model as are the number of traversals and whether the user was accepted.

3. *Actions performed by the system.*   Actions refer to any actions of significance to the user performed by the system as a consequence of a transition. Actions may include outputs produced by the system and they may include signals issued by the system to control external devices.

---

*From the system's point of view *all* input is system-initiated; otherwise the system would not know that the input was there and would not be able to accept it. In fact, if we examine the hardware mechanisms, even "interrupts," are accepted by a system only when the system asks for them. From the user's point of view the distinction between system-initiated inputs and user-initiated inputs is intuitively useful; but from the system's point of view they are the same because they can be treated identically.
†This other transition could just as well have been labeled with the null condition.

If an action is associated with a transition, the action is performed whenever the transition is traversed. By associating actions with transitions the transitions which leave a state identify the actions available in that state. Thus if an action is available in a state there is a transition that labels that state with that action. If, for example, a state corresponds to a menu the actions on the transitions leaving that state correspond to the action choices made available by that menu.

For convenience, a sequence of actions separated by semicolons may be associated with a transition. The actions are performed in the indicated sequence. As far as the user is concerned, the actions are performed as if they were a single action, that is, with no opportunity for the user to interact between them. The only reason to list them separately is if doing so it makes it easier for the user to understand them.

All system outputs, like all system inputs, must occur along some transition. This is a less strict constraint than that on inputs because an output may occur as part of a larger action; for example, prepare and print a report. Inputs may not occur as part of an action unless the action is a reference to a subgraph in which the input appears as an input selection.

User Interface Operations in Interactive Systems

Most well designed systems provide a user interface with which the user interacts directly. User interfaces typically provide two sorts of services.

1. *Local Editing and Input Assistance.* User interfaces provide local editing and input assistance while users are *within* states; that is, before making a choice to leave a state and performing an action. The services provided generally include means the following:

a. Correct typing errors, that is, a *backspace and erase* key.

b. Move around on a terminal screen while filling out a form. (If the system provides a form as part of an input request.)

c. Accept or change default values offered by the system.

d. Request input completion; the user enters part of an input and requests that the user interface complete that input if possible.

e. Request help, that is, an explanation of what is expected.

f. Validate input; that is, the user interface may be capable of detecting syntax and data-type errors (e.g., if the user enters a date when a day of the week was requested). Recall that we said earlier that an input selector may specify the desired input syntactically. It is the user interface that is responsible for these syntax and data-type checks.

These local editing activities are generally available from any state and are (or should be) the same in all states. It does not make sense to show them as separate substates of each state; therefore they should be documented separately. Local editing services should be documented as a state transition graph or a collection of graphs if they require that sophistication. The main local editing graph is entered every time the system enters a state in which user input is required. The user exits the local editing subgraph by indicating satisfaction with the input supplied. In many systems that indication is associated with the *carriage return* or *enter key* and that key would be shown as the input selector on the final transition of the local editor's main state transition graph. See the calculator example for an example of a local editing road map.

2. *Context Switching Activities: Meta-Transitions and Multiple user Activities.* Some interactive systems permit users to engage concurrently in multiple activities; for example, a user may be working with one program that takes a long time to execute while working simultaneously with another program that responds rapidly. The system may permit the user to monitor the slower program and to respond to it when it is ready but at the same time to work interactively with the faster program. These two activities may be associated with two windows on the user's terminal display, although it is not necessary. In a similar way a system may provide a *tutorial* capability as a separate activity; therefore if in the middle of doing some work a user wishes to have a lesson in the use of the system access to the *tutorial* service may be gained without destroying the status of the work.

If these interactivity transitions are permitted they must be documented separately because there is no direct relationship between the states of the two activities; that is, no transitions exist from *states* of one activity to *states* of the other. It is best to imagine the user as being in some state in both (or each if more than two activities are allowed) activities concurrently, that is, in two (or more) states at once, and that the system will permit a switch in activities (i.e., a switch in contexts). Normally it is the user interface that provides the means of making these interactivity transitions. They should be documented as part of the user interface's services.

This service, too, should be documented as a road map. It is not part of the local editing road map; the user may decide to switch focus while in the middle of local editing. Context switching should be documented as a separate road map that is available in each state of the local editing road map. (Hence the input required to follow an initial transition in the context switching road map must be different from any input in any local editing state.) Therefore just as the local editing road map is entered every time the user enters a system state that requires user input the context switching road map is entered whenever the user enters one of the local editing states that requires user input.

A Road Map for a Calculator

As a small but complete example, consider the road map for a hand calculator. The conceptual model for the calculator consists of a single number stored internally. The calculator also has a display in which it shows that number when a calculation is completed or the number the user is entering as a second argument.

A calculator is best described in terms of an operations road map and a local editing road map. Figure 5.12 is an operations road map. (Note that there are no final transitions. The calculator is always available to do something.)

Local Conceptual Model

    Internal_Number : Number
    Current_Operation : Operation

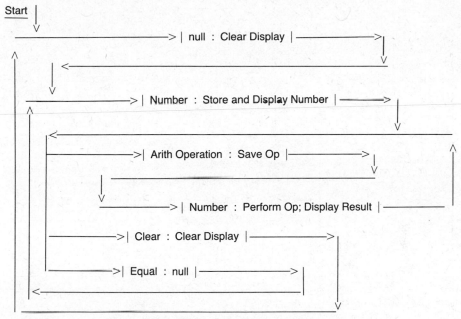

Figure 5.12.   A calculator road map.

As the figure shows, the user first enters a number which the calculator stores internally and displays. After that the user may enter the following:

1. An operation followed by a number. The calculator will perform the operation on the new number and the internal number and display the result.

2. A Clear command. The calculator will clear the internal number and the display and permit the user to start again.

3. An Equal command. The calculator does nothing, the entered operation having already been performed. The user is permitted to start again and the result of the preceding operation is stored internally and in the display.

Anyone familiar with a calculator knows that this description does not seem quite right. The road map suggests that the user sees the result of an operation when the second number has been entered. Our experience with calculators is that we see the result of an operation when we enter the *next* operation or an Equal command.

The availability of local editing capabilities explains this apparent discrepancy. The local editor reads the user's input before it is passed on to the main road map. The main road map doesn't get the user's second number until the local editor devises

Conceptual Model
  Display
  Look Ahead Operation

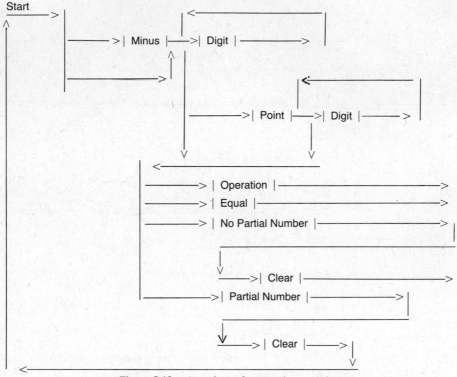

Figure 5.13. A road map for accepting a number.

a way of telling that the user has completed that number. In most interactive systems the user signals explicitly when a unit of input has been completed. That signal is often made via an Enter or Carriage Return key. In a calculator there is no such end-of-input character. The only way the local editor has of telling that the user has completed a number is if the user enters a new operation or an Equal command. Thus the main road map doesn't get the user's second number until the user has actually pressed a new operation key or the Equal key. The main road map does not see that additional key until later.

In fact, the local editor has three jobs:

1. It provides a brute force editing capability. The user may Clear a partially entered number or operation without destroying the internal number.
2. It determines when the user has completed entering a new number as we just indicated.
3. It permits the user to treat the number currently in the display as a default.

Figure 5.13 shows the road map for the local editor as it accepts a number from the user. (In this case we do not show the operations since they are obvious. The local editor's job is to accumulate a number digit-by-digit and pass it on when it is finished.)

All inputs entered by the user are displayed on the calculator's display. The internal number is not displayed while the local editor is accepting user input. As the local editor road map shows, the user may enter a minus sign for a negative number or skip the minus sign for a positive number. (It turns out that unary minus operations are possible only when the user is entering a first number on the calculator; that is, initially after a Clear command or after an Equal command. Any other minus sign is taken as a binary operation. We do not discuss this point further.)

The user may then enter a sequence of digits, terminated by a decimal point, an arithmetic operation, or an equal sign. If the user enters a decimal point another string of digits may be entered and terminated again by an arithmetic operation or an equal sign.

If the user enters a Clear command *while* entering a number the display is cleared, the road map returns to its starting point, and the user may begin again. These Clear commands are local editing commands. They are not the Clear command to the calculator we have discussed. They do not affect the internal number, only the current input. The Clear command that clears the internal number is accessible only by a Clear entered when there is no partial number. If there is a partial number the user must clear it first before the internal number may be cleared.

As the road map shows, a number is terminated by an operation or an Equal command. This termination symbol is treated as a *lookahead* symbol by the number road map. Most language processing systems are forced to look ahead one or more symbols to determine how to interpret the symbols they have already seen. The calculator is no exception. Its user interface cannot tell that a number is completed until it has been shown something to indicate the end of the number. It does not process that extra something; that is left to the next interaction with the user; that is, when the user must enter an operation. That lookahead symbol, however, must be seen by the local editor as it processes a number. This is the reason that the calculator does not seem to process a number until after the user has entered an additional arithmetic operation or an Equal command.

Note that the user interface permits the user to take the internal number (which is in the display when the local editor is entered) as a default. If the user enters an operation before entering digits the road map exits immediately and the number originally in the display is taken as the user's desired number.

This terminates our general discussion of road maps. We now return to the discussion of the behavioral specification in which we use road maps to describe a system's operational interface.

5.4.1   System Road Map

This section of the behavioral specification and the sections within it contain the system road maps. We recommend the following organizational rules:

1. Each graph (and subgraph) should represent a related collection of user operations.

2. There should be a separate subsection for each graph.

3. The graphs should be presented on the same level; that is, the subsections themselves should *not* be nested to correspond to the nesting of user operations. The nesting structure of the graphs (i.e., in which one graph is a subgraph of another) should be explained within the documentation for the graphs but the documentation structure itself should not reflect that organization. Many levels of documentation are often more confusing than useful and this part of the document is rather deeply nested as it is. The subsections should be ordered to correspond approximately to the order in which the user may encounter them.

4. The user interface graph should have a special subsection for itself.

Subgraph i

This section and the sections within it contain information about a particular subgraph. The graph itself should be presented in this introduction. The states and transitions within the graph are explained in subsections.

State i.   Each state is presented in its own subsection, which should be ordered to reflect the approximate order in which the user may encounter them. The following information should be given for each state:

1. *Name.*   Some states have names and others do not. A state name may reflect the system's entry into what we may want to identify as a mode of operation; for example, a *command mode*. A state may reflect a particular occurrence, for example, an *error state*.

2. *Intuitive Explanation.*   This section provides an intuitive description of the state's purpose and its role with respect to the other system states. A statement of purpose should inform the user of the objectives to be achieved in the given state.

3. *Appearance.*   The user should be told how the state is to be recognized; that is, how the system appears when it is in this state. Typically a state is made manifest in one of three ways:

    a. *Display.*   In a system with displays (such as an interactive terminal, lights, light emitting diodes, or liquid crystals) this section describes the values or configuration of the display elements that identify the state. If the display is not self-explanatory this section should explain it.

    b. *Menu.*   If this state is identified by a menu this section should show the menu as the user will see it. If the menu choices are not self-explanatory this section should explain them.

     c.   *Prompt.*   If this state is identified by a prompt, or perhaps a distinctive output from a previous state followed by a prompt, this section should describe the system output by which this state will be known. If the output or prompt is not self-explanatory this section should explain it.

  4. *Exiting Transitions.*   The transitions that leave this state should be explained. Each transition is described individually. A transition is characterized by the input or condition that triggers it and the action it performs. The following subsection provides details.

Transition i.   The transitions are the primary means by which users interact with the system. From the user's point of view the most important element of a transition is the action that occurs when the transition is traversed. Therefore the focus should be on the action. Each transition is presented in its own subsection. The subsections should be ordered aphabetically by transition action, which correspond to the system operations as the user knows them.

    Each transition should be described in terms that permit the user to understand its use and effects. We treat the transitions as if they were all user-requested operations, even though some transitions are simply system-requested inputs with no significant action taking place. For each transition the following information should be provided:

  1. *Action Invocation: Transition Selector.*   This section explains how the transition is selected, that is, how the action is invoked. It tells what has to happen in a given state to cause this transition to be selected for traversal. In some cases actions are invoked by commands given by a user. In others actions are invoked as a result of menu selections or by entries made on system-supplied forms that the user fills out. In still others actions are invoked as a result of internal conditions monitored by the system, and sometimes actions are invoked as a result of a particular configuration of data supplied to the system. Whatever the case, the means of invoking the action are defined here.

     a.   *Command.*   A user gives the system a command. If the command form is used the syntax of the command should be given here.

     b.   *Menu selection.*   A user gives the system a command by selecting it from a list of commands provided on a menu. If the menu form is used details about the user's method of making menu selections should be provided. The menu itself is discussed in the description of the state.

     c.   *Input requests.*   Some actions occur as a result of supplying user-input to the system. Thus in the log on example one state corresponds to entering an account name and another state corresponds to entering a password. The transitions out of these states correspond to the act of supplying requested input by the user.

     d.   *System initiated actions.*   Some actions are initiated by the system on a regular basis, for example, once every day or once every second, or as a result of the system sensing particular data or arrangements of data. In the logon example if the user fails to enter the correct password the system initiates a new logon sequence.

2. *Arguments.*   Selectors usually require arguments; for example, if the selector is a command, that command may have arguments; or if the selector is determined by how the user fills out a form supplied by the system, the entries on the form are really arguments. This section describes the selector arguments. For each argument the following information is provided:

a.   *Data types.*   The data type of an argument is the class of things from which the argument must be drawn. Typical data types for an appointment scheduling system may be Message, User, Date, and Appointment. Each data type should correspond to an element of information in the system conceptual model.

b.   *Default values.*   It is good practice to provide default values for as many arguments as possible. Defaults save the user from having to enter values that the system can assume or deduce. Default values do not limit the user because there is the option of rejecting defaults. Typically there are two kinds:

   (1)   A dynamic default is one that depends on the state of the system when the action is invoked or in some other way on preceding interactions. Use of the current date is an example of a dynamic default. Use of the most recently mentioned element of the given data type is another example.

   (2)   A static default is one that is fixed or depends only on the particular user. Use of the user's name as a default argument is an example. In an appointment-scheduling system the default assumption that appointments are 20 minutes long is another example.

c.   *Range limits.*   Some arguments and inputs are constrained to fall within a limited range of values and these range limits are not part of the definition of the data type of the argument or input. In a bookkeeping system, for example, the maximum amount that can be paid for any bill may be limited.

d.   *Amount limits.*   Sometimes arguments appear in the form of a list. There may be a limit to the maximum length of the list; for example, imagine that the current state involves filling out a form in which a list is embedded and that the form is filled out by using the user-interface's local editor. If there is a maximum length allowed for the list that limit is listed here.

3. *Effects.*   This section describes the effects the performance of the action has on the system and its environment. The effects may be classified as follows:

a.   *State changes: new state.*   If performing the action causes the system to enter a new state that information is included here. Presumably that information is also visible in the state transition graph.

b.   *Conceptual model changes.*   This section is the heart of the action description. It is here that the effects of the action on the system are described. Most actions are performed for the purpose of modifying the system's internally stored information: adding new information, deleting old information, or changing information. All the effects an action has on the system should be described here in terms of the conceptual model developed in Section 5.3.2. Actions, by their effects, provide the only way in which changes may occur in the conceptual model. Therefore, if the conceptual model is intended to change, some action whose effect is to bring about that change must be provided.

c. *Device/external effects.* A smaller but important class of action contains those intended to direct external devices controlled by the system. Many software systems are embedded within larger combined hardware/software systems, and it is the job of some of this embedded software to control some of the hardware. The software in an automobile microcomputer, for example, may be responsible for controlling the richness of the fuel sent to the engine. It exerts its control by regulating the ratio of air to fuel provided by the carburetor, in which case the effect of one of its actions must be to open or close the air inlet value by a certain amount.

4. *Outputs/Values Returned.* Many operators return a value (for the use of another operator in which this one may be nested) or provide output results. This section describes those outputs or values returned. For each output the following information is provided:

a. *Data types.* This section identifies the data type(s) of the outputs or returned values which, like the input and argument data types, should be among those defined in the conceptual model.

b. *Derivation.* This section describes how the output is derived. In particular, it tells how the output may be predicted from knowledge of the arguments and the conceptual model. The deriviation may be expressed as a formula, an algorithm, or a combination. Whatever the form, this section characterizes precisely how* the output or result is derived.

c. *Display.* This section describes how the output is displayed or otherwise made visible to the user. In many cases output is simply ''printed'' at a user's terminal. In more sophisticated systems the output is displayed in specific locations on a terminal or presented by changing a reading on a dial or gauge. Sometimes the output is highlighted by display in color, inverse video, blinking characters, or graphically, and sometimes the terminal cursor is positioned before, after, above, or below the output. All this information should be indicated.

5. *Exceptional Conditions: Special Diagnostic Messages and Recovery Procedures.* An exceptional condition is one that reflects some error, fault, or failure in the system's action. Section 4.2 of this document lists the exceptional conditions that are not specific to a particular action. This section discusses those conditions

---

*How does *not* mean that a detailed program is supplied. It does mean that a method or algorithm may be specified or simply that a formula characterizing the result is provided. This is part of providing a behavioral model of the system.

that may occur as a result of performing this particular action. For each exceptional condition the following information is provided:

a. *Interpretation.*   To the extent that it is not evident from the general discussion of this exceptional condition, this section explains how this action may have lead specifically to the exception.

b. *Recovery procedures.*   This section describes the available recovery procedures, that is, what the user should do to get back to a state in the road map.

Often exceptions can be expressed as selectors of actions that lead to error states, and recovery procedures can be expressed as actions leaving those error states. If this strategy is followed there is no need for a separate entry for exceptional conditions and recovery procedures. In many cases, however, it is more informative to document recovery procedures within the action that lead to the exception. If that strategy is followed the documentation should be provided here.

6. *Timing.*   This section discusses the timing profile of the action; that is how long it takes for this action to complete. Frequently action times cannot be expressed as a single number; they must be expressed as ranges; for example, when the system's computing resources are shared by a number of users.

Action times can be measured in a number of ways, and each may be important. We recommend the following possibilities:

a. *Response time.*   Response time occurs between the moment the user completes entering the action and the time when the system next communicates with the user and permits the user to enter a new action. Most commonly, the system's next communication is an answer developed for the preceding user action: but it may also be that the system's next communication simply informs the user that the preceding action is underway, that results will be available after a while, and that the system is ready for other work in the meantime. In both cases the user has access to the system for further work at the end of the response time period. Note that if the system is organized with an asynchronous user interface with which the user may interact at any time response time in this sense will be effectively zero.

b. *Computing time.*   Computing time is the time it takes to perform the computations required to complete the action. Computing time is concerned only with the *computations* involved. Normally, computing time is a function of the amount of computing work required to complete an action; for example, the computing time for a sort action would be a function of the number of elements to be sorted, or the computing time for a database lookup would be a function of the size and structure of the database.

c. *Effect time.*   The effect time is the time for the system to achieve the effect requested by the user. Effect time differs from computing time in that it may depend on factors external to the software. Effect time, in general, is relevant only when the system is controlling some other devices beyond itself. If, for example, the system is responsible for shutting down a nuclear reactor, the effect time is the time it takes between the request for a shutdown and the time when the shutdown can be said to be completed. Alternatively, the effect time of an action may depend on other aspects of the system; for example, if the system is distributed over a network the effect time of a command to update a remote part of the system's database may depend on the communication network in use and the load on it.

7. *Special Resources Required: Devices/Computer Resources.* This section describes any special resources needed to carry out the action. As a simple example, an action to copy a file from the system's disk storage to a tape requires that a tape drive be available and that it have a tape on it belonging to the user. In other cases actions may require special devices (e.g., for systems that perform process control and other embedded functions) or they may simply require unusually large amounts of computing resources if the action is particularly complex.

8. *Integrity.* This section is concerned with the effect of the integrity features built into the system on this particular action. System integrity is concerned with preventing unauthorized access or use of system information or facilities. Integrity is concerned with preventing unwarranted violations of the system's boundaries and with maintaining the system as a sound and complete entity. This section describes how the system's integrity controls apply to this action.

a. *User-type limitations.* This section lists any limitations on the users permitted to perform this action. An action to change the recorded salary of an employee in a personnel system may be permitted only to a small class of administrative users. An action to examine the files on a user's personal account is generally permitted only to that user. In general, any user-type limitations applicable to this action must be listed here. In addition, the means for checking the limitation must also be provided. The two most common means are the following:

(1) *Passwords or the equivalent,* in which access is permitted only to those users who can produce a password; (this is an example of a *ticket-based* security scheme).

(2) *User identification,* in which access is permitted only to users with prior authorization from an authorizing agency such as a computer-center administrator or security monitor (this is an example of a *list-based* security scheme).

b. *Data protection.* Sometimes an action may be available to any user, but some classes of data are protected from arbitrary use; for example, in a personnel record-keeping system the name, telephone number, and office location of all employees may be available for anyone to examine, but employee's home addresses and telephone numbers may not be made public unless the employee agrees to do so. Limitations like these on data with which this action may come in contact are expressed here.

c. *Audit data maintained.* This section describes the audit data maintained by the system as a result of performing this action. It is often important to keep track of all access to or modification of the elements of a system. If records are kept of this action they should be described here. There are two other reasons for keeping records:

(1) To monitor the number of times system services are used. That information can be used to tune the system so that the most frequently required services are made more convenient and efficient.

(2) To track employee productivity.

5.4.2 Exceptions: General Diagnostic Messages and Recovery Procedures

This section describes the exceptional conditions that may result when operating the system. There are two common categories:

1. *Exceptions that Allow Normal Operation to Continue.*   It often happens that the system road map can anticipate exceptional conditions and that the system can continue to operate normally even after the condition is in effect. If the user in the example in Figure 5.9 has supplied an account number and password that do not match any in the system's records an exceptional condition will have occurred but the system will continue to operate. The user is given a second and third opportunity to log on.

In some cases it may not be obvious to consider a condition an exception. In the logon example we might just as well describe the multiple attempts to log on as just another allowable path in the road map. This is a matter of judgment. Normally we would describe as exceptional any condition that appears in at least two places on the road map; that is, any that may be the result of two different actions. Similarly, we would describe as exceptional any condition that reveals a significant error or failure in the system's conceptual model; for example, a violation of an invariant.

Other conditions that develop in the normal course of operation in just one spot on the road map and that do not reflect the existence of a prior failure or error in the system may be documented as part of the normal road-map transitions. An incorrect account number and password are probably best dealt with in this way because no damage has been done.

2. *Exceptional Conditions that Prevent Normal Continued Operation.*   When an exceptional condition prevails the system is sometimes unable to continue functioning normally. Many of these errors force the system out of the normal state transitions described in the road map. If, for example, the computer on which the system is operating fails the system may not resume operation in its former state. This section should describe the state in which the system will restart itself after one of these exceptions is noted.

In particular, this section describes the behavioral manifestations of the system's fault tolerance capabilities. Thus any built-in error detection mechanisms that may impede the user should be described here. Similarly, any built-in error containment algorithms that may limit the user should also be described here.

Because restarting normally means that some information has been lost, this section must also describe the checkpointing procedures the system will take or allow so that the user can understand the state of the system when it does resume operation after a discontinuous state change.

This section lists both exceptional conditions and provides explanations and remedies for them in terms of the conceptual model developed earlier. If it is not possible to explain an exceptional condition in those terms the conceptual model should be modified. A sure sign of a poorly designed and poorly human engineered system is an exceptional condition unrelated to the ostensible operation of the system and one that requires unanticipated knowledge by the user. The sort of additional information frequently required for poorly designed systems concerns the operation of the host-computer operating system or the host computer itself.

5.4.3   Audit Information

This section describes the audit-data-gathering and reporting capabilities built into the system. Audit data normally includes aggregate information on the use of the system and specific information on who did what and when.

It is possible to specify audit information as part of the system's overall operation, but because these data are generally of interest only to a small but generally not typical class of system users it is often more convenient to confine the discussion to a separate section of the behavioral specification.

EXERCISES

1. Specify the operational interface (i.e., draw a road map and specify the selectors and actions) for a terminal session on the computer at your facility. Include neither application programs nor local editing operations. Do include at least five operating system commands, including the command that is most complex in terms of subcommand options.
2. Specify the operational interface (i.e., draw a road map and specify the selectors and actions) for the local editing operations available at the command level of the computer at your facility.
3. Specify the operational interface (i.e., draw a road map and specify the selectors and actions) for a full screen editor available at your facility.
4. Specify the operational interface (i.e., draw a road map and specify the selectors and actions) for a system that can
    (a)   accept an arbitrary form expressed as a composition of data structures;
    (b)   permit a user to traverse the form and fill in the blanks. It is not required that the user have the ability to move *directly* from one entry on the form to any other, but it is required that the user be able to move from one entry to any other *in some number of steps*. You need not wory about displaying

the form on the user's terminal. We are concerned primarily with user input and not with system output. Assume that the form will be displayed as the user traverses it.

5. Enhance the system just described so that the form entries can have associated help messages (not automatically displayed) and the user can request that these help messages be displayed. You may assume that there is a display operation that presents its argument. Again you are not required to worry about actual screen layouts.

6. Enhance the system just described to permit form entries to have default values specified which the user may accept if desired.

7. Enhance the system just described so that the form entries may have data types specified. The system is to ensure that the user's inputs will fit the specified data types.

8. Enhance the system just described so that defaults may be specified as the most recently entered value of this data type.

9. Assuming the system conceptual model developed for Exercise 3 following Section 5.3.2, specify the operational interface (i.e., draw a road map and specify the selectors and actions) for an appointment scheduling system.

5.5 OTHER BEHAVIORAL SPECIFICATIONS

Any aspects of the system's behavioral specification not covered elsewhere should be included here or in subsequent sections. Please notify the author of this book of any additional categories of procedural information. The author may be reached via the publisher.

5.6 VERIFICATION TESTS SCRIPTS

Section 5.6 describes test scripts that verify that the system performs as specified in the behavioral specification. These tests have two functions.

1. *Elaborate the Test Scenes and Scenarios in the Requirements Document.* The test scripts provide the detailed operations that are to be performed in the situations described in the requirements document. For every scene or scenario there should be a corresponding test script that shows how the system would be used to deal with that situation.

2. *Provide a Complete Set of Exercises for the System.* The test scripts should provide a complete test of the behavioral capabilities of the system. If all the tests in this section are performed successfully we should be confident that the system will in fact perform as advertised in this document.

For each test the following should be provided.

Test identification	This is the name by which the test is known.
Test conditions	This describes the conditions that must be established before the start of the test.
Test events and expected responses	This describes the events that make up the test and the responses expected from the component. Events consist of external communications to the system. Expected responses consist of responses the system is expected to make. The events and expected responses should be described exactly. It should be possible in principle for a computer program to administer the tests and to compare the actual results with the expected results. A test observer should not be required to interpret the results before determining whether they are correct.

EXERCISES

1. Develop test scripts for the appointment-scheduling system you defined in earlier exercises.

═6

PROCEDURES MANUAL

This document tells how the system in the behavioral specification fits the organizational needs described in Section 3.2 of the requirements document. It refines the planned use of the system and describes the information (and often material) flow structure within the organization that is best suited to the system; it discusses the various interfaces the system has with (a) the user-organization in terms of that information and material flow structure and (b) with the environment; it lists the demands made on the system at those interfaces and describes any other processing the organization must perform to make use of the system. Finally, if a transition from a current to the new system is required it presents the transition plan.

6.1 OVERVIEW OF DOCUMENT, ORGANIZATION, AND CONVENTIONS

This section is similar to the first in the other documents; therefore its outline is not repeated here.

6.2 SYSTEM OVERVIEW AND ORGANIZATIONAL CONTEXT: CONCEPT OF USE

Section 6.2 is an overview of the system and its intended use. It also describes the system's expected operational context. It identifies the organization that will be using the system and the features of that organization's structure and operation that are reflected in the system's functioning.

To a great extent this section should be a more concrete presentation of the parallel material in the requirements document. Just as the behavioral specification includes a conceptual model that makes the world model concrete, this section is a concrete restatement of the organizational and policy positions set forth in the second section of the requirements document.

6.2.1   System Definition

Section 6.2.1 defines the overall goals and limitations of the system. It reflects policy decisions taken by the sponsoring organization and set out in the parallel section of the requirements document. To the extent that the system definition matches its description in the requirements document, this document may refer to the requirements document. To the extent that the system definition has changed in the course of development, this section should include those changes. Changes in this definition are often simply refinements and elaborations of ideas contained in the requirements document. If the changes are incompatible with the requirements document that document should be changed or the incompatibilities should be noted explicitly.

Purpose(s)

The statement of the purpose of the system should be a concise characterization of the intended direct result(s) or effect(s) to be produced by the system's use. On the most general level it answers the question: Why use this system? See the corresponding section of the requirements document for details. In this document the purposes should be stated in terms relevant to the system as actually given in the behavioral specification.

Scope

The statement of scope should identify broadly the functional areas for which the system is to be responsible. It should also define the limits of those functional areas by outlining the boundaries of the system's responsibilities. See the corresponding section of the requirements document for details. In this document the scope should characterize the system as actually given in the behavioral specification.

Anticipated Markets and Users

The intended markets and users are listed here. If the potential user-community is fragmented the fragments should be listed separately. See the corresponding section of the requirements document for details. In this document the anticipated markets and users should be characterized for the system as actually given in the behavioral specification.

Anticipated Uses

The primary use(s) of the system should be listed here rather than the particular operations that the system itself is expected to perform. It should be clear how these uses would achieve the purposes set out above. See the corresponding section of the requirements document for details. In this document the anticipated uses should be characterized for the system as actually given in the behavioral specification.

Range of Configurations and Options

Many software products operate on different configurations and have multiple options. See the corresponding section of the requirements document for details. In this document the configuration options for the system as actually developed should be summarized. Details are provided in the administrative manual.

6.2.2   User Organization

Section 6.2.2 and the subsections within it describes the structure and functions of the expected user organization to the extent that the information is relevant to the use of the system. The description should include all the details required to explain how the system fits into the organization.

As in the corresponding sections of the requirements document; this section describes the system's operational context from as many structural points of view as are relevant. The three we discuss are generally most important, but if there are others that matter in the operation of the system they too should be presented.

Logical Organization

This section discusses how the system will fit the logical structure described in the corresponding section of the requirements document. To the extent that the system has a logical organization to match the user organization's logical structure that fit is given here.

An example of a logical organization would be an integrated corporate personnel management system. Different parts of the company would have access to different system capabilities. The personnel department, for example, would have access to personnel information about all the employees in the company. General corporate management, on the other hand, would have access to personnel information about those employees only directly under them in the management heirarchy. The personnel department would have the authority to implement changes to personnel records that had passed successfully through the corporate approval cycle. The approving individuals in the management chain would have approval or disapproval authority only over possible personnel actions. Other individuals in the corporation would have even more limited system access and change capabilities.

Physical Organization

This section discusses the relevant details of the user-organization's physical structure. Physical organization refers to the geographical arrangement of the user-organization: for example, are there branch offices located across town that must be connected? Across the state? Across the country? Around the world? How many are there? To the extent that this structure must be known by, reflected in, and be otherwise relevant to the use of the system it should be described here.

Temporal Organization

This section discusses the relevant details of the user-organization's temporal structure. Temporal organization refers to a schedule of events relevant to the use of the system; for example, if the system were intended to support budgeting this section would explain the budgeting cycle and its associated deadlines.

6.3   CONCEPTUAL MODEL

This section presents a conceptual model of the system for use as background for the procedures manual. This model should be a simplified version of the conceptual model presented in the behavioral specification, reference to which should be provided for completeness.

6.4   OPERATIONAL PROCEDURES

This section presents the details of the operational procedures recommended for the system in one or more annotated flow diagrams. The introductory section contains the flow diagrams. Subsequent sections discuss the individual processing steps.

6.4.1   Information and Material Flow

This section describes the relevant information (and material) flow. Information flow in computer-based systems is often shown graphically by representations known as data-flow charts, activity charts, information-flow diagrams, bubble charts, and by various other names [IBM, 1961; Langfors, 1963; Martin and Estrin, 1967; Teichrow, 1977; Ross et al., 1975; Yourdon and Constantine, 1979; and Gane 1979]. An information-flow diagram is a directed graph in which the *nodes* correspond to (information and material) processing *steps* and the *arcs,* to *information and material* moving from one processing step to another.

   We generalize information-flow diagrams to permit them to refer to any commodity for whose flow the system is responsible. Therefore some of the material may be processed or produced on an assembly line. We refer to these diagrams as flow diagrams. Thus a flow diagram may show how coal and iron ore travel through a steel mill as the iron ore is smelted into steel. The same flow diagram could also show how information about that process progresses from processing unit to processing unit.

For each processing step in a flow-diagram the organizational unit that performs the step is identified. Presumably some of them refer to processing performed by the computer system, in which case *the system* is identified as responsible for carrying out the processing step. It is *not* necessary that each processing step be made by a distinct organizational unit. Individual organizational units as well as the computer system itself may complete multiple processing steps. Thus each step and the name of the organizational unit that performs it is labeled for identification.

Labeled arrows connect processing steps to reflect how the information and materials pass from step to step. The arrows entering a processing step identify the information and materials that are its input and those leaving a processing step identify the information and materials produced by it. This is done on two levels. Both the information and material and the media containing the information are identified; for example, input to a data entry processing step may consist of loan application (the information) forms (the media). Output from that processing step may be the same loan applications but now on floppy disks.

In addition to the processing steps and the paths between them, flow diagrams provide information and material *sources* (where information and materials enter the organization), *sinks* (where they leave the organization), and *storage* (where, at least conceptually, they are stored within the organization).

6.4.2 Processing Steps

The subsections within this section describe the processing steps.

Processing Step i

Each processing step is described individually. The following information should be provided.

1. *Responsible Organizational Unit.* This section identifies the organizational unit responsible for the processing step. If there is an organizational unit already capable and authorized to accept this responsibility it should be named. If there is no organizational unit that fits the processing step a unit name may be created. It may also be left until later to assign or create an organizational unit to perform the required processing.

In some cases the "organizational unit" is a device or machine; for example, the factory machines in a system that controls a factory are some of its organizational units. These machines should be clearly identified and if any special equipment is needed to perform the processing steps it should be described here.

The individuals in the organizational unit should correspond to one of the user types described in the requirements document. If they do not a revised version of the requirements document should include them.

2. *Inputs.* This section describes the inputs to this processing step. This description should be concrete and specific; that is, if the inputs are to be provided on forms the forms should be shown and the entries in the forms, identified. Each piece of information or material should correspond to some information and material in the requirements document. In general, an input to a processing step is also an output from a preceding step. If the input has been described as output it is not necessary to describe input produced by some other processing step a second time. Reference may be made to its description as output from the processing step that produced it.

3. *Processing.* This section describes the processing required in a processing step. If it includes use of the computer system reference should be made to the operations required. The actual system operations should be described in the behavioral specification. Reference should be made to the states in which they are available or to the operations themselves. If the processing is not performed by the system the processing operations should be described clearly and completely. If the processing is too complex to explain in terms of a few simple operations it may be shown in subsidiary processing step charts. In general, the processing performed by a processing step should correspond to an activity or a process described in the requirements document and reference should be made to that description.

4. *Output.* This section describes the outputs and other results produced by a processing step. This description should be concrete and specific. If the output is a form or a report the details should be shown. If the output is the result of a system operation and the results are shown in the behavioral specification they need not be repeated but reference should be made to the relevant description(s).

5. *Time Schedule.* If a processing step must be performed in a limited period of time or on a certain schedule that time constraint or schedule should be shown here:

a. *Schedule.* Many processing steps are scheduled; for example, information about retail sales may be *gathered* (by point of sale equipment) during the day and *processed* at night. Both *gathering* and *processing* should be shown as processing steps. The hours when they are scheduled to be made should be included in this part of the description.

b. *Speed.* Some processing steps must be performed within a certain amount of time; for example, after a rocket carrying a satellite is launched it must be decided quickly whether to permit the mission to continue or to abort it. If a speed constraint applies to this processing step it should be shown here. The go/no-go satellite launch decision exemplifies a processing step that is both scheduled and speed critical. The decision happens at a certain point in the schedule of the rocket launch *and* it must be completed within a certain amount of time.

6. *Integrity Constraints.* This section describes any integrity constraints implemented to maintain the integrity of the processing step.

6.4.3   Sources

An information or material source is an interface that the organization (including the system) forms with the rest of the world through which it receives information and material.

Source i

Each source is described. The following should be provided for each information or material source:

1. *External Agency.* This section names the agency beyond the interface that is supplying the information and material. The external agency may be human, for example, a customer at an automated teller machine, or it may be nonhuman, for example, the ground being monitored by a sensor in an earthquake-warning system.

2. *The Input.* This section introduces in concrete detail the input that is made to the system. If the input is described elsewhere, for example, in the behavioral specification, this section may refer to that description. If the input is not given elsewhere, for example, if this input is produced by a person for initial processing by some other person (as is often the case in surveys conducted by questionnaire), the exact form of the input is shown here. The input must correspond to elements of the world model discussed in the requirements document. If it does not that document should be revised.

3. *Integrity Constraints.* This section describes the integrity constraints implemented to maintain the integrity of the input and to ensure that the expected external agency is, in fact, the source of the expected inputs.

6.4.4   Sinks

A sink is an interface that the organization (including the system) has with the rest of the world by which it produces output or other results.

Sink i

Each sink is described. The following should be provided for each of them:

1. *External Agency.* This section identifies the agency beyond the interface that is receiving the output or other results. The external agency may be human, for example, a customer at an automated teller machine, or it may be nonhuman, for example, a container for a product in a factory control system.

2. *The Output.* This section presents in concrete detail the output that the system produces. If the output is described elsewhere, for example, in the be-

havioral specification, this section may refer to that description. If the output is not available elsewhere, for example, a factory product, or the output is produced outside the scope of the system, for example, an analyst's manually produced summary report of information generated by the system, the exact form of the output is shown here. The output must correspond to the world model described in the requirements document. If it does not that document should be revised.

3. *Integrity Constraints.* This section describes the integrity constraints implemented to maintain the integrity of the output and to ensure that the expected external agency does, in fact, receive the expected results.

6.4.5 Storages

A storage is a facility in which information or materials for which the system is responsible may be left for later retrieval. A storage facility need not correspond to actual storage but may reflect the user's view that information or materials are stored in a certain way.

Storage i

The following should be provided for each storage facility:

1. *Information or Other Elements Stored.* The information or other elements stored should be described. If they do not correspond to something in the world model in the requirements document that document should be revised.

2. *Storage Structure.* The structure of the storage should be described. If the storage facility stores information the storage structure will be some data structure. If the storage facility is described in the behavioral specification this section should refer to that description. If the storage facility stores materials the storage structure should explain how the materials are accessed and how are determined the contents of the facility and any other information pertinent to its use.

3. *Integrity Constraints.* Any constraints implemented to maintain the integrity of the storage should be described.

6.4.6 Information and Material Transfers

Each arrow of the flow diagram implies a transfer of information or materials from a producer of that information or materials to a consumer. It is often transferred automatically as a result of its being processed by the system, for example, from one storage structure within the system to another. Sometimes, however, it is important to indicate how the information or materials are actually moved from one processing unit to another; for example, information may be moved by intracompany mail. This section lists all the arrows in the flow diagram for which information or material transfer is not automatic and indicates the agency responsible for transporting its elements.

EXERCISES

1. Draw and annotate a flow diagram for registration at your school. Do not forget to include the physical elements (such as identification cards) that are processed.
2. Draw and annotate a flow diagram that would enable a bank to offer automated teller devices. Assume that the automated teller devices do not communicate dynamically with the bank's computer but that they do record transactions. Do not forget to include the steps in which money is transferred.
3. Draw and annotate a data flow diagram to describe how your school awards degrees. Include registration as a single processing step. Do not forget to include the gathering and recording of grades.
4. Draw and annotate a flow diagram to describe the steps required to get an account on the computer at your facility. Include the steps required to gain special privileges.
5. Draw and annotate a flow diagram for assignments and grading in this course. Include all homework assignments (assume that there are some that require the use of a computer), projects (assume that these are handed in a number of times during the semester, reviewed by the instructor, and returned), and tests.
6. Draw and annotate a flow diagram for an appointment-scheduling system.

6.5 TRANSITION

This section and the subsections within it apply when an existing system is being replaced by a new system. It defines the mapping from the flow diagram for the old system to the flow diagram for the new. The flow diagram for the old system appears in Section 3.2.4 of the requirements document. The flow diagram for the new system is shown in the preceding section of this document.

6.5.1   Processing Steps, Sources, and Sinks

For each processing step, source, and sink of the new system we must decide whether there is a corresponding element of the old system that can perform that function.

6.5.2   *Storage Element*

For each storage element of the new system we must decide if information or materials currently in storage elements of the old system must be transferred. Similarly, for each storage element of the old system we must decide what is to be done with the information or materials stored there. If information or materials from the old system is to be included in the new system, the processing required to make them suitable for use in the new system must be described here. As a simple example, a file may have to be reformatted. A flow diagram for any required transformations should be presented here.

6.5.3   The Flow Diagram During the Transition Process

If the system being replaced is responsible for functions that cannot be interrupted during the transition this section should include one or more transition flow diagrams to characterize the operating procedures during the transition.

   If both systems are to be operated in parallel during the transition the transition flow diagram may be a combination of the flow diagrams for the old and new systems. As an alternative, if the new system is to take over responsibility incrementally the transition flow diagrams may include selected processing steps from the old, the new, and the transformation flow diagrams.

6.6   OTHER PROCEDURES

Any other procedural information not included elsewhere should be described here. Please notify the author of this book of any additional categories of procedural information. The author may be reached via the publisher.

6.7   REHEARSALS

A rehearsal is to a set of procedures as a test script is to a behavioral specification. Both are tests. Section 6.7 describes rehearsal or practice sessions to be used to verify the operation of the system in its operational context. Although it is not necessary, these rehearsals are most realistic if they are coordinated with the test scripts described in the behavioral specification. In that way the procedures and the system may be tested together. As an alternative, simulate the system during the procedural rehearsals. This approach is taken for rehearsals held before the system is operational.

═══7

ADMINISTRATIVE MANUAL

This manual provides guidelines for system administration and operation. It describes how the system is expected to be integrated into its operational environment. We define system administration as management of the day-to-day operation of the system, including all the attendant details.

7.1 OVERVIEW OF DOCUMENT, ORGANIZATION, AND CONVENTIONS

This section is similar to the overview section in the other documents and its outline is not to be repeated here.

7.2 ADMINISTRATIVE ORGANIZATION

This section and the subsections within it explain the applicable administrative details.

7.2.1 System Ownership

This section identifies the owner of the system. Frequently the owner is the anticipated user-organization and sometimes the owner expects to run the system as a service to other users; for example, as in a time-sharing service or in one that copies floppy disks from the format of one computer to that of another. In other cases the owner provides the system on a royalty or sales basis to administrators, who run the system as a service, or directly to the users; for example, as in many leased or sold software packages. To the extent that system ownership is a factor in the system's administration and operation, the ownership should be spelled out here. Ownership may be important if we expect the owner to supply a working but not modifiable version of the system (e.g., object code) to its users.

In particular, this section should discuss the arrangements made between the owners and the administrators. It should also describe the authority and responsibility of each party.

7.2.2 Operational Control

This section identifies the organization expected to provide the basic operational support for the system. This will often be the user-organization's ''computer center;'' operating the system will be another of its service responsibilities.

Similarly, a new service organization may have to be set up to operate the system. An organization without a computer center, for example, must develop a strategy for supporting the system's operational needs, which include buying supplies and changing the paper on the printer.

In addition, operational policy decisions must be made; for example, which of two contending users has the higher priority. The mechanism for making these decisions should be considered ahead of time and specified here.

7.2.3 Modification Policy and Change Support

This section outlines the expected policy for changing the system after it is built. It answers the following questions:

1. Will the owners be the only ones with authority to make changes?
2. May the administrators, for example, the computer center, modify the system?
3. May users make their own changes?
4. If a user feels the need for a change to whom should the request for modification go?
5. What agency is responsible for tracking the various changes and for ensuring their compatibility?
6. If the system exhibits a fault who is responsible for fixing it?
7. If a system change causes a fault who is responsible for fixing it?
8. What agency has the authority to decide which of the requested changes will be made and in what order?

7.2.4 Funding Strategy

This section describes how the system is expected to be supported financially. Some systems have their own budgets. Others must depend on the budget of the administering organization. Still others are maintained by royalty fees paid monthly or yearly by the users, whereas some are supported by charges levied on the users on the basis of their use of system services and resources. Section 7.2.1 states the cost of the system; this section states its price.

7.3 CONFIGURATION

This section and the subsections within it describe the system as a coordinated collection of hardware and software components. The components described are those that the administrators are required to handle. Components embedded within the administrative level components are not mentioned.

7.3.1 Prerequisite Structure

This section shows the prerequisite structures of different versions of the hardware and software components. *Prerequisite structure* refers to dependencies between components; for example, to use a certain version of the system loader a complementary version of the system compiler must be used because only that version produces load modules in a form compatible with that loader. This section must be revised whenever a new version of a system component is produced. It must show how the new version components are dependent on one another and on components from earlier versions.

7.3.2 Hardware

This section describes the system hardware. The hardware is described from the perspective of installation and operation. The hardware may be described in terms of the following categories.

1. *Host Computer System.*   This section describes the actual computer(s) on which the system runs. If the computer is a standard, vendor-supplied system this section may be a reference to the vendor's literature. The required model and configuration options should be described. If the computer is developed or modified especially for this application the structure of that computer should be outlined here and reference should be made to more detailed documentation.

2. *Host Peripheral Devices.*   The system devices (e.g., disks, terminals, and printers) and special purpose devices should be described here. In each case

any characteristics required of the device to suit them to the current application should be described.

3. *Other Hardware Configuration Components.* Any other hardware components (e.g., a system-controlled machine in a factory) are described here or references to descriptions are provided.

7.3.3 Software

This section describes the software components that form the system from the perspective of installation and operation. The software components may be given in term of the following categories.

1. *Operating System.* This section describes the operating system(s) on which the system runs. If the operating system is a standard, vendor-supplied system this section may be a reference to the vendor's literature. If a particular version of the operating system is required that information is given here. If the operating system is developed or modified especially for this application the anticipated structure of that operating system should be outlined here.

2. *Other Software Configuration Components.* This section describes the configuration components that make up the system. The description should not be a detailed account of the specification or design of the component. It should be a brief discussion of the role of the component in the system. It should also include a reference to some other document that describes the component in more detail.

7.4 OPERATION PROCEDURES

This section and the subsections within it describe the procedures for installing a system in its environment, for modifying it when upgrades are ready, and for day-to-day operation.

If the system is a typical application program that runs on a standard computer and operating system, these procedures may be no different from those for any other application program that runs on the same system, in which case this section may consist primarily of references to the operations manual for the standard system. On the other hand, if the system is expected to require special operational support this section describes that support as fully as possible.

The information called for in this section may not be completely known at the time the initial system specification is written. If the host computer or operating system is to be built especially for this application the details of that computer or operating system are still to be determined. Nonetheless, it is important to provide an outline of the anticipated host computer, support software, and required operational support. Without an outline it would be difficult to tell whether the specified system can be used realistically in its intended environment.

7.4.1   Installation Procedures

This section describes the procedures needed to install the system in its operational environment. Again, if the system is to run on an existing computer system with well defined means for adding new programs little need be said other than to refer to existing documentation. If the system is to run on a specially designed or modified computer system, details should be provided for the installation of the system. These instructions should include everything necessary to prepare the computer system to receive this particular application and for actually installing the system, often a complex job. Installation procedures must be spelled out clearly.

7.4.2   Update Installation Procedures

This section describes procedures for installing system updates. Most computer systems are not static and new versions frequently replace the older ones. This section describes how those replacements take place. Often there are two types of update:

1. *Version Updates.*   For relatively minor improvements new versions do not completely replace the old. Instead, new components may be added to a system library to replace older components. This section describes the procedures for making these replacements.
2. *New Versions.*   For relatively major updates a new system may replace an older version. The new system is often installed in more or less the same way as the initial installation. This section describes the differences between this type of installation and the initial installation described above.

7.4.3   Generation Procedures

This section describes the activities required to produce a running system once a new version has been installed. In some cases, for example, recompilations must be made before the new modules are fully integrated into the older version.

7.4.4   Startup Procedure

This section describes procedures required to start the system. Most systems are turned on and off, if only for preventive maintenance. It also tells how to turn the system on. If the system is intended never to be turned off, the startup procedures may be included as appropriate in the system installation or generation section.

7.4.5   Initialization Procedures

Any steps necessary to initialize the system after it has been started should be described here. As a trivial example, systems that are started afresh each day must be told the date and time. Somewhat more significantly many systems need to be informed of their initial complement of users. Still more significantly some systems need entire databases installed as part of their initialization. Some initialization occurs once in the life of a system, whereas, some occurs each time the system is started. As appropriate, this section may be integrated with the system startup or system generation procedures.

7.4.6   Reconfiguration Procedures

It is often possible to run a system on various configurations of hardware and software. Sometimes these different configurations are required to provide different system capabilities; at other times different configurations result from hardware malfunctions. It may be necessary for the operations staff to participate in restructuring the system. This section provides reconfiguration instructions.

Reconfiguration may occur statically during system generation or startup or dynamically while the system is operating. As appropriate the information in this section may be integrated into the sections on system generation, system initialization, or system operating procedures.

7.4.7   Operating Procedures

Once the system is operating certain operator interventions may be required to keep it running or to support users. These are steps that are assumed to be taken by system operators as distinct from users. The subsections within this section describe those procedures.

7.4.8   Checkpoint and Restart Procedures

Computer hardware and software do fail; therefore provision should be made to recover from failures. In many cases the system should be self-checkpointing and should have built-in mechanisms to restart itself after an unexpected failure. Frequently system operators are called on to perform these functions. Instructions for taking manual checkpoints and for using them are discussed here.

7.4.9   Other Operating Procedures

Sometimes a system operator must take action in support of a system user; for example, an operator may be required to mount a tape or disc pack. These operator-required procedures are described here.

7.4.10   Shutdown Procedures

Systems that are shut down periodically, either for scheduled maintenance or because they are not in use 24 hours a day, every day, require the shutdown procedures described here.

7.5   MAINTENANCE

The subsections within this section describe the recommended system maintenance.

7.5.1   Schedule

This section sets forth a recommended maintenance schedule.

7.5.2   Procedures

This section describes the recommended maintenance procedures.

7.6   OTHER OPERATING PROCEDURES

Any other procedures required by the system and assumed to be performed by operators are described here. Please notify the author of this book of additional categories of procedural information. The author may be reached via the publisher.

REFERENCES

B.S. Chen and R.T. Yeh, Formal Specification and Verification of Distributed Systems, *IEEE Transactions on Software Engineering*, SE-**9**:710–721, 1983.

M.E. Conway, Design of a Separable Transition Diagram Compiler, *CACM*, **6**(7):396–408, 1963.

A.M. Davis and T.G. Rauscher, Formal Techniques and Automatic Processing to Ensure Correctness in Requirements Specification, In *Specifications of Reliable Software*, 15–35. IEEE, 1979.

U.S. Department of Defense, Specification Practices, MIL-STD 490, 1968.

S. Feycock, Transition Diagram-Based CAI/HELP Systems, *International Journal of Man-Machine Studies*, **9**:399–413, 1977.

C. Gane, Data Design in Structured System Analysis, In *Infotech State of the Art Report on Data Design*, Infotech, 1979.

P. Gilbert, *Notes on Program Design Techniques*, Science Research Associates, Palo Alto, California, 1983.

F.V. Guttag, E. Horowitz, and D.R. Musser, Abstract Data Types and Software Validation, *CACM*, **21**(12):1048–1062, 1978.

C. A. R. Hoare, An Axiomatic Approach to Computer Programming, *CACM*, **12**(10):576–580, 1969.

IBM Corp, *Study Organization Plan Documentation Techniques*, Technical Report, IBM Corporation, Armonk, New York, 1961.

R. J. K. Jacob, Using Formal Specifications in the Design of a Human-Computer Interface, *CACM*, **26**(4):259–264, 1983.

Piccup Jensen and Wirth B. Langfors, p. 195. Some Approaches to the Theory of Information Systems, *BIT*, **3**:229–254, 1963.

R. London, Proof Rules for the Programming Language Euclid, *Acta Informatica*, **10**(1):1–26, 1978.

D. Martin and G. Estrin, Models of Computations and Systems. Evaluation of Vdertex Probabilities in Graph Models of Computations of Interactive Systems, *JACM*, **14**(2):281–299, 1967.

G. Myers, *Composite Structured Design*, Van Nostrand, New York, 1978.

F. G. Pagan, *Formal Specification of Programming Languages: A Panoramic Primer*, Prentice-Hall, Englewood Cliffs, New Jersey, 1981.

D. Parnas, On the Use of Transition Diagrams in the Design of a User Interface for an Interactive Computer System, In *Proceedings of the 24th National ACM Conference*, 379–385. ACM, 1982.

P. Reisner, Formal Grammar and Human Factors Design of an Interactive Graphics System, *IEEE Transitions on Software Engineering*, SE-**7**(2):229–240, 1982.

G. Robertson, A. Newell, and K. Ramakrishna, *ZOG: A Man-Machine Communication Philosophy*, Technical Report, Department of Computer Science, Carnegie Mellon University, Pittsburgh, 1977.

D.T. Ross, J.B. Goodenough, and C.A. Irvine, Software Engineering: Processes, and Goals, *IEEE Computer*, **3**(5):62–72, 1975.

B. Shneiderman, Multi-Party Grammars and Related Features for Defining Interactive Systems, *IEEE Transactions of Systems, Man, and Cybernetics*, SMC-**12**(2):148–154, 1981.

J.E. Stoy, *Denotational Semantics: The Scott-Strachey Approach to Programming Language Theory,* The MIT Press, Cambridge, Massachusetts, 1977.

D. Teichrow, PSL/PSA: A Computer-Aided Technique for Structured Documentation and Analysis of Information Processing Systems, *IEEE Transactions on Software Engineering,* **SE-3**(1):41–48, 1977.

R.D. Tennent, The Denotational Semantics of Programming Languages, *CACM,* **19**(8):437–453, 1978.

R.D. Tennent, *Principles of Programming Languages,* Prentice-Hall International, Englewood Cliffs, New Jersey, 1981.

A.I. Wasserman and S.K. Stinson, A Specification Method for Interactive Information Systems, In *Proceedings of the Symposium on Specification of Reliable Software,* 68–79. IEEE, 1979.

K. Jensen and N. Wirth, *User Manual and Report,* Springer-Verlag, New York, 1974.

W.A. Woods, Transition Network Grammars for Natural Language Analysis, *CACM,* **13**(10):591–606, 1970.

E. Yourdon and L. Constantine, *Structured Design,* Prentice-Hall, Englewood Cliffs, New Jersey, 1979.

PART 3

DESIGN

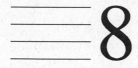

8

DESIGN DISCUSSION

8.1 INTRODUCTION

This chapter describes how software can be built to perform as specified in a behavioral specification and answers the third of the questions posed in Chapter 1:

1. *Why* is a system needed and for what purpose(s)? The requirements document answers this question.

2. *What* does a system that fills these needs look like and how is it used? The system specification answers this question.

3. *How* can a system be built to behave as described? The design document answers this question.

Thus a requirements document is a description of user-objectives for a system and the world into which an intended system must fit; a behavioral specification is a description of a system that meets these objectives and that fits into that world; and a design is a description of the inner workings of a system whose behavior is described by the behavioral specification.

This chapter differs from the others in that it includes a longer discussion. The documentation outline at the end presumes an understanding of the discussion that precedes it.

In this chapter we use notations from an invented programming language, which is like Pascal with additional constructs for software components and concurrency and resembles Ada* and Modula-2 [Wirth, 1982], from which we borrow heavily. We assume that readers are familiar with Pascal and we use without explanation those parts of our language that are similar to it. We explain, as we use them, the constructs not in Pascal.

8.1.1   Software Architecture Versus Algorithm Design

Software design may be divided into two primary subdisciplines: software architecture and algorithm design. Software architecture is concerned with the overall structure of a software system, the parts out of which it is made, and how those parts fit together. Algorithm design is concerned with the sequence of operations software takes to carry out its tasks, the control structures that organize those operations, and the program objects on which those operations are performed. In short, software architecture is concerned with the *static* structure of software *systems;* algorithm design is concerned with the *dynamic* operation of programs. As we show later, however, the static structure of a software system is *not* the same as the static structure of the system's source code.

This chapter is concerned primarily with software architecture and not with algorithm design. We concentrate less on algorithm design because several approaches to it are already widely known and highly regarded. They include structured programming [Dijestra, 1972], stepwise refinement [Wirth, 1971], and others, for example, [Jackson, 1975]; [Stevens et al., 1974]; and [Warrier, 1974]. In [Abbott, 1983], we present our own approach in which we convert a natural language description of a process into a program that uses the appropriate data-type abstractions. (We should also consider [Horowitz and Sahni, 1978], for a discussion of algorithm design techniques from the perspective of algorithmic strategies.)

 Our primary software architecture recommendation is that software should be organized as a structured collection of building blocks, that is, components, and that each should be designed to be understood on its own. In addition, the components should be designed for use in multiple software systems. Designing with components, or "modules" as they are sometimes called, has been recommended for the development of software. The approach described here extends and refines the notion of modularity as a practical tool for software design. The following is the first comprehensive discussion of software design in terms of components:

1. *Software Qualities.*   We derive our overall software design strategy from a hierarchy of software qualities; for example, software should be designed in terms of reuseable components.

2. *Software Architecture.*   We introduce the notion of an *interpreter* as anything that can be described by a behavioral specification. The notion of an interpreter is essentially a generalization such as abstract data type and abstract machine. We claim that all software systems (as well as many other interesting systems) are best understood as interpreters. We also claim that

---

*Ada is a trademark of the United States Department of Defense.

software components are best understood as interpreters and distinguish between two forms:

a. *Abstract components.* These are component definitions and are the
work of software designers. Abstract components are strictly abstractions. They must be instantiated before they can function as operational
software. They then become concrete.

b. *Concrete components.* These are instances of abstract components.
Concrete components exist as units of an operational software system.

3. *Software Component Categorization.* We divide all components into categories:

a. Data types, subunits, and data structures.

b. Operations and operation libraries.

c. Transducers.

d. Drivers.

4. *Internal Component Design.* This is the internal structure of components.

5. *Libraries of Components.* We define abstract components in terms of other
abstract components. It also discusses the library structure needed for this
sort of hierarchy.

6. *Programming Languages.* Finally, we discuss programming languages and
how they are related to our design approach.

The two final chapters of this part contain outlines for system design documentation
and component design documentation, respectively.

8.1.2 Software Design Versus Designing Software

We diverge from many of the more common approaches to software engineering in
that we focus primarily on the final software product rather than on techniques for
developing that product. Many approaches to software engineering describe how we
should *go about* designing software (e.g., [DeMarco, 1979], or [Bergland, 1981],
for a survey). In contrast, we are more concerned with the *result of* software design
than with how we achieve that result. For example, the stepwise refinement approach
to software design suggests the following steps:

1. Create a "top level" description of an algorithm expressed informally in
pseudocode and natural language statements.

2. Expand or refine the less well defined or more complex parts of the algorithm. Depending on whether we are expanding or refining, the extended version of the algorithm will include additional details or references to
subalgorithms.

3. Repeat Step 2 in the new version of the algorithm and subalgorithms until
the entire algorithm is defined to the desired level of detail.

Our concern here is not with design steps but with properties a well designed software architecture should have and how software architecture should be documented. Just as in system requirements and system-use documents we do not dwell on production techniques; we concentrate on the appearance of the product when it is finished.

8.2 SOFTWARE QUALITIES AND A STRATEGY FOR SOFTWARE DESIGN

This section discusses qualities well designed software should have and derives a design strategy for achieving those qualities. By following [Balzer and Goldman, 1979], we organize the qualities hierarchically. ([Boehm, 1978], and [McCall et al., 1977], should also be consulted for other software quality hierarchies.)

1. *Goals* for the design of software.
2. *Characteristics* possessed by software that meet these goals.
3. *Design principles* that lead to software with those characteristics.
4. A primary *design concept* derived from these principles.

8.2.1 Software Design Goals

This section describes four qualities software should possess if it is to be considered a well engineered product:

1. *Usefulness.* Software must provide the needed computational capabilities. If software does not perform the tasks for which it is needed, then, no matter what its other qualities, it's probably not worth much.

Whether software is useful is directly related to the thoroughness with which its requirements have been analyzed. In particular, the usefulness of software depends on these qualities:

a. The degree to which the written requirements accurately express the user's actual needs.
b. The degree to which the software specification documents describe software that satisfies the given requirements.
c. The degree to which the software is built to perform as promised by its behavioral specification.

This chapter is concerned with the final issue only: designing software to perform as specified by a behavioral specification. The preceding chapters are concerned with software requirements and behavioral specifications.

2. *Reliability.* Software must provide the required capabilities correctly and under all circumstances.

In one sense software is always 100% reliable in that it does the same thing every time. It doesn't wear out as hardware does; hence it does not "fail" in the same way.

As applied to software, the term *reliability* generally refers to something other than worn parts or component failures.

The term *reliability* is used with software to refer to the user's perception of it how well it works. Thus software reliability is generally concerned with whether software performs as the user expects and would like. *Reliability* is synonymous with *dependability*. Software is reliable if the user feels that it can be depended on to work correctly no matter what: "Good old system, you can always count on it." In this sense software is reliable if the following conditions apply:

a.   It is *correct;* that is, it performs as specified.

b.   It is *robust;* that is, it continues operating correctly, or at least reasonably, when subjected to conditions for which no specification is given, such as invalid inputs.

c.   It is *fault tolerant;* that is, to the extent possible it continues operating correctly even in the face of hardware or other software errors.

To be 100% reliable the software must operate correctly not only for valid inputs and on properly working hardware but also acceptably for invalid inputs and on malfunctioning hardware.

What the preceding really amounts to is an extended definition of correctness. If we adopt it we should be characterizing reliability as a notion not essentially different from correctness. To provide a definition for reliability that stands on its own we must take a different approach. This second approach defines reliability probabilistically.

The reliability of software for a particular user is the probability that the software will operate correctly for that user for a given period of time.

Although this definition does not on its face appear to be different, note that it makes reliability a function of the software *and* the user [Bright, personal communication].

Defining software reliability as a probability may be confusing:

a.   We are not implying that, given a particular input the software may perform in one (correct) way with a certain probability and in another (incorrect) with a certain probability: software always performs identically in identical situations.

b.   Nor are we implying that the probability is a measure of the likelihood of there being errors* in the software: either there are errors in the software or there are not. It is not a probabilistic matter.

The only question is whether any errors that may be in the software will be encountered by the users. If there are no errors the software will be 100% reliable. Unfortunately most systems have some errors. Therefore the probabilistic issue is whether the errors will be encountered while the software is in use. Whether a particular error will be encountered is a function of the input to the software and the

---

*We also include errors in requirements and specifications. An error is anything that causes the software to function in an unsatisfactory way.

context in which the software is operating. Thus software reliability may vary with the use made of it. A software product may have errors and still be 100% reliable for users that never cause the software to encounter those errors, but for users that do so frequently the software will seem relatively unreliable. Thus the reliability of a software product depends on how it is used:

    a.   Software that is incorrect may be considered reliable by someone whose use of that software does not depend on the part(s) that contain the errors.

    b.   Software that is nonrobust may seem reliable to someone whose use of that software does not subject it to conditions beyond its specifications.

    c.   Software that is not fault tolerant may seem reliable if no faults occur.

    3.   *Modifiability.*   Software must facilitate corrections, changes, and enhancements. Over the long term the primary reason for documenting the design of a software system is to permit that design to be modified when changes are desired. Over the life of a software system modifiability is generally at least as important as any other factor in the system's total cost.

    4.   *Economy.*   Software must be less expensive to produce and programmers must be more productive than they are now. The development and modification of software is a labor-intensive process and must become less so.

These are the primary goals for software design. Next we consider how these goals may be met.

8.2.2   Software Design Characteristics

For software to meet the preceding goals it must possess two primary characteristics.

    1.   *Understandability.*   It must be possible for programmers to understand the structure and intended functioning of the software. Understandability is a measure of the ease with which people are able to comprehend software design. Understandability contributes to the goals listed above in the following ways:

        a.   It is easier to determine whether software will behave as intended when the software is easy rather than difficult to understand. In this way understandability contributes to usability.

        b.   We can more easily identify the software parts that are used if the software is understandable than if it is not. We can more easily make those parts correct, robust, and fault-tolerant if the software is understandable than if it is not. In this way understandability contributes to reliability.

        c.   Understandable software is easier to modify than software that is harder to understand. In this way understandability contributes to modifiability.

        d.   It is less expensive to develop and modify understandable software than it is to develop and modify software that is harder to understand. In this way understandability contributes to economy.

2. *Reusability.*   Software should be developed from reusable components; and software developed for one system should be built of components that can be used on others. Reusability contributes to the goals listed above in the following ways.

   a.   The capabilities of used software components are better known than those of software that have never been used and their usefulness is easier to gauge.

   b.   Having a track record, reusable software has a known reliability.

   c.   Reusable software should have a documented history of modifications that will facilitate future modifications.

   d.   Because it has already been developed and tested once, reusable software as part of a new system is less expensive.

8.2.3   Software Design Principles

There are two primary design principles for producing software that is both understandable and reusable:

1. *Abstraction.*   To abstract is to focus on only those features of something that are relevant to a particular concern. Abstraction may be thought of as the creation of a simplified representation of a more complex reality in which the representation retains all the *relevant properties* of the real thing and, to the extent possible, none of the *irrelevant complexities;* for example, an organization chart in business is an abstraction of a real organization with respect to its management control.

Abstraction in programming is this and more. In programming we are always dealing with *two* realities from which abstraction is desirable (e.g., [Guttag, 1979]).

   a.   *The application area* for which an abstract model is desired. This is traditional abstraction.

   b.   *The computer itself,* a physical object, in terms of which that abstract model is to be implemented.

Given this two-poled version of abstraction, we should like a program design that is perfectly abstracted in both ways. The design should reflect the important properties of the parts of the world being modeled and it should express them in terms that are directly relevant to the model rather than those that require translation from a world of computer hardware or software details. The term *appropriate abstraction* refers to a point along a double-ended continuum:

   a.   At one end of the continuum is the real world in all its detail

   b.   Somewhere in the middle is a model of that world that reflects the elements of interest.

   c.   At the other end is the computer implementation of that model that includes all the complex hardware and software details.

Each point along the continuum corresponds to some degree of abstraction. The ideal is the following:

a.   It describes the relevant model of the world and nothing else.

b.   It represents that model in terms directly relevant to it and not in terms reflecting the implementation of the model on a particular computer or in a particular computer language.

As an example, consider developing a computer system to play a board game like chess. An appropriate abstract model will include the two players, the board as an 8 × 8 array, the different pieces and their locations on the board, and the rules of the game. Other information about a "real" game of chess, such as the material out of which the board or the pieces are made, is of no concern, and that information is *abstracted away* in developing the model.

From the other direction we must avoid adding to the model anything related to its computer implementation. Thus the model should not be presented in terms of the computer memory locations that correspond to the various board positions or of the codes used to record the type of piece at each board position.

Achieving the ideal degree of abstraction in software design is important to understandability and reusability for the following reasons:

a.   Abstraction aids understandability in that an individual reading software designed on the proper level of abstraction can see directly what user-level capabilities the software is intended to provide. If the software is a direct reflection of the model the reader is not distracted by too much application or implementation detail. Software written otherwise generally requires its readers to translate backward from computer-oriented details to the intended user-level concepts (e.g., the code *wk* means *white's king*) or to wade through unnecessary details of the application area.

b.   Abstraction aids reusability in that software written abstractly can generally be more easily integrated into a new system. This is so because its functioning can be characterized on a single level, the level of the intended user services. Software written otherwise often depends on features of its environment not directly related to its intended user services. There are two potential problems with software that is insufficiently abstract in either direction:

  (1)   Software that includes unnecessary application detail may be so application-specific that it cannot be used anywhere else.

  (2)   Software that depends on a particular hardware or software environment is generally difficult to extract from that environment.

1.   *Encapsulation and Information Hiding*   [Parnas, 1972; Liskov and Ziles, 1975]. Encapsulation is the design principle that requires each major design decision and functional capability to be isolated in a separate software design unit in such a manner that the means of implementing the capability is not visible to the user of the design unit; only the functional capabilities of the unit are known. *Encapsulation* literally means to enclose in a capsule. When applied to software, encapsulation means that each important element in the design of a software system (e.g., the structure used to store information of a certain sort or the functional capabilities of the system's terminals) should be isolated from all the other important elements. We should not, for example, decide how to *store* information in a system on the basis of how a particular terminal *displays* the information to be stored.

Encapsulation also implies abstraction of each design decision. By enclosing the decision in its own capsule we can distinguish those of its features that are relevant to the design, for example, the functional capabilities of the terminal used in a system, from those that simply implement the decision, such as the character sequences that instruct that terminal to perform various operations. Thus each encapsulated design decision should play a role in the system that corresponds to its abstract description rather than to its implementation details.

The principle of *information hiding* is another way of expressing the principle of encapsulation. Information hiding requires that no information regarding the implementation of a particular design decision be used elsewhere in the system. Only the abstract capabilities of each design decision should be used by other elements of the system.

Encapsulation and information hiding are important to understandability and reusability for the following reasons:

a. Software designed according to the principles of encapsulation and information hiding is generally easier to understand because the design can be considered as a collection of discrete units. Software written otherwise is often difficult to understand because parts of the design frequently depend on other parts in hidden and unpredictable ways.

b. Software designed according to the principles of encapsulation and information hiding is generally easier to reuse because the design is packaged as discrete functional units that can be plugged in as needed. Software written otherwise is harder to reuse because its pieces are harder to extract.

8.2.4 Software Design Concept

Finally, the single software design concept most useful for implementing the preceding conceptual design principles is *modularity*. To be modular software must be organized into separable units, each of which encapsulates a specific set of abstract capabilities.

Modularity is important for abstraction, encapsulation, and information hiding for the following reasons.

1. Modules may be used to implement an abstraction in that an abstract concept may be associated with and implemented by a single module.

2. Modules may be used to implement encapsulation in that a module serves as the "capsule" that encapsulates each design decision and separates the module's abstract capabilities from the method of implementing those capabilities. The abstract capabilities of the design decision are made available outside the module; the means of implementing those capabilities are hidden within the module.

Thus it is good practice to design software systems as a collection of interacting components or modules. Each module should be independently characterizable in terms of the particular abstract capability it offers.

Over the last few decades the term *module* has been used for many purposes in software design. Although generally consistent in the broadest sense, they differ sufficiently in specifics to lead to more confusion than clarity. For that reason we do not use *module* and adopt instead *software component*. We understand a *software component* to be

> *a unit of software that encapsulates and provides one or more abstractly defined capabilities.*

We next discuss our overall approach to software architecture and, in particular, to software architecture in terms of components.

8.3   INTRODUCTION TO SOFTWARE ARCHITECTURE

In this section we present our overall approach to software architecture. We consider all software systems to be *interpreters*. Intuitively, an interpreter is anything that can be described with a stimulus/response model. Thus any system for which a behavioral specification can be given is an interpreter. Recalling our approach to behavioral specifications, we define *interpreter* as anything with the following properties:

1.   By its existence it establishes a boundary between its "inside" and its "outside." That boundary is called its *(user) interface*.

2.   There is a *conceptual model* that characterizes the structure and content of its inside.

3.   There is a formalized means for communicating across its interface. That means of communicating is called its *language* and that language may be expressed by using road maps. Thus every interpreter defines a language, although as we shall see not all interpreter languages are written. Communication with the interpreter in the language has the following properties.

    a.   Any externally originated communication to the interpreter in the interpreter's language may be called an *input* to the interpreter. This means, in particular, that we do *not* distinguish between "data" and "commands" as two different types of input.

    b.   Any source of input may be considered a *user* of the interpreter; for example, a sensor, which in other contexts might be called a data source, we consider to be a user.

4.   Given its internal state, that is, the state of its conceptual model, an interpreter's response to any communication is determined. The response generally has two parts:

    a.   A visible external effect; that is, an *output*.

    b.   A change in its internal state.

This definition is deliberately quite broad. It permits many familiar things to be understood as interpreters:

1. *Interactive, Application Computer Systems.* The user communicates with the system across the user-interface in the system's command language. The result is generally both of the following:

a. The user affects the system's inside, perhaps by causing some new information to be stored.

b. The user causes the system to produce output.

2. *Physical Devices* (e.g., *Home Appliances and Automobiles*). The user communicates across the user-interface by pressing buttons and levers and turning knobs. The possible ways that buttons and levers may be pressed and that knobs may be turned define the language, which is not expressed in written symbols. These presses and turnings are the communications in the language and they generally affect the device's inside as well as causing it to produce output.

3. *Bureaucracies.* The user files forms (which define the communication language) across the user-interface (the place or method of filing forms). In doing so the user may cause the system to react as follows:

a. To act; that is, to produce output.

b. To affect records; that is, to change its inside.

4. *Traditional Games.* The users, or players, make "moves." These moves are the communications, the possible moves are the language; they are defined by the rules of the game. The communications are often expressed by the players as symbolic acts (e.g., moving a piece on a board) rather than as written symbols. The state of the game (the conceptual model) changes in response to the moves. Other than perhaps a report of the game score, there is usually no explicit output. If this seems like an unusual way to think about games the discussion that follows may make the ideas more comfortable.

5. *Video Games.* The users, or players, make "moves" by manipulating "paddles," "joysticks," or other system appendages. The state of the game (the conceptual model) changes in response to these moves. The output is generally a color graphics display of the state of the conceptual model. Most of these games differ from traditional games in that the game state is not static between moves. It changes in response to player moves and, more significantly, on its own. These changes are continually displayed, whether or not a player makes a move.

6. *Programming Languages.* By a programming language we mean the abstract machine defined by a programming language; that is, as if the programming language were implemented as the command and machine languages of an interactive computer. For the sake of this example we treat the programming language's abstract machine as an interpreter of the programming language, whether the language is actually implemented by an interpreter or a compiler. The abstract machine permits direct execution of lines of code (the communications) in the programming language (the language). The users are the programmers.

It is not new to discuss software design in terms of behavioral specifications. It has been recently recommended that the entire software system as well as the individual modules be specified abstractly at least on some level. (See, for example, [Liskov and Berzivs, 1979].) Most approaches to software design, however, while recommending abstract specifications, also adopt the attitude that software understood in terms of components for which we write specifications is ultimately artificial and that eventually we must get down to the real code. Not only must we get down to the real code, but the real code is different in kind from the specified design. The real code does not really consist of components with an outside, an inside, and a language that defines exactly how we can affect the inside from the outside. When we get down to it, the real code is just code.

Another significant thread in software design research takes the notion of a software component more seriously. Beginning with Simula-67 [Dahl et al., 1970] and running through CLU [Liskov et al., 1977] and Smalltalk [Goldberg et al., 1983] to Modula 2 [Wirth, 1982] and Ada [U.S. Department of Defense, 1983], we find that some real programming languages have adopted the notion of a component with a well defined interface. This is the approach that we take. In fact, we consider the component to be the central construct in our notation for software design, and because we are interested in the notion of an interpreter as a design and programming language construct we shall spend a bit of time looking into it.

8.3.1 Interpreters: Objects with Insides

The distinguishing feature of interpreters is that they define an inside that is insulated from direct intervention by external forces. Only through communication can anything outside an interpreter affect the interpreter's inside. In other words, the interface between the outside and the inside is understood to be impenetrable to anything except the defined communications. Nothing outside can perform an operation directly on anything inside.* Thus an interpreter is completely protected from direct external intervention. We can only ''request'' that it perform an internal operation. It is then up to the interpreter itself to interpret and carry out this request. There always remains an interpretive interface that separates the outside from the inside and we communicate through that interface in the interpreter's language.

In insisting on a completely linguistic interface, we force a closer look at some aspects of familiar systems; for example, when we claim that a game, say checkers, is an interpreter and that the moves are the language of the game we are saying that there is a distinction between the following:

1. The physical act of moving pieces on a board.
2. The change in the game's state represented by that new configuration of pieces on the board.

When a player moves a piece he or she is communicating in the language of the game and requesting that the internal state change as the move indicates. The internal state,

---

*However, well-designed user interfaces, as in a good, full screen editor, may make us think that we have direct control.

however, does not change until the game itself (in this case the referee who acts for the game or the two players acting as referee) takes the following action:

1. Acknowledges the communication.
2. Agrees that the requested move is valid.
3. Changes the agreed state of the game.

When playing a game we can move physically any piece anywhere, but if the move is not legal according to the rules it does not count and the game's (internal) state is not changed.

This might be easier to understand if we think of the game as automated. The interface to an automated game may be an instrumented board or some other control panel on which we request moves. In an automated game it is much clearer that these requests must be expressed in some language. We ask for a move by communicating in that language, but it is not made until the system senses the request and responds by changing its internal record of the game.

In "friendly," nonautomated games we rarely differentiate between the external event (the communication) and the interpretation of the communication that actually changes the internal state. In professional games, in which more is at stake, there are almost always referees, and the distinction is clearer.

8.3.2 Programmability

Our concern here is not with games but with programming languages and with the systems that are built by using them. Programming languages are a special kind of interpreter. They have a capability that most other interpreters lack: they may be *programmed*. We understand programmability in two forms:

1. *Weak Programmability*. An interpreter is weakly programmable if it permits users to store prerecorded communications (called *programs*) and have them performed later. Some home appliances are weakly programmable; for example, we may store a set of commands for a microwave oven.

2. *Strong Programmability*. An interpreter is strongly programmable if it permits users to define new interpreters in the interpreter's conceptual model. Among the interpreters mentioned so far only programming languages are strongly programmable. We shall see that what we need for strong programmability is the ability to enhance the given interpreter's conceptual model by adding to it what we call *components*.

Traditional programming languages are not the only strongly programmable interpreters. Consider the following hierarchy of interpreters in the design of a database system.* Some of these interpreters are traditional programming languages; others

---

*Often this hierarchy is said to consist of *levels of abstraction,* in which each level of abstraction is characterized by what is known as an *abstract machine* (e.g., see Spitzen et al., 1978).

are not. All are interpreters and, except for the application system, all are strongly programmable.

   1. *Application/User Query Level.* This is the interpreter seen by end-users. The query language permits the user to interact with the system, thereby changing its internal state and causing it to produce output. As a rule these systems are not strongly programmable, but they may be weakly programmable.

   2. *Database Design System.* Imagine that the application database system is implemented by the use of a database design system. To develop the application-specific system seen by the end-user the implementers specify an appropriate data-base schema and query language. The implementers are the users of this system. They use its language to make it act like the application-specific system the end-users see; that is, they design the application database system within the conceptual model of the database design system. The database design system is strongly programmable. In fact, its main reason for existing is to permit its programmers to define new interpreters within it. In this case the new interpreters are the application database systems.

   3. *High-Level Programming Language.* Let's suppose that the database design system is written in a high-level programming language. As already noted, programming languages are themselves interpreters. The users of the interpreter defined by the programming language are the programmers who wrote the programs that define the database design system. They designed the database design system within the conceptual model of the high-level programming language. General-purpose programming languages are, of course, strongly programmable. Most programs written in them are new interpreters.

   4. *Machine Language.* The high-level programming language is implemented by a translater that translates programs in it into instructions for a particular computer. The computer is the next level interpreter. The users of this system are the translater writers who prepared the translater that makes it possible for the higher level language programmers to pretend that this computer can interpret the higher level language. Again, being a general-purpose programming language, machine language is strongly programmable. In this case the new interpreter is the high-level language that was defined within the conceptual model made available by the machine language.

   5. *Microprogramming Language.* The instruction set of this computer is implemented by the use of a microprogrammable processor, which is the next interpreter. The users are the engineers who implemented the machine language instructions in the microprogramming language. Once again, this interpreter is strongly programmable. The machine language is designed within the conceptual model defined by the microprogramming language.

   6. *Electronic Circuits.* The microprogrammable processor built as an integrated circuit forms the next interpreter. Its users are the hardware designers who chose the circuit components to build the computer. The microprogramming language is designed within the conceptual model defined by the electronic circuits.

This is an interesting interpreter. Rather than a single interpreter with a single language, it is a collection of interpreters (the various chips), each of which has its own language, enbedded in an environment that lets us join them together (the environment of printed circuit boards and wires). The language its users speak is not a written language; it is a language of electronic signals. A communication in the language is the act of presenting an electronic signal to a selected component. Each chip interprets the presence of a signal as a communication; it performs the operation it is built to perform when that signal appears.

This interpreter differs from the others we have discussed in another and more important way. It has no "central" processor; each component operates on its own. Because of this, it might be called a distributed interpreter. Yet there is no reason why the other interpreters that we have discussed could not also consist of multiple concurrent processes. We are just used to thinking about most computer systems as operating on a single computer. In fact, more and more computer systems are built with multiple processors, and even many of those built with one processor are written in computer languages that support concurrent processes; that is, as if there were multiple processors that were operating concurrently.

7. *Quantum Electronics.* The circuit components are built of physical materials. These materials are the next interpreter, a multiprocessor model similar to the preceding. Its users are the scientists and engineers who design the component parts. The language of electronic circuits is designed within the conceptual model defined by quantum electronics.

Although it is useful to understand the design of software systems as a hierarchy of interpreters, this macro model does not help a great deal in the design of most of them. The primary issue is not what the hierarchy of interpreters is (usually that is fairly obvious) but how we can construct a single, new interpreter, given an existing interpreter like a programming language; that is, how is just one interpreter constructed from the interpreter immediately below it? The rest of this chapter focuses on this question. We take the central issue in software design to be the following:

How should we design a specified, new interpreter by using the capabilities of an existing, strongly programmable interpreter; that is, a programming language?

The following, then, is our problem.

1. A description of a desired new interpreter, that is, a behavioral specification for an interpreter, is given to us as system designers. Recalling Chapter 5 and the definition of an interpreter given earlier in this section, we are given a description of the desired interpreter's specification:

   a. *Conceptual model.* How a user should understand its inside.

   b. *Language.* How a user should be able to communicate with it and how the interpreter is to respond to communications.

2. We are given a working, strongly programmable interpreter in which to build a new one.

3. Our job is to write a program in a programming language that implements the new interpreter.

The following sections explain our approach to solving of this problem. Briefly, it may be described as object- and dataflow-oriented. We show how to consider a software system as a collection of interconnected *components,* much like the collection of machines in a factory or chips on a printed circuit board. Each component is an independent operational unit; it processes data passed to it and sends the results on for further processing.

Each component itself is an interpreter and as such is protected from external intervention with its internal workings. Because of this, all communication in software systems built according to our approach is from (the outside of one) component to (the outside of another) component. Communication is never from one component to the inside of another nor from the inside of one to an external component. The following sections elaborate on this approach.

8.4   THE COMPONENT AS A PROGRAMMING LANGUAGE CONSTRUCT

Earlier we said that one of the distinguishing features of a programming language is that it provides the means of defining new interpreters. In fact, most programming languages do *not* have a construct labeled *interpreter.* In most programming languages we must use indirect means to build interpreters.

We believe that in defining a system architecture it is important to provide a rigorous means of characterizing elements of the architecture and how they are interconnected. Thus, as a stepping stone in the construction of interpreters, we define a programming language construct called the **component.** The **component** construct permits us to define simple interpreters. Like interpreters, components have two parts. One, which we call the component's *shell,* serves the same role as an interpreter's language: it mediates the interaction between the outside world and the component. The other, which we call the component's *inside,* implements the component's conceptual model.

Components are concrete objects that are used in building an interpreter. Each component, like any concrete object, is unique. Because we want to discuss components more generally, it is useful to define a more abstract notion. Thus, in addition to components, we define the notion of a *component type.* Every **component** is defined as an instance of some component type.

In creating the **component** and **component type** constructs, we use an Ada-like notation. For readers familiar with Ada the constructs are modeled closely after the Ada **task** and **task type.** Familiarity with Ada is not required; we explain our notations for readers not familiar with Ada.

8.4.1 The Component Shell

A good way to imagine a component is as a mechanism surrounded by a shell. On that shell is inscribed a set of directions which are visible to the mechanism within the shell and to external components. As such they have a dual role: they direct the internal mechanism that determines the order in which internal operations are performed: they act something like a *track* to guide the inside mechanism. In addition, at various points along the way the directions define allowable communications between the component and external components.

An analogy may be made between the directions on a component's shell and the rules of a bureaucracy that guide its functions (a bureaucracy follows its own rules*). These rules define the points at which outsiders may communicate with the bureaucracy (the forms that communications must take; e.g., you must file form X) and characterize acceptable communications (form X may be filed only after you have filed form Y).

Thus a component's directions explain how external components may communicate with the inside of a given component. Because this function is exactly the same as that played by road maps in the preceding chapter, we call a component's directions its *road map*. In addition to directing the internal operation of their components and controlling the time when external components may call on them, road maps have another function: they control the time in which their components call on other components. Every call that a component makes on another is made from the calling component's road map. Thus a road map controls calls *made* and *accepted* by its component and defines exactly how its component will interact with other components. It is because the road map is the complete definition of the component's interaction with the external world that we call it (along with the imaginary boundary on which the road map is inscribed) the component's *shell*.

We next show how component road maps may be defined as certain kinds of computer program. First a word of warning: road maps are *not* intended for standard computations. Their primary purpose is to control the operation of their components and the external access to them. In some ways they are analogous to the path expressions of [Habermann, 1979]. Because they also define computations, we express them in a language more familiar to programmers. Whereas it is true that road maps may include calls on arbitrary subprograms, hence are in some sense computationally equivalent to recursive functions (they can perform any computation), their primary intended use is to define the external interfaces of components. Strictly speaking, most road maps are neither functions (they do not return values) nor algorithms (they do not solve a problem). Most road maps are defined as infinite loops and as such they define neither functions nor algorithms.

We define road maps as programs of a certain restricted form and assume that readers are familiar with the standard control structures: **if, loop,** and **case.** We add to them an **exit** statement, a **delay** statement, a statement for **raising exceptions,** and a number of constructs for making and accepting subprogram calls, which include an

---

*Generally.

accept statement that permits a component to accept calls made to it and a **select** statement that allows a component to choose among a number of possible calls. Given these additional programming language constructs, we define a *road map* as any program that consists of any sequence of control, delay, subprogram call, and subprogram accepting statements. These sequences may be nested arbitrarily. No other statements may be included. In particular, road maps may not include assignment statements. Local program variables are permitted but only under strictly limited conditions.*

Figure 8.1 is a road map for a component that represents a simple computer terminal characterized as a standard CRT that provides programmers with the ability to send it commands. It has, say, a 24 × 80 screen. It accepts commands to insert a character at the cursor position, to backspace the cursor and erase the character backspaced over, and to position the cursor to any of the character positions.

If this terminal receives no commands during a 10-min (600-sec) interval it blanks the screen (so that no single image can be "burned into" it). Any subsequent command causes the screen to be refreshed before the command is carried out.

In addition, the terminal may be shut off by command. When a terminate command is received the terminal records that fact internally by calling the internal procedure terminate. When the internal function terminated is called it returns the value stored by terminate. When the terminal is first initialized the terminated function returns **false.**

Even without a detailed description of the road-map language we can probably imagine how the terminal described by this road map works. For completeness the following explains some of the less familiar road-map language constructs:

1. *The Exit Statement.* The **exit** statement, when executed, terminates the loop **with** which the **exit** statement appears. If loops are nested the **exit** statement terminates the innermost loop. If loops are nested and labeled and the **exit** statement refers to a label the labeled loop is terminated. The form of the **exit** statement is

exit {label}—*the* label *is optional.*

An example of the use of the **exit** statement appears in Figure 8.2.

2. *The Delay Statement.* The **delay** statement permits a component to delay its own execution for a specified period, assumed to be expressed in seconds:

delay 10;—stops the component for 10 sec.

When used in combination with other statements the **delay** statement permits components to extricate themselves from waiting forever for other components.

3. *The Raise Statement.* Components may sometimes find themselves in an impossible situation, in which they are asked to do something that they cannot do. There is nothing for them to do but to inform their callers that they cannot continue. The **raise** statement permits a component to transmit that message.

4. *The Accept Statement.* Components are similar to subprograms in that both may be called from outside to perform certain functions. Yet components and sub-

---

*Readers familiar with Ada will note that our road maps are essentially the same as the main programs in Ada tasks. We have simply elevated their importance.

```
component type Terminal_X shell is
begin
  Initialize;
  loop
    Reset;
    if not Terminated then
      loop
        select
          accept Terminate do
            Terminate;
            exit;
          end accept;
        or
          accept Move_Cursor (X, Y: Integer);
        or
          accept Insert_Character (C: Character);
        or
          accept Backspace_and_Erase;
        or
          . . .
        or
          delay 600;
          Blank_Screen;
          select
            accept Move_Cursor (X, Y: Integer);
              Refresh;
              Move_Cursor (X, Y: Integer);
            end accept;
          or
            accept Insert_Character (C: Character);
              Refresh;
              Insert_Character (C: Character);
            end accept;
          or
            . . .
          end select;
        end select;
      end loop;
    else
      exit;
    endif;
  end loop;
end;
end shell
```

Figure 8.1   A road map for a simple terminal.

programs are not identical. Subprograms are subordinate to the programs that call them; they have no means of deciding to respond to calls; whenever a subprogram is called it is executed. Components are different in that they are not subordinate to the components that call them. Components have the ability to determine whether to respond to calls. It is the **accept** statement that gives components this control. An **accept** statement is an explicit acceptance of an external call. It is only when a com-

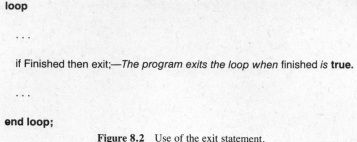

Figure 8.2   Use of the exit statement.

ponent is at an **accept** statement that it is available to receive a call from another component.

In addition to giving components control over when to accept calls, **accept** statements are like subprogram declarations:

a.   They identify the names by which the component may be called externally.

b.   They characterize the parameters that are involved in the call. They define the (data) types and the modes of the parameters. The mode of a parameter indicates whether it is used to pass information into the subprogram (**in** mode), out of the component (**out** mode), or both (**in out** mode).

c.   If the **accept** statement acts like a function it declares the data type of the returned value.

To distinguish the declarations in **accept** statements from subprogram declarations* we call the declarations embedded within **accept** statements *communication declarations*.

An **accept** statement is not just a declaration. An **accept** statement is executed like other executable statements. When a component gets to an **accept** statement it makes itself available to be called. If another component makes a call in the form that the **accept** statement declares the **accept** statement accepts the call. We use the Ada term *rendezvous* for the situation in which one component is at an **accept** statement and another component has made a call of the form declared in the **accept** statement. The caller and the component at the **accept** statement are said to *rendezvous* at the **accept** statement.

There are dangers in permitting a called component to determine when it will accept calls.

a.   When a component reaches an **accept** statement it waits there until it receives a call of the sort declared. If it never gets a call a component may wait at an **accept** statement forever. This is not really so bad as it seems. If the component is replacing a subprogram there is no difference between the component waiting at its **accept** statement and the subprogram waiting to be called.

*and from Ada task entry declarations and Ada accept statements, which they resemble even more closely (in fact they combine the functions of these two Ada statements).

b.   A greater danger develops if we consider the situation from the point of view of the calling component. If a calling component makes a call but the called component never reaches an **accept** statement that accepts such a call the calling component waits forever.

For both components there are ways to avoid getting stuck forever; they involve the **delay** statement, already discussed, and additional statements that we discuss later. First we finish our discussion of the **accept** statement.

There are two **accept** statement forms:

> **accept** communication_declaration;

and

> **accept** communication_declaration do
>   sequence_of_statements:
> **end;**

In the first form the *rendezvous* consists solely of the **accept** statement. From the point of view of the caller one action occurs: the action associated with the declared communication. The effect of this form of the **accept** statement is the following:

a.   To synchronize the calling and called components.

b.   To perform the atomic action that takes place there.

c.   To permit them to exchange values through parameters and returned values.

The second form corresponds to a sequence of actions recognizable outside the component. The sequence of statements between the **do** and the **end** delimiters are considered part of the **accept** statement. As in a subprogram call, the calling program is suspended while the called component executes the delimited sequence of statements. At the end of that sequence the two components continue separately, the called component having received any information returned to it through parameters or returned values.

Thus in both cases, after the **accept** statement finishes, the calling and the called component proceed independently. The calling component continues as it would after a completed subprogram call; the called component continues with whatever follows the **accept** statement.

In both forms of the **accept** statement the **communication declaration** is simply a standard subprogram declaration; for example:

> **procedure** procedure_name(parameter_declarations);

or

> **function** function_name(parameter_declarations) **return** value_type;

5.   *The Select Statement and the **When** Condition Construct.*   It is frequently useful to allow a component to wait simultaneously for a number of different calls; for example, we may want to develop a component that serves as a trigonometric function library to provide the capability of performing any of the trigonometric functions. This component would have to be able to accept any of number of different requests, for example, for sin, cos, tan, without knowing ahead of time which will be requested next. If the component used a simple **accept** statement that statement would have to declare which of the possible calls the component was accepting. If one of the other calls was made it could not be answered. The **select** statement provides the needed flexibility. It permits a component to provide a number of **accept** statements in parallel so that any of a number of calls may be accepted. The form of the **select** statement is

> **select**
> > select_alternative
> **or**
> > select_alternative
> **or**
> > . . .
> **else**
> > sequence_of_statements
> **end select.**

There may be an arbitrary number, but at least two select_alternatives. The **else** part is optional. Each of the select alternatives may be a **delay** statement (see above) followed by a sequence of statements or a guarded or unguarded **accept** statement. A guarded **accept** statement is preceded by a condition, cued by the keyword **when.** An example of a guarded **accept** statement follows:

> **when** Ready **accept** Go(Parameter: Type)

This guarded accept statement will accept the call go only when the Boolean variable ready has the value **true.**

When the component reaches a **select** statement it proceeds as follows:

a. It determines the *open* alternatives. These are the alternatives that have no **when** condition or have **true when** conditions.

b. If a call is waiting for any of these **accept** statements it is executed, after which the component continues with the statement that follows the **select** statement. The determination of the **accept** statement to perform, that is, which of the waiting calls to answer, is made arbitrarily.

c. If there are no open select alternatives or none of the select alternatives has calls waiting a number of subalternatives are available:

  (1) If there is an else part the component executes the sequence of statements in the else part.

  (2) If one of the open **select** alternatives is a **delay** statement, the component waits at the **select** statement for the duration specified in the **delay** statement. Again, there are subalternatives. If none of the open **accept** statements is called during that period the program executes the sequence of statements after the **delay** statement. If one of the **accept** statements is called during that period it is performed instead of the se-

quence of statements after the **delay** statement. In both cases the program then continues with the statement after the **select** statement.

(3) If neither an **else** part nor a **delay** statement occurs the component waits at the **select** statement until one of the open select alternatives is called, if ever.

It is illegal for an **else** part and a **delay** statement to be present in a single **select** statement; by definition these alternatives are mutually exclusive.

6. *Call Statements.* Three kinds of **call** statement may appear in road maps—two explicit and one implicit. The calls may be made to an operation within the component or to an external component.

a. *Explicit calls to components nested within the component's interior.* One of the primary functions of a component's road map is to call for the performance of an operation defined within the interior of that component. Normally this occurs in response to a call from an exterior component. The road map accepts the external call and passes it on to the internal mechanism that performs the service. This occurs when one of the sequence of statements in an **accept** statement is a call to a component **nested** within the component called.

b. *Implicit calls to components nested in the component: truncated* **accept** statements. Recall that an **accept** statement may be written without a *do* part. Any truncated **accept** statement is assumed to have an implicit *do* part which consists of a single statement that calls the operation within the component's interior whose name and parameter structure is the same as that specified in the communication declaration of the **accept** statement; that is, the call is just *passed through* the component's shell. The component's interior *must* have this operation defined for every truncated **accept** statement. Otherwise the component is considered syntactically illegal. In this way a truncated **accept** statement acts as a relay point by passing on external communications but only when the component is ready to accept them; that is, when the component reaches the point in the road map at which the truncated **accept** statement is located. Other than these two ways that operations in the component's interior may be called from its own road map, no access to anything in a component's interior is permitted from outside. Thus no access is permitted to a component's interior except through the component's shell as permitted by the component's road map.

c. *Explicit calls to* **accept** *statements in other components.* A road map in one component's shell may call a communication declaration in some other component's shell. Because components are not permitted to call one another from their own interiors, it is only through calls from their road maps that components may effect other components. A component whose road map includes no calls to external components is said to be **self-contained.**

Just as **accept** statements may be wrapped within **select** statements that have select alternatives, **else** parts, and time-out provisions, calls may also be wrapped in similarly constructed **select** statements. In this way components may protect themselves from calling other components that may not answer. The rules for **select** statements constraining calls are identical to those containing **accept** statements, except, of course, that calls appear instead of **accept** statements. As a simple example consider the following:

```
select
    f(X);
or
    delay 5;
end select;
```

This shows a call that will be made if the call is concluded within 5 sec. After the call is completed or if the call is not concluded within 5 sec, the road map goes on to the next sequential statement. Both internal and external calls may be wrapped within **select** statements.

Because road maps are intended strictly to control the order in which components operate, they have little need for local variables. When they are used local variables function solely to facilitate communication between the inside of a component and the external world. Thus no way is provided to declare local variables explicitly in road maps. But because they are convenient in certain situations local variables may be declared implicitly in three ways:

1. As formal parameters in the communication declarations of **accept** statements.
2. As **out** parameters in statements that make calls.
3. As **for** loop indices.

In all cases the variable's **type** is known from context and the variable's scope extends to the end of the statement in which the implicit declaration appears.

8.4.2   The Inside

Because the conceptual model of a **component** is an abstraction, it is represented only informally (e.g., as comments) and is not actually a part of the programming language construct. Ultimately it would be desirable to have a formal language to represent conceptual models. The appendix provides a sketch of one possible approach to such a language. We do not pursue this formality here. For now all we require is that conceptual models be expressed with care and rigor.

The conceptual model is *implemented* by elements inside the component. The actual inside of a component is nothing more or less than a self-contained collection of other components; that is, the components inside some other component do not access any components outside the containing component. In effect, this says that a component's shell cuts off all visibility in both directions: nothing outside the component can access anything inside the component and nothing inside the component can access anything outside the component. All communications between components inside a component and components outside a component must be mediated by the containing component's road map.

This is complete information hiding. Nothing outside a component can affect anything inside the component except as a result of an explicit call accepted by the component's road map; nothing inside a component can affect anything outside the component at all; and the component itself can affect external components only through calls made by its road map.

EXERCISES

1. Characterize each of the following as an interpreter. Define its conceptual model and write its road map:
   a. An automatic door as in a supermarket.
   b. A toaster. Treat the untoasted bread as an *in* parameter and the toast as an *out* parameter.
   c. The game of tic tac toe.
   d. The game of checkers.
   e. A television that can receive only one channel. Draw the road map that characterizes how the television receives signals from the television station and transforms them into pictures. (You may ignore sound.) Assume that television signals are received in units that correspond to pixels. This should be a simple road map. You are not showing the internal electrical design of a television.
   f. A television that can receive a number of channels. Add a second (a user) road map to the road map of the preceding exercise. Be sure to extend the conceptual model accordingly.
   g. A simplified model of a university. Assume that the operations are being admitted, filing a program of study that, when completed, will satisfy the requirements for a degree, changing a program of study, registering for courses, getting grades in courses, and graduating.
2. Reexpress in the formal language of road maps the informal road maps that you drew in exercises following section 5.4.

8.5 COMPONENTS AS SYSTEM BUILDING BLOCKS

We now show how the **component** construct can be used in building application systems. We examine various elements traditionally used to build systems and show that all may be defined as components. This means that the component construct is the *only* building block needed. We will then have shown how a large application system (which, if it has a simple enough user-interface, may also be a component) may be built by combining a number of components.

8.5.1   Object-Oriented Programming: Objects and Object Types

The approach we take in building systems is generally referred to as *object-oriented* [Goldberg et al., 1983]. This means that everything that might be considered a *thing* in the design of a system is treated as if it had a separate existence as an independent object. Under this view pure values or pure operations without some sort of embodiment do not exist. Everything is treated in some sense as a concrete object; that is, as an entity. Eventually, in defining basic data types we will find the need to distinguish between objects and values and that disembodied values must themselves be defined. For now, however, we will ignore values and deal only with objects.

We should not be too concerned that this approach differs from the more familiar ones. The object-oriented approach permits us to develop an X-ray-like picture of any software system and to see the conceptual objects that are lurking underneath the skin of the programming language.

It is interesting that the concreteness of object orientation forces abstraction, for just as we found in the chapter on requirements that entities are not useful without entity types, objects are not useful without similar classification abstractions. If everything is an object then, unless we have categories in terms of which to group these objects, each object must be dealt with individually. If, for example, we treated each integer uniquely we would not know what each one had in common with other integers. This certainly will not do. We want, for example, to be able to add two arbitrary integers with the same add operation and not have to treat the addition 2 + 3 differently from the addition 1 + 4. To define this generality we need to be able to speak in terms of a general category of integers in terms of which a general add operation may be defined. Therefore object orientation requires us to deal with the components of a system as objects and to define abstractions for classes of those objects; that is, to define object types.

We have found it useful to group object types into general categories that reflect the four basic kinds of component:

1. *Data Types, Data Structures, and Storage Units.*   These are generally the biggest and smallest system components. The data types categorize those objects that serve the roles of program variables. Storage units categorize those objects that play the roles of permanent storage such as files and databases. Data structures characterize those objects for which the structure rather than the content is most important.

2. *Operations.*   These components are the functions and function libraries.

3. *Transducers.*   These components transform data from one form to another.

4. *Drivers.*   These components direct and control other components.

It is important to note that these categories are based on the interaction of the components in them with other system components in terms of control and dataflow. The categories are *not* an attempt to categorize functionality. Although the various categories do lend themselves to certain kinds of functions (e.g., databases tend to be built as storage units and mathematical functions tend to be built as operations), we shall also see that we can define components with the same basic functionality in multiple categories (e.g., we could define a component as we would a database but one that fits the structure of a transducer).

8.5.2   Data Types and Data Objects

We use the term *data type* in the standard programming language sense. A *data type* is a category of *things* or values that may exist within a system. *Data objects* are the *things* in the data-type categories. For the most part our data types correspond to **types** in Pascal, Ada, or other modern programming languages and our data objects correspond to values or program variables; that is, things that have values.

The best way to understand data objects is to think of them as special kinds of entity—entities that are defined in the chapter on requirements. The only difference is that data objects exist within a software system, whereas entities exist in the world in general. Similarly, data types classify data objects in the same way that entity types classify entities. Examples of data types are *integer* and *character*. Examples of data objects are 37, which is a data object of a data-type *integer,* and A, which is a data object of a data-type *character*.

Note that these definitions exclude, for example, *person,* from being a data type. No person can really be inside a computer program; only information about people can be entered in a computer program. On the other hand, *message* may be a data type because messages may be stored inside computers. This suggests that whenever we use the name of an entity type to name a data type we should be clear about whether the actual entities are inside the system or whether the system contains only information about those entities, which can be a data type.

Data types are characterized by their attributes in the same way that entity types are characterized by theirs. It is most convenient to define attributes of a data type in terms of *operations* that are assumed to be associated with elements of that data type; for example, if an attribute is a measure or other static characteristic of a data object, for example, length (of a message), the operation that returns the value of that attribute may serve as its definition.

Some data-type attributes reflect capabilities rather than measures or other values; for example, one attribute of any *integer* is that it may be transformed into its successor *integer*. Thus we may define an operation *successor* that is assumed to be associated with each integer data object, as if each integer had a little button on it labeled *successor*. When an integer's successor button is pushed the integer is transformed into the successor integer.

Note how the idea that data objects have built-in operations is consistent with our component orientation. We should consider each data object as a component encapsulated within a protective shell that permits only certain operations to be performed. The allowable operations are those defined by the data type to which the data object belongs. Imagine, for example, that the protective shell of each integer permits the standard integer arithmetic operations to be performed on that integer. If A is an integer we may, for example, add another integer, B. The effect is that the object A will become the object A + B. Similarly, we may subtract another integer from it, multiply another integer by it, and divide another integer into it. Each of these operations has A as an implicit parameter and the other integer as an explicit parameter.

If this seems a bit different from our accustomed approach to integers consider a simple, four-function hand calculator. These devices are similar to the objects just discussed. A hand calculator has an internal value and a collection of arithmetic operations that permit that value to be changed. We use the calculator by providing a parameter and pressing one of its operation buttons. The internal value is the second parameter.

Because the operations for integers are defined for all integers, they are contained in the definition of integer as a data type. Figure 8.3 shows how the road map of this integer data type might look.

We have defined the data-type *integer* by displaying the shell of an *integer* **component** type. A number of other points are worth noting about the example:

1. It is natural for the road map of a data-type component to include an endless loop. Whenever an object of that type exists, that object is (presumably) performing an operation or available to **accept** a request for another operation. The object never commits suicide. As we shall see, nearly all components have road maps with endless loops.

```
component type Integer is
  loop
    select
      accept Add(B : INTEGER);
          —*Adds B to this data object.
    or
      accept Subtract(B: INTEGER);
          —Subtracts B from this data object.
    or
      accept ':=' (B : INTEGER);
          —Sets this data object to be B
          —This is simply the assignment operation.
    or
      accept Value return INTEGER;
          —Makes and returns a copy this object.
    or
          .
          .—other primitive integer operations.
          .
    end select
  end loop
end Integer;
```

Figure 8.3   Integer type shell.

*We adapt the Ada convention about comments. They begin with a dash and end at the end of the line.

2. The : = and value operations deserve further discussion. We put that off until later when we define a data structure that serves as a schematic definition for all enumeration types.

Programs may make use of the services provided by a data type:

1. Declaring objects within their own scopes of that type.
2. Performing the operations defined for those types on those objects.

For example, the program in Figure 8.4 declares local data objects I1 and I2 of **type** *integer* and then uses the defined *integer* operation Add. The line.
    I1.Add(I2)
adds I2 to I1, changing I1.

Normally we would write I1 := I1 + I2 instead of I1.Add(I2), which is still allowable. It requires only the definition of an additional + operation. We are not proposing that programmers change from a familiar notation to one that is unfamiliar; we are only showing what operations actually underly most programs when considered from an object-oriented point of view.

Data Structures and Component Skeletons

Data structures may be called higher level data types. They are generally the means for building structured collections of objects in which the following applies:

1. The objects structured are of a single type.
2. The actual type is usually not relevant.

Just as data types have associated operations, so have data structures, generally for inserting objects into or removing objects from the structure. There may also be operations for transversing the data structure. Examples are arrays, lists, files, graphs, and queues. For a more intuitive discussion of data structures see the chapter on behavioral specifications.

Because the type of elements contained in a data structure is not relevant and, in fact, because we want the same data structure for all possible different element types

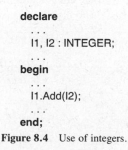

```
declare
    . . .
    I1, I2 : INTEGER;
    . . .
begin
    . . .
    I1.Add(I2);
    . . .
end;
```

Figure 8.4   Use of integers.

we introduce the notion of a component-type skeleton.* A *component-type skeleton* is, as the name suggests, a skeleton from which a component type may be built. We use component-type skeletons to define data structures as well as other constructions that are similarly abstracted from component types. For now we use data structures as an example to explore component-type skeletons.

For concreteness we consider a stack, a particularly familiar data structure, as an example. A stack is a sequence of elements that may be accessed from one end only, generally called the *top* of the stack. Intuitively, a stack is anything that is accessed on a last-in/first-out basis. To define stacks and still be careful about types we must define a different stack data type for each type of element to be contained in the stack; for example, a stack of characters or a stack of integers. Yet all stacks have the same operations defined for them:

1. A new element may be added to the stack. The element is said to be pushed onto the stack.

2. A copy of the first (top) element of the stack may be retrieved. The top of the stack is retrieved.

3. The first (top) element of the stack may be discarded. The stack is said to be popped. It would be wasteful to have to repeat ourselves if we wanted to define a stack of characters and a stack of integers. Component-type skeletons provide a way of expressing what is common among all stacks.

We shall give three component-type skeleton examples. First, in Figure 8.5 we show an example of a component-type skeleton for a stack. After that we present a component-type skeleton for enumeration types. In the section on storage units we present a file data structure.

The component-type skeleton looks like a component-type except that the first line includes a parameter. The parameter(s) in component-type skeletons indicate the piece(s) (in this case just one piece) that are required to turn the skeleton into a component type. In this case the parameter is Element_Type. Element_Type in the main part of the component-type skeleton is the element contained in the stack. What we are saying is that to make this component-type skeleton into a component type we must name an actual component type to replace Element_Type, which is not the name of any type.

Given a component-type definition of a data type, such as the integer data type in Figure 8.3, all we need to create an integer data object is to declare an instance of that component. In component-type skeletons two steps are required to create concrete data objects:

1. *Complete* the component-type skeleton definition to form a definition for a stack of a particular element. Define, for example, a Stack_of_Characters or

---

*This notion corresponds closely to a **generic** in Ada.

```
component type skeleton Stack(Element_Type : Component_Type)is
  loop
    select
      accept Push(Element : Element_Type);
    or
      accept Top return : Element_Type;
    or
      accept Pop;
    end select;
  end loop;
end Enumeration_Type;
```

Figure 8.5   A stack data structure.

a Stack_of_Integers component type.* The first step occurs completely in the world of component definitions: we create one component-type definition as a special case of a component-type skeleton definition. The following creates a Stack_of_Integers component definition as a special case of the Stack component definition above.

component type Stack_of_Integers **is** Stack(Integer)

This says that a Stack_of_Integers is a Stack with Integer substituted for Element-Type.

2. *Instantiate* a concrete object from the new component-type definition; for example, create a concrete [†] Stack of Integers from the Stack_of_Integers definition. This is done with a standard declaration:

Stack_1 : Stack_of_Integers;

An Enumeration_Type Data Structure

As a further example of component-type skeletons, we present a skeleton for enumeration types. To do so we must examine the issue of *values* in software.

A *value* is a numerical or discrete measure or expression of some property or attribute. Thus values, like entities, belong to the real world, but just as real world entities are generally not contained within computers (only references to them are actually inside the computer) neither are values. Yet values, as we shall see, are the essence of enumeration types. Therefore the first issue we must face is how to deal with values.

---

*In Ada terminology this is called "instantiating" the generic declaration. This is not our meaning of instantiating. In ada we instantiate a generic declaration into a standard declaration, which must then be used in declaring an object. We use the term *instantiation* only when referring to the creation of a concrete object.

†To the extent that any software abstraction within a computer system is concrete.

Fortunately the values for most properties or attributes may be listed in what we call a value set or the set of values that the property or attribute may have; for example,

value set grades is (A, B, C, D, F);

is the value set for grades in academia. According to this approach, every property or attribute is associated with a value that contains the values measured by that property or attribute.

Ideally, every value set should be associated with some property or attribute, but some value sets are used so frequently that they have taken on a life of their own; for example, we are perfectly comfortable discussing the integers as a value set without specifying exactly what is being counted. We all understand that integers refer to the values $(0, 1, 2, \ldots, -1, -2, \ldots)$. Thus we are accustomed to specifying value sets without necessarily mentioning the attribute or property whose value they represent. Although there may be dangers in doing so, we accept this common practice and do not insist that every time we specify a value set that we must also name a property or attribute for it.

Many of the value sets with which we deal in computations are totally ordered; that is, like the integers, given any two values in the value set, one value may be said to be *less than* the other. Value sets that are not naturally ordered [e.g., the value set of Boolean values (True, False)] may have an arbitrary total order imposed on them without doing them any damage.

Also, all value sets with which computers can deal are finite—even "real" numbers as they are treated in computations. Thus all value sets may be treated as if they were both finite and totally ordered. In other words, any value set with which we can deal in a computer can be expressed as a list of values; that is, they may be enumerated.

An enumeration data type is a data type whose objects are understood to represent values; for example, the integer data type defines a class of objects, each of which is understood to be capable of representing values from the value set of the integers. An integer data object can represent arbitrary integers and the integers that it represents may differ from one time to another. At any time, however, an integer data object represents exactly one integer.

Because all value sets may be organized as finite lists, it seems reasonable to imagine that all enumeration data types should have something in common; that is, they should all be similar to the integer data type we have defined. In fact, all enumeration data objects are similar:

1. They represent values from a defined value set.
2. They provide access to the values they represent.
3. They may have their values changed.
4. They provide access to the total ordering of the value set whose values they represent.

In saying this, we are really saying that every enumeration data type is really a special case of a simple data structure: the data structure that stores one value and provides storage and retrieval access to that value. In addition, the stored value derives from a given, finite, totally ordered set of values. Figure 8.6 shows an enumeration type data structure.

The listed operations are defined as follows:

': = '	Sets the value of this object to the value of the parameter.
Value	Returns a copy of this object.
' = '	Returns **true** if the value of the parameter is equal to that of this object; false otherwise.
'<'	Returns **true** if the value of the parameter is less than that of this object; false otherwise.
. . .	Similarly for the other relational operations.
Succ	Returns an object whose value is next in rank order, that is, next in the value set list, to this object's value.
Pred	Returns an object whose value is previous in rank order to this object's value.

```
component type skeleton Enumeration_Type(Values : Value_Set; Type : Type) is
  loop
    select
      accept ': = '(Object : Type);
    or
      accept Value return Type;
    or
      accept ' = '(Object : Type) return Boolean;
    or
      accept '<'(Object : Type) return Boolean;
    or
      accept . . . —Other relational operations such as >, < =, etc.
    or
      accept Succ(Object : Type);
    or
      accept Pred(Object : Type);
    or
      accept Pos(Object : Type) return Integer;
    or
      accept Val(N: Integer);
    or
      accept First(Object : Type) return Integer;
    or
      accept Last(N : Integer);
    end select;
  end loop;
end Enumeration_Type;
```

Figure 8.6 A generic data structure for enumeration types.

Pos   Returns the rank, that is, the numeric position in the value set list, of this
            object's value.
Val   Returns an object whose value is in the nth position in order in the value
            set list.
First   Returns an object whose value is first in the value set list.
Last   Returns an object whose value is last in the value set list.

Note that this specification implies that every object from an enumeration data type has built into it knowledge of the type's value set. In particular, it "knows" the values that follow and precede it in the list, the values that are first and last and, in fact, in any position in the list. For this to be possible the value set itself must be built into the component. We do this when we build a particular data type from this skeleton. We complete this data structure and define a data type by associating the value set of the desired data type with the data structure. The value set is shown as a parameter to the type. It is called Values.

In presenting this general enumeration type data structure, we have *finessed* the problem of values instead of solving it. We cannot show the inside of the component Enumeration_Type because it cannot be expressed. We must assume that it is primitive. There simply is no mechanism for dealing with pure values.

Given this component-type skeleton, any particular enumeration type may be created as a special case. Figure 8.7 shows a definition for the data type Color.

> **value set** Colors **is** (Red, Green, Blue, . . .);
> **component type** Color **is** Enumeration_Type(Colors, Color);

Figure 8.7   An enumeration data type for Color.

To define the component type Color we must do two things:

1. Define the value set for the type Color.
2. Create a color data type as a special case of our general Enumeration_Type. The instances of that specialized type, that is, its data objects, will have values from that collection.

In writing the line

> **value set** Color **is** (Red, Green, Blue, . . .),

we are accomplishing our first objective by defining the possible values that objects of type *Color* may have; that is, defining the value set for the data type *Color*.

We accomplish the second objective by defining a data type *Color* to be an Enumeration_Type with Type replaced by *Color* and the value set Colors replacing Values.

In making this definition, we are thus attributing to the **type** *Color* the same operations that are defined for all Enumeration_Types, but in this case they operate on objects with values from the **value set Color.**

Specialization

As we have indicated integers are also an enumeration type. Their arithmetic operations however, are defined, whereas those of the enumeration-type skeleton are not. How and when are the arithmetic operations defined?

The answer is simply that to define the *integer* data type we must not only complete the enumeration type skeleton but also specialize it by adding additional operations. In general, we may specialize any skeleton by adding to it operations that apply when that skeleton is completed in certain ways but not in others. A complete theory of specialization requires that the ways in which a skeleton may be completed be themselves partially ordered. This partial order defines what is known as a type hierarchy. Given this hierarchy, we can define operations to be included in all components created from the skeleton for all types less than (according to the partial ordering) some given type in the hierarchy. Although we do not continue to discuss specialization here, it is a powerful architectural design technique [Ingalls, 1978].

Storage Unit Types and Storage Units

To understand storage units is really to understand how they differ from data objects. Data objects and storage units look alike but are used differently. In particular, they play different roles in system architecture.

Storage units
1. Storage units appear as components in the dataflow diagram of a system.
2. Storage units may be accessed asynchronously by multiple components and must protect themselves from conflicting accesses.
3. A database is a typical storage unit.

Data objects
1. If data objects appear in a dataflow diagram they appear only as data that passes between components.
2. Data objects are accessed only by one component at a time and need not protect themselves from conflicting accesses.
3. A program variable is a typical data object.*

Like a data object, a storage unit has a set of defined operations and, like a data object, the inside of a storage unit may change when its operations are performed. Unless we can establish that it definitely does allow for multiple accesses there is no way of determining whether a component is a storage unit or a data object just by examining its structure. Because they look the same, we group storage units together with data objects in a single component class. Nonetheless, the two are differentiated by their *use* in system architecture.

---

*This implies that *shared variables* should be considered storage units and not data objects.

Storage unit types classify storage units in the same way that data types classify data objects.

The File Storage Unit

As an example of a storage unit type we consider the sequential *file*. In fact, sequential files exemplify storage unit types and data structures.

A sequential file is a sequential data structure of variable length. Elements may be written to or read from any existing position. In addition, the length of the structure may be extended or truncated arbitrarily. A ''current position'' and an implicit ''pointer'' point to the current position. Only one user may manipulate a file at a time, although different users may be expected to manipulate the same file at different times.

A sequential file data structure is defined in Figure 8.8. Like the Stack component-type skeleton this component-type skeleton has a parameter. As in the Stack component type, the parameter is the type of element/contained in the data structure. We define files in this way because, like a data structure, a sequential file is independent of the actual type of element that it contains.

Files are storage units (rather than data objects) because they have a permanence that most data objects lack. Storage units (in general and files in particular) are frequently accessed by multiple components. Because storage units (in general and files in particular) may change as a result of being accessed, it is important that they regulate the order in which these accesses occur. As the file road map shows, only one ''user'' is allowed access to a file at a time. A user must be identified on Opening a file and on each access to it. Only the user who Opens a file is permitted further access to it. Only that user may Close the file. Only after a file is Closed may some other user Open it again. To be complete this definition includes a time-out condition that stipulates that if a file is neither accessed nor Closed for a certain period of time it Closes automatically.

A Lexical Analyzer as a Storage Unit

Another example of a familiar system element that can be formulated as a storage unit is the lexical analyzer of a parser. (We show later that lexical analyzers may also be formulated as transducers.) The lexical analyzer has the job of accepting characters in an input stream and gathering them into tokens that are then parsed by a parser. Figure 8.9 is a definition of a lexical analyzer.

This storage unit is called by an input character classifying component and a parser. The input component reads characters, classifies them as digits, alphabetics, punctuation characters, or space and passes them on to the lexical analyzer. The parser calls the lexical analyzer whenever it is ready for a new token. This version of a lexical analyzer is completely passive. Other versions can be more active. This storage unit differs from the file in that the elements that are put in are not the same as the elements that are taken out.

```
component type skeleton File(Element_Type) : is
  loop
    accept Open(U : User_ID);
        —Makes the file available to this user and prevents its
        —use by other users. Defines U as the current user.
    loop
      select
        accept Close(U : User_ID) do
          if not Current_User(U)
            raise Illegal_User_Exception;
          else
            Close;
            exit; —Exit the inner loop.
          endif;
          —Makes the file available to other users.
      or
          accept End_Of_File(U : User_Id) return Boolean; do
          (similar illegal user test)
          —Returns true if the implicit pointer is at the
          —end of the file; returns false otherwise.
      or
          accept Read(E : out Element_Type; U : User_Id); do
          (similar illegal user test)
          —Reads and returns the element at the current position
          —in the file. In addition, the pointer is advanced.
      or
          accept Rewind(U : User_Id); do
          (similar illegal user test)
          —The file pointer is reset to the first position.
      or
          accept Write(E : Element_Type; U : User_Id); do
          (similar illegal user test)
          —E replaces the element at the current file position;
          —the pointer is advanced. If at the end of the file
          —a new position is created before E is written.
      or
          accept Write_End_Of_File(U : User_Id); do
          (similar illegal user test)
          —The file is terminated at the current position.
      or
        delay <some time> do
          Close;—If no action within <some time> close the file.
          exit;
        end;
      end select;
    end loop;
  end loop;
end File;
```

Figure 8.8   A sequential file data structure.

```
component type Lexical_Analyzer is
  loop
    select
      when not Buffer_Full =>
        accept Alphabetic_Character(C : Character);
      or
        when not Buffer_Full =>
          accept Digit(D : Digit);
      or
        when not Buffer_Full =>
          accept Punctuation_Character(P : Punctuation←Character);
      or
        when not Buffer_Full =>
          accept Space;
      or
        . . . etc.
      or
        when Token_Available =>
          accept Get_Token(out T : Token);
      end select;
    end loop;
end Lexical_Analyzer;
```

Figure 8.9 A lexical analyzer.

EXERCISES

1. Define a component type String. You may pattern it after the File component
    type skeleton, except that there is no parameter. The string elements are always
    characters. Allow the following as additional operations:

    a. The insertion of one string into another at the current position.
    b. Searching a string forward or backward for an instance of another string.
    c. Moving the current position n characters forward or backward in the string.
    d. Setting a marker in the string.
    e. Deletion of everything between the current position and the marker.
    f. Making a copy of everything between the current position and the marker
        and returning it as a string.

2. Let

    component type skeleton Record(Fields : Names;
                                        Field_Types : Types) **is**
    end Record;

    be a record (as in Pascal) component-type skeleton. It has no operations de-
    fined because the only operations defined on records read and write the field
    contents and the fields are not yet defined. Let

    type Name = **record** First, Last : String **end;**

    be a record in Pascal. Complete and specialize the Record skeleton to create a
    Name component type. It should have the property that, given a Name data

object, the defined operations will allow us to read and write its First and Last names. Assume that a String data type is already defined.

Define a table (data structure) component-type skeleton. Do not define a current position. Therefore an important issue will be how to refer to rows. Assume that the rows themselves are records (all of one type), as defined in the preceding exercise. Include operations to complete the following:

a. Insert a new row into the table.

b. Delete a row from the table.

c. Create and return a new table with one column deleted.

d. Determine whether a specified row is in the table.

e. Delete all rows in the table that satisfy (do not satisfy) some particular condition.

f. Return a row, if there are any, from the table that satisfies a given condition. On subsequent calls to the same operations return other rows that satisfy the same condition. Perhaps this should be defined in two operations—one to establish the condition and the second to return in sequence the rows that satisfy it.

g. Return the name of the data type from which the elements of a column are (guaranteed to be) drawn.

3. Define a set data structure component skeleton.

4. Define a multiset data structure component skeleton.

5. Define a tree data structure component skeleton.

6. Define a graph data structure component skeleton.

7. Define a counter data type component.

8. Which of the interpreters that you defined in the exercises following section 8.4 are data types? Data structures? Storage units?

9. Define time as a data base. Time is (apparently) best understood as intervals rather than points. Because any imagined point in time can really be understood as an interval (if you look closely enough at it), it is best to forget about points entirely and work exclusively with a calculus of intervals. Given this approach, the data objects will be the intervals. As operations on your data type, define the following interval relations: comes before, contains, equals, finishes, meets, overlaps the start of, and starts. Also define the inverse relations: follows, is contained in, etc. (See [Allen, 1983], for a discussion of this approach to time.)

10. Extend your time data type to include "wildcards"; for example: "Jan *, 85" means every day in January in 1985, and "*, 1, 85" means the first of every month in 1985. Define any additional relations that you need.

11. Define common time terms, such as seconds, minutes, hours, the days of the week, and the months of the year.

12. Define an appointment book storage unit. Include operations to schedule and cancel appointments, and determine what, if anything, is scheduled for a given time. Allow for the possibility of scheduling repeating engagements, such as a class every Tuesday and Thursday during the term or a department meeting on the first Friday of every month.

8.5.3 Operations and Processors

For most programmers operations are probably the most familiar of all the component categories. In general, operations correspond to subprograms (**procedures** and **functions**) in the familiar programming languages. An *operation* defines a mapping from input to effects; it is an abstract definition of an (atomic) unit of action.

As demonstrated, it was primarily in their built-in operations (i.e., the operations that made up their definitions) that we characterized data types and storage units. Frequently the operations initially built into a data type are not enough. We wish to define additional operations; for example, we may have a Float data type that includes the basic arithmetic operations. We may want to define a square-root function to extend that set of operations. These new operations are not directly associated with the original data types or data structures; they exist separately.

Operations may manifest their effects in two ways:

1. By modifying one or more of their parameters.*
2. By returning a value as a result.†

Operations, as we usually understand them in programming languages, are abstractions; they are defined as *plans* rather than as concrete objects. The plan by which an operation is to be carried out is called an *algorithm*. To include operations in our object-oriented approach we must distinguish between an operation's abstract algorithm, that is, its plan and the *thing* that performs that plan.

We imagine that operations are performed by what we call *processors*. Given an operation, a processor is a concrete instance of that operation's algorithm. Thus operations are to processors as data types are to data objects. The typical subprograms that programmers write are, for us, component-type definitions; that is, the plans. They are operations; they are not processors. Processors are created whenever an operation is executed. Thus operations are component-type definitions and processors are instances of those component types. As we said in our earlier discussion, we provide no means of defining objects of any sort directly. This includes processors. In our approach operations from which processors may be instantiated are all we can define.

As a component, an operation looks just like any other component: it has a **shell** and an internal part. In general, an operation's **shell** will protect the operation from invalid request. (This parallels the function of shells in other components). The inside of the operation will perform the algorithm that achieves the effect promised by the operation. In some cases the shell will also perform part of the algorithm. (As we have said, it is possible to express any computation in the shell language.) Figure 8.10 is the road map of a square-root operation.

---

*Normally this operation would be a **procedure** and the parameter would be declared an **out** parameter or equivalent.
†Normally this operation would be a **function**.

```
component type Sqrt is
loop
   accept Sqrt(X: Float) return Float do
   if X < 0 then raise Imaginary_Result;
   else return Internal_Sqrt(X);
   end if;
end loop;
Imaginary_Result : exception;
end Sqrt:
```

Figure 8.10 A road map for a square root operation.

Like all operations this one is defined as a **component type.** The instances of the type will be the processors that are created to perform it. This approach differs from the one that most programming languages appear to take. In most programming languages when we declare a procedure or a function we *seem* to be creating a concrete object, not a definition. We choose instead to make our operations definitions rather than objects to clarify an ambiguity found in many programming languages and to help emphasize the distinction between the definition of components and the construction of programs.

In Fortran and some earlier programming languages changes made internal to a subprogram during one execution are still there when that subprogram is executed again. In languages of this sort we are, in fact, *not* defining a type when we define a subprogram. We are defining an actual concrete component. This subprogram cannot be instantiated a second time because it wasn't "instantiated" a first time from a type definition. The original definition *is* the concrete object and the original no longer exists after it has been executed once.*

In most modern programming languages† all subprogram definitions, that is, definitions of **procedures** and **functions,** are really subprogram *type* definitions. Whenever we execute one of these subprograms we imagine that we are making a copy of the subprogram definition and executing the copy—which vanishes when it completes its execution. Any changes made internal to the subprogram during execution also vanish when the subprogram terminates.‡ Thus a subprogram definition is really a type definition that is instantiated each time the subprogram is called. Unfortunately, even in these modern programming languages we write **function** this or **subprogram** that rather than **function type** this or **subprogram type** that.

It is to make the distinction between definitions and objects completely clear that we insist on calling operations component types. Of course, operations are a special

---

*It was only later that these languages allowed for the possibility of subprogram libraries from which a subprogram could be *copied* many times. A subprogram written for and stored in a subprogram library should be labeled a subprogram type, but that distinction was never made.

†As well as any language with a compiler that produces a reentrant code.

‡We consider subprograms with **own** variables, or the equivalent, to be in a different class. They are not operations in our sense.

kind of component type: their conceptual model does not change from use to use. Nonetheless, they are best thought of as component types.

A number of points should be made in regard to the square-root component:

1. *Exceptions.* When called it (i.e., the processor instantiated from it) first checks to determine whether the number whose square root it is to find is negative. If so, it raises an **exception** because there is no real square root of a negative number. The caller's program must have a handler for the **exception.** If the number is not negative it finds and returns the square root.* It is important to be clear about the **exceptions** that a component may raise. Any component that calls this component must be prepared to handle this exception or be willing to lose control of the computation.

2. *Operations Required on the Parameters.* In testing to see if X is less than 0, the square root component is really applying the *less than* operation to the data object passed as a parameter X; that is, the condition X < 0 is more accurately written X lessthan (0). Therefore the parameter X to the square root operation must have a *less than* operation defined for it.

3. *Algorithm Stepwise Refinement.* The program that actually computes the square root is called Internal_Sqrt. It is internal to the component and is not shown. The strategy of designing components by including only the top level of its algorithm in its shell and leaving the detailed levels for the interior is called *stepwise refinement.*

In general, operation component types are defined as having three important characteristics that distinguish them from other kinds of components:

1. *Unchanging Conceptual Models.* As we have indicated, no matter how many times we use the Sqrt processor and what arguments we give it, it will respond the same way the next time we access it. Because operation conceptual models do not change, any number of processors for the same operation may exist simultaneously and all may be used asynchronously and interchangeably. This, of course, is not true of data objects. If we add something to an integer data object that object will change. Because its value is different, it will respond differently from the way it would have before the add operation.

Conceptual models are important *only* when we are able to change them. If we cannot effect something there is no need to understand it; all we ever need to know about an operation is the *external* effects it will produce. Because operator conceptual models are unchanging, users need never be concerned with them. Therefore we need not provide a conceptual model for operation component types. The relationships between their inputs and outputs are all we need to specify.†

---

*We could use a similar technique in the **integer** data type to avoid dividing by 0.
†This fact is the basis of an emerging field of computer science—applicative programming. It is also important for recursive components.

2. *Self-Contained.*   Operator components are self-contained in that they do not call other components. Two factors enable us to insist on this restriction:

a.   It is not reasonable to characterize as an operation a component that calls other components that do change, even though it does not change itself. Therefore even if we permit operators to call external components the only component that an operator component might be permitted to call should be another operator.

b.   There is no reason to have an operator call an external operator rather than to have the called operator embedded within the calling operator. In fact, there is no effective difference between calling an embedded operator and an external operator. Because the called operator does not change when called, its being called cannot be of any interest to any other component in the system; it does not matter whether it is internal or external.†

3.   *All the Work Is Performed Within a Single Accept Statement.*   Operation components have exactly one **accept** statement and all the work done by the component is performed within that **accept** statement.* Figure 8.11 shows the general structure of operation components.

```
component type Subprogram is
   loop
      accept Subprogram_Signature do
         . . .
      end Subprogram_Signature;
   end loop;
end;
```

Figure 8.11   The form of an operation component.

Operation Library Components

We can generalize the notion of an operation from one operation to a collection. An *operation library component* is one that offers a collection of operations related to one another. Typically, an operation library component provides auxiliary and specialized operations for one or more data types or data structures. An example of an operation library component is a collection of statistical analysis operations. Another is the familiar collection of mathematical operations (supplied with most program-

---

†In saying this we are not constraining the actual code generation strategy and are not forcing multiple copies of the same code. Because operators have unchanging conceptual models, all instantiations of an operator in a system, even if instantiated within mutually nonintersecting components, may be implemented by a single (reentrant) piece of code.

*If desirable for some reason operation components may be written as traditional subprograms. The subprogram would be a **function** subprogram if the **accept** statement has a **return** part; it would be a **procedure** subprogram if the **accept** statement has not **return** part. We can even take this one step farther. Because the conceptual models of subprograms do not change from use to use, there is no need to hide their implementation. In the case of operation components it is reasonable to use the standard format for subprograms and to declare local variables in component shells.

```
component type Figure_Transformations is
loop
    select
        ...
        accept Reflect(in out F : Figure; P1, P2 : Point);
            —Reflects Figure F about the axis of symmetry defined
            —by a line that passes through the points P1 and P2.
    or
        accept Rotate(in out F : Figure; P1, P2 : Point; R : Float);
            —Rotates Figure F by R radians about the axis of
            —symmetry defined by a line that passes through the
            —points P1 and P2.
    or
        ...
    end select;
end loop;
end Figure_Transformations;
```

Figure 8.12   Graphics transformations.

ming languages) that includes square root and the trigonometric operations. A third example is one that perform operations on three-dimensional graphic data objects. This operation library component is defined by Figure 8.12.

EXERCISES

1. Define an operation library of list (set, string, tree) manipulation operations. These should be operations that are not defined as primitive with the data structures but are useful. An append and a reverse operation for lists are good examples. For each defined operation show the sequence of primitive (or previously defined) operations that would accomplish it. Although we have not discussed it, you may use recursion if you wish.
2. Define an operation that takes two tables and returns their relational join on a given column. The relational join of two tables is a table that contains rows that are the concatenation of the rows of the two tables overlapped at the given column. The rows in the join consist of all combinations of rows from the two tables that have the same element at the overlapping column.

8.5.4   Transducers

The preceding categories consisted of self-contained components. (Recall that a component is considered self-contained if its road map does not include calls to other components.) Recall also that by definition components are not permitted to call other components from their interiors. Thus when a data object, a storage unit, or a processor is accessed its operations affect at most the object itself and objects passed to it as parameters. Transducers and the final category, drivers, are not self-contained. Transducers differ from data objects, storage units, and processors in that their job is not just to perform isolated operations but to mediate between objects and to permit objects to affect one another.

Transducers are components; as such, they have a shell and an interior, in which way they are no different from the other categories of components. A transducer is best understood as an active pipeline: data is fed in one end, the transducer processes it, and, by feeding it to another component, pushes it out the other end. Like storage units and data objects (but unlike processors) transducers have conceptual models that may change when their operations are performed. Typically, as transducers process their streams of data, data earlier in the stream effect the processing of data later in the stream. A transducer may change its manner of functioning in response to the data that it processes.

Examples of transducers include real-time data analyzers (i.e., programs that accept streams of, say, telemetry data and produce streams of derived results), text formatters (i.e., programs that accept streams of raw text with embedded formatting commands and produce the same text stream with the formatting commands replaced by embedded control commands for some output device), and compilers' lexical analyzers (i.e., programs that accept streams of characters and produce streams of tokens).*

```
component type skeleton Buffer_Transducer(Element : Type;
                                          Consumer : Component) is
  loop
    if not Full then—Full is internal to the buffer.
      select
        accept Put(E : Element) do
          —The producer calls when it has an element ready.

          Save(E);    — Save is internal to this component.
          end;        — I saves E in the Integral storage area.
      else
        null;         — If an element is not immediately
        end select;   — available from the Producer, do nothing.
    endif;
    if not Empty then  — Empty is internal to this component.
      select
        Consumer.Put(Next_Element);
          — This calls the consumer to pass it information.
          — Next_Element is internal to this component.
          — It retrieves next available element from the
      else    —internal buffer.
        null;       —If an element cannot be passed to
        end select; —the Consumer immediately, do nothing.
    endif;
  end loop;
end Buffer_Transducer;
```

Figure 8.13   A buffer written as a transducer.

*Our earlier example of a lexical analyzer was a storage unit rather than a transducer because it did not actively pass on its output. It waited to be called before passing on a token.

As a simple example of a transducer, Figure 8.13 shows a buffer written as a transducer. We use this example because later we discuss other methods of implementing buffers. Note also that a buffer can be written as a storage unit. (See Figure 8.15). The fact that lexical analyzers and buffers can be written as storage units and transducers simply shows that similar functions can be performed by different types of component. As we pointed out earlier, our component categorization scheme characterizes components on the basis of their functioning as elements in a dataflow and control flow architecture and not on the basis of the functions that they perform.

Note that this component is defined as a skeleton and that one of the parameters identifies a component that this component calls. Not all skeleton parameters identify elements that are stored in or processed by the component.

EXERCISES

1. Rewrite as a transducer the lexical analyzer shown in Figure 8.9 as a storage unit.
2. Rewrite the buffer shown as a storage unit.
3. Define a transducer that takes two streams of integers, both of which are ordered, and merges them.
4. Rewrite this transducer as a transducer skeleton so that the types of the input streams are not initially defined. Be sure you allow for the comparison operations to be different for different input types.
5. Select a simple text formatting language and design an architecture for it as a series of transducers. Make each transducer perform a single formatting function. *Hint:* transducers earlier in the stream should perform formatting operations that are closer to the text, such as macro substitution, and transducers later in the stream should perform operations that are closer to the final output, such as pagination.

8.5.5 Drivers

Drivers* and transducers are probably more like traditional programs than any of the other types of component. Drivers are defined by the fact that they **accept** *no* communications or only single communications that start them operating. This means that drivers function purely as control for other components.

Like transducers, drivers are not self-contained; they call other components. Unlike transducers, drivers do not respond to requests from other components; they run totally under their own control. Drivers typically use their conceptual models to keep track of how other parts of a system are operating. They use that model to determine how and when to call on other components. Thus drivers are particularly useful for

---

*The use here of the term *driver* extends the familiar use of that term in referring to test drivers and peripheral device drivers.

clarifying the *control structure* of a system when that control structure is central to understanding the system.

There are four primary driver uses.

1. *As an Executive.*   If a system is best understood as an executive control that oversees, directs, and controls the other system components, that executive is a driver. Many "main" programs are executives in this sense. So are many programs called "executives" in real-time and process control systems.

2. *As an Interface Between Storage Units.*   We can write a buffer as a driver. We call it a *pump*. Although they provide the same functional capabilities, pumps and (storage unit type) buffers are exact opposites when we consider only their control and dataflow relationships to other system components. Instead of waiting to be called, a pump calls producers and consumers. If either one is ready the pump gets or puts data as appropriate. A pump, which is a driver, is defined in Figure 8.14. It has the task of activating the storage units it serves as interface and of passing information between them.

3. *As an Interaction Manager.*   Suppose that we have a menu-driven system. We could imagine that this system is controlled by a program that offers the menus to the user and, on the basis of the user's response, presents the next menu or calls the appropriate operation. This higher level control program would be a driver.

```
component type skeleton Pump(Element : Type;
                            Producer : Component;
                            Consumer : Component) is
   loop
      if not Full then — Full is internal to the pump.
         select
            Producer.Get(E);
                        — This calls the producer to get information
            Save(E);    — from it. Save is internal to the pump. It
         else           — saves E in internal storage.
            null;       — If an element is not immediately available
         end select;    — from the Producer, do nothing.
      endif;
      if not Empty then — Empty is internal to the pump.
         select
            Consumer.Put(Next_Element);
                — This calls the consumer to pass it information
                — Next_Element is an internal Pump function.
                — It retrievesthe next available element from the
         else — internal buffer.
            null; — If an element cannot be passed immediately
         end select; — to the Consumer, do nothing.
      endif;
   end loop;
end Pump:
```

Figure 8.14   A pump.

Many language processors have similar controlling components. In language processing systems there may be three major components:

a.   A storage unit that serves as a lexical analyzer. (See the lexical analyzer example in Figure 8.9.)

b.   A set of tables (also storage units) that defines the syntax of the language.

c.   A driver that calls the lexical analyzer and the syntax tables, does the parsing, and controls the overall operation of the system.

In both cases (and in similar organizations) a driver manages user-interactions by consulting predefined structures (menus or syntax tables) that describe the allowable paths that those interactions may take. We must be careful, however, if we want to make these interaction managers true drivers. They cannot accept input themselves; they must call transducers that accept input from the user.

4.   *As a Daemon.*   A daemon is a driver that, once started, continues to perform its assigned tasks without further invocations. Typical of a daemon is a component that scans a database and reports inconsistencies; that is, data that violate specified invariants. Another example of a daemon is a component that applies a particular transformation or rule to information on a global ''blackboard'' whenever the transformation or rule for which it is responsible is applicable. This sort of component is popular in certain knowledge-based systems; each piece of knowledge is represented by a daemon. Still another simple but useful example is a timer, a component that ''counts'' a requested time period and accesses some other component when that time period is over.

EXERCISES

1.   Write a simple executive for a system that monitors machines in a factory at regular intervals. You may assume that there are exactly three machines in the factory (Machine_A, Machine_B, and Machine_C) and that each machine has a component (a storage unit) that keeps track of the machine's status. Assume also that there are only two statuses: Ok and Not_Ok. If all the machines are Ok the executive should log that fact in a system-level storage unit. If one of the machines is not Ok the executive should log that fact and shut down all the machines. For shut down purposes you may assume that each machine has a transducer that controls it and that one of the operations in that transducer shuts down the machine.

2.   Rewrite the preceding executive so that it is not necessary to know ahead of time how many machines there are. The problem raised by this added complication is that of linking the executive to the various components it must call. There are two approaches to this problem:

a.   *Dynamic Linking of Components.*   You may assume that there is a storage unit that contains the names of all the machines and that it will return those names one by one. (See part f of exercise 2 in Section 8.5.2.) The executive must then communicate with components whose names are passed to it by this storage unit; the machine-specific components with which the executive communicates are not named in the executive's road map. The components are thus linked dynamically during operation. The difficulty you face in implementing this approach is that in our language we have not allowed for communication from one component to another if the name of the component that receives the communication is not built into the communicating component's road map. To provide for this communication we need a mechanism through which communication can take place indirectly; for example, a component communicates with another component whose name is contained in a variable. The exercise, then, is to define this communication mechanism and use it to solve the problem.

b. *Static Linking of Components.*   An alternative to dynamic linking is to define some mechanism by which the names of all the machines can be built into the executive. We would then define an executive skeleton that could be completed with the appropriate names. The problem is that all the skeletons that we have seen so far have had a fixed number of parameters. We must be able to pass a variable number of parameters because we do not know with how many machines the executive will have to communicate. Not only do we need to pass a variable number of parameters, but because each parameter corresponds to a machine whose status must be determined, they must somehow be used to generate calls in the executive's road map to these components. The problem is not that we need to generate calls of an unknown kind; the communications that the executive must make with these components is known ahead of time. The problem is that the actual machines with which it is to communicate in known ways is unknown. In our language we have not allowed for skeletons to be completed in this way. The exercise here, then, is to define a completion mechanism and to use it to solve the problem.

8.5.6   Data-Driven Design

Just as we adopted object-oriented design as a guiding philosophy when considering components individually, we adopt a guiding philosophy for designing architectures for systems of interacting components. That philosophy is called *data-driven design*. *Object-oriented design* tells us to treat all systems as consisting solely of components that may be considered objects; *data-driven design* tells us to organize our system of components so that the flow of data determines the order in which the components operate.* Thus a system is said to be *data driven* when its operation depends pri-

---

*Because drivers are not data driven, they violate the principle of data-driven design. Even so, we do not dismiss them; drivers are useful in certain situations.

marily on the data that are available for processing. Data-driven systems consist of components, each capable of performing its own defined operations at any given time. To determine which components will be operating at any time we must depend on the available data for processing rather than on rules that rigidly sequence the components' operations. The stereotypical components in data-driven systems are transducer components.

The best known data-driven systems are the dataflow architecture systems that consist of a network of processors (e.g., [Dennis et al., 1980], [Agerivali and Arvind, 1982]). In the dataflow paradigm a processor performs its defined operation not when some controlling processor tells it to but whenever the parameters it needs are available. Once a processor has executed, the results it produced move along the system's dataflow network to the next processor.

One of the primary objectives of dataflow design is to permit different parts of a single system to operate asynchronously and in that way to exploit the potential advantages of distributed and multiprocessing systems. Imagine a system that includes transducers that pass data to one another. A transducer is called a *consumer* of another transducer's data if it processes data produced by that other transducer, which is called a *producer*. Whenever a system consists of multiple transducer components that operate asynchronously there must be some mechanism to buffer the information as it passes from one component to another, for there is no guarantee that the consumer will be ready to receive the information when the producer is ready to send it. Thus to permit producer and consumer transducers to operate asynchronously there must be a way to buffer information produced by the producer until it is needed by the consumer. Because buffers are so central to data-driven systems we shall spend more time discussing buffers.

How should a data-driven network of transducers be organized? There are a number of apparent answers:

1. *The transducers themselves can act as buffers.* There are two possibilities:

a. *Each consumer buffers its own input.* For a consumer to act as a buffer for its own input it must always be ready to accept input whenever the producer produces output. For this to work successfully each consumer must have an internal element that is independent of the mechanism that processes the data; that is, the mechanism that accepts input must accept it and come back for more. It may not process that data as well; that is, processing the input must not be an operation in the consumer's road map. If the input mechanism did process the data the consumer might not be ready for the next input when the producer had it ready, in which case the producer would be held up and we would not have achieved our goal of decoupling the two transducers. If we adopt this structure we will really have defined a separate input-accepting buffer that precedes the actual consumer. In other words, a consumer cannot also serve as its own input buffer.

b. *Each producer buffers its own output.* For a producer to serve as a buffer for its own output it must always be available to provide that output as input to the consumer of that data. By reasoning similar to the preceding there must be a separate buffer and a producer cannot act as its own output buffer.

2. *A separate component interfaces between the two transducers.* Clearly this is the only alternative, but even here there are choices. What form should that buffer component take? There are three possibilities:

a. *The interfacing component can be a traditional buffer.* See Figure 8.15. In this case the producer and the consumer call the buffer: the buffer itself is a storage unit. A problem with this design is that it violates our data-driven paradigm. In calling the buffer, the consumer is actively *getting* its own input rather than waiting to be driven by the data as it becomes available.

b. *The interfacing component can be a pump.* See Figure 8.14. In this case the producer and the consumer are storage units and the pump is a driver. If we take this approach the pump must call both storage units with conditional calls to avoid being stuck waiting for one storage unit while the other one is waiting. A disadvantage of this approach is that the pump is not data-driven. Just the opposite; it is a control component that pumps data through the system.

c. *The interfacing component can be a transducer that acts solely as a buffer.* See Figure 8.13. This solution keeps the system totally data-driven. The producer calls the interfacing buffer-transducer which in turns calls the consumer. In true data-driven style each transducer waits to be called. Because the interfacing transducer is nearly always ready to accept a call from the producer as well as to call the consumer, the producer and consumer are decoupled. Thus whenever either one is ready it is served.

Each of these approaches is valid and each has its advantages.

1. The traditional buffer approach is simple and familiar.

2. The pump approach permits the producer and consumer components to be self-contained.

3. The interfacing transducer approach is purely data-driven.

```
component type Traditional_Buffer is
  loop
    select
      when not Full accept Put(E: Element);
    or
      when not Empty accept Get(E: Element);
    end select;
  end loop;
end Traditional_Buffer;
```

Figure 8.15 A traditional buffer.

8.5.7   Recursion and Two Strategies for Instantiating Components

In discussing component types and concrete components we did not reveal when concrete components are *instantiated* from their component-type definitions.* The problem is the following. A system in operation consists of concrete components which are instances of components types; that is, instantiated from component-type definitions. The component type definitions are not themselves part of the operational system, although the system has access to them if needed. They are stored in a library of some sort to be discussed later. How and when are the actual components created from the component types?

The following alternatives apply:

1. *Ahead of Time.*   We could determine how many instances of a particular type of component a system will need and make them all ahead of time. This is the approach traditionally taken when dealing with systems built of physical, that is, material, components; for example, when building a circuit or a building. We build a circuit by hooking together instances of each of the circuit components. More generally, this is the approach taken by most engineering disciplines when they display a "block diagram" as the design of a system. The system is actually built when each block has been instantiated and the various blocks are linked together. This is also the approach taken by dataflow computing.

2. *As Needed.*   We could make components as needed during the course of a system's operation. Interpreted physically, it seems impossible, or at least totally impractical, to make pieces of a system while the system is operating. You would only reluctantly enter a building if you knew that the building were not completely built, but that whenever you wanted to enter a room that room would be instantiated for you on the spot. Strange as it sounds physically, this is the approach taken by most programming languages. By allocating space on a stack for the local variables of a subprogram when the subprogram is called, we are, in effect, creating an instance of that subprogram when it is needed.

Except for time, space, and recursion, there is no essential difference between these two approaches and it can usually be left to the programming language system to determine which to follow. When time is critical it is best to create all the needed components ahead of time; when space is critical it is best to create components as needed.†

When we wish to define recursive components, however, additional considera-

---

*Recall that the act of creating a concrete component from a component type is called instantiating the concrete component. The concrete component is an *instance* of the component type.
†Of course, components with conceptual models that change when the component is called must be created once and then kept. This fact still does not force a decision about when that component is first created—when the system starts to operate or when the component is first called.

tions apply. A component is said to be recursive when it calls itself, directly or indirectly. A component calls itself directly when there is a call in its shell to an **accept** statement that is also in its shell. A component calls itself indirectly when there is a call in its shell to another component whose operation may lead to a call to an **accept** statement in the original component's shell; for example, A calls B which calls A before completing the **accept** statement that handled the original call from A.

Clearly, a concrete component literally cannot call itself. A component is unable to answer its own call because, in making a call, it suspends its operation until the call that it is making is complete; while suspended it is not able to answer its own or any other calls. Thus an attempt to make a recursive call, either direct or indirect, would imply an immediate deadlock. This structure cannot work because a concrete component cannot make and **accept** a call simultaneously.

Therefore to provide for recursion we need multiple copies of all components that call themselves recursively. The number of instances needed depends on the depth of the recursion, which itself is not known ahead of time. Therefore we generally cannot tell ahead of time how many instances of a component will be needed, and with a fixed, predefined number of components recursion would be impossible. For recursive components we cannot choose the make-them-all-ahead-of-time approach; we must make them as needed.

There is a second problem with recursive components: changing conceptual models. It is only because subprogram conceptual models do not change that they may be defined recursively. If a recursively defined component's conceptual model did change from use to use and that component relied on the changes it made in its conceptual model before the recursive call to be in effect in the called instance, the new instance created for the recursive call would not be a true copy of the original component type. For this reason only operation components may be defined recursively.

8.5.8 Four Views of Road Maps

As our component categorization points out, road maps may be used and understood in four ways. The differences between these four categories depends on whether they include **accept** statements or communications with external components. Thus all road maps fall into one of four categories as summarized by Figure 8.16.

Type	Accept Statements	External Calls
Data types and storage units	Yes	No
Transducers	Yes	Yes
Drivers	No	Yes
Operations	Yes	No

Figure 8.16 Types of road map.

1. *Data Objects and Storage Units.*   Data types and storage units accept requests to perform operations but they do not call on other components. Thus these road maps include **accept** statements but no communication requests.

2. *Transducers.*   Transducers accept external requests to perform operations; they may call on other components to carry them out. Road maps for such components include **accept** statements and communication requests. Beginning programmers are usually taught to write programs of this sort. These programs read inputs, call subroutines to perform computations, and produce outputs.

3. *Drivers.*   Driver components do not accept communications. They control the operation of other components.

4. *Operations.*   Operation components are traditional subprograms. Whereas operations components may call on other components, just as subprograms call on other subprograms, the called components are also operation components. Because operation components do not change when called, the called components need not be visible to other components in the system; that is no call from an operation component has a permanent effect on the called component. Thus any component called from an operation component may be hidden within the calling component, and no call from an operation component to another component need appear on an operation component's road map.

Note that this category and the first category appear to be the same in the table. They differ in that components in this category have unchanging conceptual models, whereas components in the first category (as well as those in all the other categories) have conceptual models that may change as the component is used.

We claim that data types, storage units, and transducers are more difficult components to develop than drivers and operations. We call road maps for data types, storage units, and transducers *two-sided* because in understanding them we must keep two views in mind simultaneously:

1. *The Language Defined by the Road Map.*   In building these components we are defining a language, the language that the user (i.e., the caller) of the component uses in interacting with the component. That language is defined by the structure of the component's road map. From the caller's point of view certain sequences of calls on the component are syntactically valid; others are invalid. The road map is thus a syntax diagram of the user's language. This language view is the "outside" of the shell, the side seen by the user.

2. *The Algorithm Defined by the Road Map.*   We must think about how the road map acts when considered as a program; that is how the component controlled by the road map acts. This is the "inside" of the shell, the side seen and followed by the component itself.

As we have pointed out, this notion might be easier to understand if we imagine a component as surrounded by a protective shell on which its road map is inscribed. The road map may be read from inside and outside the component. From the outside a road map is read by the component users; it tells them about the options they have to interact with the component. It functions as a guide and definition in the same way that behavioral specification road maps function as guides and definitions.

From the inside a road map is read by the component itself; it defines the rules that explain how the component is to respond to the conditions and communications it encounters. Thus the same road map has two significantly different uses, depending on which side of the shell is consulting it.

We call road maps for drivers and operations *one-sided* because we need to worry only about the algorithm aspect of their road maps. Two-sided road maps are much more difficult to write than the one-sided because we must be conscious of two views of the road map simultaneously.

As an educational corollary we recommend that beginning programming students be taught first to write data types and storage units; that is, that student programs be called by instructor-driver programs and that students write no programs that call other components or that "read" input or "write" output. By focusing initially on constructing well defined data types and storage units students may master the basic programming skills more easily.

At the same time the focus on storage units teaches students the important lesson that most coding activity is concerned with building system components to provide services to be called on by other system components. Only after they are comfortable with the idea of writing data types and storage units should they be taught to write programs that call other components. Then they should be taught to write drivers and transducers, the most complex components, last.

In all this beginning students should *never* write input or output statements. Input and output are the most complex interactions. As implemented in most contemporary programs, input and output are incompatible with most programming theories and generally lead to much confusion.

8.6   THE INTERNAL STRUCTURE OF A COMPONENT

So far we have discussed the various kinds of components. We have categorized components on the basis of their interfaces (e.g., whether they are self-contained), whether their conceptual models change with use, and how they are used in a system (e.g., whether they are used as parameters or as nodes in a dataflow network). We have not yet discussed the internal structure of components. Although this issue is less important for high-level software architecture, it is important that we face it if we are to have a complete discussion of the component construct as we have defined it. In this section we discuss component internal structures.

8.6.1   Local Objects

The insides of most components contain a number of local data objects which are instantiated from type definitions in the library, not type definitions local to the component itself. Consistent with our object orientation, we use local data objects instead of the more traditional local variables. For the most part data objects and variables serve the same function and can be used similarly; but they do differ from one another.

1. *Variables.* A variable is a name with no permanent value or object associated with it. It can be reassigned to refer to many different values or objects. When a variable is declared it exists only as a name and, unless initialized it refers to no value or object until one is assigned.

2. *Data Objects.* A data object is a thing that generally has a name, although a name is not necessary. A data object's name always refers to that data object and cannot be reassigned to another (though, like variable names, data object names are subject to visibility rules). A data object exists as an object from the start; it need not be initialized before its name refers to something.

In most cases local data objects may be used as if they were local variables, and if we are working with most traditional languages we may want to use variables because most programming languages are defined to handle variables. We should keep in mind, however, that underneath the variable declaration we are really thinking in terms of objects. In the example in Figure 8.17 Fact is a local data object, not a local variable.

```
component type Factorial is
  loop
    accept Factorial(N : Integer) return Integer do
      If N < 0 then raise Negative_Argument;
      else return Factorial_Value(N);
      endif;
    end;
  end loop;
end Factorial;

component inside Factorial is
  Fact : INTEGER;
  component Factorial_Algorithm is
    loop
      accept Factorial_Value(N : Integer) return Integer do
        if N = 0 or N = 1 then return 1;
        else
          Fact.Set(1);*
          for I := 1 .. N loop
            Fact.Multiply(I);†
          end loop;
          return Fact.Value;
        endif;
      end Factorial_Value;
    end loop;
  end Factorial_Algorithm;

end Factorial;
```

Figure 8.17 A factorial component.

*This is equivalent to Fact := 1.
†This is equivalent to Fact := Fact*I.

8.6.2 Internal Components

For every call from a component's road map to a computation to be performed inside the component there must be an internal component that accepts that call. This is as expected; a call in a component's shell is accepted and carried out by a corresponding internal component.

As an example, consider Figure 8.17, which shows a component type *Factorial* for a factorial operation. In this component's road map the input is tested for validity; if it is negative an **exception** is raised. If the argument is valid it is passed to the inside for the actual factorial computation. This is similar to the square-root component type defined earlier.

Factorial's inside has two objects: a local data object called Fact and an embedded component called Factorial_Algorithm. Factorial_Algorithm's primary purpose is to answer the Factorial_Value call from Factorial's road map and to perform the actual factorial computation. Factorial_Algorithm's road map computes the factorial by using the data object Fact as a local object. The component Factorial_Algorithm has no inside.

The entire structure in Figure 8.16 parallels a traditional subprogram. The component *Factorial* plays the role of the subprogram declaration; *Factorial*'s inside plays the role of the subprogram body; the local object Fact plays the role of a variable local to the subprogram body; and the embedded component Factorial_Algorithm plays the role of the code in the subprogram body that uses the local variable. It may seem a little strange in this case because the code part is expressed as a component that uses a data object outside itself, but if we think of the component Factorial_Algorithm and the data object Fact as internal to the containing component Factorial, which they are, the structure should seem more familiar.

To make this organization more familiar and to let us use the traditional programming language constructs we recognize the following convention. A component, such as Factorial_Algorithm which has no inside and is the only component inside the component that contains it may be identical to a traditional **begin end** block.

Given this convention and our earlier convention about writing components, the interfaces of which have single **accept** statements as a subprograms, this component can be written as a traditional function. In fact, given our other convention of using local variables for a simple conceptual model, we could construct this entire component as a single subprogram. Having gone through the exercise of developing it as a component, we now see how components, subprograms, and code blocks are related and how subprograms and code blocks are special cases of components.

8.6.3 Dataflow Within a Component

So far we saw that the inside of a component may include our versions of two rather traditional elements: local variables and subprograms. If we look carefully at the *Factorial* example we can identify the two components in its inside as a storage unit and as a driver.

1.   The component Fact is a storage unit. It is a "database" that stores a single value.

2.   The component Factorial_Algorithm is a driver. It has no internal communication declarations and it drives the changes in values in Fact.* We might call it a *blind driver* because it drives changes to Fact without ever investigating Fact's state.

These two component form a simple dataflow network. There is a dataflow path from Factorial_Algorithm to Fact along which three communications occur: Fact is Set, Multiplied, and Copied by Factorial_Algorithm. Therefore, although it is simple, the inside of Factorial displays a natural dataflow organization when its design is understood to consist of components. The insides of more complex components will normally include a larger collection of storage units, transducers, and drivers, but they will also display a natural dataflow organization.

In documenting dataflow, it is important to document the direction of the call as well as the calls that are made. Information often flows in a direction opposite to that of the call; for example, when a call is a function call, as in the call from Factorial_Algorithm to Fact_Value, the value returned moves in the opposite direction from the call. We make the following conventions about dataflow diagrams.

1.   Each dataflow path has one arrow. It shows the direction of the call(s) represented by that path. This implies that if two components call each other, an unusual situation, there would be two dataflow paths shown between them.

2.   Along each dataflow path labels identify the calls made in terms of the called communication declaration, its parameters, and the parameter modes. In case data is transferred in two directions by a single call, as is often the case for **function** calls and for calls with **out** parameters, the direction in which data actually flows may be read from the parameter modes and whether the communication declaration is a function.

Figure 8.18 shows a dataflow diagram for Factorial's component inside.

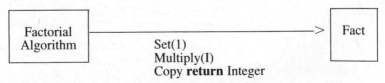

Figure 8.18   Dataflow for factorial.

*We call it a driver even though it has an **accept** statement. Its single **accept** statement simply gets it going.

8.7 THE COMPONENT LIBRARY AND THE NONOPERATIONAL COMPONENT STRUCTURES

So far we have discussed component-type definitions and concrete components. Concrete components are the operational elements in software systems as they are operating; they are the traditional operational programs, the things that do the work. Component types are definitions from which concrete components are instantiated. In addition, component-type skeletons (recall the data structures) serve as general definitions from which type definitions may be built. In the preceding sections we also discussed the various types of component, and discussed how concrete components are joined together in a dataflow network. These dataflow networks define the operational organization of software systems. In this section we discuss the structure of component type definitions; that is, the library in which component types are kept and the relationships among component-type definitions.

8.7.1 Types and Source Code Versus Objects and Object Code

As the foregoing discussion has suggested, our approach to software architecture disassociates the structure of what is traditionally called *source code* from the structure of an operational system. In those sections we discussed the structure of the operational system; in this section we discuss the structure of the source code.

As we have described them so far, components are concrete objects; each is unique. In this sense components are like physical objects, and just as it is impossible for one physical object to be in two places at the same time it is impossible for a component to be in two systems at the same time. One of the objectives of modern software engineering is to provide a way to reuse software components.

To allow for the reuse of components we must distinguish between a component and its definition. It is, of course, the component definition that is reused and not the actual component. This is really just a fancy way of saying that when we use "the same" program in two different systems it is the source code that is reused and not the linked, loaded, and relocated object code. We are simplifying here. We could use the same load module in multiple systems, but for our purposes it is simplest to suppose that programs come in just two forms: source code or linked, loaded, and relocated object code. In interpreted languages it is the allocation and assignment of storage within a system to a component's variables that is equivalent to compiling, linking, loading, and relocating a component's source code. The real distinction is between source code and an assignment of actual storage locations for variable values. Thus the distinction we are making between a component definition and the component itself is essentially the distinction between (abstract) source code and (concrete) system storage assigned for the use of source code.

What is a Definition

What is a definition of an object? An object definition is really a characterization of properties that object(s) must have if they are to satisfy the definition. Hence an object definition characterizes a class of objects. In other words, an object definition is really a characterization of an object type. Because we use source code to define components, source code is really a type definition for the class of components that can be produced from that code. This is not different from other type definitions. Most type definitions consist of source code:

type small_integer **is** 0 . . 100;

The difference is that in most type definitions the definition seems to be talking about something else. In this small_integer example the definition is talking about integers; the definition itself is not an integer. When we write the source code for a component we are used to thinking of it as ''the program'' rather than as a description of the program. In the approach we are propounding this distinction is important. The source code is a definition of the program; the program itself is the concrete storage allocated for use when running the program defined by the source code. In this section we talk about component types, that is, source programs, and the relations among them.

We never define individual components; source code defines component types only. Individual components are formed by instantiation (compilation) from component type definitions. This is not to say that our approach cannot be applied to interpretive languages. Instead of compiling source code to create a component, when dealing with interpretive languages, we simply reproduce a master copy to supply a component for use in a particular setting. For simplicity, and to highlight the difference between component type definitions and actual components, from now on we speak as if all code must be compiled before it is used.

8.7.2   System Structure Versus Component Definition Structure

In most discussions of software architecture we generally conceive of the structures of the operational system and source program as parallel to each other. Block-structured languages with their static referencing rules reflect this orientation. When building a system with such a language we are constrained to express the architecture of the running system as a transformation of the structure of the source program. This is often quite awkward [Clarke et al., 1980]; [Cormack, 1983]:

1.   To permit two subprograms nested deeply within a static hierarchy to communicate with each other we must create program variables at the level of their common parent node or add otherwise unnecessary parameters to calls of higher level programs. These variables and parameters may be irrelevant to everything else in the program; typically they are a great source of confusion.

2.   Identifying the operational program architecture with the program's static source structure leads to confusion concerning the relationship between the dataflow and control-flow structures of a program.

3. The static structure phenomena of "fan out" and "fan in" confound the principles of top-down design and stepwise refinement.

4. We do not always want program objects to come and go in exactly the same way as blocks or subprograms are entered and left in hierarchically structured languages. Most systems consist of objects with more permanence, like databases and user-interfaces. Worse, the habit of restricting our thinking to nothing but transient program elements (blocks and subprograms) frequently prevents us from even conceptualizing the structures needed. To solve this problem we resort to "common areas," global variables, or their equivalent. Often almost everything migrates to these global points of stability and they become overloaded with system details.

We eliminate these problems by separating completely the structure of a source program from that of its operational counterpart. We described the possible structure of the operational program in the preceding sections. In this section we discuss the structure of the source code. We define two source-code structures:

1. *Catalog Structure.* This is the structure in which software-component type definitions are stored. It is important for this structure to be well thought out, for any large collection of objects must be organized according to some scheme so that any particular element in the collection may be located.

2. *Definitional Dependency Structure.* This is the component type definitional hierarchy. If, for example, data type D is defined by component C_D and component P **accepts** a call that has D as the type of one of its parameters, then P is definitionally dependent on D.

Included in the definitional structure is the dependency of any component on the programming language in which it is written. We call this the *substrate* programming language. Thus these languages are also to be treated as components on which other components depend. In the next section we return to the question of the definition of programming languages in terms of other programming languages. This is our original problem: how do we build a new interpreter from a given interpreter? We now elaborate on these source-code structures.

8.7.3 Catalog Structure

We recommend a tree structure for the catalog structure of a software system. We propose that all component type definitions be kept in a single tree; and we mean **all** component type definitions!

Imagine that all the computers in the world* were joined together and that all the component definitions in these computers could be organized into a single tree struc-

---

*We are not suggesting seriously that a global tree is likely to emerge soon, but we do suggest the image to dramatize the possibilities inherent in a large library structure.

ture. The structure that we recommend for so large a tree resembles most closely the file structures available in some operating systems [Dennis and Thompson, 1974]. The tree would be organized according to some classification scheme. We suspect that, in fact, a number of different levels of organization would develop.

1. At the topmost level the tree would probably be organized politically, first by nation, then within each nation by corporation (or other organizational unit), and then perhaps by some organizational subunit. Access rights (read, modify) to subtrees at this (as well as at all) levels are the prerogative of the subtree owners. If, for security reasons, a country wished to deny external access to (parts of its) its subtree it could do so. Organizations could protect proprietary products similarly.

2. The second-level organization of the tree, within a corporation, for example, is determined by those who manage that part of it. Any number of organizational approaches are possible. Within the part of a tree assigned, say, to a software development organization the tree could be organized primarily in terms of projects and subprojects. Just as usefully, it could be organized in terms of disciplines (i.e., by the subject matter of the programs stored). Alternatively, the tree may reflect a matrix structure in which a project and discipline are contained. Finally, it may simply reflect the command structure of the organization.

3. On the next organizational level it will probably be useful to think of a node in the tree as corresponding to a more or less specialized library of programs. Each library would contain programs that are of use in its area of specialization. Some libraries may contain even more specialized sublibraries. In general, the lower we go in the tree the more specialized the subject. Some libraries may develop on higher levels; for example, national or international archives.

4. Finally, at the lowest levels there will probably be personal organizational structures, defined individually for the convenience of the individuals who own them.

In general, each node of the tree may contain any number of component type definitions and any number of references to subtrees. Again, this is similar to the file structure available in some systems in which each directory (equivalent to node of a tree) may contain any number of files and subdirectories.

Of course, given such a large tree, we would need a few simple naming conventions to prevent confusion.

1. All nodes are named.
2. All component type definitions within nodes are also named.
3. No node may contain two component type definitions of the same name, nor may a node contain two subtrees of the same name.

Any component type definition in the catalog tree may refer to any other component; that is, every component is *visible* to every other component. This differs from the standard visibility conventions in block-structured languages: only elements in the same node or in higher level nodes are visible to a element. Of course, visibility does not mean that components are executed in place in the tree. References from one component to another simply provide a means for the referencing component to acquire a *copy* of the referenced component for constructing an operational system.

Because we did not insist that all nodes in the tree have unique names (that would be out of the question), any reference to a node must somehow disambiguate among all the possible nodes with that same name. We suggest the standard approach: for identification purposes a node name may be "qualified" by the name of its parent node; the parent node may be similarly qualified; and so on. Assume, for example, that Comp_A is a component name. It is also a valid node name. If Comp_A is stored in node Library_A then Library_A.Comp_A is another valid name for Comp_A. Similarly, if Library_A is a subtree of Super_Library_A then Super_Library_A. Library_A.Comp_A is also a valid name for Comp_A. In effect, the complete name of any node is the path that leads from the root of the tree to the node.

Because the tree may be quite tall, it may be inconvenient to express the complete path at all times. To reduce this burden we establish the convention that a node may refer directly to itself and to any of its ancestor nodes. If two ancestor nodes have the same name the less distant ancestor is the one to which the name refers. (This is the same name-hiding convention found in block-structured languages.) In Figure 8.19 a reference from node I to B refers to the lower node B. For I to refer to the higher node B it must use the more complete name "A.B." For some other examples, node I may refer to node G as "C.G"; and it may refer to the two D node as "A.B.D" and "A.C.D." With this convention any node may refer to any other nodes.

The more distant in the tree two nodes are from each other, the longer the name may have to be for one to refer to the other. To alleviate the inconvenience of this name inflation we adopt another convention common in file systems. A node may have associated with it a collection of what we call *potential name prefixes*. These prefixes are to be used if a node has a name as a reference, but no node corresponding to that name can be found following the direct approach outlined. Assume that node I has "A.C" as a potential name prefix. Then a reference from node I to node D

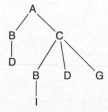

Figure 8.19   Part of a catalog tree.

applies to node A.C.D; the A.C is used as a prefix because no node D is a direct ancestor of node I.

Any node may have potential name prefixes associated with it. Assume that node I has no potential name prefixes but that node B (either one) has A.C as a potential name prefix. A reference from node I to D would again be interpreted as a reference to node A.C.D. This would occur because of the following:

1. No direct reference from node I to any node D can be found.
2. In examining the ancestors of I, B's potential name prefix of A.C leads to a valid node.

By carefully associating potential name prefixes with selected nodes we can build a network of references that encompasses useful libraries of components.

All component type definitions are kept in this catalog tree. There is no such thing as a traditional (block-structured) program that consists of a main program and nested subprograms. Each component type definition is kept separately in the tree.

There is an important consideration with respect to catalog trees: well organized access. If all component type definitions are stored in a catalog tree that tree will soon become large, and it may become quite difficult to find our way to the definitions we want. It may be easier to write our own component type definition than to find one that does the job. It is important therefore that the catalog tree be well organized; that is, that there be convenient ways of finding the component type definitions stored in it. It is these definitions that serve as reusable components and that make the component approach to software development economical. It must be easy and convenient for someone needing a certain capability to search the catalog tree for the component types that provide it.

The problem of naming, organizing, and cataloging is not new with type definitions. Consider the card catalogue of a large library, a catalogue of a large mail-order supplier, or the yellow pages of the telephone book. All have the problem of organizing references to make finding the object wanted easy. We have nothing new to add about cataloging; we simply recommend that those in charge of organizing and cataloging a collection of component type definitions take the job seriously.

8.7.4 Definitional Dependency Structure

In all but the simplest systems components are defined in terms of other components. This definitional structure manifests itself in three ways:

1. *Skeletal Completion.* A component type A is dependent on another component type B if A is built as a completion of the skeleton B. A number of examples have been made.
2. *Definitional Dependency.* There are two kinds of definitional dependency:
   a. A component type A is definitionally dependent on another component type B if A accepts a parameter of type B; for example, the square-root component is dependent on the component that defines floating point numbers.

Note that most components are definitionally dependent on their substrate programming language, the language in which they are written, as well as on other components. A component does not depend definitionally on the programming language in which it is written if it does not refer to any of the primitive data-types built into that language.

b. A component type A is definitionally dependent on another component type B if A includes an instance of B internally. An example is shown in the Factorial component. It is dependent on the Factorial_Algorithm component because an instance of the latter component is embedded in it. More generally, imagine that we are defining an operation component type and that that operation component uses other operation components to perform part of its calculation. Here, for example, we are creating a component for a mathematical function:

$$f(x) = g(x) \times h(x)$$

The operation component that computes $f(x)$ calls the components that compute $g(x)$ and $h(x)$. Recall from our earlier discussion of operation components that they never make external calls. Thus the $g(x)$ and $h(x)$ components must be embedded in the $f(x)$ component. This is accomplished simply by declaring instances of the $g(x)$ and $h(x)$ component-type definitions as local, concrete components with the $f(x)$ component.

Note that "local variables" within components are themselves components. Therefore this category of dependency includes embedded storage units as well as what would traditionally be considered local variable types.

3. *Computational Dependency.* A component type A is computationally dependent on another component type B if A calls B from its road map.

Note that most components are computationally dependent on their substrate programming languages. A component is not computationally dependent on its substrate programming language only if it does not use any of the primitive operations built into that language.

The definitional dependencies among components define a directed acyclic graph (DAG)* structure that is separate and distinct from and independent of the catalog-tree structure. It is important to keep track of this DAG structure so that if component definitions are changed the components that depend on them may also be changed.

8.7.5   Programming Language Enhancements and System Structures

In this section we consider systems that are built by incremental enhancements of programming languages. In particular, we consider how a programming language is enhanced by the definition of new component types. Although these enhancements do not create a new interpreter, our original problem, they do lay the groundwork for it.

---

*A DAG is a directed graph with no cycles; that is, there is no path that returns to its starting point. DAGs are "almost" trees. They fail to be trees because some of their branches come together instead of fanning out.

Consider a collection of component-type definitions that are written in the substrate programming language. Because they are written in a programming language, they are usable by other components written in that language; and for the sake of this example suppose that they provide a simple computer-graphics capability.

These graphics component-type definitions define new data types, perhaps *Point* and *Figure,* along with operations for manipulating data objects of those types. They make it possible to create and manipulate data objects with types that are not already defined. Thus the added component-type definitions are an *enhancement* to the substrate programming language; that is, once these new types exist in the component library it is as if the substrate programming language had them built into it originally; new components can use them just as easily as they can use the language's built-in types.

Now consider an enhancement to these graphics component-types that adds, for example, a hidden line-elimination operation and capabilities for specifying surface textures, reflectances, and light sources. This is an enhancement to the previous, more primitive set of graphics capabilities and it, too, is an enhancement of the substrate programming language. We can imagine adding more and more graphics capabilities, perhaps to support animation or some other application area, and thus defining other enhancements to the substrate programming language. It is easy to see that we may add arbitrarily many type definitions to a substrate programming language. Each provides an incremental enhancement of capabilities in a traditional bottom-up structure.

By examining this collection of definitions top-down, according to its dependency structure we can imagine that the graphics type definitions are defined in terms of other type definitions; that is, the hidden line-elimination capability is defined in terms of the *Point* and *Figure* component types. Let's also imagine that the *Figure* type was built in terms of linked lists. Thus below the *Figure* type in the definition dependency structure is a linked-list type.*

Now imagine that the graphics capabilities are to form part of some larger system, say an image-analysis and regeneration system. In implementing the image-analysis type definitions, we presumably develop subordinate types, just as the linked-list type definition was developed for the graphics type definition; for example, in image analysis we deal typically with arrays of intensity values to which various array transformations are applied. Type definitions for dealing with intensity arrays would therefore seem appropriate.

As we have pointed out, a DAG characterizes this a support structure. The root† of the DAG is the substrate programming language. It represents the primitive types and operations. Branches grow from that root upward toward increasingly specialized and sophisticated definitions. Figure 8.20 is a simplified version of a DAG.

---

*In discussing the definitional dependency structure, that is, that figures are defined by using linked-lists, are we not violating the principle of information hiding that insists that the design of a component should not be revealed? The answer is that we are not. We are *not* giving the programmer of components that use the figure type access to the linked-list structure used in implementing figures; the only operations allowed on figures are those defined in the figure component type.

†The root is shown at the bottom of the figure, even though most computer-related trees are traditionally shown with their roots at the top.

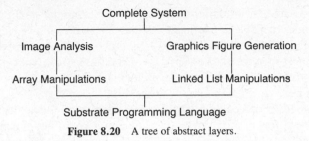

Figure 8.20   A tree of abstract layers.

Traditionally we would document this design by showing only the three levels closest to the top and by representing it as a tree with the root at the top. This approaches would suggest two subsystems, the image-analysis subsystem and the graphics subsystem, each of which is composed of its own internal subsystems.

Our approach suggests another‡ way of looking at the structure in which it is clear that the lower abstract layers, the array-manipulation capabilities, the linked-list capabilities, and the substrate-programming-language capabilities are not restricted for use in only the specific, higher level definitions shown in the diagram; they are part of the overall design environment and are available for other uses as well. We can easily imagine that in a large system many uses will occur for both general array-manipulation and linked-list capabilities. There is nothing to be gained by thinking of these capabilities as restricted to one use each. Certainly we do not want to ignore the programming language in which the system is written and pretend that it is not part of the design!

On the other hand, it is worth repeating that in representing the components in this bottom-up way we are *not* implying that the internal structure of the data objects manipulated by the image-analysis and graphics type definitions are freely available to users of those definitions. As far as these users are concerned, the image-analysis type definitions deal with data objects of (presumably) type Image, and only certain specific operations defined by the image-component type may be performed on data objects of type Image. As we said earlier, similar restrictions hold for the data objects manipulated by the graphic type definitions.

In summary, we have seen that we may enhance a given programming language by adding component type definitions do form a bottom-up structure (a DAG) in which higher level component type definitions provide more complex, more sophisticated, and generally more application-specific capabilities than lower level component type definitions. All of these definitions are equally available in the component-catalog tree for use by other programmers.

8.7.6   Cataloging Type Definitions During Development

There is a problem that must be faced by software development projects that is not of concern in other cataloging; that is, cataloging during development. Many new

‡Dare we say "bottom-up"?

type definitions are created during software development and often change as the software becomes more clearly defined. For that reason it would be inappropriate to put draft versions of type definitions into a public library. Therefore a software-development project should maintain one or more libraries of draft type definitions until those definitions become fixed. They may be maintained as restricted access subtrees of the catalog tree.

In development efforts of sufficient size and complexity, the number of different type definitions simultaneously under development may get out of hand. It may be convenient to divide the development work into separate and independent projects and for each project to maintain its own development library. Only when a component-type definition is fixed should it be transferred to a permanent library to be available to everyone.

This approach presents the risk of building duplicate copies of the same type definitions. Imagine, for example, that two separate subprojects of a larger project need linked-list capabilities. If there were a linked-list definition in a permanent library, acceptable for both uses, it could be adopted, but if there were no predefined definition of this kind and it became necessary to develop one along with the rest of the system problems might be presented.

Initially we could develop and duplicate a single linked-list type definition and put it into the working libraries of both subprojects; but to keep the two versions the same during development we would have to ensure that every change to one version would be duplicated in the other, a difficult task for large and complex systems. More likely, as the system develops (and inevitably changes), we would decide to let the two versions drift apart. One would end up with two type definitions approximately but not exactly the same.

Thus it is only by weighing the costs of configuration management and programming redundancy that we can determine how much uniformity should be required across a large project. Thus it becomes a practical management rather than a theoretical software architectural issue.

8.7.7 Creating an Operational System from Component Types

Once we have a collection of component type definitions in a component type library, how are they turned into an operational system? Because this book is not concerned primarily with the structure of operating systems, their compilers, linkers, and loaders, we have not pursued this topic in depth, but to make the preceding discussion more real we shall spend a brief time exploring this issue.

Suppose we are dealing with a compiled language.* The simplest (conceptual) way to get an operational system is "compile and run." We ask the compiler to compile some component, to load the compiled result, and to begin its execution. If the requested component refers to any other components they are compiled at the same time and loaded with the original component. According to this scheme, all

---

*If not, then in the following discussion all references to the compiled form of a component should be read as the source form.

components are stored in their source form in the catalog tree. The process of compiling and executing them treats the catalog tree as a read-only library.

In a slightly more sophisticated version of this approach we store components in the catalog tree in their source and compiled forms. When a program is compiled references to other components are left open, although the reference form (i.e., reference name and number and types of parameter) is retained. When the compiled component is needed for an operational system a copy of the compiled form is linked with the other components to form the operational system. Any components to which this component refers are included. It must be determined during the linking process that components that fill references fit the specifications defined by those references.

8.7.8   Summary

In our approach to software architecture we have made the following distinctions:

1.   *What the Components Are.*   We found that there are two general types of software component.

a.   *Concrete components.*   These are the components that exist while a system is operating, that is, the "machines" as they operate in the factory. The categories of components are:

i) data objects (such as parameters) and storage units (such as databases),

ii) processors (i.e., instances of subprograms as they carry out operations),

iii) transducers (such as user interfaces), and

iv) system drivers (such as "main" programs).

These are the objects, the "things" that we normally think of as existing within the conceptual model of an interpreter. We have used the terms *concrete component* and *object* as synonomous terms for these "things."

b.   *Component type definitions.*   These are abstract definitions of the concrete components, something like the plans for the "machines." It is these abstract type definitions that are found in program libraries. Every concrete component *must* be defined by a type definition; that is, there cannot be a concrete component without an abstract definition. This is similar to saying that every entity must be a member of some entity type. It is these component type definitions that make up the bulk of most software text; they are intended to be reusable. We have used the terms *component type, type definition,* and *component type definition* synonomously for these definitions. In addition we have defined the notion of a component-type *skeleton* as an outline of a component type that may be completed to form a component type by adding required parameters.

2.   *How the Components Are Organized.*   We showed how these two classes of components fit together:

a.   *Operational organization of concrete components.*   In operation a system of concrete components is organized as a dataflow structure, which means that the design of an operational system is best understood as a more or less fixed network of components with data flowing among them. It also means that system design is best expressed as a dataflow structure rather than, for example, a hierarchical structure.

b.   *Organization of component type definitions.*   The component type defini-
tions are organized as a traditional definitional hierarchy: the more complex types are defined in terms of the less complex types. Type definitions, how-ever, are *not* nested; they are all equally visible and available in a general catalog tree. To be useful, of course, the catalog tree, like any catalog, should itself be carefully organized. The organization of the catalog tree facilitates rather than restricts access to components.

Together these ideas form the basis for software architecture.

8.8   PROGRAMMING LANGUAGES, INTERPRETERS, AND DEPENDENCY TREES

In the preceding sections we discussed the nature of components, the types of com-ponents, and the static and operational structures by which components may be or-ganized. We suggested that components are the appropriate organizational unit for the design of software architecture, and we proposed a catalog tree as appropriate for component storage. We hope that this discussion has shed some light on the gen-eral principles of software design. Yet it has been a relatively general discussion. We did not answer the question we set for ourselves earlier. How can a given pro-grammable interpreter, that is, a programming language, be transformed into a new interpreter? How can we as programmers, that is, as users of an existing interpreter (programming language), create a new interpreter for users who are not programmers of that programming language. Nothing we have said so far has told us specifically how to build a new interpreter from a given interpreter. In this section we address this issue.

In answering that question, we shall also be discussing how, in general, program-ming languages fit into the component-dependency structure we just defined. We have already noted that components often depend (in the sense defined in the pre-ceding section) on the programming language in which they are written. Program-ming languages themselves are components in the catalog tree. What happens, then, when we use one programming language, or language A, to define another program-ming language, or language B? Clearly language B is dependent on language A, and programs written in language B are dependent on language B. Are programs written in language B dependent on language A? In this section we also address this issue.

We should also note that, powerful as our notion of *component* is, it does not tell us how to build interpreters. A component is an artifact of a programming language. Like subprograms, modules, and other structural units, components provide pro-grammers the means of building objects that they as programmers will use in their work. The objects created with these constructs exist within the environment of the containing programming language. They are accessed by the use of constructs defined in that language. They are not, in general, directly accessible by external users. Our problem is to create an interpreter that is directly accessible from *outside* the programming language in which it is written.

As we said in our earlier, more general discussion of interpreters, accessing an interpreter is the same as providing it with input. Thus to be more concrete, to create an interpreter that is externally accessible is to build means for users to provide *input* to the interpreter.* To deal with this problem we must first understand exactly what we mean by input or external accessibility. This question is not easy to answer.

In what circumstances can something access or provide input to something else? We know of one case. Within the environment of a programming language, one component can access another component. Is that sort of access different from the access that occurs when a user accesses an interpreter; for example, when a person accesses a computer program via a terminal? In both cases there is some communication between the accessor and accessee. In both cases the following questions (and partial answers) are relevant:

Question	How does the accessor send (i.e., express, externalize, make known) its communication? How is that communication received (i.e., accepted, internalized, perceived) by the thing being accessed?
Answer	In describing interpreters and components, we have imagined a "magical" interface through which they send and receive communications.
Question	Once expressed by the accessor, how is the accessor's communication carried from the accessor to the thing being accessed?
Answer	In a programming language environment it is the programming language "machine" that carries the communication from accessing component to accessed component.

Thus we have really said nothing about the *mechanism* by which communication actually occurs. We are not alone; no description of any programming language tells us anything about *how* a program really calls a subprogram. On the level of the calling program it is magic (some would say *primitive* or *built-in*); it just happens.

More generally, we may wonder how communication takes place between any two objects in any environment. Apparently there is no solution. If we think seriously about this issue it appears to be insolvable. Communication involves contact between two objects, but if two objects are truly distinct how can contact occur? The physicist's solution is to say that there are no distinct objects; everything is part of a single field. Objects are local concentrations of the field. This idea is realized in a computing context by having objects embedded in environments defined by programming languages or systems. If we look closely, the objects are not really isolated individuals; they are local concentrations of the programming environment.

_____

*Of course, we must also be concerned about output, but it is really the user's ability to reach the interpreter rather than the interpreter's ability to respond to the user that concerns us here.

Here is our paradox. Communication, we apparently observe, is possible, but we have no idea how to create a means of implementing it. Yet to build a new interpreter we must provide a way for the intended user to communicate with that interpreter. On the one hand, we cannot create an environment for communication; on the other, we know that these environments exist. In particular, means are provided to communicate with the interpreter with which we start—the substrate programming language. Therefore, because we cannot create a communication environment and one must be given to us to use, our only option is to *adapt* the given communication environment to the needs of the interpreter that we are building.

This amounts to defining an input language. An input language defines a mapping from the input capabilities provided by the substrate programming language (e.g., characters, numbers, strings, or whatever the substrate language defines as input units) to the input capabilities to be provided by the interpreter we are building; that is, the communication declarations in our new interpreter. In general, the language maps from concrete sequences (or other structured organizations of input units) in the substrate language to single, although structured, input units in the new interpreter's language.*·† As an example, consider again the collection of graphics components discussed earlier. Recall that we assumed the definition of graphics component types that were accessible to programmers in the given programming language. We did not explain how those graphics capabilities could be made available to nonprogrammers. To do so we must build a new graphics *interpreter* by writing a user-level graphics language that provides access to the capabilities defined by those components. That new language would presumably offer the same graphics data types and operations previously available only to programmers in the substrate programming language, but it would offer those capabilities to nonprogrammers in a graphics language.

By defining a language to provide access to a collection of capabilities we isolate those capabilities from the type definitions that support them and the substrate programming language. The users of our supposed graphics language have access neither to the linked-list capabilities nor to the substrate programming language. Unlike programmers, users of this graphics language are restricted to graphics; they do *not* have the use of any other parts of the original interpreter. Therefore in defining a new language we make the new capabilities, and those alone, available to the newly defined class of users who use that language.

In general, this one-level language mapping approach will work and the remainder of this section discusses how to do it. For some applications, however, we need

---

*The distinction between the *syntax* of the allowable input units in the substrate language and the *structure* of the communication declarations in the new interpreter is the same as that made between *concrete* and *abstract* syntax [McCall et al., 1977].

†Admittedly, there are some very simple interpreters, such as some home appliances, whose input language is trivially derived from the input language of their substrate interpreters. The input languages of simple home appliances are button pushes or knob twists that correspond directly to the input language of the substrate interpreter (electrical devices) on which the appliances are built. Most software systems are too complex to have communications in the substrate language correspond to communications in the language of the interpreter.

even more. We need to develop new input means that are not available in the substrate programming language; for example, if our graphics interpreter is to process images it must have the physical means of acquiring the images. These physical means may not exist in the original programming language. For another example various new user-input devices like joy sticks, "mouse" devices, and touch sensitive panels and screens are increasingly popular. Yet typically they generate input in forms not originally defined in the substrate language; there is no predefined input statement in any standard language that accepts input from a joy stick or a mouse.

The solution, of course, is to move lower in the interpreter hierarchy. Because we are always talking about physical phenomena (at least we don't have to deal with messages from ghosts as input!), there must be some level, that is, some substrate interpreter, in which the needed input capabilities are already defined. Our job then is to work our way down to that level, define the input capabilities we need, and then work our way back up the interpreter hierarchy, defining for each new interpreter new input capabilities, until eventually there is a definition for input from the desired source in the language in which we want to work.

In any case, whether the interpreter we are building will use new or traditional input devices, our problem is to translate input capabilities available in a given programming language into input capabilities for users of the interpreter we are building. In this section we examine how to build such translators.

8.8.1   The Emergence of a New Interpreter: User Interfaces

A component's language is defined by the **accept** statements in its road map. In general, there are no limitations on **accept** statements; any subprogram declaration may appear in an **accept** statement. A component can call another component simply by including in its road map a call that matches an **accept** statement in the component it wishes to call.

As far as a calling component is concerned, calling another component is a single unit of action. It does not consist of, say, spelling out the name of the communication declaration to be called and the parameters to be passed as arguments. The entire call is expressed as a single unit—even though the call may indeed consist of a component name and a number of parameters. A call is thus a single, although perhaps structured, object.

We run into trouble if we wish to let a user communicate with a component in the same manner. Users cannot express arbitrary calls as single actions. The only single actions that a user can express are those that correspond to keys or buttons on whatever communication device is made available. As we pointed out earlier, many interpreters are built with special communication panels that correspond to the interpreter's language. Consider any home appliance as an example; in addition, most arcade games, many devices with embedded computers (such as aircraft), and other (often expensive) computer-based systems have special control panels built as input devices. Yet for the most part it is not feasible to build a special communication panel for every new interpreter.

The alternative is to use an existing communication device and to build a translator that translates between that device and the language of the new interpreter. This gets us back to the issue of **accept** statements. An existing input device corresponds to communications built into the substrate programming language in which the new interpreter is to be built. We face the following problem:

> *We would like to make available to users the accept statements in the new interpreter's road map, but the only accept statements that we can, in fact, provide are those that correspond to keys on a keyboard.*

The job, then, is to build a set of translators that translates between keys on the keyboard and the accept statements in the new interpreter. The part of a system that does the translation is often called a *user interface*. (It is also called a *front end* because it is the end of the system that the user sees.)

We build user interfaces by using language transducers. A *language transducer* (in the sense defined in the preceding section) accepts communications in one language, its own, and transmits them in another, the language of the other component(s) with which it communicates. In fact, any transducer component may be considered a language transducer because all transducers accept communications in their own language and transmit communications in the language of the components that they call. The only difference between a language transducer and transducers in general is that in dealing with language transducers the focus is primarily linguistic.

To simplify our discussion we assume that the substrate programming language recognizes the ASCII character set exactly; that is, its input statements can read nothing but one character at a time. This simplification is not too strong because even analoglike user input devices such as joysticks and ''mice'' provide digitized, key-stroke-like input when read at the substrate programming language level. Because the user expresses these characters by hitting keys on a terminal, we refer to the input language as consisting of keystrokes. Thus these keystrokes define the external events to which the user interface must respond; that is, they correspond to the **accept** statements that can be made directly available to the user.

The question then is how do we translate from keystrokes to communication declarations? In making the translation, we should be aware of the following possible difficulties:

1. *Too Many Operations.* The new interpreter sometimes has so many operations that it would be unmanageable to have a separate key for each. Except in the simplest cases, there is no direct translation between keystrokes and communications.

2. *Arguments.* Many operations have arguments. Generally, there are more possible values for arguments than there are operations. It would be even more difficult to assign a separate key for each argument.

3. *Syntactic Structure.* Because user communications must often be entered as *sequences* of button pushes, they must be parsed into an operation and one or more arguments. This abstract syntactic structure defines an abstract organization. The input provided by the user has an organization in time (the

sequence of keystrokes) and often an organization in space (when the user interface provides a means for the user to fill out forms). The language transducer must map these concrete temporal and spacial organizations of keystrokes into the interpreter's abstract syntax [McCarthy, 1966].

User interfaces have typically solved these problems with the following three classes of techniques:

1. *Spelling and Parsing.*   Communications are entered as a sequence of symbols *put together* to form tokens that spell operation and argument names and *parsed* into a structure that reflects a valid communication.

Once a sequence of symbols has been analyzed a communication may be synthesized and passed on. This is the approach taken by command-driven systems.

There are two difficulties in the spelling and parsing approach:

a.   The user may not remember the names or syntactic structures to be used.

b.   Even if the user remembers the names and syntactic structures, mechanical mistakes (i.e., accidentally striking the wrong key), spelling mistakes, or syntactic mistakes may be made.

2. *Menus.*   Lists of options are presented to the user who chooses among them. In effect, menus create software defined keys. Once the user makes a choice, an appropriate communication is constructed and passed on.

Because the options represent all the valid operations and arguments and because they are presented in the appropriate syntactic structure, this approach solves most of the problems associated with spelling and parsing. It does not, of course, solve the problem of accidentally hitting the wrong key.

But if the list of options is too long, it is not feasible to present all of them to the user; for example, if an operation requires as an argument a number between 0 and 9,999, it makes no sense to list all the possible numbers and let the user choose. Even if wished to do so, the mechanism by which the user indicated a choice might be as complex as having the user spell out the desired number directly.

3. *Structurally Cued Operations.*   In many cases the system can determine what the user wants to do by noting where the attention is focused when input is entered. We call systems that use this approach *strongly interactive*. A strongly interactive system gives the user the sense of interacting directly with the interior of the system. Because it is the system itself that provides the means of focusing on parts of the system's conceptual interior, the system can identify the point at which the user is focusing.

Full-screen editors were among the first examples. These systems permit the user to move a pointer around on a display. The user is supposed to imagine that the pointer is seeking out information inside the system. The user is also supposed to imagine that he or she has the ability to type directly onto the display. The user is led to believe that whatever is typed onto the display (perhaps replacing something that was there before or perhaps new information) is being entered directly into the system's interior. Of course, a lot of work is involved in maintaining this fiction for the user, but it does create an effective user interface.

Because no approach is perfect and the various approaches complement one another, they are frequently combined. We present a framework within which all these approaches can be integrated. We see user interfaces as consisting of the following two basic components:

1. *Button_Classifier*.   Because the only preexisting contact we are allowing ourselves to assume between the user and the new interpreter is the input capabilities of the substrate programming language, and the only input capability we are allowing ourselves to assume is the ability to accept keystrokes (more generally, button pushes), it makes sense to encapsulate that capability in a component. Thus a button classifier characterizes the preexisting interface of the substrate programming language.

2. *Communication_Editor*.   The communication editor mediates between the user, as represented by the keystroke acceptor, and the interpreter itself, as represented by one or more internal components. In a sense it serves simultaneously as emissary from the user to the interpreter and from the interpreter to the user.

8.8.2   An Example of a User Interface

In this section we present a complete architectural design for a simple, infix, four-function hand calculator. We discussed this calculator in the chapter on behavioral specifications. Refer to Figure 5.11 for the user-road map. We present it here to illustrate the techniques involved in building a user-interface.

The calculator presented has a simple conceptual model that consists of storage for a single number.* It provides the means of performing arithmetic operations with that number as one argument and some other number as the other. The other number is provided by the user with the desired arithmetic operation. In effect, the calculator is a realization of our integer data type component (see Figure 8.3), except that it deals with real numbers rather than integers.

The calculator's display is capable of displaying a number and an operation symbol. At any time the number displayed may be the following:

1. A number that the user is entering initially as a first argument to be stored in the calculator's internal storage.

2. A value that the calculator has just computed.

3. A second argument to an operation that the user has already specified.

If an operation is displayed it is the infix operation that the user entered before specifying a second argument.

The calculator (Figure 8.21) is built of four components:†

---

*For this example we ignore the details of the number; for example, what its floating point precision is.
†It is not unusual for a user-interface to be as complex as or even more complex than the interpreter for which it fronts. Here three of the four components are concerned with communications between the calculator and the user. This shouldn't be too surprising. If we consider most computers the CPU and memory chips are often a small part of the entire package.

1. *Calculator Component.* The calculator component is the main component. Its road map defines the language of the calculator as the user understands it.

For reasons that we shall explore it is more convenient to write the calculator component as a driver than as a transducer or a storage unit. As written, the calculator component is *not* data-driven. Instead of waiting to be called by the communication component when a user input is ready, it calls the communication component to give it the form of the communication it now expects.

2. *Button_Classifier.* The Button_Classifier's job is to accept button pushes by the user and to pass them on to the Communication_Editor.

This component is necessary because, as we have been saying, the only capability from the substrate programming language that we can make available to the calculator user is its ability to accept keystrokes. We package that collection of **accept** statements in the Button_Classifier.

3. *Communication_Editor Component.* The Communication_Editor component translates from the user's keystrokes to the communications defined by the calculator component. Its job is to interact with the user until the user has constructed a complete communication defined by the calculator component. It then passes that communication on to the calculator component.

Therefore in the design we are presenting the user-interface input function is performed by a combination of the Button_Classifier and Communication_Editor components.

4. *Display Component.* The Display component gives the user information. It performs output for the user interface. We assume that it has the capability to display a number and an operation symbol. User inputs are made visible on the Display as the user enters them. System outputs are also presented by putting them on the Display. In general, the number displayed will be the number on which the user is currently focusing. The operation symbol will be the operation scheduled to be performed next. (Because the calculator recognizes infix notation, the user enters the operation before entering the second argument.)

We should imagine that the visible display is actually a part of this component, that is, the user can "see into" the component. If the calculator were a traditional computer system this component would be the screen part of the user's terminal. This

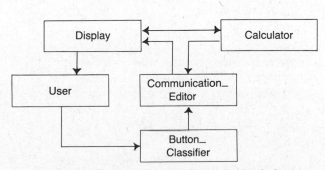

Figure 8.21 The components that form a simple calculator.

component is a storage unit; it stores the information that it displays. It is *write-only* to the system and *read-only* to the user!

Next we discuss these components in more detail.

8.8.3 Calculator Component

The calculator's road map is shown in Figure 8.22. (Of course, the lines would not be numbered in an actual program. We number them for convenience in referring to them.) This component is the core of the calculator and its road map is thought of by the user as the calculator's road map.

Although a calculator may seem to be a simple device, its road map has a number of points of interest. The following annotations are associated with the indicated lines:

Line (1)   Line (1) clears the display. The number in the Display is set to null and the operation is set to null.

The user understands the conceptual model of the calculator to consist of a number that is maintained internally. Sometimes that number is displayed in the Display; sometimes it is not. In either case that number is inside the calculator's conceptual model.

```
       component type Calculator is
(1)    Display.Clear;                    — Clears the display.
(2)    Set(0);                           — Sets the internal number to 0.
(3)    loop
(4)       Communication_Editor.
                   Communication_Request(Number, Value, Input);
(5)    Set(Input);— Set the internal number to Input.
(6)    loop
(7)       Communication_Editor.
                   Communication_Request(Operation or Operation(Number),
                                   nil,
                                   Op);
(8)       case Operation | Operation(Number)
(9)         when Equal => exit;
(10)        when Clear => Set(0);
(11)          Display.Clear;
(12)          exit;
(13)        when Plus(N) => Add(N);
(14)        when Minus(N) => Subtract(N);
(15)        when Times(N) => Multiply(N);
(16)        when Divide(N) => Divide(N);
(17)      end case;
(18)      Display.Set_Value(Value);
(19)    end loop;
(20)  end loop;
       end Calculator;
```

Figure 8.22 Road map for calculator.

Line (2)   Line (2) sets that internal number to 0.

Line (4)   Line (4) of the road map requests an input from the user. The request is made by a call on the Communication_Editor. The current value of the internal number is sent to the Communication_Editor as the default input value if the user wishes to use it. At this point the number in the display will always be the same as the internal number. Therefore the internal number is always displayed as the default.

The parameters to the call are Number, Value, Input.

Number   This is the desired data type. It is important that the Communication_Editor component know what data type is expected from the user.

Note that the entire number is returned by the Communication_Editor. We are not concerned at this level with parsing the number. That is the job of the Communication_Editor. We assume that the Communication_Editor permits the user to edit the number, albeit in a rather brute-force way. (If the user presses the clear button while entering the number the incomplete number is discarded and the user starts entering the number again.) This editing function is provided by the Communication_Editor and not by the calculator itself. It is not visible in the calculator road map.

Value   This is the default value. The calculator gives the user the option of entering a default number. The parameter Value is not a variable. It is a call to a function internal to the Calculator component which returns the current value of the number stored internally.

Input   The Communication_Editor uses the parameter Input to return the number entered by the user. In the Communication_Editor this parameter is declared as an out parameter.

Line (5)   Line (5) sets the value of the internal number to the number entered by the user. It does *not* effect what the user sees on the Display. What does the user see? As the Communication_Editor interacts with the user to accept a Number the number entered by the user becomes visible in the Display. Thus at this point the number in the Display is the number returned to the Calculator; hence it is the same as the number stored in the conceptual model.

Line (7)   Line (7) asks the user for an operation. An operation is defined syntactically as one of the tokens (Equal, Clear) or as one of the structures [Plus(N), Minus(N), Times(N), Divide(N)]. There is no default operation. We assume that while the user is entering the operation the Clear button permits the same kind of brute-force editing as earlier and that the editing is handled by the Communication_Editor and not by the Calculator. Therefore the Clear button has two meanings. It is an editing command to the Communication_Editor (ERASE THE CURRENT INCOMPLETE INPUT) and a command to the calculator (START A NEW COMPUTATION). The Communication_Editor determines which meaning is appropriate.

Notice that the Calculator asks the Communication_Editor for a possibly structured input. If the input is a request for an arithmetic operation, it is received by the Calculator as an operation with a parameter. The notation for making this request is awkward here and should be refined.

Line (8)   Depending on the user input, the Calculator selects the action to perform. If this component were written as a standard dataflow component lines (7)–(17) would appear as **accept** statements within a **select** statement.

Lines (9)–   The action taken by the calculator depends on the operation the user
(16)   enters.

Equal   The Equal operation, line (9), does nothing but exit the internal operation loop! The calculator returns to its start state with the number in the Display the same as the internal number. This seems to contradict our experience in using a calculator that suggests that the Equal operation causes the previously entered operation to be performed and the result, displayed.

In fact, pressing the Equal button causes the Communication_Editor to terminate the number that was requested the preceding time around the loop and to send it to the calculator component. It is at *that* point that the calculator component performs the requested operation and displays it in the Display.

The calculator receives that number before it is told that it was the Equal button that terminated the number. Only after performing the preceding operation does it request the next operation, which happens to be Equal.

Clear   The Clear operation, line (10), causes the calculator to clear both the Display and the internal number. It too exits the internal loop and returns the calculator to its start state.

Arithmetic   If the operation is one of the arithmetic operations
operations   the calculator performs it on the internal number

and the second argument [lines (13).(16)]. Note that we are assuming a slight extension of the standard case statement. Our case statement recognizes structures in a manner similar to unification in Prolog [Clocksil and Mellish, 1981].

Line (18)   In line (18) the result of the preceding operation is retrieved from inside and sent to the Display. The road map then returns to line (7), where the user is asked for another operation.

8.8.4 Display

Figure 8.23 shows the Display component's road map. It is quite straightforward. The Display's conceptual model provides storage of a string of characters (digits, decimal point, and minus sign) and an operation symbol.

The Display's operations provide the means of clearing the string and the displayed operation and to append characters to the right end of the string. In effect, the Display is a limited, special-purpose terminal screen.

8.8.5 A Button_Classifier

The Communication_Editor deals with conceptual units that are somewhat more general than the individual buttons on the calculator; for example it does not distinguish the digit buttons nor does it distinguish among most of the operation buttons. The Button_Classifier component stands between the actual buttons (the user's key-

```
component type Display is
  loop
    select
      accept Clear_String;
        —Clear the display of the string currently displayed.
    or
      accept Clear_Operation(Op : Operation);
        —Set the operation displayed to null.
    or
      accept Clear;
        —A combination of Clear_Operation and Clear_String.
        —This does not provide additional functionality. It is
        —provided as a convenience to users of this component.
    or
      accept Insert_Character(C : Calculator_Character)
        —Insert the Calculator_Character C at the right of the
        —current string. Other characters are pushed to the left.
    or
      accept Set_Operation(Op : Operation);
        —Set the operation displayed to Op.
    end select;
  end loop;
end Display
```

Figure 8.23 A display component.

strokes) and the Communication_Editor. It classifies the user's keystrokes for the Communication_Editor with each button push as belonging to a general category of buttons. Figure 8.24 is the Button_Classifier component's road map.

The Button_Classifier is particularly interesting in that it shows in a concrete manner the difference between traditional input and our approach. In traditional input the input receiver calls an input subprogram (such as Get) which gets the input and returns it. In our approach input is considered to be the same as any other communication. The only difference between this communication and others is that this one comes from the user, whereas others come from other components.

The Button_Classifier, as presented, satisfies the needs of an interpreter as simple as our calculator. More complex interpreters have more sophisticated needs. We discuss some of them in the following section. Here we just note that it is usually the

```
component type Button_Classifier is
loop
  select
    accept Plus do
      Communication_Editor.Operation(Plus);
    end;
  or
    accept Minus do
      Communication_Editor.Operation(Minus);
    end;
  or
    accept Times do
      Communication_Editor.Operation(Times);
    end;
  or
    accept Divide do
      Communication_Editor.Operation(Divide);
    end;
  or
    accept Clear_Button do
      Communication_Editor.Operation(Clear);
    end;
  or
    accept Equal_Button do
      Communication_Editor.Operation(Equal);
    end;
  or
    accept '0' do
      Communication_Editor.Digit(0);
  or
    accept '1' do
      Communication_Editor.Digit(1);
      . . ._Similarly for each digit.
  end select;
end loop;
end Button_Classifier;
```

Figure 8.24 A Button_Classifier for a hand calculator.

job of the Button_Classifier to serve as a buffer for user keystrokes that have not been processed further. The current Button_Classifier cannot perform that function because it is not written as a buffer. Once it receives a keystroke from the user it immediately calls the Communication_Editor to pass the keystroke on. If the Communication_Editor is not ready to accept the keystroke the Button_Classifier waits and is not available to accept additional keystrokes from the user. To make the Button_Classifier a true buffer it would have to be rewritten along the lines of the transducer buffer shown in Figure 8.13.

8.8.6   Communication_Editor

The Communication_Editor is responsible to two masters: the user and the Calculator component.

1. *To the User.*   The Communication_Editor provides the user with limited editing capabilities. By pressing the Clear button while entering input (no matter whether the input is a number or an operation) the user is requesting that the part of the input already entered be deleted and that input be started again. The Communication_Editor is responsible for performing this operation and for distinguishing this use of the Clear button from its other use as a command to the calculator, where it is a request to clear the internal storage and restart the computation.

2. *To the Calculator Component.*   The Communication_Editor is responsible for collecting user button pushes into structures that correspond to communications requested by the Calculator component. In general, there are two tasks involved here:

    a.   The Communication_Editor must gather the characters entered by the user into the tokens that form the basic elements of the communication declarations. In this case this is not difficult. In general, it may be more so.

    b.   The Communication_Editor must parse these tokens into structures that match the calculator's communication declarations. When the Calculator component calls the Communication_Editor it tells the Communication Editor what it is expecting. The Communication_Editor interacts with the user until the user has completed a communication that matches the form specified by the Communication_Editor. When the user has completed the communication the Communication_Editor returns the user's validated communication.

Figure 8.25 shows the Communication_Editor component. All the real work of this component goes on *inside* the Communication_Editor (not shown here) and not in the road map. The road map simply shows the calls the Communication_Editor is prepared to **accept** from its two masters. Note that calls from the user (through the Button_Classifier) are **accepted** while processing a call from the Calculator. Note also that the road map does not distinguish between the calls expected from the

```
component type Communication_Editor is
  loop
    accept
        Communication_Request(Comm_Type : Comm_Decl;
                            Default : Default_Description;
                            out Communication : Comm_Type));
            —This request for a communication comes from the calculator.
            —All the following communications come from the user
            —via the Button_Classifier. The Communication_Editor
            —uses these user inputs to create a communication of the
            —requested type to return to the Calculator. Note that the
            —type of the third parameter (the output parameter) is passed
            —as an input parameter, the first parameter.
        loop
          select
            accept Clear;
          or
            accept Digit(D : Digit);
                —The digit is appended to the internal number being
                —accepted. An internal flag is set so that the Display
                —will be updated.
          or
            accept Operation(Op : Operation);
                —The operation is stored internally. An internal
                —flag is set so that the Display will be updated.
          or
            accept Point;
                —The point is noted in the internal number. A flag
                —is set so that the Display will be updated.
          end select
          —After the character is processed the Communication_Editor
          —is responsible for updating or clearing the display and for
          —sending a completed communication to the Calculator component
          —if appropriate.
          if
            Display_To_Be_Cleared then
                Display.Clear;
          elsif
            Displayed_String_To_Be_Updated then
                Display.Insert_Character(Current_Character);
          elsif
            Displayed_Operation_To_Be_Updated then
                Display.Set_Operation(Current_Operation);
          elsif Data_Type_Complete then
                return Communication;
                    —Communication is a call to an internal function that
                    —retrieves the completed communication inside the
                    —Communication_Editor, where it has been constructed.
            exit;
          endif;
        end loop;
    end Communication_Request;
  loop
end Communication_Editor;
```

Figure 8.25 A Communication_Editor.

274

Button_Classifier and those expected from the Calculator. It is up to the programmer to make sure that these are kept straight.

8.8.7 A More Powerful Communication_Editor

The preceding example is a special case of a general user interface structure. The more general case is quite similar. We may imagine the same collection of components. Of course, the Display is able to display more than a single character string and a single operation symbol. Typically, it is a video display terminal, either character oriented or bit-mapped. Most important, in the general case the communication editor plays a central role. We discuss such a generalized Communication_Editor in this section.

In our prototypical system (as in the calculator) the user and the interpreter (the internal computational component(s)) interact in terms of the information presented on the Display. The Communication_Editor controls the flow of traffic back and forth between the user and the internal components. The Communication_Editor cannot ensure that the information transmitted between the user and the computational components is correct (if it could, the other components wouldn't be necessary); but what it can do is to ensure that the information is transmitted according to rules that define the type and structure of the information communicated. The Communication_Editor plays the dual role of information carrier and monitor, ensuring that the information carried fits specified formats.

It is important to be clear about the various roles played by the internal components, the Communication_Editor, and the Display. The Display actually presents the information to the user; the Communication_Editor is responsible for monitoring and transmitting the information to the internal components, the user, and the Display; the internal components and the user generate the information.

In the Calculator example the Communication_Editor was not so important as the general Communication_Editor we have just sketched. It was responsible only for the flow of information *from* the user *to* the internal component. It had no role in the flow of information in the other direction from the Calculator to the user. The Calculator component sent its output directly to the Display. In the Calculator example the Communication_Editor didn't need to know what the calculator was sending to the Display; therefore we kept it simple. In the more general case the Communication_Editor must know what the user sees on the display because one of its roles is to serve as an editor for that information.

The generalized Communication_Editor provides a number of services to the internal computational components and the user.

1. *Interact with the User to Construct the Valid Communication.* The Communication_Editor accepts a request from the internal component to interact with the user to construct a communication for the internal component. That request includes a description of the form that the communication from the user is to take, including syntax, type information, and default values. This is the function served by the Communication_Editor in the Calculator.

2. *Display Editor and Manager.* The Communication_Editor permits the internal components and the user to edit the display.

    a.   *For the internal components.* The Communication_Editor accepts from the internal components a description of information to be displayed to the user and displays that information according to the given description. It accepts not only descriptions of new displays from the internal components but also accepts descriptions of changes to existing displays. In this way the internal components need not redescribe the entire display each time a change occurs.

    b.   The Communication_Editor permits the user to edit the display as a way of constructing a new communication request. (Recall the discussion of structurally cued operations.) A request for input is often displayed to the user as a combination of information to be read and blank spaces (with associated data types, syntactic structures and defaults) to be filled in or modified. The Communication_Editor is guided by these input requests in its interactions with the user. In particular, it requires that the user enter only data of the required data types.

3. *Help Service.* The Communication_Editor is capable of interacting with the user to provide assistance in entering a communication. Most commonly this assistance consists of explanations of the data types required. The information for this service must, of course, be supplied by the internal component that requests the communication. This information need not be supplied each time a communication is requested. The Communication_Editor keeps track of all the *help* information it is sent and it uses it whenever interacting with the user about a data type for which it has information.

4. *Temporal Context for Defaults.* The Communication_Editor is able to determine some defaults on its own. We have said that the internal computational component may supply default values for any data type. It may also permit the Communication_Editor to supply what might be called a *temporal default.* When a temporal default is requested for an entry the Communication_Editor takes as the default the most recently processed value of that entry's data type. Thus the Communication_Editor keeps a record of all data types it processes and uses them as the defaults if none other is specified.

5. Specialized Communication_Editors may provide additional services, depending on the computational components they serve.

To provide these services a general communication must make multiple **accept** statements available to an internal component, not just the single **accept** statement shown in the calculator example.

It may be that the core computational components do not communicate directly to the Communication_Editor. Instead there may be one or more language transducers that define a structure for accessing operations. That structure may be more complex than the calculators; for example, there may be a menu and submenu. One way to implement a menu structure is to have components with road maps that correspond to menus. These menu components are drivers that call the Communication_Editor and the computational components.

8.8.8   A More Powerful Button_Classifier: A Screen Manager

Often we wish to permit users to interact with a number of separate processes at the same time. The user may see the terminal screen divided into windows, and the windows may have no predefined relation to one another. Each window needs its own Communication_Editor. In addition, there must be some component in charge of all the windows to permit the user to move back and forth between them, to create new windows and delete old ones, and to interact separately with the Communication_Editor in each window.

We want to let the user move from window to window easily, with, say, single keystroke commands or with a "mouse." Because keystrokes may be interpreted as communications directed toward a window or as commands to move between windows the Button_Classifier must have responsibility for this function. This enhanced Button_Classifier serves as a communication channel and distributor by channeling keystrokes (button pushes) from the user to the particular Communication_Editor for which they are intended. In addition, it interprets some keystrokes or keystroke sequences as communications to itself from the user. Figure 8.26 is a typical example of a generalized Button_Classifier.

The following points are worth noting about this Button_Classifier:

1.   *Notation.*   We use the notation C-$<x>$ to mean the character produced when the $<x>$ key is pressed with the control key depressed. Depending on the keyboard, this and other "control" characters may be produced by pressing a single key. In addition, certain keyboards are built to transmit character sequences (especially escape sequences) that begin with the escape character. These sequences are frequently interpreted as commands to the Button_Classifier.

2.   *Multiple Communication Editors.*   In this Button_Classifier the call to the Communication_Editor is really a call to the *current* Communication_Editor. The Button_Classifier maintains an internal table of the layout of the screen as the user sees it. The term Communication_Editor is not a reference to a particular communication editor but a call to an internal function within the Button_Classifier that returns the name of the Communication_Editor in charge of the window in which the user is currently working.

3.   *Display Overlays.*   Many systems permit the user to overlay windows so that they overlap on the user's display. It is the Button_Classifier that must keep track of the priorities of overlapping windows, that is, which parts of which windows are visible, so that it can determine to which Communication_Editor to send user keystrokes. The Button_Classifier must also provide some means of changing window priorities, as if shuffling through the windows.

Finally, the Button_Classifier must filter communications from the Communication Editor to the Display. Because windows may be partially obscured, a Communication Editor that was sent a communication through a part of its window that is visible may attempt to write to a part of its window that is not visible. The Button_Classifier must intercept that message from the Communication_Editor to the Display. The communication paths among the user, the Button_Classifier, the Communication_Editor, and the internal computational components are shown in Figure 8.27.

```
component type Button_Classifier is
  loop
    select
          —Keystrokes that are transmitted unchanged.
      accept 'A' do
        Communication_Editor.Text_Character('A');
      end;—Each keystroke that stands for a textual character is
      . . . —accepted and transmitted to the Communication Editor.
    or
          —Keystrokes that correspond to Communication Editor commands.
      accept Backspace_Key do
        Communication_Editor.Backspace
      end Backspace_Key;
    or
      accept 'C-Q' do
            —The character after the quote character is treated
            —as a text character no matter what it is.
        select
          accept 'A' do
            Communication_Editor.Text_Character('A')
          end;
          . . .
        end select;
      end Quote_Character;
    or
          —Keystrokes that correspond to Button_Classifier commands.
      accept '->' do
          —Move to the window to the right.
      end Move_Right;
      . . .
    end select;
  end loop;
end Button_Classifier;
```

Figure 8.26   A Button_Classifier.

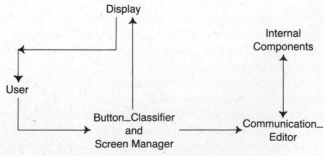

Figure 8.27   User-interface dataflow.

4. *Key Interpretations and Static or Dynamic Binding of Keys.* More sophisticated Button_Classifiers naturally recognize more classes of keystroke. In particular, Button_Classifiers that produce input to Communication_Editors generally recognize the keystrokes that function as editing commands. If, for example, the backspace key is to be interpreted to mean erase the previously entered character the Button_Classifier must recognize that key and call the associated Communication_Editor function. In well designed systems there will be a number of single button commands.

Even when a command is not a single keystroke it is often up to the Button_Classifier to recognize it and to translate it into the appropriate command for the Communication_Editor; for example, a "quote character" (in the example road map the *control Q* character) when followed by any character causes the Button_Classifier to pass the second character to the Communication_Editor as if it were a text character, even if it normally is a Communication_Editor command character.

The Button_Classifier shown in Figure 8.26 has predefined interpretations for each keystroke. An advantage of fixed interpretations is that the keyboard is forced to be used consistently in all applications programs; that is, the 'C-?' character *always* means *help*. A disadvantage of this approach is that it limits the application programs. Thus a more sophisticated Button_Classifier will maintain an internal table that defines how keys are to be mapped to interpretations; for example, one Communication_Editor may wish 'C-?' to mean a request for help, whereas another may wish 'C-H' to be a request for help. The Button_Classifier will accept a table of key bindings from each Communication_Editor and respond to it accordingly.

5. We wish to be able to accept user-keystrokes at any time; the user should never have to wait. Thus the Button_Classifier must function as a transducer buffer, always available to accept communications from the user or any of the Communication Editors.

Thus our once simple Button_Classifier becomes a general screen manager.

EXERCISES

1. Define a Communication_Editor that functions as a full screen editor. The Communication_Editor should not accept keystrokes as commands; its **accept** statements should name the commands. It is the job of the Button_Classifier that feeds it keystrokes to call the command associated with each keystroke.

2. Define a Communication_Editor that accepts a form and permits the user to fill it out. Each entry on the form should have associated with it a data type and a default value. The Communication_Editor should permit the user to accept the default value; it should not permit the user to enter information of the wrong data type. In addition, each entry on the form should have help information associated with it. If the user asks for help the Communication_Editor should present that help information.

3. Define a Button_Classifier that can handle multiple windows. It should provide operations to create and delete windows, to move windows around on a screen,

and to declare window priorities. It should provide means of writing to particular windows but it should not display information that is covered by other windows of higher priority. When a window is uncovered, the newly visible information should be displayed. It should also provide means to move a screen pointer from window to window. Given that the screen pointer is in a particular window, it should forward user inputs to the Communication_Editor in charge of that window.

8.9   SUMMARY

With this we have finally answered the question of how to build a new interpreter, given an existing interpreter. The answer turns out not to be surprising. There are two parts:

1. Develop one or more components within the existing interpreter that provide the functionality of the new interpreter.
2. Develop a user-interface that translates communications defined for the given interpreter into communications for the new interpreter.

The new interpreter is made up of the entire collection of components we have sketched.

In some sense this is not a satisfying answer. We should like the new interpreter to be a single thing, preferably a single component. That is not to be. The problem of communications prevents us from building new interpreters as single components. We find ourselves in a world in which our communication capabilities are predefined; we cannot change them. We are forced to provide a translation from the given communication capabilities to whatever new communication capabilities we want.

We can draw some worthwhile conclusions. For an interpreter (i.e., programming language) to be convenient to use for building new interpreters it should provide the following:

1. *A Component Construct.*   Clearly it is not necessary that a programming language provide a component construct for us to be able to use it to build new interpreters. We have been building new interpreters for years in languages without a component construct. That construct, however, greatly simplifies the architecture of new interpreters.
2. *Flexible Input Capabilities.*   One of the most demanding parts of building new interpreters is to construct the user interface. The user interface translates some of the communication capabilities of the given interpreter into those of the new interpreter. The more convenient the input capabilities of the substrate interpreter are to work with, the easier it will be to build the required user interface.

The second point raises a new question. Why is it that we seem to have advanced to, but then got stuck at, the character level in terms of the communication capabilities provided by interpreters? That is, in building the computer itself, we moved from communication primitives that consisted of electronic signals to communication signals that consisted of bits. In building programming languages, we moved from bits to characters, but in building interpreters on top of programming languages we seem to be stuck with characters. Any interpreter that is built on top of a programming language and that itself is a programming language (i.e., lets its users build new interpreters) provides among its primitive communication capabilities the ability to deal with characters. Why is that?

There seem to be two answers.

1. It generally requires physical devices to encapsulate the communication ca-
    pabilities of an old interpreter while making visible only the communication
    capabilities of a new interpreter; that is, we must build a device that has but-
    tons that:
    a.   Correspond to the communication capabilities of the new interpreter.
    b.   Hide the communication capabilities of the old interpreter.
    Building physical devices is generally more capital intensive than building
    software systems of the same complexity. As an industry we generally tend
    not to make that sort of investment. It is not true that we never make these
    investments. When we develop special keyboards with labeled function keys,
    for example, we are making a minimal investment of that sort. Often, though,
    the interpreters for which this investment is made are not especially useful as
    substrates for building additional interpreters. They are more often end-prod-
    uct interpreters. It seems that the less useful a new interpreter is as a pro-
    gramming language, the greater the investment we are willing to make to
    embody its communication primitives in physical devices.

2. Probably a more important reason that the alphabet persists is that the alpha-
    bet is useful. We do not know of a better set of primitives to use for building
    languages (although some interpreters enhance the set of communication
    primitives they make available by adding new ones to the alphabet). Recall
    our earlier discussion of user interface strategies. In some cases there is no
    alternative to having the user spell out names. Any interpreter that does not
    provide for character input will be difficult to use to build a new interpreter
    that needs names spelled out. Therefore most interpreters intended for use as
    programming languages provide at least the same character-communication
    capability as that found in the interpreter on which they themselves are built.

Therefore, unlike electronic signals that disappear as communication primitives as we go up the hierarchy of interpreters, characters, once developed, are replicated in all higher interpreters intended to be programming languages.

With this we have finished our discussion of software architecture. The remainder of this chapter presents guidelines for documenting the design of systems developed according to these ideas.

8.10   SYSTEM DOCUMENTATION: OVERALL STRUCTURE

The next two chapters present outlines for documenting system design and component specification and design. In this section we present a brief preview.

We define a *system* as a collection of components that has a well defined conceptual model and a well defined interface to that conceptual model but cannot be implemented as a single component. To its users a system appears to be much like a component. The calculator in the preceding section is a good example of a system. Basically a system is a (complex) interpreter.

It is typical of systems that they allow multiple external interactions to occur concurrently. It is for this reason that a system's behavioral specification includes a discussion of multiple user-interfaces. Each of these interfaces may be active simultaneously, and it is up to the system itself to keep the users from interfering with one another.

The documentation of a complete system should be given as a collection of documents that should include specification and design.

1. *System Documentation.*   A system is normally described in two documents:
   a. *Behavioral specification.*   The behavioral specification as described in Part Two serves as the system or subsystem specification document.
   b. *Design.*   The system design document discusses the interconnection of components in the system. In general, this document will include a diagram that is similar to 8.21. It shows the components that make up the system and the dataflow paths among them.
2. *Component Documentation.*   Each component should have its *own* specification and design documentation. Unless the specification and design of a component are sufficiently complex, it is acceptable to include both in a single document, although the two pieces of information must be kept separate.

Implications for Structure Charts

The design of a system (or the internal design of a component) is given, naturally enough, in terms of the specifications of the components that the system or component includes internally. (Recall that a component generally includes other components within itself. Those components are instances of component types found in the universal component library.) The design is *not* given in terms of components that these internal components include. The design of a system or of a component is a single-level construction. We argue that structure charts, diagrams that show a tree of elements with the system at the root and the lowest level elements at the leaves, are inappropriate.

Structure charts are intended to show how a component is made up of subcomponents. If we were to take this approach seriously it would lead to nonsensical results; for example, some of the components of most programs are the operations defined by the language in which the program is written. Therefore if we were to show how a program is made up of components we would have to list as leaves of the structure chart the operations used in each element at each node. We could carry the example further. We could show how the design of an application system is carried out as atoms of silicon. Clearly this is nonsensical, yet a complete structure chart would provide that information. The reason for designing with components is to hide the internal structure of the components. Structure charts defeat that purpose.

Structure charts have one possible value as parts lists. Given a system, it may be useful to know the component types that are required when building a concrete instance. There is no other need to show how the top level of a system is related to components at the bottom level. The only relationships that should be documented are those that show how any one component is implemented in terms of its immediate constituent components.

≡9

SYSTEM DESIGN DOCUMENTATION

Here we present an outline for a system design document. A system's specification is presented in a behavioral specification document.

9.1 OVERVIEW OF DOCUMENT, ORGANIZATION, AND CONVENTIONS

This section and the subsections within it provide preliminary information for the reader.

9.1.1 Scope of Document

This section describes what the document is about. Normally it may be a single sentence to the effect: This document presents the design of the software for the ABC system.

9.1.2 Scope of System

This section provides a brief statement of the scope and purpose of the system. It should acquaint the new reader with the general goals and limitations of the system but it is not intended as a complete description. It should also provide a reference to the system requirements and behavioral specification documents and should be consistent with those documents.

9.1.3   Organization of Document: Annotated Table of Contents

This section describes the remaining sections of the document and gives the reader a preview of what is to come. It should provide an abstract of the other sections and should state their purposes and goals.

9.1.4   Definitions

This section defines terms, conventions, acronyms, and other abbreviations used in the document.

9.2   SYSTEM DESIGN

This section and the subsections within it provide a guide to the top-level design of the system described in this document.

9.2.1   Hardware Architecture

To the extent that the system hardware architecture is relevant to the system design (but the hardware components are not themselves included as components in the design) this section provides a description of that hardware architecture. It is particularly important that it be described when the hardware is designed especially for the system or when the system consists of a network of interacting computers, communication facilities, and other devices. Much of the software depends on the organization of the system's hardware. It often treats the hardware components as external devices rather than as integral parts of the system and we must understand these devices to understand the system. Sometimes the hardware architecture effectively partitions the system into more or less independent subsystems. The overall structure of the system depends on this partitioning. On occasion the hardware is not relevant; the system may operate on a standard computer with no special peripherals. In these cases this section may be limited to one or two sentences.

If the hardware description is lengthy or complex it may be included as an appendix or separate document, referenced from this paragraph, in which case this paragraph should provide an overview.

9.2.2   Interfacing Software

To the extent that the system depends on any interfacing software this section provides a description of that software. If no interfacing software is assumed this section may be eliminated. In other cases when the system is designed to be integrated into an existing software system and to interact with some of the existing software elements it is important that the interfacing software be described.

If the description of the interfacing software is lengthy or complex it may be included as an appendix or as a separate document, referenced from this paragraph, in which case this paragraph should provide an overview.

9.2.3   Top-Level Nested Components

This section lists any data type components at the top level of the system. These components do not form part of the system's dataflow structure; instead they define the type of data that flows along that structure. If there are data type components they are generally application-specific data types that name and characterize the basic units of information handled by the system.

9.2.4   Design Strategy and Data- and Control-Flow Graph

This section explains the strategy used in designing the system and provides a dataflow diagram to show the following

1. *Top-level system components* which are concrete components that are not embedded in any other components in the system. Recall that a concrete component is an instance of some component type that is available in a system library. Each component type has its own documentation; therefore it is not necessary to present the complete documentation of each component here. As an example, Figure 8-21 shows the top-level components of the calculator system.

2. *The Data- and Control-Flow Paths Among the System's Top-Level Components.*   Figure 8-21 also shows the data- and control-flow paths between the components.

3. *The Information that Flows Along the Data Paths.*   Figure 8-21 does not contain this information. Refer to Figure 5-7 for an example of how this information should be presented. Each element of information whose intuitive meaning and significance is not obvious from its name should be explained in the text of this section.

The subsidiary sections provide an overview of the major components and the communications among them.

Component i

For each component a brief general description of the component's capabilities should be provided with a more detailed description of the component's role in the system.

1. *Component Name and Pedigree.* The name by which the component is known throughout the design and the name of the component type of which this component is an instance.

2. *Component Brief Abstract.* A brief, intuitive description of the capabilities provided by the component as an isolated unit. This need not be a detailed description of the component because its own documentation provides the details.

3. *Role in System.* A description of how the component fits into the rest of the system. It should be as detailed as necessary to describe the component's functioning within this particular system.

Consider as an example a system that stores some of its information in files. Each file should be implemented as a component. All files of a certain structure are instances of a single file component type; therefore they all have the same operational capabilities. Different files in a system serve different purposes, depending on the information that they store. This section describes the specific function served by this concrete component in this system.

9.2.5 Top-Level Initialization

The top-level initialization, that is, what happens when the system is first started, is described here.

EXERCISE

1. Write the system documentation for an appointment scheduling system.

≡10

COMPONENT DOCUMENTATION: SPECIFICATION AND DESIGN

This chapter presents an outline for documenting the specification and design of individual component types. It is the component types that are documented rather than the concrete components. These component types are maintained in a system component library from which concrete instances may be produced for specific systems.

Although it is the component types that are stored in a system library, when describing a component type it is natural to speak in terms of the concrete instances that a designer will actually use. For that reason we suggest that when describing the capabilities of the component type those capabilities be expressed directly in terms of the component instances rather than of "the components that may be instantiated from this component type." Only when speaking of component-type skeletons is it important to focus the reader's attention on the act of specialization.

10.1   OVERVIEW OF DOCUMENT, ORGANIZATION, AND CONVENTIONS

This section and the subsections in it provide the reader with preliminary information.

10.1.1   Scope of Document

This section explains what the document is about. Normally it is a single sentence to this effect: This document presents the specification and design of software component type ABC.

10.1.2   Type and Scope of Component

This section should acquaint the reader with the general goals and limitations of the component. In particular, it should provide two pieces of information:

Type of component   The component type should be identified; that is, whether it is a data type component, a storage unit, a transducer, or a driver. In addition, if the component is a component-type skeleton this section should indicate that fact.

Intuitive description   This section should provide a brief, intuitive description of the component's overall capabilities. It should contain enough information so that someone encountering the component for the first time will be able to understand the rationale behind the component's conceptual model and operations.

10.1.3   Organization of the Document: Annotated Contents

This section describes the remaining sections of the document and gives the reader a preview of what is to come. It should provide an abstract of the other sections and state their purposes and goals.

10.1.4   Definitions

This section defines terms, abbreviations, acronyms, and other conventions used in the document.

10.2   Component Behavioral Specification

This section does for a component what a system behavioral specification does for a system. It provides an external view of the component and tells how its behavior may be understood. (Notice that a component's behavioral specification is included in its design document, whereas a system's behavioral specification is written as a separate document.) The component behavioral specification should provide enough information to permit a designer to determine how to use the component in a design. In particular, the following information should be provided in subsections to this section.

1. *Skeletal Parameters*.   If this component is a component-type skeleton the meanings of its skeletal parameters.
2. *Imported Capabilities*.   The capabilities provided by other components that this component uses; that is, the calls that this component makes and the data types it uses.
3. *Conceptual Model*.   The conceptual model through which this component may be understood.
4. *Exported Capabilities*.   The capabilities this component makes available to other components; that is, its **accept** statements.

10.2.1   Skeletal Parameters

If this component is a component-type skeleton this section lists the skeleton parameters and defines their meanings.

10.2.2   Imported Capabilities: Other Components Referenced

To understand one component it is sometimes necessary to understand the components it uses. When one component uses capabilities made available by some other component the user component is said to *import* those capabilities. The three ways in which components may import capabilities from other components are described in the following subsections:

Imported Types

This section lists (and explains briefly if necessary) any data types that are imported; for example, assume that we wish to understand a component that gives the complex roots of equations. To do so we must first understand complex numbers. The type Complex_Number is defined by another component. To understand the complex number equation component we must first understand the Complex_Number component. Any data type that appears in a component's communication declaration, either as the type of a parameter or of a returned value, is imported.

Imported Operations

A component may make use of the operations of some other component in carrying out its responsibilities; for example, a component that provides specialized database manipulation services makes use of the component that defines the database. These imported capabilities appear as the calls a component makes from its road map to other components. This section lists (and explains briefly if necessary) any other components that this component calls from its road map.

10.2.3   Conceptual Model

This section and the subsections within it describe the component's conceptual model. It provides the framework for understanding and using the component. A conceptual model is a description of the component's internal structure intended for someone who needs to use the component. A conceptual model is not intended as a description of the component's actual implementation, although, as in system conceptual models, a component's conceptual model may provide an implementation strategy.

The description of the conceptual model may range in formality from the relatively informal (e.g., a careful natural language description) to the completely formal (e.g., in a language intended for formal verification). The appendix introduces a formal notation that may be used to describe conceptual models. Intermediate in formality, we can explain the conceptual model by producing an inefficient but understandable implementation; for example, by explaining a text data type as an array. This approach explains the conceptual model by demonstrating how that model *could* be implemented if we were not concerned about implementation efficiency. If this approach is taken we must be careful *not* to read the informal implementation as a high-level description of the *actual* internal design of the component. The informal implementation is merely a way of describing the conceptual model and not a design outline. If this approach is taken the exported operations may then be explained in terms of pseudocode programs operating on the informal model.

Static Model Description

This section describes the component's internal static architecture. It is the heart of the conceptual model. It includes descriptions of each of the objects, object types, and structures in the component and of the relationships between them. The description should be detailed and rigorous enough to allow the component to be implemented as described here if time and space resource usage were of no concern.

This section is the foundation on which the rest of the conceptual model description is built. The discussion should provide users with a conceptual framework so that the other sections can be explained in terms of the elements discussed here. If one of the other sections cannot be described without adding additional elements to the static model the static model is incomplete and should be extended:

1. Any internal processes claimed for this component should be explained in terms of operations on the static model.
2. Any exceptions exported by this component should reflect conditions expressable in terms of the static model.
3. Any operations exported by the component should be explained in terms of changes to, or values of, elements of the static model.

Internal Processes

Many components have internal processes which are best thought of as operating concurrently with one another and with the externally available operations. This section describes these processes.

Each internal process should be described separately and intuitively. Depending on the process, more or fewer details should be provided.

An example of an internal process for which more details should be provided is one that scans a database for inconsistencies and posts them within the database to make them available for external access. The "inconsistency list" should be explained as part of the static model, and the description of the inconsistency checker as an internal process should explain how elements are put on that list.

An example of an internal process that should not be explained further is a "garbage-collector" process that "recycles" used storage. As far as users of a component that includes this device are concerned, it may be important for them to know that there is one but it is not important for them to know how it works.

Often the best way to describe the important details of internal processes is with pseudocode. As usual, the pseudocode is intended to inform the reader rather than to explain the implementation. Because internal processes are invisible outside the component except through their effects on the component's static model, the pseudocode should be given in terms of objects described in the static model. If it seems necessary to describe a process in some terms not already defined by the static model those new elements should be added.

10.2.4   Exported Elements

This section and the subsections in it describe precisely how this component may be used by other components. They list and describe those things that this component makes available to other components. This part of the component's description is its actual behavioral specification since a component's behavioral specification must, in the end, be given in terms of the visible effects that result from using the component.

Dataflow Table

This section provides the component with a dataflow table* which lists the relationships between operations exported by the component and the data types those operations use as parameters or to return values. In particular, the dataflow table shows which operations take which data types as input elements and which operations produce which data types as output results. The dataflow table does not add information that is not available on the operation's road map. It simply provides access to that information in another form. A dataflow table cross references the operations (communications) the components make available and the data types the component uses. We would consult a dataflow table if we wondered, for example, whether this component ever returned an object of a particular type.

---

*Note that this is a dataflow table and not a dataflow diagram.

We recommend a table in the following format. The data types used by exported operations label the table rows and the exported operations label the table columns. An entry appears in the table element that corresponds to the row with data type d and the column with operation o if operation o uses data type d. The entry is an I if o uses d for input; that is, if the data type is associated with an **in** parameter. The entry is an O if o uses d for output if the data type is associated with an **out** parameter or if it is the data type of the returned value if operation o is a **function.** The entry is a B if o uses d for both input and output, even if used as types for two parameters or for an input parameter and a returned value.

Exported Exceptions

An exception is a condition that may occur but that the component is unable to handle. When this condition occurs the component aborts its operation and indicates the existence of the exception; for example, a car that runs out of gas stops operating and reveals the out-of-gas exception by a gauge on the dashboard. The act of aborting an operation and identifying an exception is called *raising* an exception. Any exceptions this component may raise are listed and explained here in terms of the conceptual model; that is, it should be possible for the reader to understand what went wrong in terms of the description of the conceptual model provided earlier.

Consider two examples:

1. Providing zero as a divisor to a Divide operation should lead to a Division_ by_Zero exception.
2. An empty stack should lead to a Stack_Empty exception during a Pop operation.

As these two examples illustrate, there are two primary causes for exceptions:

Invalid parameters   A parameter may not be valid for an operation, such as zero as a divisor.

Illegal operation   An operation may be requested, but the component may
for the current state   be in a state that precludes performing the operation, such as a request to Pop a stack when it is empty.

In both cases the component is unable to perform its function and has no option other than to raise an exception and force the caller to decide what to do.

Road Map and Exported Operations

This section describes the component's road map and the operations it makes available by its communication declarations. The road map should be shown with the communication declarations indicated on it in the same way that we have been showing road maps throughout this design discussion. In particular, the following information should be provided about each communication declaration.

function Complex_Conjugate(C : Complex_Number) **return** Complex_Number;
—If C = a + bi, then Complex_Conjugate(C) = a − bi.

Figure 10.1   A signature and specification of a complex conjugate function.

Signature	A communication declaration signature indicates whether the associated operation is used as a procedure call or a function call. It also gives the operation's name, its parameters and their types, and the type of returned value if it is a function.
Specification of the operation	There should be a brief, intuitive, but rigorous specification of the component's behavior when the operation is called. The specification should indicate how the operation is connected to the component's static model and the particular transformation(s) it causes. This description should include the following:
Preconditions for use	The preconditions that must hold for the subprogram to be guaranteed to function property.
Postconditions produced	The effects produced by this subprogram.
	The information need not be explicitly labeled as pre- and postconditions so long as it is clear (sometimes, in fact, there are no limiting preconditions); for example, a "complex conjugate" operation from a component implementing various complex number transformations might have the signature and description shown in Figure 10.1.
Exceptions raised	If this operation raises any of the exceptions that this component exports they should be mentioned and the conditions under which they are raised should be explained.
Real time constraints	A component may guarantee that once it **accepts** a communication it will respond within a given time. It is important to specify the computing resources that are being assumed in making this guarantee; for example, what processor will be executing the component, what fraction of the processor's time is assumed to be devoted to that execution, and, if relevant, what peripheral devices will be available and what can be expected from them.

10.2.5   Tests

This section specifies the tests that, if completed successfully, will verify the correct operation of this component. (Note that system tests are documented in the system's behavioral specification. Because a component's behavioral specification is included as part of its design document, the tests are also included here.) It is this section that takes most seriously the notion that a behavioral specification is a stimulus-response model, for it is only in observing how the component responds to stimuli that we can determine whether it is functioning correctly. Therefore this section should describe a complete series of tests which consists of stimuli (communications) and stimuli sequences along with the responses the component must produce to satisfy its specification.

For each test the following should be provided:

Test identification This is the name by which the test is known.

Test conditions This describes the conditions that must be established in this component and in any auxiliary components to allow the test to be carried out.

Test events and expected responses This describes the events that make up the test and the responses expected from the component. Events consist of external communications to the component. Expected, responses consist of responses the component is expected to make.

The expected responses should be described exactly. It should be possible in principle for a testing program to administer the tests and compare the actual results with the expected results. It should not be required that the results be interpreted by a test observer before determining whether they are correct.

Because many component communications do not produce output, the expected responses are generally not directly observable. The responses may have to be recorded and displayed by some other component. It is acceptable to document the expected responses in terms of their appearance as recorded or displayed by the other components.

EXERCISES

1. Write component specifications for the components in your appointment scheduling system design.
2. Write complete component specifications for other components defined in earlier exercises.

10.3 COMPONENT BODIES

This part of a component's design document describes the implementation of the component. The preceding parts describe how the component looks externally; that is, they provide its behavioral specification. This part describes how it is constructed internally; that is, it gives its design.

10.3.1   Design Overview and Dataflow Graph

This section is an overview of the component's design. It describes the main elements actually used in the component and the design strategy under which they are put together.

It also provides a dataflow picture of this component's implementation and includes a description of the top-level internal components in its design. It also contains a dataflow graph that shows how these elements communicate. The dataflow graph should do for this component the same job that the system dataflow graph does for a system.

Component Types Used

This section provides brief descriptions of the component types used in building this component's body.

Files Used

Files are similar to abstract object components in that they store and provide access to information in well defined and limited ways. For the purpose of system design they should be treated as components. To be clear about the actual design, however, it is important to identify files as files. Files should always be encapsulated within some component. If this component encapsulates a file the file is mentioned explicitly here.

Devices Used

Devices are similar to components in that they provide certain capabilities in well defined and limited ways. For the purpose of system design they should be treated as components. To be clear about the actual design, however, it is important to identify devices as devices. Devices should always be encapsulated within some component. If this component encapsulates a device the device is mentioned exlicitly here.

10.3.2   Initialization

This section describes any initialization the component performs when first brought into use.

REFERENCES

R.J. Abbott, Program Design by Informal English Description, *CACM,* **26**(10):???, 1983.

Tilak Agerwala and Arvind, Special Feature on Data Flow Systems, *Computer,* **15**(2);10-69–546, 1982.

J.F. Allen, Maintaining Knowledge of Temporal Intervals, *CACM,* **26**(11):832–843, 1983.

R. Balzer and N. Goldman, Principles of Godd Software Specification and their Implications for Specification Languages. In *Proceedings of the Symposium on Specification of Reliable Software,* 58–67. IEEE, 1979.

G.D. Bergland, A Guided tour of Program Design Methodologies, *Computer,* **14**(10):13–37, 1981.

B. Boehm, *Characteristics of Software Quality,* Elsevier/North Holland, New York, 1978.

P. Bright, personal communication.

Lori A. Clarke, Jack C. Wiledon, and Alexander L. Wolfe, Nesting in Ada is for the Birds, in *Proceedings of the ACM-SIGPLAN Symposium on the Ada Programming Language,* 139–145. ACM, 1980.

W.F. Clocksin and C.S. Mellish, *Programming in Prolog,* Springer-Verlag, New York, 1981.

G.V. Cormack, Extensions to Static Scoping, In *Proceedings of the SIGPLAN '83 Symposium of Programming Language Issues in Software Systems,* 187–191, ACM, 1983.

O.-J. Dahl, B. Myhrhaug, and K. Nygaard, *The SIMULA 67 Common Base Language,* Technical Report, Norwegian Computing Center, 1970.

T. DeMarco, *Concise Notes on Software Engineering,* Yourdon Press, New York, 1979.

J.B. Dennis, G.A. Boughton, C, K, C, Leung, Building Blocks for Data Flow Prototypes, In *Proceedings of the Seventh Annual Symposium on Computer Architecture,* 1–8, ACM, 1980.

D.W. Dijkstra, Notes on Structured Programming, In *Structured Programming,* Academic, New York, 1972, pp. 1–82.

U.S. Department of Defense, Reference Manual for the Ada Programming Language, MIL-STD 1815A, 1983.

Goldberg, A., D. Robson, and D. Ingalls, *Smalltalk-80: The Language and Its Implementation,* Addison-Wesley, Reading, Massachusetts, 1983.

J. Guttag, Notes on Type Abstraction, In *Proceedings of the Symposium of Specification of Reliable Software,* 36–46, IEEE, 1979.

A.N. Habermann, *Implementation of Path Expressions,* Technical Report, Carnegie Mellon University, Pittsburgh, 1979.

E. Horowitz and S. Sahni, *Fundamentals of Computer Algorithms,* Computer Science, Princeton, New Jersey, 1978.

Daniel H.H. Ingalls, The Smalltalk-76 Programming System: Design and Implementation, In *Proceedings of the Fifth Annual ACM Symposium on the Principles of Programming Languages,* ACM, 1978.

M.A. Jackson, *Principles of Program Design,* Academic, New York, 1975.

B.H. Liskov and S. Zilles, Specification Techniques for Data Abstractions, *IEEE Transactions on Software Engineering,* **SE-1**:7–19, 1975.

B.H. Liskov, A. Snyder, R. Atkinson, and C. Schaffert, Abstraction Mechanisms in CLU, *CACM,* **20**(8):564–576, 1977.

B.H. Liskov and V. Berzins, An Appraisal of Program Specifications, In *Research Directions in Software Technology*, MIT Press, Cambridge, Massachusetts, 1979, pp. 276–301.

T. McCall, *Factors in Software Quality*, Technical Report, General Electric, Syracuse, New York, 1977.

J. McCarthy, A Formal description of a Subset of ALGOL, In *Conference Proceedings: Formal Language Description Languages for Computer Programming*, Elsevier/North-Holland, New York, 1966, pp. 1–12.

D.L. Parnas, On the Criteria to Be Used in Decomposing Systems into Modules, *CACM*, **15**(12):1053–1058, 1972.

Dennis M. Ritchie and Ken Thompson, The UNIX Time Sharing System, *Communications of the ACM*, **17**(7):365–375, 1974.

J.M. Spitzen, K.N. Levitt, L. Robinson. An Example of Hierarchical Design and Proof. *CACM*, **21**(12):1064–1075, 1978.

W.P. Stevens, G.J. Meyers, and L.L. Constantine. Structured Design. *IBM Systems Journal*, **13**(2):115–139, 1974.

J.D. Warnier, *Logical Construction of Programs*. Van Nostrand-Reinhold, New York, 1974.

N. Wirth, Program Development by Stepwise Refinement, *CACM*, **14**(4):221–227, 1971.

N. Wirth, *Programming in MODULA-2*, Springer-Verlag, New York, 1982.

Appendix

ABSTRACTION AND SPECIFICATION

≡11

ABSTRACTION AND SPECIFICATION

11.1 INTRODUCTION

This appendix develops the ground work for documenting components. The difficulty we always face in the documentation of any unit of software is that we wish to expess the abstractions that the software implements without resorting to a description of the implementation. To express abstractions we need a language in which to speak. When we express abstractions that are implemented in computer programs there is an almost irresistable temptation to use the implemention programming language. This is not satisfactory; to use the programming language to specify the abstraction ties the abstraction too closely to programming language concepts. One of the main difficulties we see in many software systems is that the abstraction behind the software is lost in the forest of programming details. Yet if we do not use the programming language we are faced with two other problems.

1. What language should we use?
2. How can we tie the abstractions to the programs?

This appendix provides a general framework for the convenient expression of many sorts of abstraction.

Specifications can be expressed in any form as long as the form is sufficiently well defined. Specifications for numerical operations, for example, are usually written in mathematical terms. They include the mathematical function to be computed as well as the required accuracy and precision. Mathematical specifications are satisfactory for specifying numerical operations because they have two important properties:

They are rigorous.
They fit the subject.

Unfortunately, numerical operations are the exception rather than the rule with regard to the availability of rigorous and convenient terms for their specification. In most cases programmers and program specifiers lack the generally accepted terms for specifying the abstractions that their programs are intended to realize. To fill this void this appendix outlines a simple formalism that can nearly always be used for the rigorous specification of software.

This method combines relational database ideas with simple predicate logic. Because relational database notation is a form of predicate logic, what we are really proposing is the use of predicate logic for specifications. Because relational database notation is so easy and intuitive, the two are combined into what might be called predicate logic made simple. In addition, syntactic conventions are developed that make the notation more palatable to programmers.

We examine two examples. The first is a management system for programming projects. We use it to introduce the basic notion. In the second we develop a complete abstract specification for the data type Queue. The Queue specification takes the form of a component. A summary of the specification tools and techniques is given in the final section.

11.2   A SPECIFICATION FORMALISM: THE BASIC NOTATION: TABLES

Imagine that we are running a small programming company and that we are in the middle of a major project. The project is large enough so that we cannot manage it without a formal record-keeping system. We wish to keep track of information that will tell us who the programmers are, what their assignments are and when they are scheduled to complete them, what tasks they are performing, who is reviewing their work, and which interfaces between components have been tested. We want to develop a computer-based system to record these data.

We can use tables for recording much of this data; for example, a table (which we call the Assignments table) lists the programmers, the program components to which they are assigned, and the reason for those assignments.*

---

*Readers familiar with relational databases will recognize tables as a representation of relations, and readers familiar with predicate calculus will recognize them as a representation of predicates. For simplicity, and because they are really so simple, we continue to refer to these structures as *tables*. Readers are welcome to substitute their own favorite word.

Table Assignments

Programmer	Component	Task
Jane	Component_5	Design
John	Component_2A	Start
Jim	Component_1	Code
Joan	Component_2B	Test
Joe	Component_3	Debug
Jerry	Component_3	Design
Josephine	Component_4	Test
Joan	Component_6	Test

In the future to declare this table, instead of showing a sample, we will write:

Assignments (:Programmer, :Component, :Task)

This statement says the following:

1. We wish to work with a table called Assignments.
2. The Assignments table has three columns. The entries in the columns are of the types Programmer, Component, and Task.

Note that in this Assignments table Joan is working on two components (Component_2B and Component_6) and that two people are working on the same component (Joe and Jerry are both working on Component_3). As these examples show, the table is not required to define a one-to-one mapping in any direction. It is simply a list of assignments; and any assignments are possible.

A number of simple conventions must be remembered about tables of this sort:

1. A table is understood as simply recording facts; each row in a table represents a distinct and independent fact.
2. Because each row is an independent fact, the order of rows does not matter.
3. Because each row represents a distinct fact, there can never be two rows that are identical. To have two identical rows would mean that the same fact is recorded twice, which makes no sense, for no new information would be added.
4. A table is *not* an object that will be manipulated by the program when implemented. A table is a *meta* object: it is a specification of the relations among the real objects (Programmers, Components, Tasks) with which the program will eventually deal. The significance of this will become clearer later. For now it should be understood to mean that a table is external to the program being specified. The table records the user's conceptual model of the program's objects; but the program will never perform operations directly on the table; it will only perform operations on the objects that are listed in the table. Presumably, as the program operates on the objects, the conceptual

facts in the table will change to reflect the changing states of the relations among the objects.

5. Each column of a table is a data type—in the programming sense of data type. In defining a table we are beginning the specification of the data types with which the eventual program will work. Thus all the entries in any particular column are all the same sorts of thing: only programmers in the Programmer column, only components in the Component column, and only tasks in the Task column.

Table Entries

Because each column of a table is a data type, the entries in a column are values of that type. The possible ways of including values in a table, however, are not uniform. There are different ways, depending on the values to be entered.

1. *Attribute Values.*   A column may be restricted to values from the set of the possible values of some attribute. The Task column is a good example. Only the values start, specify design, code, debug, and test are allowed. Other value sets include numbers, if, for example we had a column that kept track of the size of modules, and strings like social security numbers or telephone numbers. In some cases the form of the values is limited: social security numbers and telephone numbers have specified forms.

2. *Entity Identifiers.*   These entries refer to something besides themselves. The entries in entity columns are references to the objects referred to from the table; they are not the values of the objects or the objects themselves. The Programmer and Component columns are entity columns. The "value" of a component is not entered; that is, the component itself is not in the table. Only a reference to it is made.

This is different from the entries already mentioned. In those cases the actual values are given in the table and will be manipulated by the eventual program. With entities, however, there are no values to be manipulated. The program does not actually manipulate the *real* programmers and the *real* components; it manipulates identifiers for them. Of course, it would be impossible to keep real entities in the table anyway. Entities as such cannot literally be stored in a computer.

It is often worthwhile to make explicit the distinction between entities and values. We can do so with an Entity_Type table:

table Entity_Type(:Entity_Type).

The Entity_Type table contains the entity types.

table Entity_Type

Entity Type
Programmer
Component

By convention we can agree that all types that are not explicitly labeled entity types are value set types; that is, types that provide the values for attributes.

Type Tables

Types label columns in other tables and may be entries in the Entity_Type table. In addition, types define tables. An entry appears in a type table if that entry identifies an entity or is a value of that type. Thus our three types give us the following:

Programmer	Component	Task
Jane	Component_1	Start
Jerry	Component_2	Specify
Jim	Component_3A	Design
Joan	Component_3B	Code
Joe	Component_4	Debug
Josephine	Component_5	Test
	Component_6	

Although we said that the order of rows in tables is not relevant, for type tables it is useful to let it define an ordering. Thus we attach significance to the order in which the elements are listed. The Programmer and the Component tables are lexicographically ordered; the Task table is ordered by the sequence in which the tasks are performed.

This ends our introductory discussion of tables. With this background it is possible to specify most of what is important in programs. The following additional specification tools are discussed next:

Linquistic constructs	These are the allowable language forms used to make claims for tables. The various linguistic constructs are introduced as needed throughout this appendix.
Functions	These are special tables. A function is a table for which there is guaranteed to be a one-to-one mapping from some of the columns to other columns.

11.2.1   Specifying Operations (Subprograms)

In this section we discuss the use of tables for specifying operations that the eventual program will implement. Three pieces of information are required:

1. The operation signature; that is, its communication declaration.
2. The preconditions that are required to hold in order for the operation to work correctly: that is, what the operation is allowed to assume.
3. The postconditions that the operation is to produce; that is, what someone (or some program) using the operation can assume after performing it.

We use tables to specify pre- and the postconditions for operations. Let's specify a few simple operations for our programming project management system.

Assume that we would like to specify an operation that, in effect, inserts a row (a new fact) into a table. We might call that operation Assign because it assigns a Programmer to a Component and gives that assignment a Task.

> **procedure** Assign (P :Programmer; M :Component; T :Task);
> —**pre:** ~Assignments(P,M,T);
> —**post:** Assignments′(P,M,T)

This specification may be interpreted as follows:

1. The signature line (first line) says the following:
   a. Assign is a procedure type operation, and not a function type operation.
   b. The name of the operation is Assign.
   c. Assign has three parameters:
      (1) The first is of type Programmer.
      (2) The second is of type Component.
      (3) The third is of type Task.
2. The precondition line says that Assign may assume that the programmer is not already assigned to the component with the given task. Literally it says that there is no single row in the Assignments table with the three given entries P, M, and T. (The '~' sign means "not.")
3. The postcondition line says that after performing Assign, we may assume that the programmer is assigned to the component with the given task. Literally it says that there is (or will be) a row with the entries P, M, and T in the Assignments table as it will be after the operation.

Initially, the pre- and postconditions may appear somewhat unusual. Actually they are fairly easy to understand and use. Pre- and postconditions are Boolean expressions. Each specifies information about the objects manipulated by the operation. They are *always* read as expressions that can be evaluated as **true** or **false.**

11.2.2   Specifying Facts as Table Entries

The Boolean value of the precondition must evaluate to **true** if the operation is to be guaranteed to work correctly. In the example given the precondition is the Boolean expression ~Assignments(P, M, T). That expression is considered to be **true** in those cases in which there is no row that consists of the entries P, M, and T in the Assignments table.

In general, the construct Assignments(P, M, T) is read as a Boolean expression that is **true** if there is a row in the Assignments table with the entries P, M, and T. It is **false** if there is none. In the precondition the not sign (~) in front of Assignments(P, M, T) negates the claim. Thus the precondition is **true** if there is no row in the Assignments table that contains P, M, and T and **false** if there is one.

The Boolean value of the postcondition identifies those conditions that the operation must bring about. In the foregoing example the postcondition is Assignments'(P, M, T) which evaluates to **true** when there is a row in the modified Assignments table that contains P, M, and T. It is exactly that situation that the Assign operation is supposed to bring about. Thus the postcondition sets forth in the form of a Boolean expression those conditions that the operation is supposed to achieve.

11.2.3   Changes Made by the Operation

Most operations cause changes in the information references by an operation. The prime (') in the postcondition is used to distinguish objects and relationships as they are before an operation from the same objects and relationships as they are after the operation; for example, the Assign operation is supposed to assign a programmer to a component with a given task. This change should be mirrored by a new row in the Assignments table as it would be after performing Assign. The postcondition specifies that new row. Note that the postcondition refers to the Assignments' (with a prime) table. We use the following convention about primes in specification:

> *An unprimed table refers to the table as it was before an operation; a primed table refers to it as it is after the operation.*

Given this convention, we never use a primed table in preconditions because they always refer to the state of things before the operation is performed. Primed tables may appear only in postconditions. Postconditions, however, may also include unprimed tables. In specifying the effects of an operation (i.e., its postcondition), it is sometimes necessary to refer to the state of things before and after the operation. Sometimes (e.g., when the operation is a function and does not change any relationships) only unprimed tables appear in postcondition specifications. We show examples of these specifications later.

11.2.4   Information that Does Not Change

Although operations often change some information, there is usually much more that does not change as a result of performing the operation. It is important to be certain about the information that is not changed. Because we are talking about tables before and after performing operations, we need to be clear about the entire contents of the table after the operation; that is, what else is in the Assignments' table (after performing the operation) besides the new assignment? Because the Assign operation is not supposed to change any of the old assignments (note that it is not an update operation; we specify an update operation later), we certainly want all the old assignments as well as the new one to be in the Assignments' table after the operation. In most cases, as in this one, the tables after the operation are nearly the same as they were before the operation. Therefore only the relevant differences should be specified, not the entire table. To achieve this effect we adopt the following convention:

> *A table after an operation (the primed (') table) is unchanged from the way it was before the operation except as specifically indicated in the operation's postcondition.*

Thus the Assignments' table is identical to the Assignments table except that it has a new row: the new assignment of the programmer to the component with the given task.

Recall the discussion in the original description of tables. There we insisted that a table was a meta object and was *not* manipulated by the program. This specification illustrates that point. The Assignments table is not an argument to the Assign procedure. Neither is it a global reference that the Assign operation refers to directly. The Assignments table is no more than a *claim* made (*external* to the program) about the relationships maintained (*internally* within the program by other means) between programmers, components, and tasks.

The Assignments table tells us the following:

1. The Assign operation has access to some sort of internal data structure in which programmers and components are related.

2. The relationships within that data structure parallel those in the Assignments table.

11.2.5   Interpreting the Pre- and Postconditions

It should be noted that pre- and postconditions are assertions about the state of the world before and after the performance of operations. As assertions, they are Boolean expressions and must always evaluate to **true.** The pre- and postconditions for an operation may be understood as conditional expressions that are evaluated before the operation (in the case of the postcondition) and after the operation (in the case of the postcondition).

If the precondition does not evaluate to **true** the operation need not operate correctly. The precondition of an operation should therefore evaluate to **true** under all conditions in which the operation is expected to operate correctly. In some cases the precondition is shown simply as the Boolean constant **true.** Because **true** "evaluates" to **true** no matter what conditions exist, a precondition of **true** means that the operation is expected to operate correctly no matter what the state of the world.

The postcondition of a operation shows what the state of the world is expected to be after executing the operation. If the operation has executed correctly the postcondition is guaranteed to evaluate to **true.** Thus by specifying appropriate pre- and postconditions we can characterize both under which conditions the operation will be expected to operate and the results it is expected to produce.

With these conventions we specify additional operations. In the process we introduce notational conventions needed for specifications.

11.2.6   The *some* Construct

It is frequently useful to be able to specify that some element satisfies a condition even if we do not know exactly which one it is; for example, assume that we want a function that, when given a Programmer and a Component, will return the Task of

the Component. To have such a function it would be useful to be able to guarantee
that there is some Task for the function to return. Consider the following specification:

    function What_Task (P :Programmer; M :Component) **return** Task:
      —pre: some T **In** Task **satisfies**
      —   Assignments(P, M, T);
      —   **end some;**
      —post: Assignments(P, M, What_Task(P, M));

The precondition is expressed in terms of a new specification construct, the **some**
construct. The general form of the **some** construct is

    some variables **in** type {; variables in type} **satisfies**
      Boolean_Expression_List
    end some;

The **some** construct is similar to the **for** statement in Ada and other languages. In
both cases new (local) variables are declared implicitly by their appearance at the
start of the construct. In this example the variable T is declared a type task. The
variables so declared exist only within the construct.

    Recall that everything in a pre- and postcondition must be a Boolean expression.
Because the **some** construct is used in pre- and postconditions, it must be able to be
evaluated to **true** or **false.** The **some** construct is evaluated as follows:

> *The **some** construct is **true** if at least one element of (each of) the **type(s)** in-
> dicated (in some combination if more than one variable is introduced), when
> substituted for the associated variable(s), makes the list of the expressions
> embedded within the **some** construct **true.** Otherwise the **some** construct is
> **false.***

In this case there is only one variable declared and only one expression in the list of
expressions. Thus the precondition is **true** if there is some Task that appears in the
same row as the Programmer and Component.

    Literally translated, the precondition is **true** if there is a row in the Assignments
table in which the following applies:

1.   P is in its Programmer column.
2.   M is in its Component column.
3.   There is some entry in its Task column.

It makes sense to impose this precondition because the function is supposed to return
the Task of the Programmer and Component. If there were no Task there would be
nothing to return. The precondition thus insists that the Programmer must be assigned to the Component and have some Task. If the precondition is not **true** there
is no guarantee about what What_Task will do.

11.2.7 Using the Function to Be Specified in Its Own Specification

The postcondition for What_Task is expressed in terms of the function result. It says that the value returned by the function must be one that is in the Assignments table associated with the Programmer and Component; that is, the Programmer must be recorded as an assignment to the Component with the Task returned by WHAT_ TASK. Literally translated, the postcondition is **true** if there is a row in the Assignments table that contains the following:

1. P is in its Programmer column.
2. M is in its Component column.
3. The value returned by What_Task(P,M) is in its Task column.

Note that What_Task is a function and its postcondition refers only to the Assignments table before execution. There is no reference to an Assignments' table because the function makes no changes to the Assignments table.

11.2.8 The *every* Construct

Just as it is frequently useful to be able to specify that some element satisfies a condition, it is also useful to be able to specify that all elements satisfy a condition; for example, assume that we are working with a one-dimensional array A and would like to specify that A is ordered. One way is to assert that

$$A(I) \leq A(I+1)$$

for every I between A'First and A'Last-1.* We can say this formally:

every I **in** A'First . . A'Last − 1 **satisfies**
    $A(I) \leq A(I+1)$;
end every;

The **every** construct is similar to the **some** construct in structure. Like the **some** construct, it introduces variable(s) of indicated type(s) local to the construct. Here the variable I is introduced and its type is a subrange of the index type of A. The general form of the construct is similar to that of the **some** construct.

every variables **in** type {; variables in type} **satisfies**
    Boolean_Expressions_List
end every;

Its interpretation is also similar, except that **all** elements of the specified type must satisfy the Boolean expressions.

*The **every** construct is **true** if all elements of (each of) the **type(s)** indicated (in all combinations if more than one variable is introduced), when substituted for*

---

*A'First and A'Last refer to A's highest and lowest indices.

the associated variable(s), make the list of expressions embedded within the
every construct **true**. *Otherwise the* **every** *construct is* ***false***.

Here there is only one variable and only one expression in the list of expressions. Thus the **every** construct is **true** if for all index values in the specified subrange the value of the array at that point is no greater than the value of the array at the next point.

11.2.9   The *if . . then* Construct

It is frequently true that we will require a condition only if some other condition holds; for example, a function that determines whether a particular Programmer is finished working might be specified by asking whether all components to which that Programmer is assigned has the Task tested. Consider the following function specification:

> **function** Is_Finished(P :Programmer) **return** Boolean;
> —**pre: true;**
> —**post:**
> —   **every** M **in** Component; T **in** Task **satisifies**
> —   **if** Assignments(P, M, T) **then**
> —   T = Tested;
> —   **end if;**
> —   **end every;**

This specification has as its precondition the constant **true**. This means that the precondition is always satisfied and the function is always guaranteed to work as specified.

The postcondition of the function is specified by an **every** with an embedded **if . . then** construct. The postcondition may be read:

> *For every combination of Components M and Tasks T, if Programmer P is assigned to M with Task T, then T is tested.*

In other words, P is not assigned to any Component with a Task other than Tested.

Notice that the **every** construct in this example has two declared variables. Both M and T are declared in the declaration clause. The interpretation of multiple declarations is that all combinations of elements from the two types must satisfy the Boolean expressions. The **if . . then** construct is used to restrict the requirement T = Tested to apply only to rows in the Assignments table with the given Programmer and not to every Component and Task combination.

11.2.10   Specifying Boolean Functions

The specification in the preceding example was not strictly correct. The function being specified is a Boolean function and as such can return a value of **true** or **false**. The specification as written deals only with the conditions that must hold for the returned value to be **true.** This is not a significant problem, for if those conditions do not hold the value returned by the function should be **false.** A full and complete specification for the function would appear:

function Is_Finished(P :Programmer) **return** Boolean;
— **pre: true;**
— **post:**
—   **if** is_Finished(P) **then**
—   **every** M **in** Component; T **in** Task **satisfies**
—   **if** Assignments(P, M, T) **then**
—   T = tested;
—   **end if;**
—   **end every;**
—   **else**
—   **some** M **in** Component: T **in** Task **satisfies**
—   Assignments(P, M, T);
—   T /= tested;
—   **end some;**
—   **end if;**

Because this specification is quite a bit longer than the original and adds no new information, we make the following convention:

*In specifying Boolean functions, only the conditions under which the function is to return a value of **true** are specified in the postcondition. If those conditions are not met the function is to return the value **false**.*

Note that the precondition of the function must still be satisfied. Otherwise the function is not guaranteed to act properly.

11.2.11 Some Additional Examples

As another, slightly more complicated example, consider a specification for a function that, when given a Programmer and a Component, determines whether that Programmer is assigned to that Component. Because the function What_Task is not guaranteed to work properly unless it is assured that there is some Task, it would be useful to define a function that makes that determination. Consider the following function:

function Is_Assigned(P :Programmer; M :Component) **return** Boolean;
— **pre: true;**

— **post; some** T **in** Task **satisfies**
—   Assignments(P, M, T):
—   **end some;**

This specification defines the function Is_Assigned. Is_Assigned has two inputs: a Programmer and a Component. The function returns a Boolean value as its result.

The precondition is shown as **true**. This means that whatever the relation between programmers and components, the precondition is considered satisfied; that is, the function will operate correctly. No specific preconditions are imposed.

The postcondition may be read as follows:

There is some Task T for which there is a row in the Assignments table containing P, M, and T.

Note that this is a specification for a Boolean function. By our convention only the conditions under which the function is to return a **true** value are given.

The Procedure Increment_Task

The following procedure increments the task of an assignment; that is, it changes the Task of an assignment from starting to designed, from designed to coded.

```
procedure Increment_Task(P :Programmer; M :Component);
   —pre:
   —   some T in Task satisfies
   —      Assignments(P, M, T);
   —      T /= Task'Last;
   —   end some;
   —post:
   —   some T in Task satisfies
   —      Assignments(P, M, T);
   —      Assignments'(P, M, Task'Succ(T));
   —      ~Assignments'(P, M, T);
   —   end some;
```

This specification is a little more complicated and deserves a complete explanation.

1. The signature says that we are specifying a procedure with two parameters, a Programmer and a Component.

2. The precondition says that there must be some Task T that satisfies two conditions:

    a. The Programmer is already assigned to the Component with that Task.

    b. That Task is not the final Task; there is something to which the Task can be incremented. The notation Task'Last refers to the last value in the value set of the attribute type Task. Recall that the value set for type Task is ordered by the order of program development.

    That is, the precondtion is **true** if the Programmer is assigned to the Component with some Task other than the last Task.

3. The postcondition for Increment_Task says that the Assignments table has changed to reflect the new Task. Literally translated, it reads: There is some Task T that satisfies all three of the following conditions:

    a. Programmer P is currently (i.e., before the operation) assigned to Component M with Task T. This was verified by the precondition.

b. After the operation (note the primed Assignments table) Programmer P is assigned to Component M and has the Task that follows S in the Task value set. The notation Task′Succ(T) refers to the successor of T within the value set of its attribute type.

c. Also after the operation Programmer P is no longer assigned to Component M with Task T.

In this specification the pre- and postconditions have multiple conditions that must be satisfied.

The Procedure Reassign

This is a specification of a procedure that replaces one programmer with another. Perhaps the first one quit (after being told to write specifications in table notation) and the second one is taking over the assignments.

```
procedure Reassign(Old_P, New_P :Programmer);
—   pre:
—   some M in Component; T in Task satisfies
—       Assignments(Old_P, M, T);
—   end some;
—post:
—   every M in Component; T in Task satisfies
—       if ASSIGNMENTS(Old_P, M, T) then
—           Assignments'(New_P, M, T);
—           ~Assignments'(Old_P, M, T);
—       end if;
—   end every;
```

The signature provides the name of the procedure, Reassign, and declares two parameters: the old Programmer, Old_P, and the new Programmer, New_P.

The precondition states that the old Programmer, Old_P, must be assigned somewhere. This precondition is not strictly required. The procedure would probably work as intended even if the old Programmer were not assigned at all, but the precondition can be used as a double check to be sure that some typographical error has not occurred on the input.

The postcondition states that all the assignments (i.e., Components and Tasks) of the old Programmer Old_P are to be transferred to the new Programmer New_P. Literally translated it says: All combinations of Components M and Tasks T satisfy the following conditions:

1. if Old_P is assigned to Component M with Task T before the operation both of the following apply:
    a. New_P is assigned to Component M with Task T after the operation.
    b. Old_P is not assigned to Component M with Task T after the operation.

2. Because we included all Components and Tasks, Old_P is not assigned anywhere after the operation.

Note that it was necessary to say explicitly that the old Programmer's assignments were no longer valid. Our convention about primed tables said that a table after an operation is identical to the table before the operation except as explicitly specified. If we had not said ~Assignments'(Old_P, M, T) in the postcondition the effect of the operation would be as if its intent were to assign the new programmer to help the old programmer; they would have had the same assignments.

11.3   A COMPLETE EXAMPLE AND MORE SPECIFICATION TOOLS

The examples in the preceding section provided an introduction to the table specification notation. This section provides a more complete example. The following specifications define operations for the common data type QUEUE. We specify the traditional Queue operations Length, Is_Empty, Enqueue, First, and Dequeue as well as a nontraditional Queue operation Split Queue.

Before specifying any operations it is necessary to decide how the information about Queues will be mirrored in tables. (Again, recall that tables are meta objects. They do not reflect the implementation of the operations; they only talk about the internal structures manipulated. Therefore it makes no difference what table organization we use as long as it permits us to say what we want to say.) For Queues we use a three-column table:

Queues

Queue	Queue Position	Queue Element
Queue_1	2	A
Queue_2	3	D
Queue_1	4	G
Queue_1	1	B
Queue_1	3	C
Queue_2	1	E
Queue_2	2	F

This example represents the information that there are two Queues:

Queue_1 = (B, A, C, G)
Queue_2 = (E, F, D)

The example further illustrates the point that the tables are not intended to indicate the form in which the program actually stores information. Internally the Queues will probably be stored as arrays or some sort of linked structures. The table simply shows abstractly the information that is being maintained.

This table would be declared

table Queues(Queue, Position, Element)

Following are the specifications for the Queue operations. We introduce a few more specification conventions along the way.

11.3.1   The *either . . or* Construct

This function returns the Length of a given Queue:

```
function Length(Q :Queue) return 1 . . Integer'Last;
—pre: true;
—post:
—    either
—        Length(Q) = O;
—        every E in Element; N in 1 . . Integer'Last satisfies
—            ~Queues (Q, N, E)
—        end every;
—or
—        some E in Element satisfies
—            Queues(Q, Length(Q), E);
—        end some;
—        every E in Element satisfies
—            ~Queues(Q, Length(Q) + 1,E)
—        end every;
—    end either;
```

The specification says that Length is a function that returns as its value an Integer in the range of 1 to Integer'Last. The number Length(Q) has the following property.

1.   The queue is empty:
   a.   Length(Q) = O.
   b.   The Queue has no Elements E at any Position N.
2.   The position returned is the position of the last element:
   a.   There is some Element at the position of the Queue returned by Length.
   b.   There is no Element at the next higher position of the Queue.

In general, the structure

```
either
    Boolean_Expressions
or
    Boolean_Expressions
or
    .
    .
    .

end either;
```

means that at least one of the sets of conditions delimited by the or's must hold. Any number of alternative sets of conditions may be specified.

11.3.2 The *no* Construct

The preceding specification suggests an additional construct. As part of the specification we included the following:

> **every** E **in** ELEMENT **satisfies**
> ~Queues(Q, Length(Q) + 1, E)
> **end every;**

Although this is a correct formulation of the desired condition, it would be easier to read if it were put somewhat differently. Instead of saying that all Elements satisfy a negative condition we could have said that no Element satisfies some positive condition:

> **no** E **in** ELEMENT **satisfies**
> Queues(Q, Length(Q) + 1, E)
> **end no;**

This construct, like the others, introduces a variable of a specified type whose scope is the extent of the construct. Its general form is similar to the **some** and **every** constructs.

> **no** variables **in** type {; variables **in** type} **satisfies**
> Boolean_Expressions
> **end no;**

The construct is **true** if no matter which Element is selected, the indicated Boolean expression(s) are **false.** Otherwise, the construct is **false.** This construct is logically equivalent to the preceding construct, which it can replace.

11.3.3 Other QUEUE Operations

The following Queue operations are also needed.

> **procedure** Enqueue(Q :Queue; E :Element);
> —**pre: true;**
> —**post:** Queues'(Q, Length(Q) + 1, E);

This specification says that the procedure Enqueue adds a new element to the indicated Queue at a position one greater than the current length of the Queue;

> **function** Is_Empty(Q :QUEUE) **return** Boolean;
> —**pre: true;**
> —**post:**
> —   **no** E **in** Element **satisfies**
> —   Queues(Q, 1, E)
> —   **end no;**

This specification says that a QUEUE is empty if (and only if) it has no element at its first position:

function First(Q :Queue) **return** Element;
    —**pre:** ~Is_Empty(Q);
    —**post:** Queues(Q, 1, First(Q))

This specification says that the function First returns an Element that has the property of being at position 1 of the Queue. The precondition guarantees that there is an Element to return. The postcondition says that the correct Element is the one actually returned.

11.3.4   The *all_or_none* Construct

The following specifies an operation to remove an element from a Queue:

procedure Dequeue(Q :Queue)
    —**pre:** ~Is_Empty(Q);
    —**post:**
    —   **every** N **in** 1 . . Integer'Last; E **in** Element **satisfies**
    —   **all_or_none**
    —   Queues(Q, N + 1, E);
    —   Queues'(Q, N, E);
    —   **end all_or_none;**
    —   **end every;**

This specification says that the procedure Dequeue removes the first Element from the Queue. The effect of removing the first Element is to take it out of the Queue and to move each of the other Elements ahead by one. The postcondition achieves this effect by saying that the two conditions Queues(Q, N + 1, E) and Queues'(Q, N, E) are both **true** or both **false;** that is, for all combinations of Elements and Positions the following applies:

1. If the Queue Q has Element E at its N + 1st position before Dequeue it should have that Element at its Nth position after Dequeue.
2. If the Queue Q has no Element E at its N + 1st position before Dequeue it should not have that Element at its Nth position after Dequeue.

The **all_or_none** construct takes the following general form:

all_or_ none
    Boolean_Expression_1;
    Boolean_Expression_2;
        .

        .

        .

    Boolean_Expression_n;
end all or none;

All **all_or_none** construct is interpreted to mean that the listed Boolean expressions are all **true** or all **false.** There must be at least two expressions in an **all_or_none** construct and the construct is **true** if they are all logically equivalent.

11.3.5   Specifying *out* Parameters

An **out** parameter is a one that has a value assigned to it by the procedure. Consider the following procedure that splits a Queue into its odd and evenly positioned elements:

procedure Split_Queue(Old_Q :Queue; Odd_Queue,
                                            Even_Queue : **out** Queue);
   —**pre: true;**
   —**post:**
   —   **every** N **in** 1 . . Integer'Last; E **in** Element **satisfies**
   —   **if** Queues(Old_Q, 2*N − 1, E) **then**
   —   Queues'(Odd_Queue', N, E);
   —   **end if;**
   —   **if** Queues(Old_Q, 2*N, E) **then**
   —   Queues'(Even_Q', N, E);
   —   **end if;**
   —   ~Queues'(Old_Q, N, E);
   —   **end every;**

This specification says that to Split a Queue is to divide the Queue into its odd- and even-positioned elements. The odd-positioned Elements are put into one output Queue and the even Elements, into a second output Queue. The next to last line of the specification states that the original Queue is destroyed by the operation: after the operation, the original Queue has no elements.

This example brings up a feature of specifications that we have not encountered before: **out** parameters. Notice that in the postcondition the two out parameters are shown with primes ('). As in the tables, these primes mean that we are speaking of the values of the parameters as they will be *after* the operation. With parameters that are strictly **out** parameters there is never a need to refer to their values as they were before the operation. For that reason **out** parameters never appear in specifications without primes.

As an example of a specification with a parameter whose input and output values both matter, consider the following procedure which increments its argument.

procedure Increment(I :Integer);
   —**pre: true;**
   —**post:** I' = I + 1;

This specification says that the operation Increment has one parameter. The value (I') of the parameter after performing the Increment must be one greater than its value (I) before Increment.

Parameters thus may appear in two forms in operation postconditions. They may appear unprimed to reflect their values on entry to the operation and primed to reflect their values on exit from the operation. As in this example, the postcondition often refers to their values both before and after the operation.

11.3.6   Invariants

So far we have discussed the specification of operations. In many cases there is more to the specification of operations than just the operation itself; for example, we might wonder what would happen in the Queue operation Is_Empty if the following occurred:

1. There is an entry in the table that says that a Queue has something at some position other than position 1.
2. At the same time there is no entry in the table for position 1 of the Queue.

That is, if both

```
some N in 1 . . Integer'Last; E in Element satisfies
   Queues(Q, N, E)
end some;
```

and

```
no N in 1 . . Integer'Last; E in Element satisfies
   Queues(Q, 1, E)
end no;
```

Would the Queue be empty or not?

The answer is that the Queue would be neither empty nor not empty: it would be incorrect. There cannot be a Queue with an element at some position besides the first, yet have no element at the first position. How do we know that? Unfortunately we do not know it from any of the operation specifications. In none of them have we specified enough information about Queues to guarantee that fact.

Should that additional information be specified? If so, where would it be included? It seems inappropriate to attempt to include this information with any particular operation specification because it is relevant to more than one. This sort of information is about Queues in general and is not tied to any one of the individual operations; for example, both Is_Empty and Dequeue depend on the fact that a Queue with some member always has a first member. Thus this fact (that a Queue that has a member at some position always has a member at its first position) should be specified in a way that makes it clear that the specification applies to Queues in general and not just to the Queue that is an argument of some particular operation.

There are two Queue invariants:

1. Every Queue with some Element has a first Element. (More generally, every Queue with some Element has Elements at all Positions from 1 to that Element.)

2.   No Queue can have two elements at the same position. That is, there cannot be two entries in the Queues table of the form Queues(Queue_I, N, Element_A) and Queues(Queue_I, N, Element_B) for the same Queue_I and N and different values Element_A and Element_B.

We can specify this information formally in terms of our table notation:

1.   If a queue has an element at position N it must have elements at all predecessor positions:

every Q **in** Queue;
        N **in** 2 . . Integer'Last;
        E **in** Element **satisfies**
    if Queues(Q, N, E) **then**
        some E_1 **in** Element **satisfies**
        Queues(Q, N − 1, E_1)
        end some;
    end if;
end every;

This says that if a queue has an element at a position N greater than 1 it has an element at the preceding position $(N − 1)$. This automatically implies that it has Elements at all Positions from 1 to N.

2.   There may be only one Element at each position.

every Q **In** Queue;
        N **in** 1 . ._Integer'Last;
        E_1, E_2 **in** Element **satisfies**
    if Queues(Q, N, E_1) and Queues(Q, N, E_2) **then**
            E_1 = E_2;
        end if;
end every;

This says that if a queue appears to have two elements E_1 and E_2 at the same position N then the two elements are the same; that is, a queue cannot have two distinct elements at the same position.

It turns out that this second sort of invariant is so common that it is worthwhile to develop a simpler notation for it. We do so in the next section.

11.3.7   Tables and Functions

A table is a function from some of its columns, called the key (from the relational database term), to its other columns if there is guaranteed never to be more than one row in the table with the same combination of values in the key columns.

By our assumed invariant about Queues no Queue has two Elements at the same Position. Given any particular Queue and any Position in it, there is at most one row in the Queue table for that combination. Therefore for the Queue table the **key** is the pair of columns consisting of the Queue column and the Position column. Thus the Queue table defines a function from Queues and Queue Positions to the Element in that Position in that Queue. In the future whenever we specify tables and the table defines a function we will indicate that fact explicitly:

function Queues(:Queue, :Natural) :Element

This says that Queues is a table that defines a function from Queues and the Natural numbers to Elements. Given this specification of the Queue table, the second Queue invariant (that only one Element may appear at any Queue Position) is declared automatically.

11.3.8   The Responsibility Imposed by Invariants

Invariants are important to specifications. Without the two invariants specified for Queues the notion of a Queue would be incomplete.

Invariants impose an obligation as well. Because an invariant is always supposed to be **true,** it is essential that the operations performed not create situations in which the invariants become **false;** for example, there cannot be a Queue operation that adds an Element to a Queue blindly at, say, its 100th position. To do so might lead to a situation in which the Queue has an Element without a predecessor Element, violating the first Queue invariant.

It is up to the specifiers and implementers of the operations that are defined as part of a specification to ensure that the effects of the operations do not violate the invariants.

11.3.9   More Complex Specifications: Separate Predicates

Although it is good practice to keep specifications as simple as possible, in some situations it is just not possible to modularize programs to keep all the specifications simple. For these situations a mechanism is necessary to allow more complex specifications to be presented in an easy to understand format. As in normal programming, a good way to make the complex simple is to break it up into pieces, with each piece representing an abstraction. This section discusses a technique for expressing specifications in a modular form.

The mechanism to be suggested is essentially the same as that used for components: give each unit of the specification its own identity. As an example, consider the situation in which three operations P_1, P_2, and P_3 each:

1.   Perform some processing on the first elements of Queues Q_1, Q_2, Q_3.
2.   Dequeue the processed elements.

To write complete specifications for these three operations it is necessary to include in the specifications that the first elements of the Queues are Dequeued by the processing. Unfortunately the symbology required to say that an element has been De-queued is somewhat lengthy. (See the Dequeue operation specification.) Rather than write that same symbology three times (once for each of the three operations), it is much easier to define a predicate

Dequeued(Q :Queue)

which means that the first element of Queue Q has been removed. We could then use that predicate in the specifications of all three operations. The following frag-ment shows how this might be done.

```
      . . .
   procedure P_1(. . . ; Q_1 :Queue; . . . )
     —pre: . . . ;
     —post;
     —      . . .
     —       Dequeued(Q_1);
     —      . . .


   procedure P_2( . . . ; Q_2: Queue; . . . )
     —pre: . . . ;
     —post:
     —      . . .
     —       Dequeued(Q_2);
     —      . . .


   procedure P_3( . . . ; Q_3 :Queue; . . . )
     —pre: . . . ;
     —post:
     —      . . .
     —       Dequeued(Q_3);
     —      . . .


   Dequeued(Q :Queue) means
     —every N in 1 .. LENGTH(Q);
     —      E in Element satisfies
     —   all_or_none
     —       Queues(Q, N + 1, E);
     —       Queue'(Q, N, E);
     —   end all_or_none;
     —end every;


              ·       —Other predicates would be defined here.
              ·


   end Predicate_Example;
```

The idea of defining predicates that are not tables but instead are defined in terms of other predicates is the basis for the programming language Prolog. [Clocksin and

Mellish, 1981]. We could use this programming language instead of our notation to write software specifications. Although our language has some conventions that are not available in basic Prolog (in particular, typed predicates, functions, a distinction between entities and values, and an ability to order elements of a given type), Prolog has the advantage that it is an operational programming language. Another currently operational specification langauge is GIST, developed at ISI [Balzer, 1977; Balzer, 1982]. It doesn't really matter which specification language is selected so long as we select some language. The field of specification languages is developing rapidly and much progress is expected in the next few years.

11.3.10   How Complete a Specification?

At this point we may wonder how complete specifications must be? If our example specification of a Queue data type is as long as it is, won't more complicated systems be even lengthier? Is it worth the trouble to provide complete abstract specifications?

Recall that abstraction always involves developing a model that can be used to characterize the essential features of something. The basic problem we must confront when doing abstraction is, in what terms will the abstract model be described?

Often, as in mathematical functions, existing models are sufficient to characterize the abstract features required of the function. In most cases, however, no model exists. Sometimes widely accepted, intuitive models do exist; for example, although there are no widely used formal models of queues, lists, and trees, most people have a good intuitive grasp of these data types. On the other hand, most programming projects require the development of new ones. The properties of these types and the behavior of operations defined on them must be carefully described.

Therefore the question comes down to the terms in which the explanation is given. There is no limit to the ways in which we can build models. Many different modeling frameworks are possible and all are useful in different situations. What we are suggesting here is that the table framework will often be useful when we describe models. It is not required that every model be defined in those terms. It is suggested that when defining an abstraction, good style requires that a description as rigorous as possible be given. We also suggest that the table approach will often provide a simple and convenient framework for expressing that description.

How complete and rigorous must the model be? It is at this point that we must leave the extent of specification up to the program designer. A complete specification would help us to prove formally that programs work correctly. Unfortunately complete specifications are often long, tedious, and (even worse) sometimes difficult to understand.

The primary stylistic goal in programming must always be maximum understandability. The guidelines suggested here are that formal specifications be used to the greatest extent possible but that when formality gets in the way of clarity then clarity must take precedence.

11.4   SUMMARY AND CONCLUSIONS

This appendix has described tools and techniques for abstract specifications. This summary section reviews these tools and techniques and then provides some final conclusions and gives some specification advice.

11.4.1   Specification Tools Summary

Tables

A table is a collection of facts about objects of a fixed set of data types. Each "fact" is maintained as a "row" of the table where the "columns" are the data types about which the facts are maintained.

In some cases there may be multiple columns of the same data type and the columns may be given names (as in operations in which the parameters are given names).

Pre- and Postconditions

Pre- and postconditions are Boolean expressions that characterize the action of operations.

The postcondition to an operation explains the conditions under which the operation is guaranteed to function properly. If a precondition is shown as the constant **true** its operation is guaranteed to function properly no matter what the state of the data.

The postcondition for an operation characterizes the state that is brought about by the operation. In one case, Boolean functions, there is a special convention. For Boolean functions the postcondition specifies the conditions under which the function is to return the value **true.** In all other conditions the function returns the value **false.**

Predicate Logic Notation

Pedicate logic notation is a programming language-like notation that permits the expression of Boolean conditions. The constructs include the following:

Predicates	A construct parallel to Boolean functions in many programming languages that consists of a table name and a possible row entry. A predicate is **true** or **false,** depending on whether the indicated row entry is in fact in the table.
The some construct	A construct that resemble the **for** statement in many programming languages. It is **true** or **false,** depending on whether some element in the specified type(s) satisfies the indicated conditions.

The every construct	A construct that resemble the **for** statement in many programming languages. It is **true** or **false,** depending on whether every element in the specified type(s) satisfies the indicated conditions.
The no construct	A construct that resembles the **for** statement in many programming languages. It is **true** or **false,** depending on whether the conditions specified are **true** or **false** in the appropriate combinations.
The either . . or construct	A construct permitting the specification of alternative sets of conditions. It is **true** or **false,** depending on whether one of the sets of conditions is **true.**
The implicit and construct	A construct that permits the specification of multiple conditions. Conditions strung together with semicolons (;) are required to be **true** for the set of conditions to be considered **true.**
The all_or_none construct	A construct that permits the specification of logical equivalence among conditions. It is like the implicit **and** construct in that it is **true** if all the conditions specified are **true.** Unlike the implicit **and** construct, however, it is also **true** if all the conditions specified are **false.** If some of the conditions specified are **true**, whereas others are **false,** the **all_ or_none** construct is **false.**

Functions and Keys

If a table has the property that one or more (but not all) of its columns uniquely define the rows of the table the table is said to be a function and we refer to those columns as a key. There are guaranteed to be no cases in which two rows have exactly the same values for those particular columns; that is, no two rows have the same values in their key columns.

Invariants

An invariant is a piece of information that is specified to be **true** at all times. Invariants may be relied on to update the tables as a result of other specified changes; that is, if an invariant links the contents of one table to the contents of another and a specification states that the second table is changed by a procedure, the first table is also assumed to be changed by the procedure. Likewise, if a procedure specifies a particular value to be associated with an element by a function, any other value that may have been associated with that element by that table is assumed to be deleted. In specifying operations, we must be careful not to create conditions that violate stated invariants.

Separate Predicates

It is sometimes convenient to define predicates (i.e., specification statements) independently of any particular specification. It is useful to do so when (a) the specification statement is likely to be used more than once or (b) the specification statement is complex or significant enough to deserve an independent statement.

The practice of defining separate predicates is similar to the practice of defining separate components. We do so because the predicate makes sense on its own or because the predicate may be referred to multiple times (or both).

Invariants, as discussed in the preceding subsection, are separate predicates that are declared always to be **true.**

11.4.2 Conclusions and Final Advice

This appendix has set forth a framework for the specification of software elements. The goals of specification are the following:

1. To make software easy to understand.
2. To make software portable.

To some extent these goals conflict. Portability is not possible without complete specifications, for without complete specifications it is not safe to use a foreign software element in another system. Yet complete specifications are sometimes tedious and difficult to understand. It is up to the software customer and designer to decide together just how complete and rigorous a specification should be provided for each software system.

Our advice is the following:

1. The first priority should always be understandability.
2. Completeness is important and should be achieved if at all possible.
3. If necessary for understandability completeness may be achieved by additional documentation.

REFERENCES

R. Balzer, N. Goldman, and D. Wile, Informality in Program Specifications, In *Proceedings of the Fifth International Conference on Artificial Intelligence.* ACM‖y‖, 1977.

R. Balzer, N. Goldman, and D. Wile, Operational Specifications as the Basis for Rapid Prototyping, In *Proceedings of the Second Software Engineering Symposium: Workshop on Rapid Prototyping.* ACM, 1982.

W.F. Clocksin and C.S. Mellish, *Programming in Prolog,* Springer-Verlag, New York, 1981.

INDEX

329